Collected
Writings
of William Still

Collected Writings of William Still

Volume 2: Studies in the Christian Life

Edited by Sinclair B. Ferguson

RUTHERFORD HOUSE BOOKS
Edinburgh

Published by Rutherford House
17 Claremont Park, Edinburgh, EH6 7PJ, Scotland

ISBN 0 946068 48 8

Printed by The Cromwell Press, Broughton Gifford,
Melksham, Wiltshire SN12 8PH

CONTENTS

Preface   VII

Towards Spiritual Maturity
  1. He is our Peace   1
  2. The First Dimension of the Cross
     The Removal of Sins   3
  3. The Second Dimension of the Cross
     Sin's Reign Overthrown   6
  4. The Third Dimension of the Cross
     The Defeat of Satan   13
  5. The Military Training of a Soldier   19
  6. Christian Service and Warfare   32
  7. Spiritual Maturity   35

What it is to be a Christian
  1. The New Birth   41
  2. The Godwardness of the Gift of Faith   53
  3. The Personalness of Salvation   65
  4. Justification   78
  5. Grace Abounding   88
  6. The Sheer Excess of God's Extravagant Gift   99
  7. The Divine Discontent   108
  8. Sin and Guilt   121
  9. Made to become Sin   130
10. Adoption   140
11. Sanctification   149
12. The Indwelling Christ   159
13. Into Christ's Likeness   169
14. The Spirit Within   179

15. Recognising the Enemy   189
16. Resisting the Enemy   200
17. On to Glory   212

Prayer   225

Two Sermons on Morals
   1. Ethical Questions   237
   2. Overcoming the Flesh   251

The Christian in the Home, Church and World
   1. Foundations   263
   2. Primary Evangelism   273
   3. Into the World, to the End of Age   282

Rhythms of Rest and Work
   Preface   295
   1. Rhythms of Rest and Work   297
   2. The Content and Substance of Our Peace 307
   3. Simultaneous Rest and Work   319

PREFACE

Volume 1 of *The Collected Writings of William Still* was sub-titled 'Theological Studies'. Its focus was on the work of Christ and the ministry of the Holy Spirit. In Volume 2 we have selected material from William Still's ministry which can be conveniently grouped together under the rubric 'Studies in the Christian Life'.

It has been said of the great North American pastor-theologian Jonathan Edwards that he had the ability to take an idea and hold it in his mind, turning it round like a diamond to view it from every possible perspective. William Still would make no claim to rival Edwards; yet one of the obvious passions of his ministry has been to take several fundamental biblical insights and explore how these apply in a variety of areas of Christian thought and life.

The result is striking. For the reader of Volume 2 will discover that some of its chapter titles correspond to chapter titles in Volume 1! This is not due to any lack of originality on Mr Still's part, nor even to an oversight on the part of the editor! In fact these materials present the same topics set within a quite different theological context, viewed from a new perspective and expounded in a fresh and independent fashion. In this way, the 'whole picture' of the grace of God presented in the rich tapestry of Scripture becomes ever more vivid.

No attempt to publish the 'collected writings' of William Still could afford to omit *Towards Spiritual Maturity*, his most seminal work. First circulated privately in 1957 as a summary of teaching he found himself giving frequently in a period of his ministry when he was much in demand to speak at conferences and conventions, it is here reprinted by the kind permission of Christian Focus Publications, the present publishers of a paperback edition.

The themes expressed in *Towards Spiritual Maturity* are more fully worked out in a wide variety of areas of the Christian life in *What it is to be a Christian*, originally a series of seventeen sermons preached in Gilcomston South between 11 June and 1 October 1972. This is followed by an address given on 3 October 1988 to The Crieff Brotherhood (a gathering of colleagues which Mr Still has convened at Crieff since 1971) on the subject of *Prayer*—an area of individual and church life in which Mr Still has provided special leadership in the second half of the twentieth century.

The final pieces deal in very different ways with the practical application of this teaching to specific areas of Christian living. They include *Two Sermons on Morals*, preached on 3 March 1968 and 16 March 1969 and later privately circulated. The addresses on *The Christian in the Home, Church and World* were given on 25 to 28 July 1977 to a group of young people in Northern Ireland with whom Mr Still had close associations over a number of years.

The closing piece, *Rhythms of Rest and Work* is, in its own way, as seminal and remarkable as the first. Originally printed privately in 1977, it sets out to apply elements of biblical teaching to the practical rhythms of Christian living in the high-paced modern world. It well conveys how wide-ranging William Still's ministry has sought to be in its practical application of the whole of Scripture to the whole of life.

As this volume goes to press, William Still has already passed his eighty-third birthday and continues to minister with joy and vigour. We join with readers worldwide in saluting him and wishing him continued health and strength and continued blessing in his ministry.

Sinclair B. Ferguson

TOWARDS SPIRITUAL MATURITY

1. He is our Peace

The fundamental blessing of salvation is peace. From it flow all God's richer blessings of love, joy and glory. It is not only the foundation stone of the Christian life, 'the peace of God which passes all understanding' (Phil. 4:7), but also the top stone, 'the peace of God which presides in our hearts' (Col. 3:15). But before we consider the 'peace of God' (Phil. 4:7) we must consider the nature of the 'the God of peace' (Phil. 4:9) whose work in men's hearts is to make peace—first his person, *then* his work.

God is the God of peace. He is at peace, in and with himself. A fundamental implication of the Holy Scriptures is that the triune God was, is, and ever shall be in perfect accord with himself, person with person, office with office, and that he is. satisfied with himself in the fullness and perfection of his wisdom, love and power. When infinite intelligence finds infinite perfection in itself, infinite stability and integrity of character are assured. This integrity is simply another name for God's righteousness, or rightness.

The righteous nature and character of God is, by implication, expressed in the demands he makes upon men in the Ten Commandments. The tablets written with the finger of God are the focus of his Shekinah glory which hovered over the Tabernacle in the wilderness. The rays of the Lord's glorious light were shining down upon them, pointing to them. Beyond his laws, we see the character of the God who gave them. The laws tell us what God is like. They also imply that since God is like this, holy and righteous, he desires his creatures to be like this also.

We know that God is love. But his character is often expressed in the

---

Scriptures in terms of righteousness (*e.g.* the theme of Romans). This righteousness is no mere rule, or form, but is of the essence of his being. Righteousness with God is not only a rule, but his life and his passion. He is not only righteous himself, but loves righteousness. He rejoices in it so much that he desires righteousness for his creatures, and that, not only for its own sake as a seed, but for its fruit which is peace (Is. 32:17; Heb. 12:11).

But we do not say that God is only righteousness. The Bible does not say that, but assumes that righteousness belongs to the divine heart as well as to the divine mind. Although in Exodus 20 we see the righteousness, holiness, and wrath of God at their sternest (God cannot look upon sin, Hab. 1:13; 'the soul that sinneth, it shall die', Ezek. 18:4), yet, wonder of wonders, embedded in the most alarming chapter of the Old Testament we find mercy and love. What a discovery this is, there! The God who gives the commandments is first of all the Saviour who has delivered his people from bondage (Ex. 20:1, 2). The heart of God which burns with righteousness and holiness also burns with love and mercy, grace and forgiveness. He who is righteous, and desires righteousness for his children, makes them righteous by imputation and by impartation through his redeeming love. To our amazement we discover that the rock of his law and truth which is so hard on the surface, is molten underneath with his love.

But, having ventured to consider the 'God of peace' with a view to considering the 'peace of God', we unconsciously slip from the one to the other. This is not surprising, for what God is by the energies of his divine nature, he necessarily desires to impart to his creatures.

It is astonishing that studies of the work of Christ have not yielded clearer and more systematic distinctions between the different dimensions of the work of his death. Evangelical Christianity does distinguish between sins and sin, fruit and root; but the third dimension, the work of Satan, is seldom acknowledged, even where Satan and his work are recognised. Yet for a total unmasking of evil in the human heart the third dimension is necessary, since the person and work of the devil is the greatest hindrance to mature Christianity. Satan loves it so. That is doubtless why it is so, and why so many are suspicious of talk about the devil and demons. Yet it is a strange blindness with which the god of this world has blinded so many professing Christians (2 Cor. 4:4). We propose to challenge it by setting forth in sequence the three dimensions of the work of the death of Christ.

TOWARDS SPIRITUAL MATURITY

2. The First Dimension of the Cross

The Removal of Sins

We have already said that what God is by the energies of his divine nature, he necessarily desires to impart to his creatures. How does he do so? That is our first theme.

Those who review the history of the doctrine of Christ's atonement generally conclude that no single view covers its whole range. But some views are nearer the heart of the truth than others, in which the greater includes the lesser. For example, it is not wrong to regard the death of Christ as the supreme example of sacrificial love; but his death is more than that. Failure to see this accounts for the spiritual listlessness of many who hold a mere exemplary view as the whole truth. For the death of Christ is no mere display of love in action. It is the putting away of the sins which set up a barrier to the very possibility of love between God and man. It is not only an exhibition, but a removal. Indeed it is more a removal than an exhibition, for it is one thing to show sinners what they ought to do, and quite another to do it for them when they are helpless to do anything for themselves. We need not only pictures, but power; not only diagrams, but dynamic. This we have in the death of Christ, which is nothing if not an actual, factual, objective putting away of our sins.

Let us look at the fact as plainly stated in Scripture. Isaiah 53:6 tells us that whereas, 'all we like sheep have gone astray', 'the Lord has laid on him the iniquity of us all'. Paul corroborates this in Romans 4:7, 8 when he quotes from Psalm 32: 'Blessed are they whose transgressions are forgiven (removed), whose sins are covered; blessed is the man whose sin the Lord will never count against him' and 4:25: '(Jesus our

Lord) was delivered over to death for our sins'. Peter says: 'He himself bare our sins in his own body on the tree' (1 Pet. 2:24). There is no evading the plain and repeated words of Scripture: Christ took our sins.

But John 1:29 takes it a step further: the Baptist declares that the Lamb of God, on whom our sins are laid, takes them *away*. Do we question this? Let the Bible answer our questions: 'I have swept away your offences like a cloud, your sins like the morning mist' (Is. 44:22). 'You have put all my sins behind your back' (Is. 38:17). 'You will again have compassion on us; you will tread our sins underfoot; and hurl all our iniquities into the depths of the sea' (Mic. 7:19). 'As far as the east is from the west, so far has he removed our transgressions from us' (Ps. 103:12). 'This is the covenant I will make with them after that time says the Lord. I will put my laws in their hearts and I will write them on their minds. Their sins and lawless acts I will remember no more' (Heb. 10:16, 17; also Jer. 31:33, 34).

Thus Christ takes our place, and bears our sins with their guilt, punishment and shame 'in his own body on the tree', and on the third day rises without them, so that they are gone, for ever. Every sin we have committed, from life's beginning to its end, is *for ever* put away, never to be brought against us again. Christ the sinless One is God's appointed substitute 'Criminal', to take our place. He is God's 'Dustman', carrying away man's filth with his own pure hands. What unutterable love, in action!

Objection may be raised to the assertion that God forgives sins before they are committed. But, it is as simple as this, that no question of penalty and eternal separation from God can be raised in respect of a forgiven sinner in a state of grace.

Two things must be distinguished: God's dealing with sinners, and his dealing with saints. Conversion necessarily involves the once-for-all forgiveness (removal) of sins. But it involves much more. By it the believer is declared to be righteous in Christ, having been brought to new birth. He is not sinless, yet: as John says, the seed of God dwells within him and he cannot sin (1 Jn. 3:9). Because his mind and will are united to Christ his attitude to sin is radically altered. The enmity and rebellion against God are slain, and sin is no longer a cause of wilful pride and perverse pleasure, but a cause of sorrow, shame and self-loathing.

Thus, God's attitude towards saints in their sins is different from his attitude towards sinners in their sins (although he hates sin equally in both—more in saints!). But further, the saints' own attitude to their sins is different from sinners' attitude to their sins. There are no penal consequences of sin after conversion, for the child of God is in a state of grace, and although chastisement may be severe, he knows he is free from final condemnation (Rom. 8:1). If we cannot lay this great stone of eternal peace at the foundation of our Christian life, what assurance have we that anything we may build upon it will stand?

But, are not the sins of the saints serious? Yes, indeed! They cause estrangement between the Father and his children. And while God will not disown them, however provocative they may be (the history of Israel proves this—see Hosea 11), he withdraws from them—even while he stands firm on the verities of forgiveness, justification and sanctification—and refuses to have active fellowship with them. The Father remains their Father and the children remain his children, but there is no communication until sin is confessed and repented of, and cleansing and fellowship sought. This is set forth clearly and fully in 1 John 1:6–2:2, and careful study of the passage should end all confusion as to the two forgivenesses, once-for-all for sinners concerning penalty, and daily for saints to preserve fellowship. Both forgivenesses are provided for in the death of Christ, who is the Mediator and Saviour of the sinner, and the Advocate of the saint.

Roman Catholics distinguish between mortal and venial sins, and we may recognise this distinction if we know what it means, for the true child of God cannot sin a mortal sin, since all his penalty is paid by Christ. Yet child of God though he be, he cannot have blessed communion with the Father while he remains in a state of disobedience and unrepentance. But we have continual access to the Father through the advocacy of Christ our great High Priest, who 'always lives to intercede' for us, and we ought thereby to learn to keep 'short accounts with God'. This is what John calls 'walking in the light' (1 Jn. 1:7). It is, of course, assumed that the saint knows himself to be a saint, although prone to fall. Yet the claim to be a child of God goes ill with a lack of Christ-likeness. It is by our fruits, not our roots which are not commonly open to sight, that we are seen to be the children of God.

TOWARDS SPIRITUAL MATURITY

3. The Second Dimension of the Cross

Sin's Reign Overthrown

The second dimension of Christ's redeeming work is his death *to* sin. He not only died *for* our sins to take them away, but died to sin's dominion, to defeat it for us in order that the root as well as the fruit of sin might be destroyed. Paul says to the Corinthians that 'God made Christ who had no sin to be sin for us; so that in him we might become the righteousness of God (2 Cor. 5:21). Some scholars discredit this verse as revolting and unthinkable; but it does not stand by itself. Paul says to the Romans, God sending 'his own Son in the likeness of the flesh of sin, and for sin, condemned sin in the flesh' (Rom. 8:3 RSV).

This second dimension of the work of Christ is far from easy to understand, and determined efforts are necessary to think through the paradoxes involved. To help us we can employ the old distinctions of fact, faith, and feeling. If we do not build our Christian doctrine upon the *facts*, and rest our *faith* in them, our wayward *feelings* will never be brought into captivity to Christ. It is one thing to know that Christ has dealt with our sins (the things we have done wrong in thought, word and deed), but quite another to believe that Christ on the cross dealt with the dominion or reign of sin, and that finally.

We start from the facts. There are not two orders of mankind, Adam and Christ (Rom. 5:12–21). Adam fell away to God's enemy and was lost. Jesus the second (or last) Adam (1 Cor. 15:22, 45), came to overthrow the reign of sin inaugurated by the first Adam that he might in exchange give his own holy nature, the new and true humanity. We must not think of our salvation as less than a complete exchange, for there is nothing good in fallen Adam, he is totally and incurably corrupt in all his parts and passions. There is therefore no hope for him; death is the only 'cure', for it is by death only that Adam can be saved from his fallen self and become a new creation. This is what Christ has done for Adam. He took his place, not only as his Substitute to take away his sins, but as his Representative to crucify his fallen nature, that in his sinless body he might slay and remove the old, and by his resurrection replace it with the new.

The ground of this truth is in Romans 6:3–8. There, Paul repeats the truth verse after verse in varying forms of words: we are 'baptised into his death'; we are 'buried with him by baptism into death'; we are 'planted together in the likeness of his death'; 'our old man was crucified with him'; 'he that is dead has been justified from sin'; we are 'dead with Christ'. Could anything be more plain? Paul says that when Jesus died, we died with him. The negro spiritual is not wrong when it asks, 'Were you there when they crucified my Lord?' We were all there.

But we must take time to ponder it. Does it mean that when Jesus died on the cross we all died to sin with him, before we were born? The answer can only be, 'Yes', although the actualising of the fact awaits our birth and our conversion. The only way to grapple with the fact is to let its incredible statement strike home to our hearts with stark and daring force. That is why we like the title of the book which declares unequivocally that Christians are *Born Crucified*. Yet it is not so incredible when we remember that that same Spirit by which Christ offered himself to God on our behalf (Heb. 9:14) brings us to new birth and indwells our heart. The eternal Spirit of God is not limited by time and space.

Having established that we died in him, Paul goes on in Romans 6:9, 10 to emphasise the finality of Christ's death. 'Christ being raised from the dead'—an immortal Man—'dies no more': 'death has no more dominion over him. For in that he died, he died to sin, once and for all'. 'Likewise ye', says the Apostle (v. 11 AV); for if Christ died to sin once and for all, then we also died to sin once and for all, being united to him as those who are for ever dead to sin. Christ has given us from the beginning—since it happened before we were born—a finished work. His work is therefore complete before we receive it, and when we receive it by the Spirit it is a fully accomplished fact.

This takes some believing. If we think we have taken it in our stride and know it all, it may be that the grandeur and wonder of it has not yet struck us. But it must be believed with the whole heart and mind before

it can profit us one whit. Many children of God possessing this
wonderful finished work do not know it, save in the vaguest and most
impractical sense. It must be known and believed if it is to change our
lives.

Is it hard to believe? Look at the word 'count', or 'reckon' in the
crucial eleventh verse of Romans 6. It belongs properly to the sphere of
the accountant and book-keeper, and means that we are to take stock of
what we have. We are therefore to say to ourselves a thousand times a
day, 'I am dead indeed to the reign of sin. I have been born into, and am
now in, a perfect state of absolute and final death to the reign of sin'.

Do you find this easy to believe? Of course not, for at this point
doubts and questionings crowd into the mind thick and fast. We argue,
'But I am not dead indeed to sin, for I feel the motions of sin in my
members. I sin every day. It cannot be true that I am dead to sin'. Well,
it is God's Word against ours. But this argument is a side-track, a
satanic side-track, strange as it may seem, to blind us to the spiritual and
eternal fact which resides in our breast by the indwelling Holy Spirit.
For we cannot have any other Christ within us than that eternal One who
came to die our death that he might give himself to us, a blessed gift
which we could not acquire of ourselves. Our doubts and fears, with all
their thoughts, feelings and experiences, must therefore bow to the
Word of God and to the Spirit's witness within our hearts and be silent
and believe. Of course, if we come to the conclusion that we are not
children of God, that is a different matter, and nothing here stated will
then be true of us. In that event we must come to God in repentance, and
to Christ in faith (Rev. 3:20), and be converted. But if we know that we
are born of God, we must accept that we are born crucified. We are no
longer 'slaves to sin' (Rom. 6:6). It no longer rules our lives.

At this point the transcendent finality of it all may stumble us, so that
we cannot believe with child-like minds. May we not argue it out? Why,
yes. The truth has nothing to fear from the most formidable attack of
reasoned incredulity. Think away.

Can our salvation be perfect before it is well begun? The answer is
simple. Yes, by virtue of the perfection of the gift that God has given us.
We begin perfect in the sense that God has from the beginning done a
perfect work in us. But we are not perfect. No, but only a power which
is perfect could hope to bring us to perfection. Does not the seed contain
within itself the germ of the flower and the fruit? We work from inherent
perfection to out-wrought perfection. We do not deny the process of

sanctification, but the process is but a drawing upon the resources imparted in the crisis, the new birth. The working out takes time, it may take a lifetime (Phil. 2:12, 13), but the work is from perfection to perfection, from faith to faith, and from glory to glory.

This we must believe before we can begin to grow. The problem of frantic sectarians is often that they refuse to see that the process of sanctification is not something to be wrought into the believer, but to be wrought out. In the new birth we receive *all* that God has to give us, even unto glory (Col. 1:27b). 'What we will be has not yet been made known' (1 Jn. 3:2). Let us learn humbly and gratefully to draw upon this 'all' for everything. We are therefore not dying, but have already died. The process is not *to* death, but *from* death *to* mortification, from inward fact through working faith to outward reality.

Can your heart still not rest in humble and grateful acceptance of this mighty blessing? Do not be surprised; for all the powers of hell will resist your attempts to stand upon Romans 6:11. Every thought and feeling will rise to shout you down as the rankest hypocrite for saying you have indeed died to sin while the motions of sin are still present in your members. We must ignore them all, for 'God is greater than our hearts, and he knows all things' (1 Jn. 3:20). What we ask ourselves is: Lord, are you there? And when he answers, 'Yes' by the inward witness of his Spirit (1 Jn. 5:10), let us acknowledge that we are united to him by eternal and indissoluble bonds and are dead indeed unto sin. Let us believe with all our hearts.

But a voice from beneath says, 'It is one thing to believe it. A man can believe anything if he tries hard enough: but it may not be true. Try putting it into practice and find out if you are really dead to sin'. This sounds reasonable, but it is really devilish, and we are not to listen to the devil even when he sounds reasonable. Can we doubt the mischief he intends? Is his name not deceiver? And is he not obliged to deceive to conceal his vile intents? Never mind his taunts.

Nor should we be over-worried about practice at this stage, for if we accept the enemy's challenge and try to 'die to sin' and fail by a hairsbreadth, Satan will laugh in our face and ridicule the whole idea. We are not ready yet to be concerned with practice: we are still engaged in the war to establish faith upon facts. Our chief concern is to know what sort of Jesus dwells in our hearts.

When we are utterly convinced against the apparent evidence of our fluctuating feelings, and against the fiery darts of the wicked one, that we are dead indeed to sin, then is time enough to begin to put faith to the test and prove the mighty power of Christ's death within us; for faith, which then grasps fact, taps power. For if Christ crucified is within us, this means he is there *with all the power of his death*. Paul in 2 Corinthians 4:12 says, 'Death works'. Is it not natural, then, to draw upon what is there? We therefore conclude with Paul in Galatians 2:20 that we 'have been crucified with Christ', and in Colossians 3:3 that we 'are dead'.

But the devil is not done yet. If he cannot shake our faith, he will go to the other extreme (he is fond of extremes). Now, shrewdly acquiescing in what we believe, he will try to draw us away into working it out in our own strength. We must therefore be sure that we are really drawing upon Christ by faith, and not trying to work it up on our own. This does not mean that we sit back and let Christ work within us as an independent worker. He won't. We have our part to play, which may involve moral sweat, toil and tears; but always on the understanding that we are drawing on his resources and not working on our own. To co-operate with him does not mean to dispense with him, as if he gave us a push and then left us to ourselves. What makes a motor car go when the driver operates the levers? It is its inherent power, not the man. He sits, almost idly, and makes a few easy, although all-important movements; but he knows that it is not his power which makes the vehicle go, but its own power. It is by works of faith through grace only that we work out our own salvation.

This brings us to Romans 6:12, 13 where we see how perfectly the Scriptures provide knowledge leading to faith and practice. We are not to 'Let sin reign in your mortal body'. This command is addressed to us, but only on the ground of what we have received. It is for lack of strict training in the facts of Scripture that men's faith and feelings go awry. Let us know better, and smash the arrogance of our unbelief by the hammer of God's Word. This is his power to us.

But some will ask: How do we do this? If Christ has done all, what is left for us to do? Well, we must believe, for one thing; but much more. He has broken sin's dominion in his finished work, and while there is nothing left for us to do in that respect, it is only when we 'count' on it that we are ready to do our part, namely that of mortifying what Christ crucified. 'Ah', you say, 'so we mortify'. We do it after all! You must not say that, in view of Christ's mighty work. He has slain, we must mortify (Rom. 8:13). Do you think this is playing with words? Believe it and try it: there is no other way to prove its truth and power. We are to 'count', and let not sin reign, and as we do, the risen life of Christ takes possession of us and his mighty negative of death leads to his glorious positive of life.

There is one further suggestion. What of the dominion of sin? It is slain, but is it rooted out? Yes; but the dregs remain, otherwise salvation would be automatic and would leave no room for the exercise of faith, and heaven would be populated with infants. The remnants of corruption are still there (Rom. 7:14b), but Christ gives us power to keep them in the place of death (Col. 3:5) until they are cast out for ever. If we prove unfaithful to what Christ has made us and let these dregs manifest themselves, we must suffer the consequences. Some people, on account of constant struggling and frequent defeats, have concluded that these remnants are as strong as the new nature, and therefore see no hope in their lives of anything better than a perpetual 'tit-for-tat' of indecisive conflict. This is not so. We may modify the words of John and say, 'Greater is Christ within me than the remnants of sin within me' (1 Jn. 4:4).

Paul also has something to say about this in Romans chapters 5 and 7. Three times in chapter 5, verses 15, 17, 20, he says that Christ is 'much more' than Adam; and in chapter 7, verses 17 and 20, he indicates that a new Christian 'I' has taken the place of the old man. Before Christ came, sin was the householder or owner-occupier: now that Christ has come, sin is dispossessed, and the remnants of corruption remain on sufferance until death parts us for ever from their presence. 'I' am now a Christ-one, committed to live the Christian life, and no longer defer to the Adamic influence. We must accept the fact of the presence of the flesh (Rom. 7:25c), but must refuse its influence in our lives as a power cancelled by Christ's death; and we must regard that potential for evil as an unwelcome residue which we are to mortify by faith in Christ's death, and keep it near the fringe of our lives until we are finally separated from it at death.

Here again, faith must take hold of fact. Do we really believe that Christ within is greater than the presence of sin within? Then let our faith take hold of the fact, even resisting the sin of unbelief to 'blood'. Then we will experience the power of Christ's salvation, not only *from* sin, but for holiness. To this end, we yield to God the new Christian life, whose dregs must be kept down continually because God has no use for them; for who can feed the life of Christ in our soul, and fit it for his purposes but God himself who made it?[1]

---

[1] See *The Westminster Confession of Faith*, chapter 13, Of Sanctification. See also
John Owen, *Works* Goold Edition, III, pp. 386, 465, 488.

TOWARDS SPIRITUAL MATURITY

4. The Third Dimension of the Cross

The Defeat of Satan

When the sin-nature is effectually dealt with and the new Christ-life yielded to God (Rom. 6:3–13), it might be assumed that Paul's next step in Romans would be to unfold the riches of the Spirit-filled life. Not so: there is a chapter-and-a-half yet on the subject of sin, before we read of the Spirit-filled life in chapter 8. Why? What remains to be said about sin, after it has been destroyed? If we read Romans 6:14–7:25 we shall see Paul's continuing preoccupation with sin. Note that *sin is characterised in increasingly personal terms*. In 6:14 it is dominion; from 6:16–23 it is a tyrannical master, a slave-driver; in 7:8 and 7:11 it is an unscrupulous and wily opportunist standing ready to use what is good (the Law) for its own evil purposes; in 7:13, 17, 20, 23 it is a deadly enemy warring against the new man in Christ.

What is this baneful power which Paul cries so desperately to be delivered from? Surely it is more than the power of inbred sin? It is: it is the devil, lurking behind the remnants of corruption and using them to cloak his presence and working. He is the third dimension of evil which Christ dealt with on the cross. Our present task is to expose him as deceiver.

'A man sowed good seed in his field; but while men were sleeping, his enemy came and sowed weeds among the wheat... And the servants of the householder came and said to him, "Sir, did you not sow good seed in your field? How then has it weeds?" He said to them, "An enemy has done this"' (Matt. 13:24–28 RSV). *Satan is essentially a deceiver*. Our Lord declared that he was not only a liar, but the father of lies. And he needs to be; for his person and works are so vile that no one

---

would be attracted to him in his own hideous guise. He must needs deceive; and his present deception conceals from sincere but guileless Christians that he is there and at work at all. He does his best (or worst) work in the dark.

To accomplish this he lies so close to the dregs of what we were, that his personal presence is not suspected, and he is consequently able to work upon souls committed to the truth of Romans 6:11 by insidiously stirring up their mortal flesh and (as soon as he has done so) accusing them of sin. We cannot know too much about his wiles. Paul declared that the Christians of his day were 'not ignorant of his devices'. But, today, some professing Christians do not believe in the devil's existence at all, and most Christians have only the haziest notion of his being, location, and working. Some even think it impious and cowardly of us to blame Satan at all for their sin.

It is too easy, admittedly, to blame the devil for our sin; but we are considering those who are free from the reign of sin, and who are taking their stand resolutely against its remaining corruption. For it is to the godly soul, or to him who would be godly, that Satan comes—Job, for example (see Job 1 and 2).

The devil knows that a soul justified by faith in Christ is lost to him for ever. But he can still work much ill in our life, hindering growth in grace and interfering with training for Christian warfare. And this Satan does by instituting a new campaign of temptation and accusation, which consists of injecting new depths of evil thoughts into the mind, to cast down the godly soul utterly, and make him fear that the truth declared in Romans 6 does not work. This leads to despair, which appears to be Paul's own remembered condition in Romans chapter 7 after Romans 6. That is why he cries out in mortal agony for deliverance from this new, greater, and more virulent 'sin'. But it is not sin, as such, but Satan, hiding in the folds of the fallen nature; who must be dealt with, personally and specifically, before the soul can be delivered from this new and terrible bondage.

Yes, but do we realise the supreme importance of this doctrine of Satan in the biblical unfolding of the meaning of the cross? The first promise of the Saviour in Genesis 3:15 speaks of deliverance, not from sins, nor from inbred sin, but from Satan, when the seed of the woman shall bruise the serpent's head. This explains the true nature of the conflict between good and evil as all-out war between God and the devil, the battleground being the life of man. Paul confirms this in the climax of the epistle to the Ephesians when he declares in 6:12 that our wrestling is not with flesh and blood (whether our own or that of others), but with spiritual foes still dwelling in the heavenly places which they have defiled. This is made even plainer by our Lord who, when Peter remonstrated with him concerning the prospect of his coming death, turned and addressed his beloved Peter as 'Satan': he saw the devil lurking in Peter's personality.

Does this not set the Christian's after-consecration struggles in a new light? Or do we still think it is too easy to blame the devil? Apparently, for some consecrated Christians prefer, piously and heroically, to blame themselves alone. How wrong and unhealthy! What a shame to turn our gracious Saviour into a policeman. How many are there who crack the legal whip before young Christians and spread the injurious heresy that God is a petty tyrant and slave-driver? What a monstrous travesty of the truth that is! Who is it, then, that Christians are dragooned into worshipping as a superthrasher of saints, with such devastating results? It is the devil, that dread 'angel of light', the accuser of the brethren, 'who accuses them before God day and night' (Rev. 12:10).

This insight is far too little known. But it is not novel. It is at least as old as *Pilgrim's Progress*! Wrote John Bunyan:

> One thing I would not let slip. I took notice that now poor Christian was so confounded, that he did not know his own voice: and thus I perceived it. Just when he was come over against the mouth of the burning pit, one of the wicked ones got behind him, and stepped up softly to him, and, whisperingly, suggested many grievous blasphemies to him, which he verily thought had proceeded from his own mind. This put Christian more to it than anything that he had met with before, even to think that he should now blaspheme him that he loved so much before. Yet if he could have helped it, he would not have done it; but he had not the discretion either to stop his ears, nor to know from whence these blasphemies came.[1]

But how are we to know when Satan is working in our thoughts? Surely the answer lies on the surface of Bunyan's passage. Christian knew that these were not his own thoughts, certainly not the thoughts of his

---

1 See Bunyan's *The Pilgrim's Progress*, Part 1, from the place at which Little Faith lies asleep in Dead Man's Lane, to the place where Christian meets with Atheist. *Cf.* also the passages quoted below, pp. 195–197. See John Owen, *Works*, Goold Edition, VI, pp. 190, 191, 193, 194, 203, 204, 212-214.

regenerate heart. After all, he, the regenerate one, was the real man, not fallen Adam. This, doubtless, Bunyan learned from the two illuminating verses in Romans 7 (17, 20), where the Apostle distinguishes between the one voice and the other speaking within him. This is good enough for us. We know that all that is not congruous with the holy law of Christ belongs to the other world, whether of sin or of Satan. Tracing it to its source and author, we ought always to refuse it, even when it subtly tries to mingle itself with what is pure, and gives us certain emotions which we normally associate with the truth. We must not put trust in our feelings. Only emotions which accompany the contemplation of the pure truth of God are to be trusted, and these, not of themselves, but only when accompanied with the truth that gives them rise.

But how are we to deal with this element in our lives if it is not only sinful but demonic? Is the thought that we are moved by perverse and malign spiritual intelligencies not unnerving? Not if we know the truth. Satan and all his crew have been dealt with. Jesus, who died to take away our sins and to overthrow sin, also died to defeat Satan and his powers, for us. For us! Just as we have wrestled with the paradox which says that we are dead to sin but must yet keep down the remaining dross, so we must now wrestle with the further paradox that Christ has finally defeated Satan for us on the cross, but we must make his victory our own by battling in his strength.

Take the fact of Christ's victory over the ultimate person of evil, the devil. Hebrews 2:14, 15 bluntly states that 'since the children share in flesh and blood, he himself likewise partook of the same nature, that through death he might destroy [bring to nought] him who has the power of death, that is, the devil, and deliver all those who through fear of death were subject to lifelong bondage' (RSV). And 1 John 3:8 is plain: 'The reason the Son of God appeared was to destroy the devil's work'. Colossians 2:15 says that Christ stripped, or disarmed 'the principalities and powers and made a public example of them, triumphing over them in it' [the cross], or 'in him' [Christ].

What do these Scriptures mean? That Christ took upon himself the very human nature in which Adam succumbed to Satan's power, and gained victory over the foe in it for Adam. John H. Newman's hymn helps greatly:

> O loving wisdom of our God!
> When all was sin and shame,
> A second Adam to the fight

And to the rescue came.

O wisest love! that flesh and blood,
Which did in Adam fail,
Should strive afresh against the foe,
Should strive and should prevail...
O generous love! that he who smote
In Man, for man, the foe,
The double agony in Man,
For man, should undergo.

Easter hymns love to trumpet forth the clarion note of Christ's victory over the enemy, but Newman's hymn goes further than many in declaring that the victory was *for man*, that is, *for us*.

To understand what this means we must remember that Christ the eternal Son of God and Co-Creator with the Father had no need of personal victory over the devil: he was not in his power. Rather, the devil was a creature of the three-in-one God, whom he could destroy in a moment. It is unthinkable that Christ should need to inhabit a human body to gain victory over the devil for himself. It is Christ who holds all things together in his hands (Col. 1:17; Heb. 1:2, 3). He won the victory for us: that was the length to which his love went to retrieve our ruin. Hence Paul cries out in the great resurrection chapter, 'Thanks be to God. He gives us the victory through our Lord Jesus Christ' (1 Cor. 15:57).

He gives us the victory! The Easter hymns are largely content to shout Christ's own victory, as if he won it for himself, and not for us. It was for us, and its great purpose begins to be realised only when we see it, and enter into its fruits, as did the saints in Revelation 12:11.

That whole passage describing God's victory in Christ over Satan ought to be studied (Rev. 12:7–12). Its climax declares that our brethren, who are accused day and night by Satan, overcame him through the blood of the Lamb, and through the word of their witness (to that fact), which witness they maintained, not loving their lives even to martyrdom. Think what this means: *Men overcame Satan*, through Christ's victory over him. Therefore, *we may overcome him, too*. Is it not tremendous that mere sinners, formerly under absolute bondage to God's implacable enemy, may now, by trusting in Jesus' death, overcome him, because Jesus died to procure that victory for them?

This is why James challenges us: 'Resist the devil, and he will flee from you' (Jas. 4:7). Peter also warns us that our 'enemy the devil prowls around like a roaring lion looking for someone to devour'; adding, 'Resist him, standing firm in the faith' (1 Pet. 5:8, 9). But let Jesus have the last word: 'No one can enter a strong man's house, and carry off his possessions [the enslaved souls of men, including believers still partly in his power], unless he first ties up the strong man. Then he can rob his house' (Mark 3:27).

Christ has given us the power to bind the strong man, the devil, and spoil his goods, and this includes the freeing of our souls, and the souls of others, progressively from his thrall. But first we must let the facts of Christ's power sink deep into our minds until faith rises to take hold of them. Then faith will take hold of the enemy where his influence lives, and shake him until he flees for his life.

The victory Christ gained for us over the enemy is full and final, but we must, none the less, battle our way into it, inch by inch, through his power. We must therefore lay our plans in full Bible knowledge. If we do, we shall soon see three clearly discernible stages in the development of the Christian life, from childhood to soldierhood.

1. A believer is born of Christ as a babe, and is spiritually in need of milk food because he cannot stand strong meat (1 Cor. 3:1–3; Heb. 5:12–14; 1 Pet. 2:2). Infants cannot serve.

2. A true babe in Christ, if nourished in God's Word, will grow and become fit for the service of God. (There were forty hidden years in Moses' life, thirty in our Lord's, and ten in Paul's after his conversion.) He will then serve according to his calling and gifts.

3. A servant cannot fight until he knows the enemy, within and without, and has been trained in the use of Christian armour, weapons, and strategy: then he becomes a soldier. This is the theme of our next chapter.

TOWARDS SPIRITUAL MATURITY

5. The Military Training of a Soldier

As there are three stages in the development of the Christian life from childhood through servanthood to soldierhood, so there are three stages in his training as a Christian soldier. They are:

1. Strategic Retreat.
2. Unyielding Defence.
3. All-out Attack.

We must learn *how, when* and *where* to *run for shelter* from overwhelming danger; *stand for resolute defence*; and *advance to confident attack.*

1. Strategic Retreat

It may seem contradictory to what we have stated concerning victory in Christ, immediately to counsel young soldiers to run from the enemy; but it is necessary. Discretion is often the better part of valour, especially when God lets Satan loose upon us for our training. He is, of course, never really loose: God simply lengthens his chain, and allows him scope to try us. But it is a frightening experience to face his snarling advance, and at first we may want to turn and flee, not into Christ, but away from the whole terrifying business of being a Christian at all. Many have tried to do so and have striven to maintain an uneasy compromise between Christ and the devil and heaven and hell, but without success. Besides, God's Word strictly and sternly forbids us to fear Satan. How many 'Fear nots' are there in the Bible? Yet part of our training is to know the enemy, and before we have the unspeakable thrill of putting him to flight, we must learn what a terrible foe he is. As we learn we will realise that it is important to know where to run for shelter, for there are days of Satan's power (see Luke 22:53b) when

---

even the strongest is well advised to run to Christ for safety. The Scriptures teach this.

David in his Song of Deliverance from his enemies says: 'The Lord is my rock, my fortress, and my deliverer; my God is my rock; in whom I take refuge, my shield, and the horn of my salvation. He is my stronghold, my refuge and my saviour—from violent men you save me' (2 Sam. 22:2; see also Ps. 18:2). The same great soldier says again: 'Hear my cry, O God; listen to my prayer. From the ends of the earth I call to you, I call as my heart grows faint; lead me to the rock that is higher than I. For you have been my refuge, a strong tower against the foe. I long to dwell in your tent for ever, and take refuge in the shelter of your wings (Ps. 61:1–4). And the mighty general's son Solomon: 'The name of the Lord is a strong tower: the righteous run to it, and are safe (Prov. 18:10).

Much is said about the increasing tendency to escape the pressures of modern life, and some escapes, like those into drugs or suicide, are bad. But escape is sometimes necessary. No man is able to cope with the evil in the world unaided. But the Christian is not unaided. He has Christ for his shelter, and must learn, especially in the evil day (Eph. 6:13), to beat an ordered retreat from him and hide in the Rock of Ages until Satan's fury is past (see Ps. 57:1).

We need to be forewarned of Satan's attacks when we enter the training school for spiritual warfare, for they usually come suddenly, and from the least expected quarter. It may be an inward attack, or it may come from without, as a bolt from the blue, to demoralise us before we know where we are. It is a real enemy we are fighting, who will stop at nothing to knock us out of the fight before we are in it.

Many Christians who accept this kind of teaching in general without personal knowledge of the devil's malevolence, and who are therefore innocently sceptical of it, are alarmed when he cuts across their path, or makes them fall flat on their faces on the threshold of a great campaign. Consequently, they reel and wonder what has hit them. But we must not panic, nor become morbidly preoccupied with dread of Satan, but set a serious watch, and reckon that without looking for trouble, he will attack.

2. Unyielding Defence
It is wonderful to run into Christ in the evil hour and, with the enemy roaring all around, know that he is powerless to touch us. Only then,

when we have learned in practice what we know in theory, do we realise that *Jesus is stronger than Satan.* With this new confidence in our Saviour's power we are ready for the next stage in our training, and we graduate to a higher class in the Captain's school. There is a paradox here; for we must always run into Christ in danger, since we are ourselves defenceless souls. Yet God is not only our refuge, but our strength. Sheltered in him and made aware of the armour he provides, we are soon encouraged to don its several pieces and think about facing the foe. When Satan next attacks, instead of cowering in the corners of our shelter, we dare to stand forth and resist him bravely. Hebrews 2:14, 1 John 3:8, and Colossians 2:15 have already afforded us typical ground for believing in Christ's victory: now we begin to accept the fact that the power of Christ to shelter us from the devil may also fortify us in confronting him.

But before we go to the battlefield, we need to be reassured that Christ's victory will be personally available to us. To believe this calls for a tremendous effort of faith, and we must learn to grapple to our hearts such words as 'gives us' in 1 Corinthians 15:57 and 'they overcame him' in Revelation 12:11, to know that his victory is ours. This is not easy, even if we have the example of the heroes of faith in Hebrews 11. However many saints have trusted in God's power and found it effectual, this is *our* first attempt in a new dimension. It is as if not only we, but Christ also, were being tested anew. In fact, it demands a trust in Christ's deed and Word which in the critical event is nothing less than the dying of a death to all defeatist, emotional rationalisations that are likely to assail us in the conflict. This is simply a matter of following Christ into that death by which he gained his victory. We gain ours likewise, by following where he first victoriously led. If it does not work with us, then not only do we fail, but he fails also, for his Word is proved ineffectual. God cannot take that risk, and is as much concerned that his power works with us as with his Son; for it is wrought for his Son in his death, that it might work for us in ours. 'For us' is our fortification, and thus fortified, we go forward confidently to face the foe. And we had better, as Jeremiah the most timid of prophets found when he was commanded to face the whole evil might of decadent Jewry.

Jeremiah sought to excuse himself to the Lord because, he said, he was a child and could not speak (Jer. 1:6). But God said: 'Now, I have put my words in your mouth' (v. 9). 'Do not be afraid of them; for I am with you and will rescue you' (v. 8.). And, lest he falter, God added: 'Get yourself ready! Stand up and say to them whatever I command you. Do not be terrified by them or I will terrify you before them. Today I have made you a fortified city, an iron pillar, and a bronze wall against the whole land…. They will fight against you but will not overcome you for I am with you and will rescue you' (vv. 17–19).

Thus exposed to the blasts of the enemy, there is no alternative to naked faith in the Word of the Lord, no alternative but complete demoralisation, and defeat!

Turn to David again. Here is a hardy word of encouragement for such a time, and from a surprising place—the Shepherd Psalm. The writer is in the valley of the shadow of death, not knowing, apart from their occasional growls, where the wild beasts lurk amongst the surrounding crags; and he is calmly sitting down to a sumptuous meal while his person is groomed, even to the anointing of his head (Ps. 23:4, 5)! Could we enjoy a feast if a roaring lion were about to leap upon us?

But the fullest and most helpful passage on the exploit is in Ephesians 6:10–18. Following the introduction (10–13), note the four 'stands', in 11, 13 (twice), and 14. It is easy to say 'Stand', but when all the demons of hell are let loose it is not easy to stand, let alone sit and indulge ourselves. But in Christ we do not stand defenceless and exposed to the enemy's onslaughts, but are provided with suitable dress for the battle. To this we now turn.

(i) The Belt of Truth
The first item of defensive armour is the belt of truth. The Scriptures have much to say about 'girding the loins'. They bid us gather ourselves together for action as soldiers gird themselves for battle. The girdle or belt applied to truth reminds us that only the truth can prevail in the war against falsehood.

> Fain would we join the blest array,
> And follow in the might
> Of him, the Faithful and the True,
> In raiment clean and white.
> Yet who can fight for truth and God,
> Enthralled by lies and sin?
> He who would wage such war on earth
> Must first be true within.
> (Thomas Hughes)

The apostle is probably referring both to the whole body of biblical truth and to particular truths declaring God's power and victory over the forces of evil. What are these? They concern the nature of God and the devil and the different dimensions of their activities:

1. God the Father is the uncreated and unbegotten One, whereas Satan is a creature gone wrong, whom God could destroy in a moment if he chose.

2. Christ the eternal Son, the only-begotten of the Father, has gained final victory over Satan, as Newman says, 'in Man for man'. See Hebrews 2:14; 1 John 3:8; Colossians 2:15; Revelation 12:7–11.

3. God the eternal Spirit, following Pentecost, brings the efficacies of Christ's victorious death to the hearts and lives of those who believe in him.

If in the face of the enemy's attacks we bind these truths to us and refuse to let them be torn from us, we will repulse the enemy, and rejoice to see him driven defeated from the field.

(ii) The Breastplate of Righteousness
But Satan is not done with us by any means, and we must be prepared for further attacks. We must put on the breastplate of righteousness, to withstand his attack both upon our standing and our state in Christ, for he will try to deny both our imputed and our imparted righteousness. The breastplate particularly guards the heart, and it is in the heart that we must believe that Christ is our righteousness (see Rom. 10:10; Jer. 23:6; and 1 Cor. 1:30). This is our standing.

But it is perhaps especially in respect of our moral state, or state of actual righteousness, that we are assailed by Satan. We shall not be *perfect* while we are in this mortal body, but we can be *blameless*.

It is only as we preserve moral integrity before God by the Spirit's aid that, as to basic virtues of honesty, purity, humility and charity, we can withstand the enemy's assaults.

At this stage we may expect massive attacks upon basic virtues. We should not be surprised even although we are appalled, at some of the impure and dishonest thoughts that he causes to pass through our minds. These are not ordinary temptations of the flesh, although they come through the flesh. They come from the enemy himself. Further, their sudden coming is generally related to some opportunity about to present itself for fruitful witness or service. The fact that Satan is trying something on in relation to the (possibly) immediate future should encourage us to resist his emotional enticements. It is far more exciting to resist a sudden pleasurable sensation or tempting thought and subsequently discover where the devil was trying to gain an advantage over us, than to yield to it without a struggle!

This is a common attack on young servants of God, as is plain from Paul's words to Timothy: 'I give you this instruction in keeping with the prophecies once made about you, so that by following them you may fight the good fight, holding on to faith and a good conscience. Some have rejected these and so have shipwrecked their faith' (1 Tim. 1:18, 19). Again, a leader 'must not be a recent convert, or he may become conceited and fall under the same judgement as the devil' (1 Tim. 3:6, 7). Peter adds, 'as aliens and strangers in the world...abstain from sinful desires, which war against your soul' (1 Pet. 2:11). Again, says Paul, 'Do not give the devil a foothold' (Eph. 4:27).

We must guard our inward moral integrity as our life; for, if we fail here, we fail utterly. Yet if we begin to see how cunningly occasional, or tactically planned these temptations are, we shall soon be wise, not only to them, but to him (Satan).

(iii) The Gospel of Peace
We are taking the pieces of defensive armour in Ephesians 6 in progressive and culminating sequence, although some think this goes beyond the scriptural warrant. Perhaps; but that there is a progression is plain from the fact that the defensive comes before the offensive; the shield, *etc.* before the sword of the Spirit and the weapon of all-prayer. We shall maintain this progression, but those who reject it need not reject the truth associated with it: we are not trying to impose an arbitrary pattern of diabolical attacks upon the spiritual progress of every soul— even a little knowledge of human psychology shows how foolish that would be.

The attack upon our personal, moral integrity is a serious one, and the devil, successfully repulsed, may now retire to devise new and more cunning tactics against us. If he cannot shake our moral convictions or undermine our moral character, he has other weapons in his diabolical armoury, and will doubtless try more powerful means to move us, in the hope that he may shatter our peace of mind.

He may now assail us with a sense of restless foreboding, and with irrational fears, until we seriously doubt God, ourselves, and, in fact, everything that is good. All joy goes out of life, nothing seems to matter, a vague, gnawing, cynical dread underlies all we formerly thought secure; the whole world begins to heave and turn like an ocean giant plunging to its doom. These are not ordinary feelings of unhappiness; indeed, they can be so enveloping and total that it is hard to believe they are real. But they are only too real—yet they seem so unlikely that it is impossible to talk about them; people would not understand.

Not many understand, although many suffer. But God who permits them understands, and he has a word, several words, for them. Here is one, whose bedrock dependability has been proved for ages by those in dire need: 'You will keep in perfect peace, him whose mind is steadfast, because he trusts in you. Trust in the Lord forever, for the Lord, the Lord is the' rock eternal' (Is. 26:3, 4). This is not biblical jargon with meaning only for the initiated, but an anchor of truth for all to hold on to when the whole world seems to be giving way.

Here is another word, this time from Paul: 'Do not be anxious about anything; but in everything by prayer and petition, with thanksgiving, present your request to God. And the peace of God, which transcends all understanding, will guard your hearts and minds in Christ Jesus' (Phil. 4:6, 7). And again, 'And over all these virtues put on love, which binds them all together in perfect unity. Let the peace of Christ rule [preside] in your hearts' (Col. 3:14, 15).

With Scriptures such as these—and it is not the number of them but the penetration of their truth that counts—the sorely tried soldier, his feet well shod with the good news of God's care and provision, can take his stance and hold his ground against the most hellish attack. This is especially true, since the Father is watching that he may not be tempted beyond what he is able to bear (1 Cor. 10:13). After all, it is not only our faith in Christ which daunts Satan, but the watchful eye of the Almighty. He will not suffer us to be overwhelmed by him. It is well to remember that when we are tried, and tempted to resign ourselves to the darkness of defeat, the enemy also may be almost played out. If we can hold on, he will collapse and let go. He must and will, because we are trusting in him who has vanquished him, once and for all. Jesus' own heart-rending cry was just before the end. What devilish pressure was laid upon him we do not know, but it was 'for the joy that was set before him' that 'he endured' (Heb. 12:2). He had all to gain or all to lose, and he emerged triumphant in victorious death and resurrection. So shall we, if we endure, and be ready to fight another day, with strengthened faith.

(iv) The Shield of Faith

The enemy will at this point need to regain his breath. He is not
invincible, and more easily shaken by those in Christ than we realise.
But while he calls an infernal conference (*cf.* C. S. Lewis' *Screwtape
Letters*) and desperately tries to plan new and more deadly attacks, we
may list, not proudly, but humbly and thankfully, the growing tale of
our victories—all to Christ's glory. Yet these will not suffice for his next
attack: we must also set ourselves to test our defences, and seek to found
our faith more securely on the Rock of Ages, so that we may stand
together with Christ against the further demoralising attacks the enemy is
about to launch. We need a huge shield of faith to quench all the fire-
tipped darts which he is about to hurl at us from all directions, in an all-
out blitz.

But what does the imagery of the fire-tipped dart represent in
experience? A series of sudden, totally unexpected attacks, usually very
different from one another, aimed at shaking our faith in God, his
revealed Word and will to his children, and our judgement, obedience
and sincerity.

For example, a young servant of God awaiting news of an
examination is seized with a feeling of vile and impure hands laid upon
her, and the feeling persists and grows until she is well-nigh demented.
Exhorted to resist in faith and believe for success (having done all she
could to merit it) she does so, and when the good news about the
examination comes through, the attack ends as suddenly as it began.

Another example: a young missionary, his leave long overdue, looks
forward eagerly to the voyage home to relieve the almost unbearable
strain of a trying tour of service. The days before embarkation are spent
in a hospitable home where the children are suffering from an
exceedingly infectious disease. On the night of the embarkation the
awful thought strikes him that he is a carrier of the disease and dare not
go on board. There were no symptoms, nothing to ground the obsessing
fear upon but the overpowering thought, confronting him like a barrier at
the gangway. Almost mad with tension, he nevertheless resists the
thought, and the next day, with trepidation, goes on board.

The first few days on ship were hell to his tortured mind: he avoided
every one, especially the children, as if he were a leper. No symptoms
appeared, however, and the gripping fear began to relax, and the

remainder of the voyage was pleasant, beneficial, and fruitful in spiritual profit to others. Only those who have experienced this kind of thing can appreciate the inward agony.

Here is another story of a tried and trusted servant of God. It has two parts, one comparatively trivial, the other more serious, illustrating the varied stratagems of the enemy. A young man intent on serving God had begun to prepare for Christian service. He had a happy nature with a normally healthy outlook on life, but had become increasingly obsessed with the morbid suspicion that to be too happy was sinful. One day he saw something he wanted in a shop window and went in to buy it. The shopkeeper appeared, and instantly the inward tyrant hissed, 'You cannot have it: it is sin!' Dumbfounded at the violence of the warning, he fled from the shop leaving the astonished shopkeeper gaping.

The other part of the story concerns a university grant. Financial assistance was not easily come by then, and the young man's parents were not able to finance his education. But he was assured he would receive a grant, and was about to sign the application form when the sinister voice spat out, 'You cannot do it, it is sin!' Several years of financial aid were thereby unsigned away, leading to years of hardship.

This form of attack came with increasing frequency and ferocity until a sane and balanced young man became almost demented, not only by its unpredictableness, but by the horrid discovery that the 'God' he had believed to be so loving was really a monster. (Compare the experience of Job, for example, in chapters 9 and 10.)

It is all very well to say that Satan's bluff should have been called earlier; but he is a spirit, and when he comes in this way, and young Christians have no teaching on the workings of evil spirits, the very force of the attacks is frighteningly impressive, and his victims are driven to comply in sheer terror, lest they fight against God.

As this form of attack developed increasingly in the young man's life, his early ministry was periodically overwhelmed by a pall of spiritual darkness completely enshrouding his soul. He had to preach the Word even while the black conviction gripped him that he himself was lost, a Christless soul; and others were converted through his preaching even while this was his own experience. Eventually, although it took years, the ground comparatively innocently conceded to the enemy was retaken, albeit with painful failures and setbacks, until at last there was full deliverance. The fruits of this man's ministry are now well known, and the reason for Satan's desperate attempts to stop it before it had well nigh started is fully exposed.

It is the suddenness and unexpectedness of the attacks which are alarming, as also the imperious demand that the spirit is to be obeyed instantly without question—and without reason.

How then are we to distinguish between the voice of God and the voice of Satan? We know, of course, that God can give his servants swift guidance, but he never 'blitzes' them. He has no need; for even when he comes suddenly, he is sweetly reasonable and identifies himself by his loving wisdom, and thus we recognise him. Normally he takes his time to tell us something new, and allows his gently growing pressure to convince us that it is indeed our heavenly Father who is speaking. He never dragoons, least of all those who are being trained to be his valued servants. He has a specially tender care and regard for them.

(v) The Helmet of Salvation
This is the last piece of defensive armour—salvation for the head. The attack which it serves to ward off is certainly the devil's worst. Indeed, true children of God, who are not, all of them, old and senile, can be attacked. Evil can assail those who are normally sane, whether they have a predisposition to mental illness or not.

It is too painful and embarrassing to discuss modern examples, but a notable scriptural example illustrates the possibility, that of Israel's first king, Saul. To understand the example fully we must read his life story in 1 Samuel, chapters 10–26, when it will be hard to escape the conclusion that that magnificent specimen of manhood was attacked by the devil, or some demonic spirit or spirits, to his ruin.

But surely the intimate stories of missionaries who have challenged the kingdom of darkness and have paid for their pains, tell of what the wrecker can do to God's soldiers if the head is not protected from his diabolical attacks. Nothing less than the helmet of salvation will save in this situation. The last piece of defensive armour must be a scriptural word defying the total ingenuity and might of the devil himself. Such a word is, 'submit yourselves, then, to God. Resist the devil, and he will flee from you' (Jas. 4:7; also 1 Pet. 5:8, 9).

But the helmet needs to be firmly fitted to protect the whole mind. We must boldly react against the desperate wiles of the devil until he is thoroughly shaken. This is a tremendous thing to do, for it involves nothing less than standing between God and the devil, and daring to declare that we intend to prove in our own mind and body that Jesus is stronger than Satan. Furthermore, that brave attitude must understand that the salvation of the mortal life is at stake, for it has its back to the wall, is faced by an implacable foe, and is fighting for nothing less than survival as a practising Christian. The devil must yield.

Do we ask what will happen if he does not? Well, if we were to draw on the victorious resources of Jesus Christ in the evil day and found that they did not work, we would have proved Christ's claims false, and could trust him no more. But he cannot fail: his integrity depends upon him delivering his people in the 'evil day'. Why, even the survival of the universe, and his own survival, depend upon that! We may be called with the Apostle to be 'exposed to death again and again' (2 Cor. 11:23), but through it all there must be resurrections, either in this world, or, in the case of martyrdoms, in the next. We can be as sure as God that in Christ there is victory for us (1 Cor. 15:57).

3. All-out Attack
We are almost weary of the word 'attack' as applied to the enemy. It will be a change to re-apply it to ourselves in Christ. When the devil, who cannot destroy the servants and soldiers of God, but only render them unfit for service, sees that we have won our spurs, he will withdraw from us for a little. He is not gone for ever, but has retired to plan fresh attacks. But we have learned that in the strength of Christ he can be repulsed. We have gained something of his measure, and the lesson is not lost on us. We are now ready to wield the sword of the Spirit which is the Word of God.

(i) The Sword of the Spirit
We have used the Word of God before in our defence (Eph. 6:14). We are now to learn to hurl it at the enemy as Jesus did in his temptations. How do we do it? Just as he did (Matt. 4:1–11). He took three 'rocks' of holy Scripture (Deut. 8:3; 6:16; 6:13) and flung them at the devil until he departed, beaten. The devil can quote the Scriptures, too, but if we compare Matthew 4:6 with Psalm 91:11, 12, we shall see that Satan, like so many, leaves out what does not suit his purpose. He uses the Scriptures to deceive, trap and destroy us if he can: whereas Jesus uses them to destroy what is evil. We see who uses them successfully in the temptation account.

The difference between Jesus' use of the Scriptures and the devil's use of them is this: Satan tinkers with them and loses their force by leaving out God's promise to keep his people while they walk in his ways. Jesus uses them simply, and, united to the Father and the Spirit speaking in holy Writ, resists him effectually. It is, therefore, identification with the triune God speaking in Scripture which is our strength, not trying to add or to subtract from God's Word (*cf*. Rev. 22:18, 19). To prove the power of God in his Word we must stand foursquare upon it with Jesus.

We are now in a realm where we may not only withstand the enemy on our own behalf, but on behalf of others. This is a tremendous thrill, which will be even more obvious when we come to the use of the other offensive weapon, all-prayer. The writer to the Hebrews tells us that, 'The word of God is living and active, sharper than any two-edged sword, piercing to the division of soul and spirit ... discerning the thoughts and intentions of the heart. And before him (note the unity of God with his Word) no creature is hidden' (Heb. 4:12, 13a RSV).

When we use God's Word in accordance with his will, we have all the consent and power of the Almighty behind us. We therefore take the Word of Jesus which commands us to bind the strong man (the poetic figure of binding is not congruous with that of swiping with a sword, but the truths belong together) in order to spoil his goods (the souls of men held in his thrall). We shall find that when we exert ourselves to do this with an energy and devotion at least as keen as we apply to selfish pursuits, lo, people begin to respond to God's Word, perhaps to our great surprise. It is not to be wondered at. The truth is that men's hearts and lives are in fact in bondage to Satan (1 Jn. 5:19) and when his power is broken, they are free to hear and heed God's Word.

This is a great secret; and yet many of us go on in Christian work year by year, dealing with men as if they were normally free agents willing and able to do what we say, or what they themselves will. They are not (Rom. 7:14–20), until God frees them in answer to prevailing prayer.

(ii) All-Prayer
The connection of the sword of the Spirit with prayer is clear. It is not in direct witness, public or private, that the battle for souls is won, but in the closet and prayer room (Matt. 6:6). Far too many who are engaged in Christian service do not appreciate this. They also are blinded by Satan, and we may wonder whether they believe in God at all, except as some rudimentary, vague spirit who sits content with perfunctory religion.

There are two possible meanings of all-prayer: (1) that it includes all forms of prayer; (2) that it means all-out prayer. This seems to be what the Apostle has in mind in Ephesians 6:18. It is *total war*, demanding *total dedication*. The plain truth is that as Christ did not save us short of his death, neither will we save others short of his death in us, whatever that death may be or may mean for us personally.

The most searching word on this is found in 2 Corinthians 4:10–12, where Paul speaks of dying and rising on his own behalf (vv. 10, 11), and for others (v. 12). This is the death which defeats Satan. It defeated him fundamentally and finally on the cross, and it defeats him in our lives and in the lives of others as we stand with the Crucified and Risen One resisting to 'blood' (Heb. 12:4).

This 'death' in prayer has two effects, which Scripture describes as 'fasting' and 'prayer'. 'Fasting' indicates the negative part of it in temporarily denying ourselves the legitimate pleasures of life, whereas 'prayer' indicates the positive part of entering into the intercessory death-throes that bind Satan. Such intercessory death enables God to open men's hearts and minds to receive the Word of Truth with unblinded and unbiased honesty. It also gives utterance to witnesses to the truth (whether speaking in private, or in public), who let the Holy Spirit through from the throne of God to their hearts, and then to the hearts of their hearers, and back again to heaven. The whole sequence and circle of the divine purpose is thus wonderfully threaded through to its completion.

'All-Prayer' is therefore not an 'added extra' to evangelism. It is so vital a part of evangelism that no true evangelism can exist without it (see Eph. 6:19, 20).

TOWARDS SPIRITUAL MATURITY

6. Christian Service and Warfare

It cannot be too clearly stated, or too often repeated, that God has only one Worker, the Holy Spirit. In all we hope to become and do for God we never take over from him.

God will not surrender his sovereignty to his creatures. Indeed, in all our Lord's amazing 'homecoming' to sinful humanity by his incarnate, saving love, he is always careful to make the distinction between God and man. Jesus does not pray or speak to the Father as we do, saying 'our Father', but, 'my Father' (Jn. 20:17). It is only in the Only-Begotten that we are adopted into the Father's family. Even so, we remain creature-sons and daughters, as he ever remains the Creator-Son. This means that our dependence on God's power must be constant and absolute, as Jesus' stark statement shows: 'When you have done everything you were told to do...say, "We are unworthy servants; we have only done our duty"' (Lk. 17:10). Whereas Paul declares, 'I can do everything through him who gives me strength' (Phil. 4:13), Jesus says, 'Apart from me you can do nothing' (Jn. 15:5).

There is great danger of the intrusion of the flesh (fallen humanity) into Christian service. It is surely for this reason that in moments of high spiritual strategy God makes indubitably plain that the authority, initiative and execution of his will remain always and only in his hands.

An illustration of this is provided in Exodus 14 when the Red Sea barred the escape of the Israelites fleeing from the Egyptians. Something had to be done—and quickly! Moses turned to the panic-stricken people and shouted, 'Do not be afraid. Stand firm and you will see the deliverance the Lord will bring you today. The Egyptians you see today, you will never see again. The Lord will fight for you; you need only to

---

be still' (Ex. 14:13, 14).

But they did not stand idle. God said, 'Go forward, right down to the shore, and see what I will do.' And they did; for salvation, all of grace, is nevertheless of faith, the gift of God's grace. In this instance, the fact that redemption was all of God was acknowledged later by Moses and Israel when they sang their song of triumph:

> I will sing to the Lord, for he is highly exalted.
> The horse and its rider he has hurled into the sea.
> The Lord is my strength and my song; he has become my
>   salvation.
> He is my God, and I will praise him,
> my father's God, and I will exalt him.
> The Lord is a warrior;
> The Lord is his name (Ex. 15:1–3).

We find the same emphasis in the story of David. In gratitude for his victories over the enemies of Israel, he desired to build a house for the Lord. God said, 'The Lord himself will build a house for you' (2 Sam. 7–11).

The house David intended, and which Solomon eventually built, was of wood and stone. The house God promised to build for David was his lineage, even to 'great David's greater Son', then to us and all the children of God. That house is *God's* building, although we help to build it and are part of it and shall dwell in it one day. The fine balance of God's working and of our co-operation with him is perfectly expressed in Paul's exhortation: 'Work out your salvation with fear and trembling, for it is God who works in you to will and to act according to his good purpose' (Phil. 2:12, 13).

A God so great in power will not share his honour and glory with us. 'I am the Lord; that is my name! I will not give my glory to another' (Is. 42:8). 'Therefore if any one is in Christ, he is a new creation; the old has gone, the new has come. All this is from God' (2 Cor. 5:17, 18a). 'Whether you eat, or drink, or whatever you do, do it all for the glory of God' (1 Cor. 10:31).

God is the only Worker, for all that we do in him is by his power. Those who seek to serve him and fight for him must be morally, intellectually and emotionally convinced that all the glory is his, and that the uncreated God will never share his sole prerogative with his

creatures. What he shares are his blessings, and the man in Christ can
have his fill of them—certainly more than he seeks.

TOWARDS SPIRITUAL MATURITY

7. Spiritual Maturity

We have called this collection *Towards Spiritual Maturity*, not *Towards Spiritual Victory*. Why? Because spiritual maturity is more than the achievement of victorious service. Certainly, none can serve God without a measure of maturity, as none can fight for him without a measure of understanding of, and training for the realities of spiritual conflict.

We have heard the claim, and have supported it, that the highest divine service on earth is intercession. Is there not a higher? Not higher, but different, which necessarily belongs with fruitful intercession. It is love to Jesus, and enjoyment of God. This is highest worship, highest maturity, and highest service, all in one. It runs side by side with the mighty warfare of intercession and with effective public service for Christ. It stands to reason that we cannot be often at the throne of grace without coming to know the occupant of the throne. We cannot be much on active service in the interests of his glory without enjoying the fruits of that co-operation with him. Indeed, this both precedes all we can say, and is the sum of it.

> *The love of Jesus, what it is*
> *None but his loved ones know!*

There is a zeal for God (*cf*. Rom. 10:2–4) and for the honour of his name which may work itself to death in sacrifice and endurance ('if I surrender my body to the flames', 1 Cor. 13:3), but whose motive is neither high enough nor pure enough to gain the Lord's co-operation, or his commendation. Such was the case with the Ephesians in Revelation 2:1–7. They had left their first love, Jesus, and consequently their highest and best was at least suspect. There is no loyalty, faithfulness, obedience, endurance, or suffering that can pass the all-seeing eye of heaven's Majesty except it springs from love to Jesus.

Let us look further into this in connection with what we have been saying. We have seen that God hates three elements in fallen man—his sins, his sin, and the influence of Satan on him. Having learned from God's Word of Christ's complete provision against all three, and that there is nothing and no one to fear beyond these, we may enter into the infinite and eternal inheritance which Christ's victory has gained for us, namely that of the 'peace that passes all understanding'.

'Where sin increased, grace increased all the more' (Rom. 5:20). There is no doubt about the pleasure we have in God when we see the real size of the enemy, for all the evil which God implacably hates we then see to be but serving his purpose, by evoking responses of divine grace to deal with it.

We know, of course, that we must not sin that grace may abound (Rom. 6:1, 2). Yet we must nevertheless rejoice that all the evil and sin which God permits he purposes to use to his glory. When Simon the Pharisee inwardly despised Jesus for regarding the woman 'who was a sinner', Jesus replied, 'I tell you, her many sins have been forgiven for she loved much. But he who has been forgiven little loves little' (Luke 7:47). The grace of abundant forgiveness of many sins evokes a commensurate love in the forgiven sinner. This turns the so-called problem of evil not only into a mystery solved, but into such a cause of rejoicing and thanksgiving to God as surely makes the vaults of heaven ring and its courts resound with angelic praise.

We have sometimes thought the laughter of God at the attempts of Satan to hurt him must be so hearty and incredulous as to be too much for over-serious Christians to hear! The amazement of heaven at the devil's niggling attempts to do despite to God and his work must be astonishing. No one who knows that God is on the throne and that 'all things work together for good to them that love God' can possibly have a qualm or fear about anything. Things being as they are by the victory of Christ, there remains nothing to preoccupy the heart and mind beyond Jesus.

Let us be sure about this. If we look at Exodus chapters 7 to 9 we shall see that six times Pharaoh hardened his heart (7:13, 14; 7:22; 8:15; 8:32; 9:7), but in 9:12 'the Lord hardened the heart of Pharaoh', which suggests that God ultimately confirmed Pharaoh in his chosen path of sin. But Pharaoh's sin, confirmed by God, does not frustrate the Almighty (see Rom. 9:17, 18). The Egyptian king resisted God to his own destruction, and to the destruction of his army.

'In the morning watch the Lord looked down from the pillar of fire and cloud at the Egyptian army and threw it into confusion. He made the wheels of their chariots come off so that they had difficulty driving. And the Egyptians said, "Let's get away from the Israelites! The Lord is fighting for them against Egypt." Then the Lord said to Moses, "Stretch out your hand over the sea so that the waters may flow back over the Egyptians and their chariots and horsemen." Moses stretched out his hand over the sea, and at daybreak the sea went back to its place. The Egyptians were fleeing towards it, and the Lord swept them into the sea' (Ex. 14:24–7). Mark the point of the quotation, which is not the deliverance of Israel, but the glory of God. The Egyptians saw that the Lord was fighting for Israel, and glorified him (Matt. 5:16), not them! Further, Exodus 14:31 says, 'When the Israelites saw the great power the Lord displayed against the Egyptians, the people feared the Lord, and put their trust in him and in Moses his servant'. Here are two testimonies to the glory of God: one from the Egyptians, the other from Israel. All this, then, is to his glory, and nothing that is ultimately to his glory comes amiss, however calamitous it may appear to be at first.

We have referred to Romans 9. Paul there argues that we must let God be God and not ask impertinent questions. 'Who are you, O man, to talk back to God?... What if God, choosing to show his wrath and make his power known, bore with great patience the objects of his wrath—prepared for destruction? What if he did this to make the riches of his glory known to the objects of his mercy, whom he prepared in advance for glory—even us...' (9:20–24). That is the Almighty's business—glory. Evil only provides the friction to produce it, and when grace triumphs over every evil thing, what is there to fear? Nothing, absolutely nothing.

> *Jesus! the Name high over all.*
> *In hell, or earth, or sky:*
> *Angels and men before it fall,*
> *And devils fear and fly.*

What, then, is the peace of God? A negation? The mere absence of the undesirable? God forbid! God's peace is a positive blessing, not a vacuum. But what sort of a blessing is it? At the very least it consists of undistraction, which, blessedly, affords complete freedom to enjoy

God. We must therefore strive to remain undistracted, not only by evil,
but by all that evil would use to distract us. That will include turning
aside from some of the highest and best gifts of God. 'The time is short.
From now on those who have wives should live as though they had
none; those that mourn, as if they did not; those who are happy, as if
they were not; those who buy something, as if it were not theirs to keep;
those who use the things of the world, as if not engrossed in them. For
this world in its present form is passing away.... I am saying this for
your own good, not to restrict you, but that you may live in a right way
in undivided devotion to the Lord' (1 Cor. 7:29–35).

Spiritual maturity, then, is in sight when we begin to know that
freedom from sinful and carnal distraction, high or low, which affords
the soul leisure for the enjoyment of God. 'Man's chief end is to glorify
God and enjoy him for ever' (*Westminster Shorter Catechism*). Is this in
conflict with human duty, or with Christian warfare? Not at all! It is the
inspiration of both, and of every good work, and is prior to them all.
Without love to Jesus, as the Spirit says to the Ephesians (Rev. 2:1–7),
there is nothing. But with it, all things are possible.

Let us end with these words of Jesus, simple and profound: 'I have
told you this so that my joy may be in you, and that your joy may be
complete' (Jn. 15:11). Note, '*my* joy' becomes '*your* joy'. The promise
is nothing less than fulness of joy.

And what is the Psalmist's response to such a sweet challenge? And
what is yours, and mine? It ought to be: 'You are my Lord; apart from
you I have no good thing.... Lord, you have assigned me my portion
and my cup; you have made my lot secure. The boundary lines have
fallen for me in pleasant places; surely I have a delightful inheritance....
Therefore my heart is glad and my tongue rejoices; my body also will
rest secure.... You have made known to me the path of life; you will fill
me with joy in your presence, with eternal pleasures at your right hand'
(Ps. 16:2, 3, 5, 6, 9, 11).

This is the voice of spiritual maturity!

WHAT IT IS TO BE A CHRISTIAN

1. The New Birth

We commence this series of studies on 'What it is to be a Christian' with the most embracing and positive of themes—the new birth. This is what Jesus did. He did not start with the negative; he started with the positive. Sadly, that is not always what evangelicals do in their preaching. In evangelistic circles there is often an emphasis on seeking to bring people to Jesus Christ by means of an *unbalanced* stress on the 'sin' issue, as if to say: the first thing you must know when you come to Jesus Christ, or even approach him, is that you are a sinner. This, of course, is absolutely true and must never be forgotten, omitted or diminished in the slightest. I would be the last one to want to do so. But there is something greater than that. That I am a sinner is not good news, however vitally necessary it is to the full declaration of the gospel; it is bad news. But there is good news! I can be saved.

There will come a day, a time (if 'time' you can call it) when sin, as far as believers are concerned, will be done away with completely. Perhaps we will be able to forget it entirely—I don't know. Won't it be wonderful if we can do then what we cannot do here and now, namely, forget our past! It still comes up. Some unkind so-called friend may do it, or our own conscience, going back through the years, may remember things that fill us with loathing and pain. But the devil principally does it, the accuser of the brethren (Rev. 12:10), and it can be exceedingly painful. It may be that in the midst of some blessed moment, some holy experience, thoughts will dart into our minds. Those who are involved in Christian service know how often the enemy can dart into the mind, even while we are engaged in Christian service, thoughts that fill them with dismay, and almost take the breath away. The accusing finger points and the voice says: 'You? How dare you stand on a platform or in a pulpit, or sit with a Bible Class or Sunday School class and tell them about holiness and truth? You?' We wonder if there will ever come a day when the bliss of heaven is such that all that will be blotted out. That is on the positive side. Yet, in another sense, we would not want to forget what we have been saved *from*, would we ?

We begin, then, with the new birth. For our sins are forgiven and we are justified within the context of the new birth. You cannot be born of God without the forgiveness of sins. These two, the negative and the positive, are like the two sides of a penny; they belong together. You cannot have the one without the other. Put it like this (startlingly as some may think, and yet it is perfectly true), the whole work of our Lord Jesus Christ in dealing with our sins, and our sin (our evil nature, the Adamic nature) and the devil behind it all—this sequence of three—is but a means within and to an end. The end is that we might be Christ's.

I want to try to bring together two opposites here: on the one hand the simplicity of the new birth, and yet, on the other, its tremendous significance—the hidden grace of this work of God in the heart of man.

Take Nicodemus: he could not understand the new birth, so Jesus said, 'Well, Nicodemus, you shouldn't really be surprised. Don't marvel that I said to you, "You must be born anew." The wind blows where it wills; you hear the sound of it, but you do not know whence it comes or whither it goes: so it is with everyone who is born of the Spirit' (Jn. 3:7, 8).

He says it is like the wind. But the wind (and we are not quibbling with our Lord) or the sound it makes passing through such as trees, can be *heard*. The wind in the trees yesterday afternoon as we celebrated a wedding in the cathedral of the trees up the Dye Valley, was very, very audible and very, very wonderful. You can hear the wind, but the spiritual wind, the breath of God, is not audible. You cannot see it, you cannot hear it. You may not even recognise it. The Spirit can come so suddenly.

The breath of God can also come overwhelmingly, although it may not be seen or heard. It can come unexpectedly. Very often, sitting listening to the Word of God, or singing praise to God, or bowing one's head in prayer in some meeting or service, or at home meditating, the Holy Spirit of God having made his own preparation in the heart, steals gently in. One may have something like the experience of John Wesley when the Spirit came to him so manifestly in a meeting in Aldersgate Street in London, so that one feels a strange warmth in one's heart. But one may not even feel that to begin with, at all.

The breath of God can come upon us and bring us to the birth suddenly and unexpectedly in some seemingly chance encounter. Our thoughts may be far from religious or spiritual, but we suddenly meet someone at the corner of a street, or in a house, or wherever, and suddenly a seed thought is planted in our minds. We may not realise, although we go away to ponder it or think about it, that that seeming chance encounter has altered our whole life. When we say 'whole life' we mean, not only our mortal life but our life for ever and ever.

It is as we rummage through the Word and come to the Letter to the Ephesians that we see that what began with a seeming chance encounter, a sudden confrontation out of the blue, undreamt of and unthought of, was in God's heart and mind before the world began (Eph. 1:4). Yet, it can begin so modestly, so simply, so hiddenly. The Spirit of God may steal into the heart of somebody in this house of God, and those sitting on either side of that person may not know anything about it. That person may get up at the close of the service and go away and no one will know it until they testify (and they will need to testify, for the Spirit of Christ, born within us, will never come alive and leap into blessed salvation until they open their lips and confess to someone. That has to be, as Romans 10:9 teaches us.)

If, however, it starts so inauspiciously and so modestly, simply and hiddenly, there are *certain* signs. The seed begins to grow. The realisation dawns that the Christ who stole quietly into the soul is a real person. He was inviting himself into our hearts, wanting us to reckon with him and take cognisance of him. We see not merely the historical Christ of two thousand years ago come to us, but the present living Christ, by his unseen Spirit. This thought begins to grip us. The thought-process and all concerning it, especially what we read of it in the Bible, becomes so prominent that it begins to dominate us. It may be that someone who lives with us says, 'What's wrong with you? What are you thinking about? Why are you so happy? What is different about you?' We find, before we have fully realised it, that we have entered into a new way of life. We have new interests. We no longer go the same ways, to the same places, meet the same people. Not, of course, that we ought cut off our friends, whoever they are. Paul advises us about this in 1 Corinthians 7:20–24: 'Everyone should remain in the state in which he was called. Were you a slave when called? Never mind. But if you can gain your freedom, avail yourself of the opportunity. For he who was called in the Lord as a slave is a freedman of the Lord. Likewise he who was free when called is a slave of Christ. You were bought with a price; do not become slaves of men. So brethren, in whatever state each was called, there let him remain with God' (1 Cor. 7:20–24).

But he has brought us to the birth in Jesus Christ that we might live for him exactly where we are—as in time, so in place, in our home, at our work. Too many Christians, as soon as they begin to grow and realise Christ is within their hearts say, 'I must change and do something different.' I know that Christ himself redirects many young people as to their calling, after they come to him; necessarily so. But the first thing is to make him known, to manifest him (and that is not necessarily to talk about him to begin with) where one is. One's interests change and one seeks other friends, but not to the exclusion of, or because one despises, one's old friends. They need us all the more if we have found something new. We have found Christ. We must not forsake them nor despise them: very much the reverse. At the same time, we are looking for those we can talk to and with whom we can share Jesus Christ.

These, then, are the two marks of a Christian, the essential marks: first that we want to seek out Christian fellowship, and secondly that we do not withdraw from the world. Christ has come to you and brought you to himself so that you might live for him and manifest his grace where you are, doing a better job at work and living graciously at home and abroad.

Our codes begin to change. There are certain things we no longer do. It is always better if people don't tell us what not to do. Better if the Word tells us, or better still, Christ by the Spirit, working through the Word: 'Now you ought not to do that; Jesus Christ will not be pleased with you for doing that. You cannot go there. You cannot carry on like that.' So, our code changes, our habits change, our thoughts and our desires and our ambitions change. We live an entirely new life.

Do you see what needs to be emphasised first of all, as we realise the magnitude of it all? I am stressing how simply, modestly, imperceptibly the Spirit of God can steal into our heart. Precisely because we do not know what the Spirit of God may be doing, even in answer to our own prayers, we need to be careful. We need to be guided often for even the shrewdest of us can be mistaken. What mistakes we all make with ourselves, and other people too, don't we? What misunderstandings!

I want to ask you this question: Why is it that such a radical change, such an elemental transformation can begin so simply, modestly and even inauspiciously? You know what Jesus says in the parable: 'The kingdom of heaven is like a grain of mustard seed which a man took and sowed in his field (he is talking about the whole kingdom, but it applies also to the individual). The mustard seed is the smallest of all seeds (one seed? It seems so ridiculous—you could almost lose it in your hand), but when it has grown, it is the greatest of shrubs and becomes a tree' (Matt. 13:31, 32).

This is another thing that so many involved in evangelistic work forget: the experience of Jesus Christ is something which grows, and growing things take time to grow. Sometimes, I think, we have far more patience with our pot plants than we have with our babes in Christ. Mind you, we can be impatient with our plants too! Here is a particular seed we have planted and we go and look at the soil, even rake in it a little to see if a shoot is coming through, and we are equally impatient at every stage. When it shoots up, we look for leaves, then we are looking for the bud and thinking how slow it is to open. What colour will it be? Patience, patience! Nature will take its time, because God has made time, and uses it and loves it. Time has been contaminated, of course, and is often our enemy, but it should not be. It is we who are disorientated. Patience, patience! It is God who says the smallest seed grows to the greatest of shrubs.

Why so? Because however simply and imperceptibly and hiddenly the seed of God is planted in the heart, however gently and inaudibly, the life-giving breath of God breathes upon a soul, what he has breathed into us is everlasting. We read in John 3:16, 'For God so loved the world that he gave his only begotten Son, that whoever believes in him should not perish but have everlasting life.' *Everlasting* life! Think of the eternality of God. He never had a beginning. He is forever and ever. It is frightening. We like to see the uttermost of a matter. We like to know the beginning and the end of many things. He has no beginning: 'In the beginning, God [was].' Go back as far as you can and try to think in the dimension of eternity (which with our finite minds we cannot really do) and God is there. You cannot reach back to a place where there was not God the Trinity: the Son with the Father and the Holy Spirit with the Father and the Son, eternally. Is it new life of *that order* he has given us? Have we, mortal creatures that we are, here for sixty, seventy, eighty, ninety, maybe even a hundred years, clay, flesh and bone, have we this life in us? Is it possible that the soul has the life of God in it and will go on forever and ever?

Take another thought from Ephesians 1:4, 'even as he chose us in him

before the foundation of the world, that we should be holy and
blameless before him.' Did we really exist in the heart and mind of God
before the world began? Was there any point in eternity when we came
into existence in his thought and mind? It is possible that God lived a life
in his eternity for a long, long time before we came into his thought. He
certainly conceived us, brought us to the birth in his heart and mind
before he brought us to the birth here. All this grips us practically,
experimentally, at the moment when we meet somebody at the street
corner and are perhaps invited, even hustled (although I hope not) to a
church service or whatever. For the first time our minds are taken up
with the thought: Jesus Christ. Then we are led on until we feel the
breath of God breathing so sweetly upon us that, although in a sense we
scarcely feel it, we *know*. 'We are partakers of the divine nature' says
Peter (2 Pet. 1:4). Now think about this. Even though we hurt our heads
a little it will not do us any harm! We hurt them thinking about other
things—too much sometimes, as some of the student folk will tell you.
How big is this? Only the Book can tell us; it says that when we come to
Jesus Christ or he comes to us (however we put it) we become new
creatures in Christ Jesus.

I want to discuss that: *new creatures*. What does it mean? It will help
us to understand if we trace a certain thread of teaching through Paul's
words in Romans 5:12–21. Paul speaks here about our sinful nature in
relation to the first possessor of it—Adam. He says, 'Look at it like this:
as far as the Christian life is concerned, there are only two orders of
manhood and two heads of the human race: Adam and Christ; the first
Adam, and the second or last Adam: two men. Not only so, but Paul
here discusses one action of each of these two men. Adam in the Fall
and Christ on the Cross. We have therefore two orders of manhood, and
two actions.

All we need to take from verse 12 are the two words 'one man,' (that
is, Adam) because of whose sin, 'death spread to all men because all
men sinned.' In verse 15 Paul is contrasting these two men in their two
actions: Adam in the Fall and Christ on the Cross, to retrieve the ruin of
the Fall. It is by the action of Adam in the first instance, that we are first
made sinners, and then by the action of Christ that we are justified and
born again.

As we read through these verses we see a contrast as well as a
similarity: 'But the free gift is not like the trespass. For if many died
through one man's trespass, much more hath the grace of God and the
free gift in the grace of that one man Jesus Christ abounded for many'

(v. 15). The first 'one man' is Adam in his action, his trespass; the second 'one man' is Jesus Christ.

We find the same thing in verse 16. 'And the free gift is not like the effect of that one man's sin.' He is making a comparison. He is not only setting forth two men and comparing them, but he is comparing the results of their two separate actions. They are unequal because Adam was mortal and became a sinner. Christ is the eternal Son of God and is righteous and perfect and the Redeemer of men. So, as they themselves are unequal, their actions are likewise unequal. True, Adam has created an awful lot of trouble in the world, for all sin stems from him. 'Ah but, here is a better man (as Paul says and the writer to the Hebrews says)— much better.' That word 'better' recurs and recurs throughout the Letter to the Hebrews. Here is a better man, and being a better man, he is able to do a better job!

Thus, Paul continues, 'And the free gift is not like the effect of that one man's sin. For the judgment following one trespass brought condemnation but the free gift following many trespasses brings justification. If because of one man's trespass death reigned through that one man, much more will those who receive the abundance of grace and the free gift of righteousness reign in life through the one man Jesus Christ' (Rom. 5:15–17). Sin reigned, because it was in control before Christ came. How then does the free gift of righteousness reign? How does this take place? Christ came to deal with Adam. He put him to death in his own body. He took the old Adam upon himself sinlessly (and that is a mystery). He was born in the likeness of sinful flesh (Rom. 8:3). He was made to become sin (2 Cor. 5:21) for us. He assumed the life of Adam, although he remained perfectly sinless and went down into death and died Adam's death. That is what Romans chapter 6 goes on to speak about.

Look at some of the phrases there. 'Those who are in Jesus Christ are made partakers of his death' (Rom. 6:3–6). This is because Jesus died this death for us. Why did he come and assume Adam's nature? He came to assume Adam's nature to take it away forever. He did not need to take it away on his own account. He assumed it, and was personally perfectly sinless, for he never sinned one sin in our human nature throughout his thirty-three years. He did not need to go down to death when he assumed Adam's nature, since he did not assume its sinfulness: it was for us. FOR US—two of the greatest words in the world—it was for you and for me, he did this.

When we come to him, Jesus Christ can steal simply and hiddenly, sweetly and imperceptibly into our hearts. But it is an almighty thing that has happened, because it involved Jesus Christ's death to our Adam. In his coming to us he not only breathes sweetly on our souls and gives us new life, but in that miraculous moment he brings our old Adam to death. Oh yes, sin remains in us, but not Adam. We are no longer 'in Adam'. Adam is dead. We have to distinguish between the state of being 'in Adam', and the continuing reality of indwelling sin, but we will come to that later. When Jesus Christ comes into your life he 'kills off' your old life 'in Adam' absolutely.

This is Paul's emphasis in Romans 6:3: 'Do you not know that all of us who have been baptised into Christ Jesus were baptised into his death? When we are baptised into Christ Jesus (and of course the baptism goes beyond water baptism. That is the symbol of being baptised with the Holy Spirit) we are baptised into his death.' In fact Paul goes further and says, 'We were buried with him by baptism into death....' We are not only dead, but buried. Verse 5: 'We are united with him in a death like this.' Verse 6: 'our old self was crucified.' When he died, we died with him, but it only comes home to us, the potential of it, when Christ comes into our lives. Follow the sequence of implications Paul draws: verse 7: 'For he who has died is freed from sin.' Verse 8: 'But if we have died with Christ we believe that we shall also live with him.' Verse 11: 'So you also must consider yourself dead to sin and alive to God in Christ Jesus.'

Take this a step further. Turn to Romans 7:1–4, and put it in a different context. Here is Paul's analogy: 'A married woman is bound by the law to her husband as long as he lives.' The 'husband' here is Adam. Paul is speaking about all that we are in our fallen nature. But 'if her husband dies she is discharged from the law concerning her husband.... She is free from that law, and if she marries another she is not an adulteress.' You see, when Jesus Christ comes into our life, the Jesus Christ who died and rose brings the potency, the vitality of both his death and his resurrection into my life by the Holy Spirit. He brings Adam to the death and Christ to the life. There is a great exchange!

John Henry Newman put it like this:

> O loving wisdom of our God!
> When all was sin and shame,
> A second Adam to the fight
> And to the rescue came.

O wisest love! that flesh and blood
Which did in Adam fail,
Should strive afresh against the foe,
Should strive and should prevail.

O generous love! that he who smote
In Man, for man, the foe,
The double agony in Man,
For man should undergo.

That is it! It is an exchange, which Paul has wonderfully brought out in 2 Corinthians 5:21: 'For our sake God made Christ to become sin, who knew no sin (he was personally sinless, but took our sin upon him) so that in him we might become the righteousness of God.' He became sin to take away our sin as if to say, 'Here, I am taking away all you are in Adam, and in place of that I am giving you myself, the Christ.' That is why our desires change. That is why our lives change. That is why people say, 'What is different about you?'

This exchange, by itself, is bound to make a difference. Do you mean to tell me that you need to go and brandish a New Testament before your father and mother or be tactless and unwise before your friends to let them know you have become a Christian and that Jesus Christ is really in your heart? If you are scared to say that you have become a Christian because the seed is so small it does not seem to have any effect on your life to begin with, let it grow a little. Am I unwise in saying that? Better that than the other way, at any rate. If he is really there and the seed is nourished by God's Word, the time will come that people will see.

One thing I am absolutely sure of, and I wish all who are engaged in evangelical and evangelistic work would believe it. If Jesus Christ is in your heart he must reveal himself, unless you are hiding him, unless you are pulling down the blinds. Oh that we would believe it and trust him to manifest himself because he has given us this exchange. Our indwelling sin remains, but see that you make the proper distinction: Adam doesn't remain; he is dead, he is gone. Sin is now a *thing*. It is less than a person. Before you were converted you were a sinner. You are still, in the sense that you sin. But you are not Adamic any longer. Adam is slain. Christ has come to slay him, not merely to hurt him, nor to wound him, but to slay him. He is dead.

Think then of what God's Word says about the possibilities of growth, and God's patience as we grow. First, the author of Hebrews

2:8 tells us that 'in putting everything in subjection to Christ, he left nothing outside his control. Jesus deals with the whole universe totally, radically, and finally. But as it is now, and until Christ comes, we do not see everything in subjection to him. Everything has been put in subjection to him—even tyrants and dictators are under his thumb and breathe only by God's permission. The devil is not in the burnings of hell yet, but that is only because of God's permission. He knows he is going there, that is why he is so mad and troubles you and me so much. But we see Jesus, who for a little while was made lower than the angels, crowned with glory and honour. For God is using time; we are therefore not to be impatient. We are sometimes piously and sanctimoniously far too impatient, even with ourselves. True, we are sometimes too patient with ourselves, but that is another story! Sometimes, sensitive, keen, zealous, eager souls are far too impatient with themselves, and indeed Satan uses that to mar their lives. He comes in and makes us too ambitious for God. We are sometimes more ambitious to serve God than God wants us to be: self comes in and that is bad. God made time and he wants us to learn his patience about it.

Then, secondly, think of the teaching of 1 John 3:2: 'Beloved, we are God's children now.' That is what we believe, of course. This is not said indiscriminately. I don't go up and down Union Street stopping people and saying, 'We are God's children now,' if I don't know they have God's Christ in their hearts. This is written to Christians. 'Beloved, we are God's children now; it does not yet appear what we shall be (This refers to the resurrection and the new bodies we will have, but we can take it a little nearer, and apply it to our relative condition now, in these days) but we know that when he appears, we shall be like him, for we shall see him as he is.' This is the point! 'It does not yet appear what we shall be.' Will you learn, then, rather than be caught up by the enemy and made too zealously ambitious, particularly in Christian service? Will you learn patience with God? It is not easy when you are young, but learn it, so that in the fulness of time God may reveal to you and to others what he purposes to do in you.

Thirdly, think of 1 Corinthians 15:35–41, particularly verse 38. 'But some will ask, "How are the dead raised? With what kind of body do they come?" You foolish man! What you sow does not come to life unless it dies. And what you sow is not the body which is to be, but a bare kernel perhaps of wheat or some other grain. But God gives it a body as he has chosen, and to each kind of seed its own body. For not all flesh is alike, but there is one kind for men, another for animals, another for birds, and another for fish (you can link that to Genesis 1).

There are celestial bodies and there are terrestrial bodies; but the glory of the celestial is one, and the glory of the terrestrial is another. There is one glory of the sun, and another glory of the moon, and another glory of the stars; for star differs from star in glory (brightness).'

'To each kind of seed its own body.' And as he grows within us Christ shows himself authentically Christ. This is a tremendous thing. Christ is within us, not constricted, stunted, but watered and fed by the Word and prayer. He shows himself in each one; some more, some less, I suppose. It is the same Christ. It is the very same Christ, and yet each one is different. Different facets of the infinite variety of growth and wisdom and truth and everything wonderful in Jesus Christ are being seen. Even in glory, you will be able to show facets of Christ that are not possible to me at all. Let me put it like this: if you want to see Christ in his fulness, gather the saints. How many? Every one. Surely you do not need every one? Yes, myriads and myriads. Bring them together like an absolutely gigantic jig-saw puzzle, with not one missing. Come on— every one. Somebody missing? A few there? Come on; the face is not perfect. I can't see Jesus' face. I can't see his personality; for it takes every saint that will be in heaven to show forth the fulness and the glory and the brightness of Christ. You see, each saint is a reflection of the complete Christ. But it takes every saint to reflect him fully.

The fourth text to notice is Ephesians 1:18–23. Paul hopes and prays that the eyes of our hearts may be enlightened, 'that you may know what is the hope to which he has called you, what are the riches of his glorious inheritance in the saints, and what is the immeasurable greatness of his power in us who believe, according to the working of his great might which he accomplished in Christ when he raised him from the dead and made him sit at his right hand in the heavenly places, far above all rule and authority and power and dominion, and above every name that is named, not only in this age but also in that which is to come; and he has put all things under his feet and has made him the head over all things for the church, which is his body, the fulness of him who fills all in all.' You know what this means: God so loved his Son that he wanted to fill the whole heavenly universe with him. And the only way he could do that was by creating in Christ Jesus, innumerable miniature Christs to show forth every facet of Jesus Christ. You see, this is for the glory of God. Our redemption in Jesus Christ is to the glory of God. The glory of God is the effulgence, the manifestation of God. We shall see the greatness of God—how big, and great, and wonderful, and manifold, and infinite God is, when we see all the saints together, everyone indwelt by Christ and everyone needed to show forth the fulness of Christ. And this can all begin with us sitting in a meeting, or church, or encountering someone at a street corner, getting a wisp of words from the gospel, or even a kind look, or a smile, or something that brings the breath of God stealing into their hearts and they hardly know what has taken place. How marvellous!

One further thought occurs to me: Let us be patient with those we are praying into the kingdom, the youngsters and those belaboured with one kind of sin or handicap or another. Let us be patient; not pathetically patient but hopefully and believingly patient with a constructive and purposive, directed patience. Because we are believing, waiting to see what God will do, we let them fall, and trip up, disappoint us, go back a thousand times; but don't let us be daunted. I wonder if some 'fall away' and never really come to Jesus Christ because Christians never persisted in prayer in love, and patience, and forgiveness. Oh God, give us grace to woo and win them to Christ that they also, with their immortal souls saved, may show forth facets of his glory.

It can happen so imperceptibly. Let's be patient and wait to see what God will do in our day, not only here in Aberdeen but in many other places. Oh, let us patiently woo and win the young folk to see this hidden work come to view in their lives, as Christ is formed in them!

WHAT IT IS TO BE A CHRISTIAN

2. The Godwardness of the Gift of Faith

We have begun to consider what it means to receive new life in Christ. It is important to stress the godwardness of this act, and its sovereignty. God comes down to make us new: we do not reach up to gain it or effect it in any way. Take what Jesus says to Nicodemus: 'We speak of what we know' (Jn. 3:11). If you do not know, Nicodemus, how can you understand? Are you a teacher of Israel, yet you don't know about the new birth? You could have read about it in the Old Testament, in Jeremiah 31:33, or Ezekiel 18:31, or 36:26, 27. 'We speak of what we know, and bear witness to what we have seen: but you do not receive our testimony. If I have told you of earthly things (that is about the new birth and the work of God's grace in human hearts, changing them so that men suddenly become aware of their brothers, have a care for them and are honest towards them; that sort of thing—practical things!) and you do not believe, how can you believe if I tell you of heavenly things?' What could the heavenly things be? If the new birth is earthly (of course it is heavenly in origin; but it is heaven come down to earth) possibly our Lord means by heavenly the whole plan of redemption, all that is in God's heart and mind from all eternity, that no man knows. 'Eye hath not seen nor ear heard what God has planned' (1 Cor. 2:9). God has revealed some of those things to us by his Spirit. Our Lord says, 'But what would be the point of telling you all these heavenly things if you can't understand this earthly, elementary thing that God has done in men's hearts to bring them to new birth?' How can you believe the one if you don't understand the other?

Jesus then goes on to say: 'No one has ascended into heaven but he who descended from heaven, the Son of Man' (Jn. 3:13). Now, in that context, what does he mean? Simply that to understand the earthly thing that he is speaking about, the new birth, and to understand the whole plan behind it all and God's purpose from all eternity, man blinded by sin (2 Corinthians 3:14) cannot know a thing unless God himself (here in human flesh, or otherwise by the Spirit) had come down to reveal it to him. 'Eye hath not seen nor ear heard...but God has revealed to us' many of these precious things by his Spirit, chief among them being his Son. This is the next thing we are to understand; it is all to do with God coming down, not anything to do with our reaching up. Paul has something to say about this in Romans 10:5–8. 'Moses writes that the man who practises the righteousness which is based on the law shall live by it.' That is, if he fulfils it and practises it perfectly. Moses is saying, if a man can live perfectly according to the Ten Commandments he shall live in God's sight thereby. But that is not the gospel. This is the gospel which Paul sets over against that, 'But the righteousness based on faith says, Do not say in your heart, "Who will ascend into heaven?" (that is to bring Christ down) or "Who will descend into the abyss?" (that is to bring Christ up from the dead.) But what does it say? The word is near you...'. We do not have to go anywhere, up, nor down, nor round about; the 'word is near you.'

How can it be near us? We are fallen sinners and our eyes are blinded and our ears stuffed so we cannot see or understand divine things. Even Nicodemus, teacher of the law, could not understand the earthly things of the new birth. The word of faith is near us, 'on your lips and in your heart' because God has come down with it, given it to us, put it on the tip of our tongue and thrust it into the midst of our heart. No need to ascend, no need to descend, no need to look at all, but only to let God speak to us, just where we are so that we discover his Word.

Think about Noah: 'Noah *found* grace.' He did not need to sail round the world to look for it! He found it just where he was. I want you to see this. Romans 10:5–13 is a marvellous passage. It goes on to speak of the result of someone being made aware, by God's coming to them, that the word of faith is on their lips and in their heart, inclining them to believe because God has come to enable them to believe. No man can believe of himself. 'The word is on your lips and in your heart, because, if you confess with your lips that Jesus is Lord and believe in your heart that God raised him from the dead, you will be saved. For man believes with his heart and so is justified, and he confesses with his lips and so is saved. The Scripture says, "No one who believes in him will be put to shame." For there is no distinction between Jew and Greek; the same Lord is Lord of all and bestows his riches upon all who call upon him.' You see, there is no distinction between Jew and Gentile. When man becomes aware that Christ has come down and the word of faith is on the tip of his tongue, he confesses Christ and 'every one who calls upon the name of the Lord will be saved.'

It is God coming down. This is the point of the gospel: God is near enough to enable us to believe, and calls on us to believe because he has come near us. He pleads with us, saying, 'Believe, believe, believe!' This is the wonderful theme of Ephesians chapter 2:

> And you he made alive, when you (the Gentiles) were dead through the trespass and sins in which you once walked, following the course of this world, following the prince of the power of the air, the spirit that is now at work in the sons of disobedience. Among these we all once lived in the passions of our flesh, following the desires of body and mind, and so were by nature children of wrath like the rest of mankind. To you God came equally (no distinction) as to us; to the Jew first but also and equally to the Gentile. God had come in the wealth of his mercy, out of the great love with which he loved us, even when we were dead through trespass and sins, and has made us alive together with Christ (by grace you have been saved) and has raised us up with him, and made us sit with him in heavenly places in Christ Jesus, that in the coming ages he might show the immeasurable riches of his grace in kindness towards us in Christ Jesus. For by grace you have been saved through faith.

We have then God coming down in all the wealth of his love, his grace and his kindness, promising to pour out the lavishness of his kindness in his grace, mercy, forgiveness, his care and consideration, the supreme value he sets upon us, to bless us. We see God giving his Son that we might have pleasure in God. God loves us so much that there is nothing too much even for him, the almighty God who has all power in his hand, to do to please us. This is what the Christian life and the Christian church is about. This is why we are called to serve and suffer. It is because there is given to us in the gospel, the privilege of enjoying the lavishness of God's grace for our pleasure, our holy pleasure, for all eternity.

Look, the chief and supreme incentive to being a Christian is that God wants absolutely to flood our lives with pleasure. If someone rather cynically says, 'Aye, but what pleasure?' God says to them (and I would say to myself, as doubtless you would to yourself—'Are you sceptical about his offer of pleasure, that God would give you all he has in his heart to delight you for all eternity?'): 'What do you know about true pleasure? Are you the judge of true pleasure? Are your pleasures so absolutely satisfying that you are sure they are far better than any pleasure I can give you? Could it be that your miserable pleasures which lead you so often to be far more unhappy than you were before you began to indulge in them, are not pleasures at all? Indeed, they are the very antithesis of pleasure, misery in fact.' The very cessation of the things we do to titillate our senses show how unsatisfying and transient they are. What do we know about it? He is saying, 'You don't know what pleasure is. You don't know what pleasure the human heart can enjoy, even in this vale of tears. You don't know what I will pour into your hearts.'

Oh how absolutely wonderful it is to see the grace of God coming to men and women, to young men and women and to boys and girls; to see the love of God dawning in their souls and the light of Christ shining out of their eyes, when they realise how wonderful it is that God loves them and cares for them.

So, you see, when we take all the theory as we read it in the Scriptures, and research the Old Testament and the New ultimately we begin to see that there is a living God far more real than we are. He is far more real than the person we see when we look into the mirror, or when we look at someone else. We see there is a living God who cares as no one in the world can care.

It is strange how long it takes some of those who have truly believed, to see this. I wonder why. With some it takes years of seeking in the Word, or perhaps going astray, trying other ways, maybe becoming cool and then being brought back by a gracious and loving and patient God to begin to see. Before that so many people in the church today, ministers, elders, office-bearers, members, Sunday School workers, see the church and its activities and its services as such a dreary round. I suggest there is a lot of truth in that; far too much truth in it. But if this is so, it is simply because our eyes have never really been opened to the glory and the wonder of the kindness of God: not the satisfactions that are found in Christian service and church work, even the joys of Christian fellowship, marvellous as that is; but rather the knowledge that he who made all things, cares. He cares for this lump of quivering flesh with all its feelings, its pains, its aches, its pangs and longings and frustrations. He cares! I cannot sigh but he cares and bends down and like some nurse, or doctor, or loving mother towards a sick child says, 'What is it, my dear? Can I help you?' We seem to refuse to see God like that. We just refuse to see it, his kindness with all its human-ness and all its gracious divinity. Even the angels get a few shocks when they see what he will do for the sons of men, the redeemed ones, his chosen ones! They will get a few surprises as they see 'the plan of the mystery hidden for ages in God who created all things; that through the church the manifold wisdom of God might now be made known to the principalities and powers in the heavenly places' (Eph. 3:10).

So you see his kindness to us (his present kindness as well as what he is to show us in the ages to come, the immeasurable riches of his grace) is that he has saved us by grace. He has come to us and put his arms round us and said, 'You are mine. You are mine.' He has breathed his life into us and given us the gift of response, given us to know he is there, given us to realise it so that we say, 'Oh God, it is you. These are no temporary feelings these deep, profound heart-searching feelings that run through me like an electric shock, and even more wonderful than that, fill me with an awe that is more than physical, emotional and psychological. This is truly spiritual. This is you O God, you. It is you yourself. You have come to me.'

I love these four words, 'By faith we understand' (Heb. 11:3). He makes us understand. He comes to us and fills and floods our lives with something new as we respond. However gently it begins (as we saw in our first study) and we make response, God becomes alive to us. Think of it in these terms: some dear old soul, sitting in their home of an evening, not expecting anyone to call, just sitting there musing, dozing by the fireside, soon to go to bed, perhaps just lingering to hear the news or wait till the fire burns down and suddenly there is a knock on the door. There is somebody there. The old soul becomes aware—partly fear and dread and wonder—Who can it be? Did I hear? Yes, she hears it again, the second knock. 'Behold, I stand at the door and knock.' He knocks, and like a visitor loaded with Christmas gifts to a poor, old soul who has very little to feed herself on, so he comes and knocks at our door, loaded with kindness. He says, 'Let me come in and let us have supper together. Let me sit down with you and be with you.' The old soul would get up, full of fear and dread and wonder—perhaps it is a dear friend. Eagerly, yet fearfully she calls, 'Who is it?' She has responded to the knock. Somebody is there and she can't sit and doze and wonder or go to bed. Somebody is there. What do they want? They are wanting something with her. That is how it is with us.

I want to call faith the totality of man's response to God. If we are saved by grace through faith, then faith I take to be the completeness, in all its different dimensions, with which we respond to God when he comes to us, and we realise he has come. I want faith to stand for all our responses, including the gift of repentance because this is a total gift of God. It is first life (regeneration, the new birth) then faith, with the gift of repentance and the gift of forgiveness of sins. On the other side it is the gift of righteousness—Christ's righteousness—sanctification, and ultimately glorification and a resurrection body. It is all these, it is a total gift. He comes and gives himself to us and says, 'Look, I am going to live my life with you.' It is total. It is all gift. And it is by the gift that we are enabled to respond.

Let me give you a few Scriptures. 'For all have sinned and come short of the glory of God, they are justified by his grace as a gift, through the redemption which is in Christ Jesus' (Rom. 3:24). Or this, later on: 'It depends, not on man's will or exertion, but upon God's mercy' (Rom. 9:16). It is God's mercy. No man decides he is to become a Christian, to be saved, although he may think it at the time. God has been there before him. This is regeneration. God is working in a man's heart from the beginning. God must be working in a man's heart before the man knows it. Paul writes to the Philippians: 'You are all partakers with me of grace' (Phil. 1:7). Then later on, in verse 29, 'For it has been granted to you that for the sake of Christ you should not only believe in him but also suffer for his sake.' Of course the emphasis there is on the 'suffering for Christ's sake.' But it is the first part I want: 'It has been granted to you for the sake of Christ that you should believe in him.' It has been *granted*. It is a gift. It is by God that we are enabled to believe. He has done it. Oh, recognise that. Don't see your Christian life as a struggling after God, feeling after God; see it the other way. Say to yourself, How is it that I am here? How is it that I am interested? Is it something I have taken into my head to be interested in, or is it God who is drawing me on? That is the question to ask.

Peter says, 'By God's great mercy we have been born anew to a living hope...to an inheritance in heaven...kept for you, who are kept by God's power through faith for salvation' (1 Pet. 1:3–5). Kept by God's power. How does God's power work in human hearts? By faith, enabling us to respond. That's it. Isn't it marvellous! Jesus says to the woman of Samaria, 'If you knew the gift of God and who it is that is saying to you, "Give me a drink", you would have asked him and he would have given you living water' (Jn. 4:10). What I am saying quite simply is: gift, gift, gift from beginning to end, gift to open hearts, gift to open doors. 'If any man...', 'Behold, I stand at the door and knock' (Rev. 3:20). Here is Jesus standing at empty homes, homes of empty hearts and he is saying, as he walks along the road, stopping at each one, 'Oh, these houses could be full of light, and joy, and warmth, and food, and pleasure, and purpose in life. Oh, that I could fill these hearts with my love; that I could lavish and pour out my gifts upon men.'

Gift, gift, gift. I see this as the prime essential in living the Christian life, that we have to learn in new ways to open our hearts to God. God is all around us. His Spirit is pressing in upon us all the time, everywhere present, pleading with us by many tokens, many hints and intimations, pleading with us, 'Respond, Respond! Open, Open!' He is saying at many places, many points in the course of a day, 'Listen, listen!' He is tugging at our coat sleeve, whispering in our ear, pulling our coat: 'Listen, listen, listen!'

'Oh, I am too busy', we say, 'I'm too busy. What do you want?' And all he wants to give is this, and this and this, and this... What is all this? It is *himself*, nothing less. So, the gift begins to operate, the light begins to dawn, or, if you like, the seed begins to take root. However you put it, faith is not a work, it is a response, the inevitable and essential response of the human heart to God's coming. Just as the old soul we spoke of earlier will get up because she wants to know who is rapping at the door. She has heard someone is there and it is as spontaneous as that: he is there and she is there, and the two must meet because she wants to know who is knocking. Faith is not a work.

Now, look at Romans 10:4. 'For Christ is the end of the law for righteousness to everyone believing.' There is a great deal in that. It means that Christ is the end of striving to climb by ourselves into heaven, striving to reach after God, (I'm speaking to Christians) striving to live the Christian life, doing our part duteously. 'I suppose I had better go to church tonight.' Christ is the end of all that. It is all turned into pleasure to everyone believing. 'Christ is the end of the law for righteousness to everyone believing.' The fact that the sentence ends with 'everyone believing' indicates that Christ is the end of striving. Believing is not striving. Believing is simply, purely responding to God's grace, and that is not a work. It is no task to run and open a door when a dear one is there.

Yesterday I saw some people arriving at a door in my street. I know they had not been there for ages. I expect the mother had been watching from the window, for the car had scarcely come to a halt when she was down on the doorstop, down the path and her arms around her laddie. That was not work; it was a pleasure. So, it is not work to respond to him when he comes. And because the gift is so great, Paul counts everything else loss to gain it in its fulness and richness: 'But whatever gain I had, I counted as loss for the sake of Christ' (Phil. 3:7). Too busy reading a newspaper or watching television to open the door and see who is there? Not Paul. Away with the papers, away with the television, away with everything and everyone else; 'Excuse me, I must go. Pardon me, I must run.' We cannot read this with sufficient convicting power, but let us try. 'Indeed – I – count – everything – but – loss – because – of – the – SURPASSING – worth – of – KNOWING – CHRIST JESUS – my LORD.' The affection in that 'my Lord' is tremendous. 'For his sake I have suffered (perfect tense) the loss of – all things, and count them as – rubbish – RUBBISH! – in order that I may gain – CHRIST, and be found – in – him, not having a righteousness of my own, based on the law, but that which is through faith; that I may know him, and the power of his resurrection and may share his sufferings, becoming like him in his death, that if possible I may attain the resurrection from the dead' (Phil. 3:8–11). Paul says, 'I will go to all lengths to have him and enjoy him.' When the glory of God's incoming is realised, all loss for it is gain, absolute gain.

In 2 Corinthians 4:1 Paul is speaking about the ministry. 'Therefore, having this ministry by the mercy of God, we do not lose heart.' How in the world could we lose heart in the Christian way? Do you really lose heart? Well, either you are falling away and growing cold, sliding back, or Satan is working very hard on you. If so, you need to share that burden with someone who will pray and care for you. There is no need to lose heart even if it means you have to resist Satan. The gift is so great Paul goes on to say: 'We have renounced disgraceful, underhand ways; we refuse to practise cunning or to tamper with God's Word, but by the open statement of the truth we would commend ourselves to everyman's conscience in the sight of God. And even if our gospel is veiled, it is veiled only to those who are perishing. In their case the god of this world has blinded the minds of unbelievers, to keep them from seeing the light of the gospel of the glory of Christ who is the likeness of God. For what we preach is not ourselves, but Jesus Christ as Lord, with ourselves as your servants for Christ's sake (for he is all and in all. For it is God who said (and this harks right back to the very beginning of Genesis) "Let light shine out of darkness" who has shone into our hearts to give the light of the knowledge of the glory of God (Where? Oh, where is all this to be found?) in the face of Jesus Christ' (2 Cor. 4:2–6).

You see, it comes down to the humanity of God again. Aren't you glad we have such a human religion? I'm glad because I am a human being and I love human religion. I hope I do not forget or underestimate Christ's deity. But how glad I am, as a human being, that he became a man. Hence, you see Paul magnifies the privileges of receiving this gift of the grace of God. So, the response: faith, repentance, conviction of sin, obedience—whatever it is—is easy, so wonderfully easy and pleasurable because we are responding to a living God who has come and taken us in his arms and crushes us to his breast until we say, 'Oh God, give me a chance; you are killing me with love.'

It is thus that Paul magnifies the privilege in particular of the Ephesian Gentiles joining equally with any Jew, even Paul the apostle, Peter or John, because God has come near to both Jew and Gentile. That is it. He has come near to both of them. We read in Ephesians 2:10, 'For we are his workmanship, created in Christ Jesus for good works which God previously prepared that we should walk in them.' Think for a moment again of these Gentiles feeling they are not 'up to' these Jews. They may have thought, 'These Jews believed first, and they are superior to us, because, of course, they have got the Bible, the Old Testament. They are so proud of it and they make us feel inferior.' Gently and kindly Paul says, writing to these Ephesians, these Gentile believers, 'Remember that at one time you Gentiles in the flesh, called the uncircumcision by that which is called the circumcision which is made in the flesh by hand, remember (his mind is too full) that you were at that time separated from Christ, alienated from the commonwealth of Israel and strangers to the covenant of promise, having no hope and without God in the world. But now in Christ Jesus you who once were far off have been brought near in the blood of Christ. For he is our peace (and 'our' here means Jew and Gentile) who has made us both one, and has broken down the dividing wall of hostility (between Jew and Gentile) by abolishing in his flesh the law of commandments and ordinances, that he might create in himself one new man (in Christ Jesus) in place of two, so making peace (between them), and might reconcile us both to God in one body through the Cross, thereby bringing the hostility (between Jew and Gentile) to an end. And he came and proclaimed peace to you who were far off and peace to those who were near' (Eph. 2:11–17).

Is it not beautiful how he puts the Gentiles before the Jews here? Ah, that is kind. Oh, you tactful man. But, the grace of Christ makes us tactful and thoughtful—not merely polite with conventions and all that kind of thing, and suave, with polished manners, but genuine with heart care for others so that we think what we say and how we say it, because we want to bless those who are with us and share Jesus Christ. 'So, he came and preached peace to you who were far off and peace to those who were near, for through him we both have access in one Spirit...' (Eph. 2:17, 18).

Paul begins the third chapter of Ephesians with, 'For this reason I...' but the poor man's mind is positively full of truth, and the third chapter is so rich that he goes on and on about the privilege he has whereby God has revealed mysteries to him in a fulness not revealed to men of the Old Testament time at all. It is only when he comes to verse 14 that he makes another attempt at saying what he wants to say and goes a little bit further. 'For this reason, I Paul, a prisoner for Christ Jesus on behalf of you Gentiles (and there is a dash and he is away at a tangent, like some preachers I know!). Verse 14, 'For this reason I bow my knees in prayer before the Father from whom every family in heaven and on earth is named, that according to the riches of his glory he may grant you (he is telling them what he is praying for them, but he is not speaking to them directly. Paul does that. He is writing, telling people what he is praying about them to God. That is interesting.) that according to the riches of his glory (the wealth of his glory? Oh dear, the wealth of his grace is enough, but the wealth of his glory!) he may grant you to be strengthened with might through his Spirit in the inner man, and that Christ may dwell in your hearts through faith; that you, being rooted and grounded in love, may have power to comprehend with all the saints (all the saints, as it were, in a circle, joining hands, hand in hand trying to embrace the eternal Christ. It takes every saint, in all the ages, stretching their hands out to embrace the fulness that there is in Christ. Christ's church is the fulness of Christ, it says at the end of the first chapter. Isn't it tremendous!) what is the breadth and length and height and depth, and to know the love of Christ which surpasses knowledge (How can you know the love of Christ which surpasses knowledge? It will take all eternity, but we have to try and stretch ourselves, saying, 'Come on, there is more – more – more.') that you may be filled (What in the world does that mean? It is like the end of the first chapter, 'the fulness of him who fills all in all.') with all the fulness of God' (Eph. 3:14–19).

Then he ends with this tremendous ascription of glory: 'Now, to him who by the power at work within us is able to do (Ah, here is the theme, God's gift makes us respond.) far more abundantly than all that we ask or think, to him be glory in the church and in Christ Jesus to all generations, for ever and ever. Amen' (Eph. 3:20, 21).

He has not come to the point even yet. Before he tells them what he wants them to do, he tells them what he is praying God to do for them.

'For this reason I pray...he may grant you...'. In Chapter 4:1 he comes to the point and tells them what he wants them to do: 'I therefore, a prisoner for the Lord beg you to lead a life worthy of the calling to which you have been called, with all lowliness and meekness, with patience, forbearing one another in love, eager to maintain the unity of the Spirit in the bond of peace' (Eph. 4:1–3). Even here he is saying. 'I want you to recognise what God has done to you and given to you so that you may learn to live according to it.'

This is the whole thing: it is a matter of realising what he has given us. I heard the other day of two ladies who live together, and one had gone on holiday. When she came back she found her friend had decorated the rather shabby house in which they lived. It had been decorated in her absence from top to bottom—and she was absolutely dismayed because she didn't like it! But, suppose you went away on holiday, leaving the key with someone you could trust and when you came back you found the place just as perfect as you could have it. There is work to do, things to arrange. You respond to the whole thing and you say, What am I going to do with all this? You are overwhelmed with the lavishness of what has been given. Your heart has been filled with pleasure not only at the bounty of the gift, but with all the love behind it. It is like that with God. He comes and pours himself with all his grace into our hearts. He says 'Here you are.' We have to take stock (This is what all the Bible reading and all the Bible study are about). If we are Christians what are we searching for? I hope we are looking for what we have already got. It is, in a spiritual sense, like opening your bank book to see what you have. To go back to the earlier illustration, what is the value of what is in your home? Do you know? Are you so busy looking round for something new you cannot appreciate some of the treasures you have, the gifts that loved ones have given you? So with him. Take stock of what he has given you, and the lavishness of his grace. This is the way to live your life in constant communion with Jesus. This is the life. This is all there is to life, because everything flows from it: Jesus in the heart. The more you realise his presence and the wonders of his grace, his kindness and his care, quite spontaneously, without thought, you respond. That is what faith is, in all its different aspects.

I wish I could express it the way I feel it. I doubt if I can, but I am really trying to speak of this from experience. I am only at the beginning of learning this myself, but I see that for me, in my life, which gets busier as it goes on and looks as if it will, as long as the Lord gives me strength, the first essential is this: to live my life, beyond all the busyness, with him in a chamber, a hidden place where no one can intrude.

So, I am just thinking about him, and the wonder of his love and grace
to me. And this is necessary for two reasons: firstly, because this is
what I am going to be doing in eternity for ever and ever; and secondly,
this is the way I am going to serve him better and be able, perhaps, to be
busier without strain. So, I do it and let him tell me more and more about
the lavishness of his grace and his kindness to me. Oh, it is heart
melting, when you think of his kindness!

WHAT IT IS TO BE A CHRISTIAN

3. The Personalness of Salvation

In these studies in 'What it is to be a Christian' we are beginning with the positive. We will, eventually, come to the negative; but our first concern in expounding the biblical teaching is with the positive.

The origins of the systematic exposition of Scripture in Gilcomston South Church commenced—it seemed at the time, by accident—with a series on salvation. But then I began with the negative. Here we are changing the order because it is so important for Christians, both spiritually and psychologically, to understand what God has given us in his grace.

The negative is vital, of course, because there is so much that needs to be removed from us. Sometimes it is particularly necessary to stress that. But we must always remember that the negative is a means to an end. What our Lord did on the cross was negative (taking away sin and guilt, overcoming the devil); but it was a means to a gloriously positive end: that he might have us as his own and that we might live with him to all eternity. Never again, from the point of the new birth through to all eternity, will the painful question of my sin arise. God has put it away; he does not like to poke about in our past guilt! And he does not want us to poke about in it either!

Indeed, false views of the Christian faith have gained credence at different times because people have been too preoccupied with sin and sins, and getting rid of it and them.

It is quite clear even in his encounters with individuals in the gospels, that Jesus deals very summarily with sin. He wants to deal with it as quickly as possible, have it out of the way and talk about something better because he wants us to be his own; that is what being a Christian is all about.

You see, when people have professed a gospel which is largely forgiveness of sins, or even justification, to put it more positively there has often been a tendency to a negativeness in their lives. There are people who have professed this kind of thing for years, and if you profess intimacy with the Lord Jesus, that you know his presence, his kindness, his love, they are obviously embarrassed. Oh yes, they know all the ins and outs of the doctrine of justification in gospel terms, I mean 'evangelistic gospel terms', but when there is any suggestion of intimacy with the Lord, it embarrasses them.

There is a sentimental and obnoxious way of talking about him; I do not mean that. But if we live our lives closer to him than to anyone else, if our life is largely communion with him we should talk of it and get others to know of it. Mind you, this has hazards. We do not want people to be absorbed with each other's experiences; but sometimes when I am chatting with somebody personally and alone it helps to share and talk about one's own experience of Christ. Sometimes those who have seen the preachers only in their pulpits, so seemingly assured, authoritative with the authority of God's Word, get an exaggerated idea of them. Simply to confess one's need of a heavenly Father to come and put his arms round one, as a child is comforted and reassured, seems to surprise them. But this is part of the essence of being a Christian. I would lose a lot of things: health, friends (God forbid!) and a whole lot of things very precious to me in the context of the Christian life, but I couldn't lose that; that would be death before I was dead. Ultimately, of course, we will talk about other doctrines (people are most concerned lest we are not faithful to the whole gospel), but it is this I want to stress at the moment, the personalness of salvation.

Salvation is Jesus Christ coming into our hearts; but it is a change of relationship, not merely a change of inward state of heart and life. The ultimate aim (I am not saying this in a derogatory fashion) is not mere goodness, or holiness, or saintliness, but all of these things in the context of having fellowship with God, knowing God, communing with him, living our life with him, and understanding how kindly and sweetly he comes to us along the line of our own personalities.

One of the things we have to learn is that God is just as much with us when we do not feel him emotionally as when we do. There are times when you may feel rather cold in respect of Christ and God and religion, when you could really wonder whether God is real and there is a God; you do not *feel* him. Or, it could be sometimes when you pray you do not feel him and it is like praying against a brick wall. People regularly speak to me about this and how it distresses them to have no sense of the presence of God. But, you see, God is there, whether you have the sense of his presence or not, and God is just as kind when we have no sense of his presence as when we feel him come and put his arms around us and hug us.

One of the reasons why he withdraws the conscious, felt senses of his presence is that we might learn to live by faith, and trust his Word and grow in grace and steadfastness. He wants us to know that he always loves us like that, whether we feel it or not. This will establish our lives with such strength and stability and resoluteness that we will not be weak-kneed, wobbly, shiftless sorts of Christians, up one day and down the next. Of course, our emotions and our digestions affect us, and we *are* inclined to be up one day and down the next, but our faith in God will not be up one day and down the next, nor our love to Jesus. It will not fluctuate, because we are holding on to the fact he is within us and he never changes within us. He is not one colour one day and then another, however we feel it; he is always the same. He does not need to change. He is absolutely everything. There is no need for him to change. Sometimes I'm sure he says to us. 'What do you want? What are you craving for? Why are you so disgruntled? Why are you so discontented? What are you wanting?' And we give him a shopping list of our needs. But does he look at it and ask, 'I'm not here? not here?' You see, it is so easy in the Christian life with all its concerns, applying it to our vocation and all that, to forget *him*.

Therefore, every problem of the Christian life is a personal or an inter-personal problem. It is a problem of personality, of human beings, living, intelligent, feeling, thinking, conative (trying) and cognative (thinking) persons. I want to look at that in a few persons in the Old Testament.

Adam. When Adam sinned, under the influence of Satan through Eve, he no longer wanted to be friends with God, the God who had made him and had given him everything in the Garden that was lovely. Because he knew God would be displeased with what he had done, he knew that to have fellowship with a God who would be grieved with him, and indeed angry with him for his sin, would be far too painful. So, having sinned, he wanted to run away. So when they 'heard the sound of the Lord God... the man and his wife hid themselves from the

presence of the Lord God among the trees of the Garden' (Gen. 3:8).
God had to go out and look for Adam. Let me put it like this: God had
perfect fellowship in himself, Father with Son and with Holy Spirit; but
he made man to be his created friend. He lost his friend.

When a child comes in from school in the afternoon, and calls out
'Mummy!' but Mummy does not answer, what does he do? He calls out
'Mummy! Mummy! Mummy! Where are you?' Home is not home
without mummy. So it was with God, 'Adam, where are you?' And
Adam replied: 'I heard the sound of thee in the garden, and I was afraid,
because I was naked; and I hid myself.'

Cain. Cain did not want to have fellowship with his brother, so much
so that he slew him (Gen. 4:2–11). God had welcomed Abel's offering
because it was given in faith; Cain's was not. Thus Abel's life had made
Cain feel badly about his relationship to God. The end result of that is
murder, of one kind or another.

Enoch. 'Enoch walked with God; and he was not, for God took
him' (Gen. 5:24). 'Ah,' said God, 'I have a friend here. Come on,
Enoch! Come on!' Enoch lived a long life (three hundred and sixty-five
years, according to Gen. 4:23!), but one day the Lord said to him,
'Enoch, come on; let's go for our usual walk.' And God walked Enoch
right off the face of the earth! Like Elijah, who went in even more
spectacular fashion! But what were they taken for? More fellowship!

Abraham. 'The Lord said to Abraham (in Ur of the Chaldees, down
by the Persian Gulf), go from your country and your kindred and your
father's house to the land that I will show you. And I will make of you a
great nation, and I will bless you, and make your name great, so that
you will be a blessing. I will bless those who bless you, and him who
curses you I will curse; and by you all the families of the earth shall
bless themselves' (Gen. 12:1–3).

This is wonderful! Do you notice the I's and the you's? God is saying
to Abraham: 'Abraham, give up everything for me—land, house,
family, everything. Go out from here, and I will show you the way.
Trust me. I will bless you, and make your name great so that you will be
a blessing. Do you see how personal this is? God is telling Abraham, 'I
want *you*, Abraham, to do this: give up everything, except me, and
come with me.'

In a sense, God said to Abraham, as he said to Enoch: 'Come and walk with me.' So they took a long walk, along those two arms of the triangle going right up by the River Euphrates and down into Syria. They walked up the right arm of the triangle to Haran, and then down the left, into Canaan. Isn't that wonderful?

Moses. 'Now Moses was keeping the flock of his father-in-law, Jethro, the priest of Midian; and he led his flock to the west side of the wilderness, and came to Horeb, the mountain of God. And the angel of the Lord appeared to him in a flame of fire out of the midst of a bush; and he looked, and lo, the bush was burning, yet it was not consumed. And Moses said, "I will turn aside and see this great sight, why the bush is not burnt." When the Lord saw that he turned aside to see, God called to him out of the bush, "Moses, Moses!" And he said, "Here am I." Then he said, "Do not come near; put off your shoes from your feet for the place on which you are standing is holy ground." And he said "I am the God of your father, the God of Abraham, the God of Isaac, and the God of Jacob." And Moses hid his face, for he was afraid to look at God. Then the Lord said (Oh, when we have an awe of him, and fear to draw near to him because he is very terrible and very great, God always comforts. He did to Daniel. He did to John on Patmos. He said, 'Now, don't you be afraid. Don't be afraid.' He is constantly saying that to those who have an awe of him. 'Don't be afraid.') "I have seen the affliction of my people who are in Egypt, and have heard their cry because of their taskmasters; I know their sufferings, and I have come down to deliver them out of the hand of the Egyptians."'

By the way, reading this, I wonder if sometimes Moses and the children of Israel thought: our God doesn't care a rap about all we are going through. We have been here four hundred years; why doesn't he do something? But look at what this is saying. If you live by your feelings, not by your faith in God's good work of love, you will never believe these precious things. There are times when you think you are deserted; God has forgotten. What rubbish! 'I have seen (perfect tense, relative to all the past) the affliction of my people...and come down to deliver them out of the hand of the Egyptians, and to bring them up out of that land to a good and broad land, a land flowing with milk and honey.' (Oh, the kindness! God is always doing kind things, good things for us.).

'Come (he says to Moses) I will send you to Pharaoh that you may bring forth my people, the sons of Israel, out of Egypt.' But Moses said (And he has a lot of 'buts' before he is done, the naughty man, because he doesn't want to do it. You can see this right through the next chapter.

But, of course, this is what we do, too. 'But Lord, you have forgotten this, and you have forgotten that, and I'm not suitable, and there is this, that, and the other.') 'Who am I that I should go to Pharaoh, and bring the sons of Israel out of Egypt?'

I imagine that here the Lord might have said, 'Well, you are nothing, but go and do it nonetheless.' That is what he says to us all. We say, 'Who am I?' He says, 'Nothing, but go and do what you are told' (Ex. 3:1–12).

It is as simple as that. God is not looking for important people to do his work; he is looking for obedient people and faithful people, even if they are nonentities. In one sense God loves nonentities because he can pour all his wisdom into their hearts and minds. There are not enough nonentities of that kind; we are all so confoundedly opinionated.

Moses said, 'Who am I?' God said (and this is it) 'But I will be with you. You are not going alone.' Remember the other place where Moses said in his desperation in an extreme situation with Israel, 'Oh, God, if you are not going up into Canaan with us, we are not going.' The Lord said, 'But, I would not dream of sending you up to Canaan without going with you' (Ex. 33:12–17). He never sends us on any errand without going; never, never, never. 'But, I will be with you....'

Samuel. 'And Samuel grew and the Lord was with him and let none of his words fall to the ground. And all Israel from Dan to Beer-sheba knew that Samuel was established as a prophet of the Lord' (1 Sam. 3:19). 'He was with him.' Just that; it is so simple. But it is this simple thing that is the whole thing. This is what gave these men strength. This is what made them giants in the faith. They knew that they were not alone, left to their own helpless nonentity. 'I will be with you.' And the Lord was with him.

David. 'Behold, I have seen a son of Jesse the Bethlehemite, who is skilful in playing, a man of valour, a man of war, prudent in speech, and a man of good presence; and the Lord is with him' (1 Sam. 16:18). This concerns the anointing of David. Samuel had seen Jesse bring in all his great tall sons, all handsome chaps: but he had not thought to bring in the youngster David. I'm sure he did not despise him, but he did not think of him as a candidate for the throne.

'Have you any more sons?' asked Samuel. 'Oh, yes, there is the wee one.' 'Send him in. Let us have a look at him, because God has not chosen any of these.'

Well, in comes the wee one. He was ruddy and had beautiful eyes and was handsome. And the Lord said, 'This is the fellow. Arise, anoint him; for this is he'. 'Then Samuel took the horn of oil, and anointed him in the midst of his brothers; and the spirit of the Lord came mightily upon David from that day forward (1 Sam. 16:13).' And so on to verse 18 'and the Lord is with him.'

Elijah. I am trying to recall how they used to present Mendelssohn's *Elijah* in the Royal Albert Hall. Now, if I were the producer, I would begin like this: an absolutely bare stage, then suddenly this great giant of a man strides on to the middle of the stage. That is how it was: 'Now Elijah the Tishbite (Tishbe is a rugged place, and a rugged people came from this part of the country) said to Ahab, "As the Lord God of Israel lives, before whom I stand"' (1 Kings 17:1). 'Before whom you stand, Elijah? What in the world do you mean by that?' 'Well, I mean what I say, "Before whom I stand..."'

Isaiah. Isaiah 'saw the Lord' in his vision 'sitting on a throne, high and lifted up and his train filled the temple' (Is. 6:1). Now here is where we touch on the whole question of sin and unworthiness. When Isaiah saw the Lord it was like looking into a mirror, for he saw himself. When you see the Lord over against yourself you say, 'Lord, I'm unclean.' You don't know how unclean you are until you have seen the Lord. 'Woe is me! For I am lost; for I am a man of unclean lips, and I dwell in the midst of a people of unclean lips; for my eyes have seen the King, the Lord of hosts' (Is. 6:5). To Isaiah, even in a vision, it was an experience of confrontation with the Lord himself.

Later in Isaiah 8:11, he writes: 'For the Lord spoke thus to me with his strong hand upon me.' What does that mean? Have you ever experienced anything like that? Perhaps your father, or your teacher, or someone concerned for you is rebuking you, or showing particular care for you, or admiration of you, and they stand and put their hand on your shoulder, and it becomes heavier and heavier till you feel weighed down. I wonder if Isaiah felt God really there and his hand becoming heavier and heavier upon him. Although that could be awesome and alarming in a sense, the point is the intimacy of the experience. It is a man and God, and God is pressing him down, so much so, that that is how he describes it. He says, God has got his hand on me and is pressing me down. You say, 'God isn't like that; the invisible God is a Spirit. He is not like that.' Yes, but that is how it feels. 'His strong hand was upon me, warning me not to walk in the spirit of this people' (Is. 8:13). 'But the Lord of hosts, him you shall regard as holy; let him be your fear and let him be your dread.... I will wait for the Lord who is hiding his face from the house of Jacob, and I will hope in him' (Is. 8:17). The Lord had said to Isaiah, Judah is falling away from me, just as the ten northern tribes fell away. Isaiah is really fed up with the people of Judah, but then he is called to be the prophet among them until at last the Lord says, 'Ugh! Leave them alone. Shut the Book. Don't speak the Word of God to them any longer. Shut the Book. Keep it only for those who have a taste for it.' 'Seal the teaching among my disciples' (Is. 8:16). And Isaiah says, 'All right, I will wait for the Lord, who is hiding his face from the house of Jacob (But he is not hiding his face from me.) and I will hope in him' (Is. 8:17).

Jeremiah. Jeremiah beautifully describes how the Lord came to him (Jer. 1:4ff.). Think how intimate it is. Think, if the Lord should come to you tonight, just before you sleep, and such thoughts and words as these came into your head—and they could. 'Before I formed you in the womb, I knew you.' What? Yes. 'And before you were born I had set you apart. I appointed you a prophet to the nations.' 'Then I said, 'Ah, Lord God! Behold, I do not know how to speak, for I am only a youth.' (Speak in public, I suppose it means. Lots of folk cannot speak in public, but have plenty to say in private!) 'But the Lord said to me, "Don't you say, I am only a youth (I wonder if God is saying this to some young person. Is somebody despising you? Is there somebody making little of you and it is hurting you? I hope not in your own home—father, or mother,—a big brother? It can be sore. A sister? A teacher? Surely not, though there are teachers and teachers! Someone making you feel small? That is not the way God comes to you. Even if you are a very little chap he says, 'Don't say, I am only a youth.') for to all whom I send you you shall speak. Be not afraid of them, for I am with you to deliver you," says the Lord. Then the Lord put forth his hand and touched my mouth.' Now, do you think it incredible that Jeremiah felt that? 'The Lord put forth his hand and touched my mouth; and the Lord said to me, "Behold, I have put my words in your mouth."' Isn't that great?

Daniel. It gets better as it goes on! In Daniel chapter 10 we find him in the middle of a vision: 'Behold, a hand touched me and set me trembling on my hands and knees.' Oh, the intimacy of God, even when he comes in the Old Testament in angelic form. 'And he said to me, O Daniel, man greatly beloved, give heed to the words that I speak to you, and stand upright (not flat on your face which is the right position for us before a holy God). Stand up on your feet. Fear not, Daniel. Stop shaking, man. Get up on your feet and stand upright. Stop shaking.' What a God this is, who is going around all the time saying, 'Don't be afraid. Don't feel small. Don't think you are nothing.' Isn't that wonderful? I wish I had been told all this when I was crippled with feelings of inferiority from the age of thirteen onwards, through all my youth, made miserable because nobody really told me there was a God who cared in this personal way. 'Fear not, Daniel, for from the first day that you set your mind to understand and humbled yourself before your God, your words have been heard, and I have come because of your words.' Oh, there is so much more—think of Nehemiah, too! But we must come now to the New Testament.

We come to Jesus. Think of Matthew 11:28–30. *Now* we come to it! These are the words set down in the Church of Scotland *Book of Common Order*, to be read at the Lord's Table. I don't do anything necessarily *just* because it is in the *Book of Common Order*, but I love to read these words. I love them at any time, but particularly at the Lord's Table. Savour this! Maybe I shouldn't say it, but savour these words like the rarest wine—even if, like me, any time you have ever sipped wine, even the rarest, it has always tasted like vinegar! But savour the words as appeal to you best. Make music of this or something visual; for these are the choicest, the rarest words. Handel usually finds the right music for the right words and his certainly brings these out. 'Come unto me all who labour and are heavy laden and I will give *you* (See him standing, pointing to you) rest. Take my yoke upon you and learn from me; for I am gentle and lowly in heart, and you will find rest ('relief' as it has been translated) for your soul. For my yoke is easy, and my burden is light.'

Again, turn to John 17:20, and Jesus' 'High Priestly Prayer': 'I do not pray for those only, but also for those who believe in me through their word, that they may all be one; even as thou, Father, art in me, and I in thee, that they also may be in us, so that the world may believe that thou hast sent me.' You see his emphasis on the fellowship. From this you have the clearest definition of one vital kind of evangelism. The world outside sees how united we are, how we love one another, the quality of fellowship that is between us, the trust, the care. Somebody is sick and everyone says, 'Oh, we'll need to pray.' 'I'll need to see what I can do.' 'Can I visit or send a note or ring up?' People see all this, and they say, 'These people are pretty close, aren't they?' Would it be real, think you? That is what Jesus means when he says, 'that the world may believe that thou hast sent me...and hast loved them even *as* thou hast

loved me.' Is this true? God loves you *as* he loves his Son, his perfect
Son who never sinned, the divine eternal One? Jesus, is that what you
are saying to your Father in prayer? Can it be true? 'Thou hast loved
them *even as* thou hast loved me.' (My word, I can't take that in, but I
must begin to try.) 'Father, I desire that they also whom thou hast given
me, may be with me where I am, to behold my glory which thou hast
given me in thy love for me before the foundation of the world.'

This love is everlasting. There is no change in it. Even when people
change it goes on loving. It is very difficult to do. I find it very difficult.
I am convicted about this kind of loving. I can think of people who were
here twenty years ago, some of them as children, now grown men and
women in the world, and my heart bleeds for them. I do not know
whether they are following the Lord and loving him. I can still see them
as bairns in the Children's Church. And sometimes because of
disappointments or long delayed response to the Word on their part one
grows weary, sometimes a little sore and even perhaps a little bitter. One
who caused me pain for years subsequently wrote and said, 'Will you
forgive me? I am sorry for all the hurt I caused you.' You know what it
made me feel? It made me feel a worm because sometimes I was sore,
and it hurt, and I fear I magnified it because I was hurt. And I felt small,
and asked, 'Oh God, was it because I didn't love him enough?'

'Oh righteous Father, the world has not known thee, but I have
known thee; and these know that thou hast sent me. I made known to
them thy name, and I will make it known, that the love with which thou
hast loved me may be in them, and I in them.' This personalness of
Jesus coming to be one with whom we commune, with whom there is
such intimacy of friendship (on the basis of fact, not feeling), who is
always tender even when we feel cold or angry with him, whose
tenderness is over us all the time, this kind of thing is called by so many
long names.

On one occasion when I had made reference in a sermon to various
scholars, a dear woman said to me at the close, 'I dinna like all these
long words; Jesus used small, short, simple words.' I said, 'Yes, my
dear, and that is what we should use too.' But you see, some of these
long words are used in the Bible and on that account they are not to be
despised. They are to be revered. But, admittedly, some of them are
difficult. For instance, if I were to say, 'Write down in a sentence or two
the definition of justification and then after you have done that write
down the definition of sanctification,' I wonder what kind of answers
we would get. What fun it would be looking at them! Anyway,

salvation, fellowship with Christ, is described in so many different terms, with abstract words designating some of the blessings and the advantages which come to us through having Christ as our Saviour. But when you go over them, you find they can all be expressed in personal terms, and need to be. Let me show you that this is the case.

Take *conviction of sin*. That is one of the most painful ones. It is by conviction of sin that we come to Christ, confess our sins, forsake them and receive forgiveness. We experience conviction of sin in relation to God. It is not a mere unpleasant feeling but a conviction that overmasters us and can be absolutely terrible in its working. When God comes to someone and convicts them of sin, it is with his wrath and anger that he comes. It is therefore personal. It is God being angry with me. It is not a mere feeling: it is a profound experience in relation to God who is grieved with me and is telling me what I have done wrong. 'Look what you have done. Look what you have done!' he says.

Repentance. Repentance means change of mind, and more especially a change of mind in relation to God. It is God who comes and changes our minds with regard to himself, with regard to ourselves, and with regard to others. This also is personal; it is not some kind of mechanical work within us. It is not like taking one piece of mechanism out and putting another in. He changes us in relation to himself and in relation to our own selves. We see God differently. We see him as we have never seen him before. We see ourselves differently and have a different attitude towards ourselves. And we have a different attitude towards other people.

The forgiveness of sins, or as we should say, the removal of sins by Christ. By Christ we have the forgiveness of sins through his blood, or redemption through his blood. Well, it is God who removes our sins; that is personal too. Jesus comes to take them on his back and dies with them and takes them with him. Annihilation! He blots them out and comes up without them. Yes, he did that. He removed our sins.

Salvation. What is salvation? Salvation is Jesus. 'Neither is there salvation in any other' (Acts 4:12). Salvation is Jesus; it is not a thing. It is not a feeling, it is not a mere experience, it is not a doctrine (although it involves doctrine): salvation is Jesus, nothing less.

Justification (righteousness). This is in relation to God. We are made right in God's sight. We cannot go into this in detail here, but he declares us, through faith, to be right. He marks our paper, Right. And right means right, not half-right. There are no comparatives to right. Right is an absolute. Something good can be better, and beyond better is best, but you cannot really speak about something being righter than right! So, God marks our paper, the paper of our lives, Right. He does it. He says it. It is personal, you see. You have the mark of it in your life.

Redemption. To be redeemed is simply to be delivered. Delivered from what? From sin, and all that. From whom?—the devil. By whom?—by God. What for?—for God. Christ comes and delivers us. He says, 'Come on now, into the arms of God.' It is all personal.

Reconciliation. Well, that is obvious enough. We are reconciled to God. He takes us into his arms like the father in the story of the Prodigal Son. Think of the son running back from the far country where he wasted his substance in riotous living. Back he came, and his father, standing on the tower of the house where probably they watch for the foxes in the vineyards, peering into the horizon and yearning and saying, 'Oh my laddie, when are you coming back?' And he sees him; down the steps he goes, and lifts the skirts of his robes, and takes to his heels. My, he had never run like that since he was a young lad! He comes to his son, and he clings to him and clasps him in his arms. He is reconciled. That is reconciliation.

Sanctification. Lastly we have sanctification (holiness). Now, ultimately, sanctification or holiness is not so much to do with being pure, true, good, and clean, like a statue, as it has with being set apart to God. Of course it has to do with being pure, good, true, and holy and all that. I am not taking away from that. But the word itself means 'set apart'—'to set apart to God'—and that is a relationship. To be holy is to be his, to know that you are his and to live for him. So, you see, it is all personal.

There is no part that is not personal. It is not abstract. By all means, go to college and study theology and be involved in all that, but never forget that it is all personal. What is *theology*? It is the study of God, and God is a Person, who loves us. That should be wonderful, to study the Person who sent his Son into the world to redeem us so that he could take us into his arms.

There are two last texts therefore. Here is the first: 'This is life eternal, that they may know thee the true God, and Jesus Christ, whom thou hast sent' (Jn. 17:3). Sitting at my desk before I came out to preach on this theme, I said, 'Lord, there is not enough here, not enough to help folk; give me another word to clinch this.' And this is what he gave me: 'He that is joined to the Lord is one Spirit' (1 Cor. 6:17). Now, you are a believer (or you are going to be, I hope, soon, if you are not)—you are a believer, that is to say Jesus Christ has come into your heart, by his Holy Spirit (for his resurrection body is in heaven) and he takes your spirit (for you have a spirit which is dead to God until he comes) and his Holy Spirit; and he joins the two together in perfect communion until you cannot see the join, and you are one. I have never put it like that before, I don't know why. But that is the heart of it. It could not be more personal, or intimate than that, could it?

WHAT IT IS TO BE A CHRISTIAN

4. Justification

Justification is a long word which one should never use in public without explaining what it means! It has to do with making right what is wrong. It is as simple as that. Our concern in the beginning of this series is not with the justification of men but the justification of God. No man can demand justification of God. Who dare try? But he is so great that he demands justification of himself.

Think about it like this: God is a perfectionist, an absolute perfectionist. Now you know it is sometimes difficult to live with perfectionists because they are never happy until everything around them is just as perfect as they can make it or they can see it could be. They are unsatisfied with anything that is less than the very best they can do, or give, or have. That is quite right. Some of the geniuses of history—musicians, sculptors, architects, poets and so on have spent long hours perfecting, perfecting, perfecting, and have still not been satisfied. We all know that there is a kind of perfectionism that is a sickness. A psychiatrist may ask a patient, 'When you see a picture squint on the wall do you feel absolutely compelled to straighten it?' But our God is a balanced perfectionist. He cannot be satisfied with anything less than absolute perfection because he is of that order himself. When he made the world he insisted it should be perfect. Read through the story of creation in the first chapter of Genesis, and you will see how often God declared his creation to be good (Gen 1:3, 9, 12, 18, 21, 25, 31). That was good and the other was good until when it came to man himself, Adam and Eve, God said they were 'very good.' You see, God is a perfectionist.

Just imagine the Father the perfectionist and the Son with the Holy Spirit, the divine, the eternal, the holy Family in eternity before the world began, discussing something. The Father loved the Son (Jn. 17:24). Because he loved his Son he wanted to do everything he could for his Son's pleasure (as every right father does) and because he thought his Son so wonderful, beautiful, infinite in wisdom (wisdom personified as Proverbs 8 in the Old Testament tells us), grace, goodness, righteousness, integrity, he wanted in a sense, both to extend the range of that virtue, and to show it forth. He wanted others to see the glory of his Son. So, we may imagine, in discussion with his Son he said, 'Let us create a race of creatures through whom we may display and make known my love for you, because you are so wonderful. Through them we may display your being, your nature, and your character, not in pictures, not in puppets, but in living, true representations (miniatures, if you like) of yourself.' A worthy race, you see, would not be puppets nor servile beasts of the lower order at all.

So they created (and there is a hint of this in the Book of Job) first, the angelic world. There is indeed a great deal in the Old Testament about angels. Almost from the beginning God revealed himself to the Jews in angelic form. And we later find the Letter to the Hebrews setting angels in their true perspective and domain, in relation to men and to God, as do the closing verses of Psalm 103:

> The Lord has established his throne in the heavens,
> and his kingdom rules over all.
> Bless the Lord, O you his angels,
> you mighty ones who do his word,
> hearkening to the voice of his word!
> Bless the Lord, all his hosts
(and here hosts means his ministers, his servants; compare Heb. 1)
> his ministers that do his will!
> Bless the Lord, all his works,
> in all places of his dominion.
> Bless the Lord, O my soul.

Who, or what, are angels? They are creatures who are exceedingly numerous, whose power is inconceivable and whose place is about the throne of God. But we know that some of them fell, one of them in particular. This must have been a tremendous blow to the Almighty, although in his discussion with his Son he had foreseen the whole thing. The question was whether they would dare to make creatures with real free will which would enable these creatures, if they wanted, to go their own way and turn their back on the God who had made them. It is here we see that God could not be satisfied with puppets; he wanted creatures, who, if they were to be like his Son, would respond fully and happily as his Son did, obey his every word and give him full pleasure and fellowship. They had to take the risk; and the risk they took. Many have believed that this is portrayed under the figures of kings in Isaiah 14 and Ezekiel 28; the creation of the angels and the fall of one who was very likely the brightest angel of all. He is called there (AV) Lucifer, the 'light bearer', the most resplendent angel of all because of the very beauty and authority God gave him over all creation. We know this is true from our Lord's lips. Three times in John's Gospel the Lord speaks of the devil (for this brightest angel, Lucifer, became the devil by his fall) as the 'prince of this world', the universe (Jn. 12:31; 14:30; 16:11). The Apostle Paul speaks similarly of him, too (2 Cor. 4:4; Eph. 2:2).

So God gave the great angel free will and he chose to aspire to God's eternal throne and sought to take God's seat. For this he had to be cast down. Now, of course God had a great problem on his hands (albeit foreseen): what was he to do? Was he to destroy the angelic world? Destroy this creature who had rebelled against him? No; he would try again. Oh the daring, oh the courage of the Almighty! He would try again but even more wonderfully this time: he would make another race, of clay, of animal substance but into which he would breathe his breath, his Spirit. He would also give him intelligence, free will, power to choose, power even to choose the God who made him (as the angels had been given) or refuse. If this creature fell under the influence of the first to fall, Lucifer the angel, two catastrophes would be on hand. How could God cope with that? All this was seen in eternity before the world began. He and his Son together had foreseen it all and they bravely said, 'We will go through with it all. We will take the risk. We will take the double risk. We shall not wipe out the angels nor shall we wipe out the men but when Lucifer falls and then drags Adam down too with him and he falls, then (says the Father to the Son who nods his perfect assent) you will go down and retrieve the ruin, repair the disaster and redeem man.'

That is not easily done, to redeem the evil, in a sense self-inflicted by the man through the power of the enemy. How do that? How is it to be done? How could a God of the highest integrity, the most sublime, perfect and infinite righteousness, live with himself and with his handiwork thereafter, if, to try to repair the ruin caused, he sought to cover up the cancerous growth with a bread poultice? Never. If he was to repair this ruin to his own satisfaction (leave everyone else out of it) he must deal with it radically—to the very root. To right the wrong of human sin he must do so to his own conscientious satisfaction. He must please himself.

This is where some of the great New Testament texts come in. Let us look at them: Romans 1:16, 17. 'For I am not ashamed of the gospel: it is the power of God for salvation to everyone who has faith, to the Jew first and also to the Greeks. For in it the righteousness of God is revealed...'. Now, I know that this includes the righteousness of God's actions in procuring our justification, in curing what was wrong; but first it states the integrity of God himself, that this must be done according to his satisfaction. 'The righteousness of God' is first the demand of God to please himself in what he did to an absolutely perfectionist standard.

You have this again in Romans 3:26. From verse 23 the apostle has spoken about the redemption that was in Christ Jesus, whom God put forward as a propitiation by his blood, to be received by faith. This was to show God's righteousness, because in his divine forbearance (which is part of his righteousness) he had passed over former sins.' He had been prepared in the meantime, as a temporary measure during the Old Testament ages, simply to cover up from his sight the sins of the Old Testament saints. Put it simply like this: although they went to God, Abraham, Moses and Elijah were not objectively saved until Jesus Christ had died and had been raised from the dead. Notice I use the word 'objectively.' They were not objectively saved. Their sins were not removed, they were only covered up from God's sight. The very word 'atonement' in the Old Testament means 'to cover up.' They were not objectively saved until Christ came to blot out their sins and annihilate them, to cause them, with their guilt and shame and penalty, to cease to be. Paul says, 'This was to show God's righteousness because in his forbearance he had passed over the sins of the saints of the Old Testament; and it was to prove at the present time (that he was going to fulfil all that he desired to satisfy his own integrity) that he himself is righteous and that he justifies him who has faith in Jesus.' He justifies the ungodly (Rom. 5:6, 8, 10).

No one is to inspect him doing this. No one is above him. This he is doing to his own satisfaction, and so, if he is to right the wrong of human sin, he must right it righteously. He must right it to his own satisfaction. It must be fully and finally and radically dealt with but it must be dealt with upon principles that satisfy his integrity, his conscience of what is right and wrong. God cannot produce laws for men unless he has laws for himself; and he has laws for himself. He is that kind of being. He cannot sin; that is against his own law. So, the act

must be done to his satisfaction; someone must righteously contain the
evil and destroy it. Who is big enough for this? Who do you think? Cecil
Frances Alexander is absolutely correct:

> There was no other good enough to pay the price of sin.
> He only could unlock the gate of heaven and let us in.

This is where Jesus' earthly life and his cross are so crassly
misunderstood in the world. Men simply do not understand why Jesus
turned away from worldly power and worldly popularity and the
crowds. They fail to understand what he planned to do. Even to the end
of his ministry his disciples could not understand what he had come to
do. Jesus might have said, 'Peter, Peter, blind and stupid Peter, can't
you understand that I came to die, not to sit on a great golden throne
with you on one side.' Oh, the blindness of men as to what Christ came
to do. In his cross he is not only showing men by his costly death, how
bad men are to need to be so died-for by the death of the Son of God,
but it was the only way to get rid of man's sin. God himself had to take
it away for there was no other fit to take it away. He alone could take it
away to his own satisfaction. He alone could bear the cost by taking it
on himself, loading it on his back in Jesus Christ and carrying it away as
if he were the sinner. People who are very proficient in their job may
teach others and so encourage them till at last their pupils achieve
something of their perfection, but there are times when they say to
themselves, 'If you want a job done right; do it yourself.' That is what
God said. And the cost? The cost is seen in Isaiah 53. How remarkably
that prophecy is fulfilled in Jesus!

Notice in the first flush of popularity with the healing of the sick and
the feeding of people's bodies they crowded to Jesus, but when he
offered them bread for their souls, you couldn't see them for dust! So he
said, 'What is the good of giving you bread for your bodies if only to
feed you as fodder for hell? I came here to feed your souls, to transform
your lives, but you won't have it. What is the point of feeding your
bodies like beasts for the kill? What is the point of that?' He therefore
turned away to feed the souls of those who would have it. Sometimes
there were only twelve, and one of those was a disaster and a devil.
Thereafter, Jesus was 'despised and rejected of men, a man of sorrows
and acquainted with grief' (Is. 53:3). Even when it came to the point that
he was led to the cross he was deserted by all; even the three, even
Peter. 'As one from whom men hide their faces, he was despised and
we esteemed him not' (Is. 53:3). I think the prophet was wonderfully
inspired when he so described Jesus' experience on the cross. There

were criminals on either side, you remember. I am not saying that the sight of him, the visual aspect of our Lord was like this, although it must have been horrible to view if you had any feeling at all. But the prophet is going deeper than that. He says, 'Many were astonished that his visage was so marred beyond human semblance and his form beyond that of the sons of men' (Is. 52:14). I am inclined to think that there is a hint of the angels here somewhere, marvelling at what men do to a perfect Man. What do you think the holy angels could have thought of what men did to Jesus? It must have shocked them and taken their breath away.

Yet, says Isaiah 53:4; 'Surely he has borne our griefs and carried our sorrows.' This was the only way. Do you recall strikes in the past, when we have had to cope without the dustmen? The streets of London and other great cities resembled those of the east; quite shocking. Sin is like that. Who is going to take away the dirt? 'I will,' says Jesus (Surely he has borne our griefs and carried our sorrows) because only he could do it perfectly, only he could make us clean. He alone could bear the punishment that was due because of God's holy, righteous condemnation of the sins we had committed and the rebellion of which we were guilty.

'Yet we thought he was stricken, smitten and afflicted by God' (Is: 53:4). We wondered why God was doing this to him. He was doing it to him to save us. 'He was wounded for our transgressions, he was bruised for our iniquities: the chastisement of our peace was upon him and with his stripes we are healed. All we like sheep have gone astray; we have turned every one to his own way; and the Lord has laid on him the iniquity of us all' (Is. 53:5, 6). In the Old Testament the word 'iniquity' is the deepest word for sin. It means perversity, not merely acts of sin but the disposition to sin, the disposition of rebellion against God.

If you know Handel's Messiah you will doubtless remember what follows: 'He was oppressed and he was afflicted yet he opened not his mouth: he was brought as a lamb to the slaughter, and as a sheep before her shearers is dumb, so he opened not his mouth' (Is. 53:7). Why did Jesus refuse to defend himself before Herod, before Pilate and before the Jews? Paul sought to do so when he was almost lynched on his visit to Jerusalem (Acts 21:27ff). Not that he always sought to defend himself; he refrained later on, but he did then. Why did Jesus not defend himself? Why did he not justify himself? Because he was saying to himself, 'For their sakes, I am guilty. I am the sinner. I am the criminal.

I am to be put on that cross to bear the punishment of others.' It is not the devil's doing. This was the only way that God could justify himself, satisfy himself that our salvation would be achieved perfectly. So Jesus shut his mouth. He pled guilty for us. Oh God, it is too much! It is more than we can take in or understand.

Then Isaiah continues: 'By oppression and judgment he was taken away; and as for his generation, who considered that he was cut off out of the land of the living, stricken for the transgression of my people?... Yet, it was the will of the Lord to bruise him' (Is. 53:8). It was God who did it. It was he who put him to grief. You see why? It is for his own satisfaction. 'When he makes himself an offering for sin, he shall see his offspring, he shall prolong his days; the will of the Lord shall prosper in his hand; he shall see the fruit of the travail of his soul and be satisfied' (Is. 53:10). There it is: the Suffering Servant became God's criminal, God's dustman, to take away the dirt of others and to do it perfectly, righteously and to his own satisfaction.

In his Letter to the Romans, Paul makes a radical diagnosis of sin and sinners. In the first three chapters you have a thorough-going diagnosis of the sin of men, apparently in three categories. The apostle begins with the rank pagan to whom God has spoken although he is blind to it. He has revealed himself to him in nature, in the things he has made, and man turns away from God as he sees him in nature. Paul makes it quite plain that this is a sin against Almighty God to turn away from the handiwork of God as one sees it in nature, because it speaks of God. Psalm 19 says so: 'The heavens are telling the glory of God', and preaching the wordless gospel of his glory. If men were not blind, they would see that it is all made by God. The only argument one needs, in the first instance, for the reality of God is the beauty of his handiwork even now, fallen as it is by sin.

The next category is the so-called moral man who turns his back against God. At the end of Romans 1 Paul tells us that the pagan, refusing to see God in nature, goes down into the filth of Sodom, but in chapter 2 he turns to another man, equally bad. This man looks at the vile pagan, soused in filth and perversity, and with horror he says, 'Look at him. Look at him, the dirty dog.' But Paul whips round on him with, 'You are just as bad!' 'Me? Me just as bad? I am a moral man and I wouldn't do, couldn't do the things he does.' 'Ah but,' says the apostle Paul, 'you are just as bad in your heart because the standard, the rule with regard to what is sin, is only in respect of God.'

That is what David said when he had defiled Bathsheba and murdered her husband, he said he had sinned only against God. He was not denying that he had sinned against the man and the woman but, as he now saw it, he had sinned against God. So, the apostle Paul, by the Holy Spirit, turns against the so-called respectable man and says, 'You are just as bad as the vile pagan in God's eyes, for you do the same things in your heart. You don't know the vileness of your own heart yet.'

You find the third category of man in the second half of Romans 2. He is the Jew who has the Ten Commandments and the Old Testament law. He is teaching the law to others, but he is breaking it all the time himself. He is a teacher of the law, the sacred law of God but he is living as sinfully as the other two, so to him God says, 'You are an equal sinner with those two.' Take the vile, the respectable, and the religious; in their hearts they are all equally vile. Indeed, the respectable man is more vile than the other, for he has more light. He has an informed conscience. The vile pagan has practically no conscience; it is darkened, almost dead and inactive. But the moral man has a conscience and some idea of what is right and what is wrong. He sees and knows what he can and should do. He even despises those who do not do it; but he is not doing it himself. Therefore, if he sins, having more light than the vile heathen, he is a greater sinner. The same with the religious man. He is sinning against God's holy law, the Ten Commandments, a clear revelation of God's will, which apparently the moral, respectable man does not have: he has only conscience. The first man only had nature speaking to him of God, the second conscience, but the third has God's holy law, so he is infinitely worse. The higher you go, the worse you are, the further you fall. You see, you climb the wrong hill, the hill of self-effort, which says in effect, 'I will work my way up to God. I'll please God by my own efforts.' That is not the hill that leads to God, that is the hill that leads to the precipice of hell.

Therefore, with this radical diagnosis of sin, Paul comes to the conclusion in chapter 3 that no one has a ghost of a chance before God unless God himself does something. 'What then? Are we Jews any better off? No, not at all; for I have already charged that all men, both Jews and Greeks, are under the power of sin; (He is telling the Jews to read their Bibles and see whether they are any better than others) as it is written, "None is righteous, no, not one; no one understands, no one seeks after God. All have turned aside, together they have gone wrong; no one does good, not even one." "Their throat is an open grave, they use their tongues to deceive." "The venom of asps is under their lips." "Their mouth is full of curses and bitterness"' (Rom. 3:9–14).

You say, 'Oh, but we are not like that.' What about Northern Ireland? That is what men are like when they get the chance. 'Their feet are swift to shed blood, in their paths are ruin and misery, and the way of peace they do not know.' 'There is no fear of God before their eyes.' 'Now, we know that whatever the law says it speaks to those who are under the law, so that every mouth may be stopped (And if the heathen's mouth is shut up, then the so-called respectable man's mouth is doubly shut) and the whole world may be held accountable to God. For no human being will be justified in his sight by works of the law, since through the law comes knowledge of sin' (Rom. 3:15–20). The more you know about being good, the greater your responsibility to fulfil it. But you lack the power. No human being has the power. God has to do something. And this is the turning point in Romans: 'But now the righteousness of God has been manifested...'.

What a gospel we have to preach! What a Bible! What a New Testament! Isn't it thrilling! Not much wonder we sing with the joy of what God has done for us.

Thus, having radically diagnosed sin and sinners, Paul goes on to reveal how God took away man's sin, since he could not take it away himself. Man could not pay, therefore he could not take part in this. You know, when Jesus went to the cross to take away our sin and guilt and punishment, there is a sense in which he said: 'Stand back. No Apostle Paul can stand here. No Jeremiah, no David, not even almost blameless Joseph can stand here. Stand back. Stand back.' As the hymn says, 'There was no other good enough to pay the price of sin.' Aye, alone. We are never so far from Christ as when he is doing the deed to bring us to himself. He has to put us right out and say, 'Stand back. Don't meddle. Don't interfere. Stand back. Don't spoil, don't sully what I am doing. Stand back and I will do it perfectly.' And he did.

I conclude with a few verses from the New Testament. 1 Peter 2:24: 'He himself bore our sins in his body on the tree.' Nothing could be more explicit. But even more illuminating in relation to Romans is 1 Peter 3:18: 'For Christ also died for sins once for all, the righteous for the unrighteous, that he might bring us to God...'. Then this, in 1 John 2:1: 'My little children, I am writing this to you that you may not sin; but if anyone does sin, we have an advocate with the Father, Jesus Christ the righteous (That is the one who did it all with perfect, divine integrity); and he is the propitiation for our sins, and not for ours only but also for the sins of the whole world.'

1 John 4:10: 'In this was love, not that we loved God but that he loved us and sent his Son to be the propitiation for our sins.' And when he has dealt with them objectively (remember what I said about the sins of the Old Testament saints only being covered up until Jesus died) they are removed and destroyed. That is what the forgiveness of sins means.

I believe that if you were to go to God as a Christian and speak to him about your past sins (apart from the fact that he would not want to hear about them because he does not like to hear about sin, to think about it or to be taken up with it) he might very well say, 'Oh I died to take all that away, didn't I?' 'Yes.' 'Well, is it not taken away? I don't know what you are talking about.'

Is it like that with you? He has taken your sins away to his satisfaction; never mind *your* satisfaction. It is with him we have to deal. We are not going to judge ourselves on the last day. We are not going to judge one another. It is all to be to his satisfaction. Has he taken your sins away to his satisfaction? That is the point!

WHAT IT IS TO BE A CHRISTIAN

5. Grace Abounding

In the previous study we began to discuss the subject of justification and said we must constantly explain what we mean by that word. The basic idea of the word is simply 'right'. Justification is the work of God in Jesus Christ on the cross by which he is able to declare those who believe in his Son to be righteous in his sight. Since right is an absolute term, we began to consider the perfection of God with regard to it. Before we considered the justification of men through Jesus Christ, we considered the justification of God. God revealed his righteousness in that what he has done for us is something that satisfies his own integrity. What Jesus Christ does on the cross, first of all pleases him and satisfies him. It must do that, for God, as we have said, is a perfectionist and will have nothing but the best. Nothing can enter his heaven but that which is absolutely perfect. His righteousness, then, is seen in that he does a perfect work for us, first of all to satisfy himself.

We find this in Romans 1:16, 17: 'The righteousness of God is revealed in the gospel' and in Romans 3:26: what God did was 'to prove at the present time that he himself is righteous and that he justifies him who has faith in Jesus.'

God deals with sin according to his own integrity and perfection, which is to say that he does the deed of justification (declaring us to be righteous) himself. That is why, in the prophecy of Jeremiah, you have these words: 'The Lord our Righteousness' (Jer. 23:6). Interestingly enough, further on in Jeremiah 33:16 he calls Jerusalem and Judah, that is the saints, Israel, God's people, 'The Lord is our righteousness'. 'In those days Judah will be saved and Jerusalem will dwell securely. And this is the name by which it will be called: "The Lord our righteousness."'

First of all he is our righteousness; it is he himself giving himself to us who is our righteousness. This is the wonderful exchange of which we read in 2 Corinthians 5:21: 'For our sake he made him to be sin, who knew no sin, so that in him we might become the righteousness of God.' Then he gives his righteousness to us and so speaks of his people as 'The Lord their righteousness.'

He does the deed himself. He takes the sin of the world upon himself and does the deed that no other one is able or worthy to do, and having done it himself, does it perfectly to his own satisfaction.

But now we must look at what follows from that. If God himself did the deed then it is well done; it couldn't be better because God is perfect, absolutely perfect. In fact, Jesus says, in the Sermon on the Mount, 'Be ye perfect, as your heavenly Father is perfect' (Matt. 5:48). He is perfect and he has done his deed so well that man who is the benefactor of this deed to whom justification came, can have no complaint with what God has done. The perfection of God's deed in justifying us in Jesus Christ is beyond all praise, beyond all understanding and imagination. This is what makes us so thrilled with the gospel that we not only stand and sing praise, but could dance with our feet as well as with our hearts, it is so wonderful. This is the marvel of what God has done; but we don't see it; by nature we are blind to it and even as Christians we scarcely see it clearly. We are not discussing theological theories, although it may seem like that when we use words like justification. I want to tell you that God has done such a marvellous thing that you cannot possibly exaggerate it. It is too big for us! Nevertheless when God, by the Holy Spirit, gives us glimmers of light and shines into our hearts, we begin to see what he has done for us and then our joy knows no bounds.

This is the answer to so many problems of our lives. A great many of your problems, your practical, daily problems, physical problems (of health, sickness, weakness and all that sort of thing), psychological problems (not having peace in your heart, not getting on well with your fellows at home, work, or whatever), spiritual problems (problems of demonism and all the rest of it), are greater than they ought to be. If our hearts were more full of the joy of the Lord, if we lived constantly, or even intermittently in the light of the wonder of what God has done for us then the joy of it would so fill our souls that we would forget our troubles. Then when we went back to cope with them (as we have to) we would view them differently. But, alas, we don't live like that; we live on the very edge.

You know the story of the little boy who kept falling out of bed at night? He got quite puzzled at this and his mummy said to him: 'Why is it, son, that you keep falling out of bed? Why can't you lie safely in your bed?' He said, 'I suppose it is because I stay too near the place where I get in.' That's true. That is the danger; we don't go on. The wonder of grace does not grip us more and more. Sometimes as we grow older it grips us less, and the devil is behind that. I have heard Christians confess it, sometimes with a kind of hopelessness, and I am amazed. I know a dear man in Aberdeen with whom I was involved as a student in the Christian Union, who is now a rank backslider. He said to me, 'You know, as you get a bit older, your food and your comfort and all that kind of thing mean more to you.' I nearly said, 'And Christ less.' He has come to mean nothing to him; partly to the satisfaction of his wife; God have mercy on her soul. More not less! If you want to maintain your youth, whatever you look like in the mirror (don't worry about that!), then get a grip of the truth of the gospel. Get a grip of the wonder of Christ as your Companion, and you will go on and on, and life will get better, every day.

Indeed, so perfect is the deed God does for man that it is far beyond man's need. God has done more than man could possibly need. You could say to me, 'That is a peculiar way of putting it.' Well, I like to put it like that; so just suffer it. It is far beyond what man needs: that is to say, there is an excess of virtue accruing to man in his justification from the very quality of the deed God has done for him. Since God became very man for us and for our salvation (the second Man, to do this deed) the excess of virtue accruing to men from it can be expressed in terms of the comparison of the first Adam's deed of sin (Gen. 3) with the second Adam's deed of justification.

Paul expounds this in magnificent detail in Romans 5:12–21. Take verse 12 and the last part of verse 14 together. 'Therefore as sin came into the world through one man and death through sin (Paul, in a sense you might have stopped there, and finished your sentence, but you are a preacher!) so death spread to all men because all men sinned', that is, in Adam and through Adam. Break off there. Adam is not mentioned until verse 14 but then he is mentioned twice. Pick this up: 'Who [*i.e.* Adam] was a type of the one who was to come.' Adam and Adam: the Bible doesn't speak of the *second* Adam; it speaks (1 Corinthians 15:45) of the '*last* Adam.' That is the right way to put it because there will not be any Adam following him. Only two orders of manhood: Adam and Christ, the first and the last Adam.

Here they are then: sin came into the world through this one man, Adam, who is a type of the One who was to come. He is really and truly a man, tempted in all points, as we are (Heb. 4:15). Think of the temptations in the wilderness, Satan tempting Jesus in his flesh on account of hunger—and this is only one of the temptations Jesus suffered.

There was not a temptation to which man is subject through the fall and through Satan (every temptation; including those we would not mention in public) that Jesus did not know. I sometimes say that, as carefully, guardedly, chastely, and yet as plainly and practically as I can, to young people struggling with their passions. He knows it all. He was truly and properly, thoroughly, absolutely man: the only proper, true, perfect man who ever lived; the only fully human man who has ever lived. There never has been a man so fully human. To the extent that man is a sinner he is less than God intended him to be; much less. He comes short of the glory of God. That is to say, he comes short of the purpose for which God created him. He is not fully human; Jesus alone is.

So, the first Adam is a type of the second One. They are alike in this, that they are both fully human but they are absolutely unlike in that Adam fell into sin through the temptation of Satan, whereas Jesus did not. He resisted evil; he resisted sin absolutely to the end; that is the difference between the two lives.

Come now from Christ's general resistance to temptation and sin and Satan right through the three years of his ministry beyond the Temptation, to the cross itself. It is the one deed of our justification without which all that Jesus came to be and do would be of little value. The sins of the Old Testament saints would still be only covered up; they would still be there; God would know they were there and they would not have been objectively removed. So, we come to the great deed of our redemption in the cross. Take this deed of Jesus Christ, the second Adam, and compare it with the deed of the first Adam. We see, then, that the one is (and this is almost feeble language, though the best human language can do, used by the apostle Paul, inspired by the Holy Spirit) 'much more' than the other.

Bear in mind that God suffered two seeming defeats following creation: his disappointment with the angelic governor, Lucifer, who sought to usurp his throne and had to be cast out though still retaining his authority as prince of this world; that was God's first disappointment, his first 'defeat'. His second was with man. He made a man to compete with this false and fallen governor of the universe, Satan, the prince of this world. He made a man in his own image with dominion over all things, but he also fell under the spell and power of Satan. Thus God had his second, dangerous, disastrous defeat. Two defeats: first with the angels and then with the man.

God foresaw and planned all this before the world began. We talk of the perfections of God: God is so big, God is so great, God has such tremendous creative resources within himself that he says, 'One defeat? Another defeat? I can stand them both, and deal with them, thoroughly.' It is as simple as that. So, it is in his heart and mind to send his only begotten Son, dwelling with him in eternity as a second Adam, truly and properly man, born of Mary, the virgin. He says, 'I will reveal the Godhead in that human body, that human frame and human mind, and in that fully and proper human form, I will get the better of Satan who has caused these two defeats, and he will be defeated and overthrown. The greatness of the victory is what we are singing about and our hearts leaping and dancing about today. The victory is all the more glorious because God first suffered what seemed like defeat. When you are studying the art of war, it is not merely tactics, not merely battles you consider; many a victor has lost many a battle, especially the first ones. That was true in the two Great Wars. It is he who can sustain the conflict to the end who wins. 'He who endures to the end shall be saved,' and be victor; none else.

It is the end that tells, not the beginning. That, incidentally, is why we have to pursue the truth of the Bible right through until we come to the glorious consummation. We have to study and probe, think and wonder; and that is what many people will not do. They will take a crossword puzzle and sit and puzzle it out; they will find dictionaries; they will ask this one and that and phone up and ask, 'What do you think this one would be?' But the Bible? No, it has all to be on the surface. It has all to be handed to them absolutely on a plate with no thought, no effort. What infernal cheek! It is worth probing. Certainly, if you want the joy in your heart of knowing the wonder of Christ's friendship, you have to probe and probe until the joy wells up because you say, 'I see. I see it!' There are Christians who have never come to the stage when they would jump out of their chair and dance, and say, 'Oh, I see it. I see it. How marvellous what God has done!'

Does someone, maybe a little older, think, a little cynically, 'Oh, I have heard that for forty years, or fifty years'? Beware! If the biblical gospel is not still fresh to you, something has happened to you. Something has happened to you if your heart is not singing and dancing as if you heard it for the very first time. In a sense, every time we hear it, it is for the very first time, because it *is* new. That is how I feel. My heart leaps up to God and says, 'Oh, God!' Get it? You see, in a sense we become more incredulous at the incredible act of God. It becomes more fabulous and fantastic as we probe it. We say, 'Could it be? Could it be?' And in that blessed sense our seeming doubt or scepticism could increase, not in the cold, bitter, disinterested sense but in the sense: 'I can't tell. I can't believe it. It is more than I can grasp. Can it be so?' Yes, yes, we cannot grasp it fully, nor will we until we get to heaven. Who knows what progress there is in our knowledge of God in heaven? I suppose it would take us to the end of the endless ages of eternity, and perhaps not even then, as finite creatures, to grasp it.

But to return to these verses! John Murray (in his commentary on Romans 5:18) completes the sentence that is broken off at the end of verse 12: 'Therefore, as through one man, sin entered into the world and death through sin, and so death passed on to all men in that all sinned' in this way: 'even so through one man righteousness entered into the world and life through righteousness, and so, life passed on to all men, in that all were accounted righteous.'

In verse 15 Paul begins to make comparison between the two deeds. 'The free gift (righteousness) is not like the trespass. For if many died through one man's trespass (all men die; if you want proof that man is a sinner, it is that: all men die), much more have the grace of God and the free gift in the grace of that one man Jesus Christ abounded for many. And the free gift is not like the effect of that one man's sin. For the judgment following one trespass brought condemnation, but the free gift following many trespasses brings justification. If, because of one man's trespass, death reigned through that one man, much more will those who receive the abundance of grace and the free gift of righteousness reign in life through one man Jesus Christ.

Then as one man's trespass led to condemnation for all men, so one man's act of righteousness leads to acquittal and life for all men. For as by one man's disobedience many were made sinners, so by one man's obedience (Christ's obedience unto death) many will be made righteous. Law came in, to increase the trespass; but where sin increased, grace abounded all the more, so that, as sin reigned in death, grace also might reign through righteousness to eternal life through Jesus Christ our Lord.'

'Law came in to increase the trespass': God can set up any barrier to what he seeks to do that he likes. He sets up this barrier to his purposes. God likes, loves obstacles. He likes to make things difficult for himself. Why? Shall I tell you? So that he may show how great he is. That is why he set up the obstacle of angelic free will. He said, 'You, angel that I appoint as governor of the universe, I give you free will (or what corresponds to it angelically).' Then in the fulness of time to man, the competitor for the governorship of the universe, he set up the same free will, that obstacle; and in both cases these creatures fell at the obstacle. But God can deal with all obstacles and overleap them all. 'Law came in to increase the trespass'; first Lucifer, then Adam, then Moses bringing in the law to say to men, 'You have sinned. You have sinned. Look at the Ten Commandments; you have sinned.'

'Grace abounded all the more': grace overstepped all the barriers of Lucifer, Adam, Law, and Moses; everything, because God has such an excess, such a superfluity of power and ability to do what he wants to do that he is hindered by nothing, and overleaps the whole lot to do a superabundant work of grace in our hearts. He loves the whole thing. He is a joyous, triumphant athlete, is our God! He overleaps all the barriers.

So he says, 'Look at this deed of Adam that has caused so much trouble, look at it and the fruit of it in many sins in all the men who have ever lived. Look at the fruit of it everywhere.' God says, 'I can deal with all that. I can deal with the source of all that evil. I can deal with the root sin, the primal sin, that which set man on his evil course, setting apart from me man whom I intended to be my dearest companion next to my Son and in my Son. I can deal with the whole thing.' And he has done.

'Much more, much more'—he sends his Son to do this deed. God becomes a Man and takes his place on the cross as God's criminal, God's dustman to take away man's dirt, that he may say to men, 'Look, it is all away. It is all away. I have dealt with it all.'

I believe in one sense in what is called 'limited atonement', and yet in another sense I think the truth of the Bible transcends it. I believe in them both, in that I believe Christ knew who he was dying for, but also I do not believe he could give a genuine offer of the gospel to every man in life unless there were resources in Christ's death to deal with the sins of all. Nor have I found anything in Scripture to contradict that.

The resources, then, are infinite to deal with all the sin as well as with this first sin and so to put it away with its effects and harvest. God puts it away so that he can justify man and declare him to be righteous through faith. It is incredible, but we must not be incredulous, because not to take it in, or to set God so far above sinful man that it seems scarcely credible, is to magnify God and his holiness and his righteousness in a wrong kind of way that produces the wrong kind of conviction of sin. To magnify God in the wrong kind of way sets him over against us. Too many preach the gospel in such a way that they set God so over against us as to make it seem impossible for us to come to him or even he to us. There is a way of emphasising the holiness, the righteousness and the wrath of God that leads, as I said, to the wrong conviction of sin which sets God over against us only as our enemy. We must not be incredulous of the incredible. We have to take it in and believe it, humbly. Ah, there's the rub. There's the rub: believe it humbly that this that God has done for us in Jesus Christ is greater than we will ever be able to grasp.

Think through the meaning of these two verses: Romans 2:4: 'Don't you know that God's kindness is meant to lead you to repentance?' and James 2:13: 'Mercy triumphs over judgment.'

Mercy triumphs against judgment. You can set out the holiness, and the judgment, and the wrath of God in such a way that it just appals man. That is not a preaching of the Good News; it is a preaching of the Bad News. We do not deny it is an essential part of the gospel and a prerequisite of the gospel, but it is not itself the gospel. The good news is, that that holy God, that wrathful God against sin, that holy, righteous God up in heaven who cannot look upon sin, has come down to earth as a man to become his own criminal, to suffer the pain, the guilt, the shame and the hurt to himself in taking the punishment for all the sins of men that he might bring us to himself. The incredible is true. Too good to be true? Too good *not* to be true!

This gospel makes you an optimist, not a pessimist. You have to bring the blessed truth of the Bible right home to your heart and really believe that God cares. Now, this is very difficult. Christians, the aim of your life should be to bring others to Jesus Christ. How are you going to do it? By telling them how bad they are? Well, that was not Jesus' way. Certain categories of people he dealt with very severely of course; they were the agents of the devil. To men and women belaboured with sin and by Satan he came with infinite compassion and showed them respect and care.

A boy I had once met at a student meeting came to be in such psychological throes that he had to give up his course, and so desperate was he that on a fleeting visit to the south I had to make arrangements to see him. I spent hours with him, seeking to help him, and ultimately brought him up here to Aberdeen so that he might meet some of the fellowship and we might try to help him in his difficulties. We spoke for hours. He knew the Scriptures and could discuss them very intelligently and there was a good deal of that over the course of a few days. (I mention this only because it is an example of what we have been speaking about.) Finally he said to me, 'You know, the striking thing was that you took me to your home and made a meal for me.' Now I don't take people to my house and make meals for them, because I live alone and need all my time to make meals for myself before getting on with the world! But you see, it was absolutely necessary. All the rules and all the work that was lying to be done, had to be swept aside because a young man in desperate straits had to be helped. No matter though the world came to an end, he had to be helped; even to making a meal for him, which is not easy for a chap who can hardly boil a kettle! So often, you see, it is the human thing that tells most. Something of the same order was true for a foreigner our congregation knows—one who had married a Scottish girl. His loved ones were desperate for him to become a Christian and they witnessed to him in every way. One day, at a funeral, when the service was over I nearly trampled on his hat, lying on the grass at the cemetery. Knowing it was his, I picked it up, said, 'Is this your hat?' and smiled at him. He says (not I) *that* was the moment when Christ came alive to him. You see?

God has shown us that he cares in that he came down to us to do our dirty work. This is how he did it. Listen to some of the phrases: 'He justifies the ungodly' (Rom. 4:5). Think of that. 'He justifies (declares to be righteous) the ungodly.' Are you taking this in? Again Paul says in Romans 5:6, 'Christ died for the ungodly.'

You say that is dishonest, immoral, illegal as far as God's holy law is concerned. *Not if you take the penalty yourself.* And he did. He paid the penalty. He bore it all himself. That deed is so far beyond merely compensating for or repairing Adam's deed. It is not a mere repair; it is a new thing of such fabulous wealth and glory that there is absolutely no comparison between what Christ does for us and what Adam did against us. The marvellous thing (and this is where you begin to see what the gospel is all about) is that the barrier to God's taking us into his arms, into his heart, into his life and finally into his heaven, is removed. The barrier of our sin he removes himself. This is why the Apostle here speaks of 'justification unto life' (Rom. 5:16, 17). The sinner is absolutely and righteously justified unto life. Now, justification is not life. Righteousness, in a sense, is not life, but it is unto life. God has to do this so that he can take us into his arms. He will not take us to his home if we are dirty. He is perfect, and we have to be perfect before we get there. How can we be? He does it by his own blessed deed, in Christ. He does it; and, having dealt with the sin he says, 'Come away. Come away into my arms and be mine forever, and ever, and ever.' That is justification unto life.

Now, that is something to sing and shout and be happy about! It is something to change your life. If that does not make you better tomorrow (indeed give you sounder sleep tonight), and make people say, 'Dear me, what has happened to her (or him)? What a change!' then nothing will. If that doesn't send you to your work with a smile, a spring in your step, joy in your heart to cope with, more than adequately, all the problems, and all the difficulties, and all the temptations and the trials of life, then you must be blind to its reality and its glory. This is literally life-transforming.

I wish I had time to particularise in what ways this could make a difference to your life. This is what I spend my time preaching about, preparing to preach about, writing letters about, meeting with people, and speaking to them on the telephone about, practically all the time. You see, it is all very well to try to know a bit about this Book and teach it and preach it, but the fruit of it has to be seen in lives. If the fruit of it has not begun to be seen in my life, you would need to come and tell me; otherwise I am living a lie, a delusion. And if I don't see the fruit of it in the lives of those who sit under this ministry and teaching, I want to know why not. I must first ask myself, Why? and then I must ask those who are not benefiting and profiting from such ministry, Why not?

We are not concerned with mere theories; we are concerned with something that works. This justification unto life has to work. How does it work in your case? This is what worries me. I don't know if the Word is not watered enough with prayers but there is often something in the ministry and preaching of the Word that doesn't distil the meaning of the words, written black upon white, into life-giving and life-transforming essence; which is what it is meant to do. This Book is life because it ministers Christ, and he is life; life, not in the abstract sense, but life in the sense that Christ's life has application to every problem and difficulty in our daily life. Whether your particular problem is physical, psychological, social, political or spiritual; whatever in the world it is, Christ has a solution.

Of course, there are things that will not be perfectly solved down here, but whatever your situation or whatever your problem, Christ has something relevant and practical to say to you about it. After years of experience now, I would dare to say that whatever your particular problem, by God's grace we can say something practical and helpful to you about it, no matter who you are or what your problem is. God's Word works; it applies, all because of the glory of this deed of Christ that is infinite in its fruits, and so far above the deed of Adam.

This is what I see in the gospel. We are too much taken up with the negative, too much taken up with sin and all that; we are not taken up enough with Christ and his glory and wonder; his kindness, his love and his grace; his power and the solutions he brings to our problems.

You know, the Christian church, for a time, in its discussion groups, its assemblies, its convocations, rode the word 'problems' to death, until we were all sick of it; 'the problem of this, and the problem of that, and the problem of the other.' What about a few solutions, because this Book is full of solutions to problems, whatever they are. This is because there is infinite virtue, and power and grace in this deed, and the fruit of Christ's deed, to apply to your case. I want to see in this fellowship, and beyond it to the wider fellowship, scattered all over the place, an increase in Christian grace. I want us to see in one another a development, a growth in the grace of Jesus Christ. I want us to be able to deal with our problems in living, working and worshipping together: the same at home, at work—solutions, solutions! Salvation, not problems! Salvation is what Christ has to give. May God help us to take it.

WHAT IT IS TO BE A CHRISTIAN

6. The Sheer Excess of God's Extravagant Gift

If God is pleased with what he has done for man, what right in the world has man to be displeased with it? Man's responsibility is to find out what a marvellous thing God has done for him in taking all his guilt and his shame upon his own back, in his own body on the tree; then, having realised it (or begun to, for it will take all eternity to realise what God has done for us in Jesus Christ) to silence ourselves as far as criticism is concerned, so that we bow humbly, and abase ourselves before him and say, 'Oh God, it is too much. Too much; but how grateful I am that it is true;' and thus receive the free gift. Oh, it is humbling!

Some people cannot receive a gift gratefully; they are too proud to receive charity. The only thing we can do with charity such as this is receive it and acknowledge that it is all of grace. Having sinned in Adam, and having sinned in ourselves with the same spirit of rebellion as that of Adam, what we deserve is everlasting hell. So, as guilty, hell-deserving sinners it is ours simply to marvel and thank God for this gift. Man may be abundantly satisfied with what God has done; that is why in Romans 5: 15, 17 and 20 we have these words, 'much more.' Jesus is 'much more' than Adam, and his deed on the cross is 'much more', far greater, far more wonderful in its range, effect, application and fruit than Adam's deed. If Adam did a terrible deed (not to speak of the damage and injury it caused to God and his kingdom), the deed of Christ to cancel it, overleap it, and blot out all remembrance of it, is infinite.

Now we must consider what is so satisfying to man about this wonderful redemption and justification by God. When the wonderful notes in the symphony of the gospel in the Word of God are repeated, some people are cynically inclined to say, 'We have heard all that

before!' Do you say in a musical symphony when the first subject and
then the second subject recurs, possibly in a different form but the same
tune, 'Oh, we have heard all that before'? You scarcely ever hear the
melody of a great composer like Bach, Mozart, Beethoven, Brahms, but
it is in a new dress of harmony, orchestration, or pitch. Similarly, if
your heart is attuned by the grace of God to the gospel, you never hear
the *leitmotifs* (the expression used for wisps of tunes in Wagner) but
they are fresh, and you say, 'Ah, new orchestration, new nuances, new
light and shade, sonority, sweetness.' So let us repeat the blessed notes
of the gospel, not least because even as you hear the Word read or read it
yourself, the devil is at your ear trying to snatch away the words as soon
as they penetrate your mind and conscience; that is why there is need for
constant repetition of the blessed gospel. What, then, is so satisfying
about this blessed gospel? It is the sheer excess of God's extravagant
gift.

What do Paul's 'much mores' in Romans 5:12–21 really signify?
What do we gain in Christ? To see this we must go back to the
beginning and see first what God originally made us. God made man
unique in his creation. He made him 'in his own image', with dominion
over the universe. Genesis chapters 1 and 2 recall how he lavished
absolutely everything he could upon a creature made of his own breath
and of the dust of the earth.

The thing that strikes me most about these chapters, when one is
reading with the kind of sanctified innocence, open-heartedness and
open-mindedness one needs, is the sheer lavishness, the sheer
prodigality of the gifts God poured out on man. As with his Son before
the world began, there is nothing too good for man. At the same time
(and this does not detract in the slightest from what I have said about the
lavishness of grace of his gifts to him) he is a creature, although made in
the image of God and the climax of creation; and he is on probation.

God lavished on man his very best, but he also placed him on
probation: 'Then the Lord God formed man of dust from the ground,
and breathed in his nostrils the breath of life; and man became a living
being. And the Lord God planted a garden in Eden, in the east; and there
he put the man whom he had formed. And out of the ground the Lord
God made to grow every tree that is pleasant to the sight and good for
food, the tree of life also in the midst of the garden, and the tree of the
knowledge of good and evil' (Gen. 2:7–9). 'The Lord God took the man
and put him in the garden of Eden to till it and keep it. And the Lord God
commanded the man, saying, "You may freely eat of every tree in the

garden; but of the tree of the knowledge of good and evil you shall not eat..."'

Now, look back to verse 9 where 'the tree of life...in the midst of the garden' is mentioned. It is not mentioned further down, but there it is in the midst of the garden. There is only one prohibition. You may eat of all the trees, and the fruit of all the trees of the garden, including the tree of life. Surely; but of that tree apparently they did not eat. God made man in his own image, lavished upon him all the gifts of his grace and set him in the midst of the garden on probation. 'Here: have all this—but as to these two trees, I warn you not to touch that one; it is death to you, but here is the other; choose it, for it is life.' Choose eternal life. Is that what it means? In a sense it ultimately means choose Christ, the eternal Christ (see Rev. 2:7). Is not that what it means? But man and woman chose wrongly.

Think what we lost. It is interesting that after the Fall God is deeply concerned lest Adam and Eve, having eaten of the tree of the knowledge of good and evil, thereafter should eat of the tree of life and live forever and become, apparently, eternal men, and eternal enemies of God! 'Then the Lord God said, "Behold, the man has become like one of us, knowing good and evil; and now, lest he put forth his hand and take also of the tree of life, and eat, and live for ever"—therefore the Lord God sent him forth from the Garden of Eden, to till the ground from which he was taken. He drove out the man; and at the east of the garden of Eden he placed the cherubim, and a flaming sword which turned every way, to guard the way to the tree of life.' So man lost what apparently it was God's good pleasure to offer him. He lost the dimension of eternal life, having partaken of the wrong tree.

What then do we gain in Christ? Not only recovery of all man has lost but what he never gained, because he chose wrongly, eternal life, in the Son of God. We gain no mere salvation as any kind of qualitative abstraction, although that is included, but we gain Jesus Christ. What else in the world can the tree of life mean than life in fellowship with the eternal Son of God? So, in the fulness of time, Jesus Christ came to retrieve our ruin by the eternal second Person in the Trinity's personal intervention.

Let us think for a moment what he came to do. He came in the first place to understand our condition (Heb. 2:10, 18; 4:15; 5:7–9). He came to feel our woes and the weight and power of them; yet without sinning. 'Being tempted in all points like as we are', he came to understand.

This, by the way, is what we are committed to as Christians in the world. Jesus did not need to sin to understand the woes of men; he just needed to be man; and we too are committed to understand. It is not easy these days when some of our fellows find themselves in fearful conditions, in subhuman, almost bestial conditions. Yet we are committed by Jesus Christ himself who went as far, further than we thought he might have dared go, to assume the 'likeness of the flesh of sin' (as Paul says in Rom. 8:3, 4); to be made to 'become sin for us' (says Paul again, in 2 Cor. 5:21). We are committed, following him, to understand our fellow men. But, back to our point: Christ came to understand.

Then, he came to take our place. Let me put it quite simply, drawing on Isaiah 53:6 and John 1:29. I hope you hear Handel here; I do. 'All we like sheep have gone astray; we have turned every one to his own way; and the Lord has laid on him the iniquity of us all.' The word used for iniquity is the deepest word in the Old Testament for sin: 'perversity'. John the Baptist goes a step further in John 1:29 when he points to the Christ making his way to Jordan to be baptised; and says, 'Behold the Lamb of God, who takes away the sin of the world,'—not only upon whom the sin of the world is laid, but which, being laid upon him, he takes away by his death.

Christ came to expunge all our shame and guilt and the penalty written down by a holy God against us. Listen to Paul writing to the Colossians: 'You, who were dead in trespasses and the uncircumcision of your flesh, God made alive together with him, having forgiven us all our trespasses (that is, having removed them, blotted them out), having cancelled the bond which stood against us with its legal demands; this he set aside, nailing it to the cross. He disarmed the principalities and powers and made a public example of them, triumphing over them in him' (Col. 2:13–15). So Christ, by personal intervention came to understand, and to take our place, blotting out all our shame, and guilt, and penalty; all that stood against us. He thereby prepared the way righteously to provide us with the satisfaction of his perfect righteousness. He prepared the way for God to honour us—not with any honour—but with his honour.

One of the things that grips me more and more as I read the Word and pore over it, and ponder it, and seek to preach it, is the way the glory of its truth takes my breath away. Take John 17, which is so often called the 'High Priestly Prayer' of Christ. Christ came by personal intervention to understand and take our place and blot out all that stood against us, thus preparing the way for him righteously to honour us with his honour. Notice the words in John 17:11 'even as.' They re-appear in verse 21, and again in verse 23. Read them in context. 'And now I am no more in the world (he says in prayer to his Father and someone eavesdropping records it), but they are in the world, and I am coming to thee. Holy Father, keep them in thy name, which thou hast given me (he had already said: for they are thine; all mine are thine, and thine are mine, and I am glorified in them' vv. 9, 10). That they may be one, *even as* we are one.' He has prepared the way by his work righteously to honour us with his honour. Verse 13: 'But now I am coming to thee; and these things I speak in the world, that they may have my joy fulfilled in themselves.' Notice, 'My joy.'

Jesus continues (in v. 20) 'I do not pray for these only, but also for those who believe in me through their word, that they all may be one; *even as* thou, Father, art in me, and I in thee, that they also may be in us, so that the world may believe that thou hast sent me. The glory which thou hast given me I have given to them, that they may be one *even as* we are one, I in them and thou in me, that they may become perfectly one, so that the world may know that thou hast sent me and hast loved them even as thou hast loved me.' Are you taking that in? 'hast loved them EVEN AS thou hast loved me.' Rebel Adam, under the influence of that horror, Lucifer, disobeys God and turns his back on all the lavishness of his grace and says with Eve, 'We will do this and follow that one.' And despising all of God's grace they say, 'Take your grace. Away with it! We are going this way.' And Jesus says, 'I have come down to tell them, my chosen ones, that you love them as *you* love me.' Oh, who can take that in? Who indeed!

I speak about his personal intervention with tremendous emphasis on the word, 'personal'. We must never fail to stress that this is a personal intervention, for it is all in his Person. It is the Person doing the work, but it is not the work, once the Person has done it. It is not like a workman coming into the house to adjust something: your clock, or your television, or your 'fridge, or whatever, and then as he goes, saying, 'It is all right now, madam,' and shutting the door. This One brings his work and he is pleased with his work. His work is part of his identity now. He is absolutely integrated with his work, but you can only have his work in the context of his personal Presence. You do not want your workmen to live with you. You do not want your doctor to live with you. I don't suppose you want your minister to live with you! But I hope you want *him* to live with you—Christ. We receive himself; his manhood in place of your rotten manhood. He gives us himself. This is the good news! He gives us himself in giving us his righteousness. He gives us lots more, but this is what we are discussing. He gives himself in his righteousness, not his righteousness as a mere accreditation, you see. He personally stands in. He says, at the door, as it were, 'I have come with your righteousness.' You say, 'Give it to me.' 'Well, *I am it*; take *me* in.'

But where is the accreditation? Is it on paper? Is it in anything subpersonal or subhuman? Oh no; it is in himself. It is not in gifts, nor signatures, nor documents; it is not in any subpersonal authorisation; it is in himself, absolutely. He comes to give himself in exchange for our unrighteousness. Look at that blessed verse, 2 Corinthians 5:21. You could live here! 'We beseech you on behalf of Christ, be reconciled to God. For our sake he made him to be sin who knew no sin (we cannot begin to talk of that; it would take too long. It is a whole subject. But it is wonderful. It melts my inmost heart. How could God do it?), so that in him we might become the righteousness of God.'

Now, if we become the righteousness of God in him, that is no abstraction. It is no mere certificate. It is not an authorisation. Nor is it an entrance within the gate of heaven; it is Christ, Christ, Christ; nothing less. It is himself. 'That we might become (Take in the words. Be shocked and startled by them. Do you know what we do when we do not allow the Holy Spirit to work deeply in our midst? We say, 'I know it. I know it.' But the trouble is we don't know it. You don't know it. I don't know it.) might become the righteousness of God in him.' The sheer stupendousness of what he is saying drives us back. We would want to go right back and go over it all again to reassure ourselves that this is being given to us on a sound, legal, moral, spiritual basis, according to the integrity of the perfect, holy God.

In that connection, consider 2 Peter 1:1, 'Simon Peter, a servant and apostle of Jesus Christ, to those who have obtained a faith of equal standing with ours in the righteousness of our God and Saviour Jesus Christ.' What does he mean when he says 'an equal standing with ours in the righteousness of our God and Saviour Jesus Christ'? We have already seen that it is Christ himself who is our righteousness (Jer. 23:5, 6; 33:16). God has made 'Christ Jesus...our righteousness' (1 Cor. 1:30).

The Bible discusses the gift of Christ's righteousness to those who believe, in various pictures and in symbolic language. It speaks of the righteousness Christ gives to his own as a 'divine dress.' You remember the 'wedding garment' in Matthew 22: 1–14, and the one who came into the feast without the wedding garment? 'But when the King came in to look at the guests, he saw there a man who had no wedding garment; and he said to him, "Friend, how did you get in here without a wedding garment?" And he was speechless.' Well, Christ provides his own with a wedding garment, or a priestly garment.

This is how his righteousness is described in Scripture—as a garment. Psalm 132:9 uses that imagery: 'Let thy priests be clothed with righteousness, and let thy saints shout for joy.' So does Isaiah 61:10: 'I will greatly rejoice in the Lord, my soul shall exult in my God; for he has clothed me with the garments of salvation, he has covered me with the robe of righteousness, as a bridegroom decks himself with a garland, and as a bride adorns herself with her jewels.' Righteousness, you see, is a positive thing. If the forgiveness of sins that we speak of is negative, in the sense of sending something away, righteousness is positive. It is something he dressed us in; he dresses us in himself.

There is a third Old Testament illustration of this in the Book of Job. Job is speaking about his integrity as a godly man, as a righteous man before his affliction came upon him. He is saying how God blessed him in those days and how men revered him, listened to him and were advised by him; now it is different. In the course of it he says, 'I put on righteousness, and it clothed me; my justice was like a robe and a turban. I was eyes to the blind, and feet to the lame. I was a father to the poor, and I searched out the cause of him whom I did not know. I broke the fangs of the unrighteous…' (Job 29:14–17). A marvellous chapter; read it sometime. But this is the point, 'I put on righteousness and it clothed me.'

There is another intriguing reference, in Revelation 19:8, although I do not think it applies so pertinently to what we are saying here to include it in quite the same category: 'it was granted her to be clothed with fine linen, bright and pure'—that seems to convey the idea of sanctification. This is the fruit of Christ's righteousness. You see, he dresses us in his righteousness. We cannot put on the robe ourselves. He dresses us in his righteousness; but in another sense, having been dressed perfectly, fully and finally in his righteousness, we proceed in another manner, to dress ourselves in that righteousness by our deeds. I think I could expand the figure a little by saying that we could think of ourselves adorning the righteous garment, the garment of his righteousness. Think about that!

Well then, righteousness is a dress put on; but the dress is Christ himself. Dressed in Christ; isn't it beautiful? That is exactly what our Lord is speaking of in the Sermon on the Mount: 'Let your light so shine before men that they may see your good works and glorify your Father' (Matt. 5:16). They say, 'Ah, there is a quality about that fellow's deeds, a quality about that woman's life and what she does that is not of earth at all. There is an aura, an atmosphere, a dimension of grace and eternity about the Christian. That is the result of being dressed in Christ.

Then, the righteousness that is God's gift to us may be described in terms of marriage. This may not seem so clear, but it is very beautiful. I want you to think of Christ's righteousness as given to us in a marriage bond. Let us look at Hosea, chapter two (you could also read Romans 7:1–6). The story of Hosea is a parable of Israel as the wife of Jehovah and of her backsliding. Hosea's wife, Gomer (Israel, the wife of Jehovah) falls away from her husband. She said, 'I will go after my lovers, who give me my bread and my water, my wool and my flax, my oil and my drink' (Hos. 2:5). To that unfaithful wife, the Lord, the true Husband, says, 'They feed you, do they! Therefore, I will hedge up her way with thorns; and I will build a wall against her, so that she cannot find her paths. She shall pursue her lovers, but not overtake them; and she shall seek them, but shall not find them. Then she shall say "I will go and return to my first husband, for it was better with me then than now"' (Hos. 2:6, 7).

Says the Lord, making comment on this, 'She did not know that it was I who gave her the grain, the wine, and the oil, and who lavished upon her silver, and gold which they used for Baal (the false husband). Therefore I will take back my grain in its time (This is how God afflicts his own when they depart from him.) and my wine in its season; and I will take away my wool and my flax, which were to cover her nakedness. Now I will uncover her lewdness in the sight of her lovers and no one shall rescue her out of my hand' (Hos. 2:8–10).

Do you see what this means? God exposed Israel in all her poverty and nakedness before the nations of the world. God said to these pagan nations: the Chaldeans (Babylonians), the Assyrians, the Medes, the Persians, the Greeks and the Romans, 'Look at her, my unfaithful wife. Look at that horrid woman.' And he exposed her on the streets of the world. 'Look at her and the mess she has made of her life.' That is what he is saying. 'And I will put an end to all her mirth (her wild, carnal goings on), her feasts, her new moons, her sabbaths, and all her appointed feasts. And I will lay waste her vines and her fig trees, of which she said, "These are my hire, which my lovers have given me." I will make them a forest, and the beasts of the field shall devour them. And I will punish her for the feast days of the Baals when she burned incense to them and decked herself with rings and jewelry, and went after her lovers, and forgot me, says the Lord' (Hos. 2:11–13).

Then what will he do? He will take her to Nineveh. He will take her to Babylon. He says, 'I know what I will do, then, when I thrash her within an inch of her life.' 'Therefore, behold, I will allure her (like the prodigal son in his hunger and need), and bring her into the wilderness, and speak tenderly to her. (Jesus never made sinners smart for their sin when they were as pathetic as the Woman of Samaria, or Zacchaeus, or the Woman taken in adultery. Christians sometimes mistakenly sear people.) I will speak tenderly to her. And there I will give her her vineyards, and make the Valley of Achor a door of hope. (The Valley of Trouble a door of hope!) And there she shall answer as in the days of her youth' (Hos. 2:14, 15). She shall answer to me in blessed, faithful response. It is a domestic scene; the husband coming in for his meal, calling out, 'Are you here?' She responds, 'Yes, my dear.' She is not sulking, ashamed and hiding from him for what she did in the night. 'And in that day, says the Lord, you will call me, "My husband," and no longer will you call me "My Baal." For I will remove the names of the Baals from her mouth, and they shall be mentioned by name no more. And I will make for you a covenant on that day with the beasts of the field, the birds of the air, and the creeping things of the ground (remember that after the Fall, childbirth was painful to woman and the ground would not yield its harvest to Adam because of their sin. God turned the whole of nature against man for his sin; but now he says) and I will abolish the bow, the sword, and war from the land; and I will make you lie down in safety. And I will betroth you to me for ever; (here it is!) I will betroth you to me in righteousness and in justice, in steadfast love and in mercy. I will betroth you to me in faithfulness; and you shall know the Lord' (Hos. 2:16–20).

Justification: in a sense it is an inadequate word, perfect though it is! 'You shall know the Lord.' *Know* the Lord; that is righteousness!

WHAT IT IS TO BE A CHRISTIAN

7. The Divine Discontent

I want to begin with a summary of what we are going to look at. It is this: faith is a gift, and then faith is an instrument of our salvation. Faith is not a work of merit, yet it works. It works through the divine discontent, which God communicates to us, working in us. It is the *sine qua non*, the absolute essential for salvation. It comes to the poor of this world and works by love which 'believes all things', and it rests on God and his power. It works in time. It rests, and yet it works because eternity works in time, 'striving to enter into rest' as Hebrews 4:11 puts it. That is the message. Faith is God-given and it is a God-given response. It is an authentic, spontaneous, full-blooded act of consent of the total personality, whereby God inclines persons to close absolutely with his offer of righteousness and sanctification in Jesus Christ.

Faith is a gift. Look again at Romans 5:12–21, the passage we kept returning to in these studies. Within the scope of three verses, 15, 16 and 17, the words, 'a free gift' or 'gift' appear five times. It is interesting to notice that these words translate different words in the original. Twice in 15 you have 'free gift'; that is the word *charisma*. 'Free gift' the second time is the word, *dorea*, meaning something that is given. Then in 16 the word 'free gift' is *dorema* from the same root. Later in 16 we have *charisma* and then once in 17 *dorea*.

Now, read the passage, from verse 15 to the end of the chapter. 'But the free gift (of righteousness through Jesus Christ) is not like (to be compared with) the trespass. (And you remember that here the apostle is comparing Adam's sin in which man fell at the beginning of the story of man [Gen. 3] with the one perfect deed of Christ on the cross for our justification. The trespass of Adam cannot compare in extent, range, quality and power with the free gift.) For if many died through one man's (Adam's) trespass, much more have the grace of God and the free gift (of the grace of God) in that one man Jesus Christ abounded (or overflowed) for many. And the free gift is not like the effect of that one man's sin. For the judgment following one trespass brought condemnation, but the free gift following many trespasses brings justification. If, because of one man's trespass, death reigned through that one man, much more will those who receive the abundance of grace and the free gift of righteousness reign in life through the one man Jesus Christ. Then as one man's trespass led to condemnation for all men, so one man's act of righteousness leads to acquittal and life for all men. For as by one man's disobedience many were made sinners, so by one man's obedience many will be made righteous. Law came in, to increase the trespass; but where sin increased (by the law declaring us to be sinners. We were sinners before, but we did not know it until the law came in with Moses.), grace abounded all the more, so that, as sin reigned in death, grace also might reign through righteousness to eternal life through Jesus Christ our Lord.'

That is saying over and over again, among other things, that righteousness, justification, is the free gift of God although, notice, faith is not mentioned as such there at all. Righteousness is a gift. But we know from Ephesians 2:8 that it is 'by grace we are saved through faith; and this is not of our own doing.' Salvation by grace and the faith whereby we receive salvation are a gift of God. It is all a gift. 'Not all men have faith' (2 Thess. 3:2), says Paul. Faith is a gift of God.

Peter addresses his second letter to, 'those who have obtained a faith of equal standing with ours in the righteousness of our God and Saviour Jesus Christ.' It is something to be obtained, and to be received. Let me read some Scriptures again that speak of this.

Romans 3:23: 'since all have sinned and fall short of the glory of God, they are justified by his grace as a gift through the redemption which is in Christ Jesus.'

Romans 9:16: 'So it (salvation) depends not upon man's will or exertion, but upon God's mercy.'

Philippians 1:7: 'For all are partakers with me of grace,' and later in 1:29: 'For it has been granted to you (as a gift) that for the sake of Christ you should not only believe in him, but also suffer for his sake.'

Peter 1:3: 'By his great mercy we have been born anew to a living hope through the resurrection of Jesus Christ from the dead, and to an inheritance which is imperishable, undefiled, and unfading, kept in heaven for you, who are kept by God's power through faith (it is God who keeps us) unto a salvation ready to be revealed in the last time.'

Jesus himself, speaking to the Woman of Samaria, says; 'If you knew the gift of God and who it is that is saying to you, "Give me a drink", you would have asked him and he would have given you living water' (Jn. 4:10).

Faith then is a gift of God, pure and simple, a sheer, sovereign gift of God. It is nothing that fallen man can work up, or create, or generate of himself at all. It is a pure gift of God. But it is also the instrument of our salvation. This is well expressed by the (Westminster) *Confession of Faith* when it speaks of justification.

> Those whom God effectually calleth he also freely justifieth; not by infusing righteousness into them, but by pardoning their sins, and by accounting and accepting their persons as righteous; not for any thing wrought in them, or done by them, but for Christ's sake alone: not by imputing faith itself (as actual merit, or as a work), the act of believing, or any other evangelical obedience, to them as their righteousness; but by imputing the obedience and satisfaction of Christ unto them (it is Christ's goodness that is given to us; nothing else. Christ's righteousness, Christ's rightness; that is what is imputed to us), they receiving and resting on him and his righteousness by faith: which faith they have not of themselves; it is the gift of God.

> Faith, thus receiving and resting on Christ and his righteousness, is the alone instrument of justification; yet is it not alone in the person justified, but is ever accompanied with all other saving graces, (that is to say, faith is not dead, but living. It is not of men, it is of God, but once God plants faith in a man's heart it begins to grow; there are no dead seeds there) but is ever accompanied with all other saving graces, and is no dead faith, but worketh by love.

It 'works by love', but it first begins to work, of course, (since this is the nature of faith) by believing. Do you believe? Do you find it hard to believe? Are you sometimes rather proud that you find it hard to believe and think you are rather clever trying? Or are you sometimes rather inclined to go further and be proud of not believing? This is an age (there have been other similar ages when men were very, very proud of their scepticism, cynicism and unbelief) when it is fashionable not to believe. But that is against the Word of God, which asserts that believers are, in the summary of the whole of Paul's Letter to the Romans, not ashamed of the gospel; it is the power of God for salvation to every one who has faith, to the Jew first (in time) and also to the Greek (the Gentiles). For in it the righteousness of God is revealed through faith for faith (from faith to faith); as it is written, "The righteous shall live by faith"' (Rom. 1:16, 17).

The gospel is the power of God for salvation to everyone who believes, and to no one else. But if it is the power of God unto salvation to those who believe, then it is consistently the power of God unto salvation to everyone that believes; and no one can believe without being saved. Paul is saying two things, you see: first that salvation is by faith (through grace, of course) and secondly that you cannot believe without being saved! 'The righteous shall live (that has a double meaning too, if we went back to Hab. 2:14!) by faith.'

What we are looking at now is the fact that salvation, and particularly justification, are by faith to everyone who believes, without exception: 'But now, the righteousness of God has been manifested apart from the (Old Testament) law, although the (Old Testament) law and the prophets bear witness to it (pointing forward to it), the righteousness of God through faith in Jesus Christ for all who believe' (Rom. 3:21).

Notice in neither of these instances does Paul say, 'For believers', but rather he stresses 'for everyone (for all) who believes.' You cannot be saved without believing. 'For there is no distinction (between Jew and Gentile); since all have sinned and fall short of the glory of God, they are justified by his grace as a gift (given freely—*doron*) through the redemption which is in Christ Jesus, whom God put forward as a propitiation (RSV's 'expiation' is inadequate here) by his blood, to be received by faith. This was to show God's righteousness, because in his divine forbearance he had passed over former sins (he overlooked the sins of the Old Testament saints until he could put them away); it was to prove at the present time that he himself is righteous (his integrity) and that he justifies him who has faith in Jesus' (Rom. 3:22–26).

So, faith is a gift. It is the instrument of our salvation, although not the ground of it. The ground of our salvation, including justification, is Christ, because faith is not a work of merit. We cannot feel proud of ourselves because we believe; because, if you believe, it is because God has given you the power to believe. Faith is not a work! This is brought out wonderfully in Romans 4:1ff. It is a marvellous passage: 'What then shall we say about Abraham, our forefather according to the flesh? For if Abraham was justified by works he has something to boast about, but not before God, (he may boast behind the back of God for a little if he dare, but he cannot boast before God if he is justified by works). For what does the Scripture say (Gen. 15:6)? "Abraham believed God, and it was reckoned to him (his believing) as righteousness (yet his believing was not a work of merit for which he may be applauded and rewarded for his faith). Abraham believed God and it was reckoned to him as righteousness." Now to one who works, his wages are not reckoned as a gift but as his due. And to one who does not work but trusts him who justifies the ungodly (see the contrast: the opposite of 'working' is 'trusting' or even, if you like, 'resting'. Do you see that?) his faith is reckoned as righteousness. So also David pronounces a blessing upon the man to whom God reckons righteousness apart from works: "Blessed are those whose iniquities are forgiven, and whose sins are covered; blessed (happy) is the man against whom the Lord will not reckon his sin (but has blotted it out)" (Ps. 32:1, 2).'

Then he goes on to ask this question: 'Is this blessing pronounced only upon the circumcised (the Jews), or also upon the uncircumcised? We say that faith was reckoned to Abraham as righteousness. How then was it reckoned to him? (Do you see what he is coming to?) Was it (reckoned to him) before or after he had been circumcised?'

Let me read that again and instead of 'circumcised' let me put in 'baptised' and see what that says. 'Is this blessing pronounced only upon the baptised or also upon the unbaptised? We say that faith is reckoned as righteousness. How then is it reckoned? Is it reckoned before or after we have been baptised? (For baptism in the New Testament corresponds to circumcision in the Old; you will see them together in one verse in Colossians 2:11). It was not after, but before we are baptised. We received baptism (and these are the very words we use in our baptismal service) as a sign or seal of the righteousness which we had by faith while we were still unbaptised.

The purpose was to make him (Abraham) the father of all who believed without being circumcised, and who thus have righteousness reckoned to them, and likewise the father of the circumcised who are not merely circumcised (as an outward rite) but also follow the example of the faith which our father Abraham had before he was circumcised. (You see grace comes before faith.)

The promise to Abraham and his descendants, that they should inherit the world, did not come through the law (fulfilling the law, or trying to) but through the righteousness of faith (the righteousness that comes to those who believe). If it is the adherents of the law (the workers of the law) who are to be the heirs, faith is nullified and the promise void. For the law brings wrath, but where there is no law there is no transgression (we don't know we are sinning, although we are).

'That is why it depends on faith, in order that the promise may rest on grace (that is, rest on God, not on anything man does) and be guaranteed to all his (Abraham's) descendants—not only to the adherents of the law, but also to those who share the faith of Abraham, for he is the father of us all. (He is the father of all those who believe).'

Paul continues in verse 20, 'No distrust made him (Abraham) waver concerning the promise of God, but he grew strong in his faith as he gave glory to God, fully convinced that God was able to do what he had promised.' You see, faith is a work of God, which when God plants it in our hearts, must energise and operate; but it is to God's glory not to man's. Yet, it is that response that God gives to man whereby he may hold out his empty hands and receive God's gift of salvation and righteousness in Christ. If you find Paul's thought difficult to follow here, just be patient and we will come through to something that will become clearer.

Now turn on to what Paul later says in Romans 10:1: 'Brethren, my heart's desire and prayer for them (Israel, the Jews; that is what he is concerned about in chapters 9–11) is that they may be saved. I bear witness that they have a zeal for God, but it is not enlightened (their minds are blinded and darkened). For, being ignorant of the righteousness that comes from God (as a free gift) and (therefore) seeking to establish their own (that is, instead of waiting for Christ to come from heaven and save them, they are trying to scramble up on their own helpless, feeble, little ladders to God, trusting in their own efforts), they did not submit to God's righteousness.'

This is the essence of the sin of man. Man says, 'Oh, I'll do it myself'—like little children who become very confident and cocky after a time, once they have tried out their faculties a bit. Mummy or Daddy says, 'Now, let me help you, dear' (sometimes this is overdone we know, but sometimes one doesn't get the chance to overdo it). 'No,' the child says, 'Don't you touch it, Mummy. Don't touch it, Daddy. I'll do it myself.' And then he or she makes a mess of it. That is the proud

spirit, 'I'll do it myself.' That is the essential spirit of rebellion that Satan
sowed in the heart of man, and we should see it for what it is, not
something virtuous but something horrid and wicked. We should hate it,
all our rebellion against God, all that 'I'll do it myself.' We should hate
it; it is from the pit. 'Those who are ignorant of the righteousness that
comes from God, seeking to establish their own, do not submit to God
(they do not let God make them clean, and right, and nice, and good and
lovely). 'For (says Paul, here, in a tremendous statement) Christ is the
end of the law for righteousness to everyone believing' (that is the pure
Greek; obviously believing is not a work of merit). He continues:
'Moses writes that the man who practises the righteousness which is
based on the law (working for it) shall live by it (if he can. And this is
promised a number of times in Deuteronomy). But the righteousness
based on faith (the righteousness that comes to men from God through
faith) says (Oh, don't try to get at it yourself. Don't try to scramble up to
heaven and get it yourself), do not say in your heart, "Who will ascend
into heaven?" (that is, to bring Christ down) or "Who will descend into
the abyss?" (that is, to bring Christ up from the dead). But what does it
(faith) say (and this is quoting the Old Testament, the Book of
Deuteronomy: 30:14)? "The word is near you (the work of faith
whereby you believe and receive), on your lips and in your heart", that
is, the word of faith which we preach (He is saying to anyone who may
be an unbeliever, 'Go on; believe.' You say you cannot believe. But,
supposing he is putting faith on the tip of your tongue and at the door of
your heart saying, 'Go on, go on; believe); because, if you confess with
your lips that Jesus is Lord and believe in your heart that God raised him
from the dead, you will be saved (you will be a Christian). For man
believes with his heart and so is justified....

(This justification is no legal fiction. Faith marshals the whole
personality. When God gives the gift of faith to a man he does not stick
it in some part of his being that operates apart from the rest. When God
gives man the gift of faith he marshals the total personality so that man
flings his arms wide and throws himself into the arms of God and says,
'Take me: totally, wholly, absolutely, with no reserve and no delay; take
me.' That is what the passage is saying.)

'And he confesses with his lips and so is saved. The Scripture says
(Is. 28:16) "No one who believes in him will (ever) be put to shame"
(disappointed, embarrassed). For there is no distinction between Jew
and Gentile (that was his subject); the same Lord is Lord of all and
bestows his riches upon all who call on him (with that faith that is placed
on the tip of your tongue). For, "every one (here it comes again) who

calls upon the name of the Lord (everyone without exception) will be saved.'"

This is brought out magnificently by Paul in Galatians 3:2ff. He says to the Galatians: 'Let me ask you only this: Did you receive the Spirit by works of the law, or by hearing with faith? (Note that works of the law and hearing with faith are contrasted; they are set over against one another. Hearing with faith is not a work of the law, it is responding to a work of God in your heart.) Are you so foolish? Having begun with the Spirit, are you now ending with the flesh? Did you experience so many (Christian) things in vain?—if it really is in vain. Does he who supplies the Spirit to you and works miracles among you do so by works of the law, or by hearing with faith? (Is it by your works that God comes down upon you and does such mighty works in your midst?)

'"Thus Abraham believed God, and it was reckoned to him as righteousness." So you see that it is men of faith who are the sons of Abraham. And the Scripture, foreseeing that God would justify the Gentiles by faith, preached the gospel beforehand to Abraham, saying, "In you shall all the nations be blessed." So then, those who are men of faith are blessed with Abraham who had faith....

'"He who through faith is righteous shall live"; but the law does not rest on faith, for "He who does them shall live by them." (It is by your works, not your faith, that you would be saved according to the law). Christ redeemed us from the curse of the law, having become a curse for us—for it is written, "Cursed be every one who hangs on a tree"—that in Christ Jesus the blessing of Abraham might come upon the Gentiles, that we might receive the promise of the Spirit through faith.'

The 'blessing of Abraham' is God blessing Abraham. There are two words for 'blessing' in the New Testament: one is the word in the Beatitudes, 'Blessed are the pure in heart...' *makarios*, which means 'happy'. Here, blessing is *eulogia*, which comes from *eulogeo*, to speak well of. Let me read it to bring this out. 'In Christ Jesus, the blessing of Abraham (God speaking well of Abraham) might come to the Gentiles so that God might speak well of the Gentiles that we might receive the promise of the Spirit through faith (that as God speaks well of Abraham to his salvation, so he might speak well of the Gentiles unto salvation).'

We said faith is a gift, yet it is at the same time an instrument of salvation that the believer must use, for 'salvation is to everyone who believes.' Faith is not a work of merit, yet it works, as 1 Thessalonians

1:3 makes clear: 'remembering before our God and Father your *work of faith* and labour of love and steadfastness of hope in our Lord Jesus Christ.'

James 2:14 is the last of the passages to which I draw your attention. 'What does it profit, my brothers, if a man says he has faith but has not works (that is to say he believes in his heart, but he doesn't do anything about it)? Can his (*i.e.* that kind of) faith save him? If a brother or sister is ill-clad and in lack of daily food, and one of you says to them, "Go in peace, be warmed and filled," without giving them the things needed for the body, what does it profit? (What is the use of your blessing to him if you send him away without any help?) So faith by itself, if it has no works, is dead (as blessing in words without deeds to a hungry man is nothing, is dead and sends him away down your path cursing you; so faith by itself, if it has no works, is dead also.). But some one (the apostles know that there are always arguers; those who are proud of their unbelief—the sin of sins) will say, "You have faith and I have works. Show me your faith apart from your works (*show me* it; he can't look into his heart, can he?) and I by my works will show you my faith. (That is to say, You can't look into his heart to see his faith, but then you don't need to look into his heart because you know what is in his heart by his deeds. He opens his pocket! says James, rather sarcastically). You believe that God is one; you do well (very good for you, believing that God is one). Even the demons believe (that) and shudder. (The faith the devil has doesn't help him very much). Do you want to be shown, you foolish fellow, that faith apart from works is barren? Was not Abraham our father justified by works, when he offered his son Isaac upon the altar? (He didn't sit at home and say, 'God has told me to go to Mount Moriah and offer my son; I approve of that, I obey that in my heart but I am not going. What would be the good of that?) You see faith was active along with his works (he gathered materials for the fire. He took his son and his servants and walked step by step up Mount Moriah. Faith was completed by works until the man had lifted his knife to slay his son and God stopped him.) and the Scripture was fulfilled which says, "Abraham believed God, and it was reckoned to him as righteousness"; and he was called the friend of God (because he not only believed with his heart, but he did it with his hands and his feet). You see that a man is justified by works and not by faith alone.'

Go back to James 2:21. Every time you read 'works' in what James says, add the words 'of faith'. 'Was not Abraham our father justified by works (of faith), when he offered his son Isaac upon the altar? You see that faith was completed by works (of faith), and the Scripture was fulfilled which says, "Abraham believed God and it was reckoned to him as righteousness"; and he was called the friend of God. You see that a man is justified by works (of faith) and not by faith alone. And in the same way was not also Rahab the harlot justified by works (of faith) when she received the messengers and sent them out another way? For as the body apart from the spirit is dead, so faith apart from works is dead.'

We are, in a sense, trying to do the impossible—to get this balance whereby we see that we are saved by faith, and yet see that this faith is totally, from beginning to end, a work of God. It begins with God, as everything begins with God.

God has a divine discontent. I know that God in three Persons, as the Creeds and the Scriptures indicate, is absolutely self-sufficient and in need of nothing. He did not need worlds at all. He could have lived, Father, Son and Holy Spirit without worlds, without angels and without men forever and ever unto all eternity. He had no need of anyone, yet he planned further fellowship—not because he was dissatisfied with the fellowship of the Son, but he wanted the fellowship of his Son extended. It could not be increased, but extended in range, to innumerable creatures. You see, his fellowship with his Son was so infinite that he said, 'I could take the qualities, the virtues of my Son Jesus Christ, and put elements of them in myriads of creatures, different elements and compositions of the virtues of my Son into different creatures by the million and not two of these would be quite the same; every one would be unique. Every one would reflect my Son's glory, but every one in a different but yet authentic and complete way. So, because he longed to see his eternal Son reproduced in many creatures, so he longed to create them and, after the Fall, recreate them. This is the divine discontent.

Various writers have spoken of this. Here is what Gordon Graham says: 'There are two kinds of discontent in this world, the discontent that works and the discontent that wrings its hands. The first gets what it wants and the second loses what it had. There is no cure for the first but success; there is no cure for the second at all.' Think about that in relation to God! Charles Kingsley says: (and this, I think, is where our phrase comes from) 'To be discontented with the Divine discontent and to be shamed with noble shame is the very germ of the first upgrowth of virtue.' Ella Wheeler Willcox speaks of the 'splendid discontent of God.'

God, desiring fellowship with creatures, creatures of a particular personal quality, because of that 'discontent', created, thereby incurring disappointments, first with Lucifer and then with Adam, but not with Christ. So, there is hope, you see, and there has been hope from the beginning, because God knew from the beginning what he would do, namely see his Son reflected in creatures of men—Abraham, Noah, Abel. 'Of his own will he begat us by the word of truth that we should be a kind of first fruits of his creatures (the first creatures of the whole new creation).' 'Worthy art thou O Lord God to receive glory and honour and power (quotes John in the Revelation) for thou didst create all things and by thy will they existed, and were created.'

God places his divine discontent in us and thus we begin to search for God. We think we are searching for God, as if God weren't searching for us! Somebody in another city in Scotland said to me, 'I met a chap who says he is looking for God. He is coming to Aberdeen and he is going round all the churches looking for God.' I hope he finds him! But of course if he is really searching for (and not running from God), it is God who is drawing him on to search for him. And if it is God who is drawing him on he *will* find him, wherever it is he finds him. For God, planting that in a man's heart, draws that man to himself because he injects into him his own *divine* 'discontent' and communicates that to him. Thus he works in an individual and makes him dissatisfied in his life.

This is a wonderful thing. It comes sometimes suddenly, sometimes gradually. Our congregation is full of those who, whether suddenly or gradually, began to feel discontented with their lives—seeking satisfaction in themselves or others, or in exercise, sport, art, music or whatever.

I know a lot about seeking satisfaction in music. I went to the fountainhead of music, John Sebastian Bach in my teens and would sit at the organ in the Methodist Church right into the late hours of the night until the church officer would say, 'Aren't you cold?' And, 'Aren't you going home?' I would not have told him I was seeking for satisfaction in John Sebastian Bach. At length I got fed up of John Sebastian Bach, although I still think his works are wonderful—his B Minor Mass in particular—but it didn't satisfy that part of the heart that was made for God. I had to come to God to satisfy that. That was the divine discontent planted in me by him.

Faith is the *sine qua non*, the absolute essential. 'Without faith it is impossible to please God. Whatsoever is not of faith is sin.' James says in his marvellous Letter, faith comes to the poor of this world. 'Blessed are the poor,' says the Beatitudes. Happy are the poor. What in the world does that mean? Oh, tell that to the modern man of our day in the welfare state. My goodness, get the Trade Union leaders together and preach a sermon with the text, 'Blessed are the poor'—you would have an empty kirk. Wouldn't they go mad! But it is still in the Bible, Trade Unionists or not (and I am not against Trade Unions). It is the poor to whom God gives this gift.

But what does 'the poor' mean? Preeminently it is those who begin—and this is a work of God—to feel dissatisfied with their materialistic life, so they search and search until they come to God by faith which works by love. Then they say, 'Ah, this is it. This is it.'

What is all this I am talking about? Are you perhaps bamboozled? We are simply talking about this, that when God loves us and Jesus Christ loves us he comes and, as it were, sits down in our heart and says, 'Love me. Love me.'

So faith comes home to rest in God. Yet, resting in God (and here is the paradox of Hebrews 3:4), faith rests in him and his power and his grace *actively*. When you are on holiday and seeking a rest you don't sit all the day with your feet up, do you? You do get up, however late, because the rest you are needing is a new kind of activity to refresh you and change you. This rest we speak of is a striving after God. You see you have three tenses here. When the God of eternity invades time, finite creatures in time must see him in three tenses. That is what John expressed in Revelation. 'Holy, holy, holy, is the Lord God Almighty who was, and is, and is to come.' He has come in the past but he has also to come to us in the present. It is all very well for God to come to Abraham, but what is the good of that to me? Come now to me.

The Psalmists are constantly crying, 'It is all very well for you to come to Moses and Israel in the wilderness and help them, but come to me, now.' Not only so but there is a striving that goes out into the future. God is the one who was and is, and *is to come*'. We are still longing for him. Even when he comes to us and blesses us we say, 'It is not enough. Come more. Come more.' Oh, we are greedy for his presence because we are his children. 'Come more. Bless us more.'

All this blessed striving, straining and longing will never end until we reach heaven; it is part of the activity of the rest of faith. When you rest in God it is a resting of purposive, fruitful, creative and character-building activity. Peter explains this when he speaks about people 'waiting for and hastening the coming day of God' (2 Pet. 3:12). You see the rest and the activity: 'waiting for and hastening.' This work of God whereby his divine discontent is planted in our hearts enables us by striving and straining at last to come and find God. Then, having found him and cast ourselves upon him, entrusting our whole souls, our life and hope to him, we go on, striving to enter into deeper rest. Thus we will strive until we reach our goal in heaven.

So we can be quite sure that our salvation does not depend upon our works and merit, because the faith whereby we receive, embrace and love God, is something new that has come into our lives that never was there before. You just need to see the difference that faith makes to some people. If there is one thing I am sure about and that becomes an increasing pleasure and thrill every day that I live, it is to hear by conversation, telephone or letter of this radical, deep and thorough-going change that faith, the work of God in men's hearts, makes. I could believe anything for anybody, once God has begun to work in their heart by faith. There is no end to what we can do and become, once God fastens on us and says, 'I'll have you. Come to me and let me change your life radically.' When he comes to us like that we cannot resist. But then we do not want to; for there is the thrill of transformation!

It is a wonderful thing to see the light of Christ dawn in the eyes of the young—and of the old too. But to me, I suppose because of my particular calling, the great thrill is to see characters growing more and more Christ-like. That's it!

WHAT IT IS TO BE A CHRISTIAN

8. Sin and Guilt

We have been considering the righteousness which God not only is, but that he is prepared to give to unrighteous men who have faith in his righteous Son and in his righteous work for us the unrighteous. It is time now to look back to see just how needful this is for sinful man, and to see from what depths we have been retrieved from multiple ruin, by that one act of Jesus Christ. The presupposition of God's gift of righteousness is the fact of man's sin.

I start from three references, which you could call texts, if you wish. The first one, Romans 3:19, is where Paul sums up three categories of men: the vile, the professedly respectable, and the religious. He says that all men, Christ apart, are guilty in God's sight. In fact it would seem that if all are guilty in God's sight, then, because the respectable have more light of conscience than the others, they are in a sense more guilty. And if the religious (referring, of course, to the Jews who have the oracles of God and the light of the Mosaic law) are alike guilty with the so-called respectable who look down their noses at the vile, then they are even worse than them because they are sinning against greater light. Paul does not quite say this, but surely it is implied. In any event, Paul sums up these three categories of men by saying that all men who ever lived are guilty (*hypodikos* = under judgment) before God.

There are two other references, and it is the word 'guilty' we should notice in them. One is in the passage on the Lord's Supper, 1 Corinthians 11:27. Paul says there that those who eat the bread and drink the wine (representing the body and the blood of our Lord) unworthily, are *guilty* of his body and blood, and drink condemnation to themselves. The word is *enochos*, from which we derive the English 'obnoxious'. Obnoxious to God! The second reference is James 2:10.

James speaks about those who try to fulfil the whole Mosaic law in every point except one, and says, 'For whoever keeps the whole law but fails in one point has become guilty of all of it.' That is, if you fail in only one point, because God is a God of perfection he will not be satisfied with anything less than perfection. If you keep all the laws except one, you are 'guilty', says James, 'of all.' And the word 'guilty' here also is 'obnoxious.' You are 'obnoxious' to God.

It is clear, then, that man, in his fallen state, 'born in sin and shapen in iniquity' is totally objectionable, utterly unacceptable and completely intolerable to a holy God. So much is this the case that the Almighty has had to prepare a place of everlasting burning for those whose sight and presence he cannot bear. After all, he made all things for his pleasure, and if you made something for your pleasure and it turned to your shame, what would you do with it?

We must probe this: How deep is God's objection to us as fallen creatures—as sinners? Does it go from the fruit of our sin to its root, our disposition? Is it the case that we are evilly disposed towards God and will not let him rule over us? We are prepared to acknowledge him, if he stays up there, but not if he interferes with us. Says the creature to the Creator, 'Oh yes, You can stay up there: You can please Yourself up there, as long as You don't interfere with me.' What infernal impertinence!

If that is our attitude to God, and we are so hostile to him who made us, we must then ask this question: How deep is this disaffection of our disposition? Are we so deeply disaffected towards God that we become to him totally objectionable and obnoxious (the word used in the Scriptures)? Is it temporary? Is it something that is due to our human flesh? Is it something that is due to our animal flesh? Are animals the worst sinners on earth? Would beasts in the depths of the jungle do what men have done? No, nature, in that sense, does not sin. Listen to this: 'For the creation was subjected to futility, not of its own will.' It is not a deliberate sinner; it is different from man. And it is God's purpose (provision having been made for fulfilment of that purpose in Jesus Christ) to transform, regenerate and recover the whole of the natural creation, including the beasts. The elemental things of nature did not sin. It was man, through Satan, who pulled the creation down around him. Man is the sinner, not only in respect of himself, but in respect of the creation. If the creation is all wrong, and we suffer calamities and catastrophes: tidal waves, earthquakes, tornadoes, volcanic eruptions— man has done it by bringing down the whole creation over which God had set him as governor.

Do you think this disaffection is accidental—one for which we were not really responsible? I know no one who, through the years, has stressed as much as I have the responsibilities of Satan for man's fall—a fact often forgotten. Man's responsibility and Satan's must, of course, be delicately balanced, but that doesn't reduce one whit man's responsibility, for God gave Adam and Eve absolutely everything possible. The lavishness of his provision, as shown in Genesis chapters 1 and 2, is beyond description. There was, as you might say, only one tiny prohibition, and the serpent came and fastened on that. Therefore, Adam and Eve sinned heinously against the light of God's revealed command. No sin could have been more terrible, more reprehensible and responsible than Adam's sin. You cannot conceive of a more bare-faced disobedience of God's holy commandment than theirs, disobedience of a God who had given them everything. No, it is no accidental disaffection for which we are responsible.

What does 'born in sin and shapen in iniquity' mean (Ps. 51:5)? It goes very deep. It means nothing less than that we are guilty with a guilt so deep that we are set in a solidarity of evil with Adam in his sin! We are federally joined with Adam; we are his sons and daughters, aren't we? We are joined with him federally, not only in becoming sinners in that we sin after him, but we are bound in a federal solidarity with Adam in his own sin. We are guilty of his one sin by imputation. You may regard that as a deduction from the imputation of Christ's righteousness to us. Well, even so I think it is logically acceptable, and I have little doubt that this is the fact. That is why we find Romans 5:12–21 so difficult because Paul is saying something that is almost un-understandable unless we accept the fundamental fact, so shattering, so radically deep that we cannot begin to understand the passage unless we accept the fact that there have only been two races of men on the face of the earth: one the race of Adam, the other the race of Christ. It is because we are joined with Adam in his one sin that God in his mercy has sent another Man to perform one adversative or opposite act, that of our redemption. Thus by imputation and then by impartation (although we have not come to that yet) we partake of Christ's righteousness and can therefore be declared by God to be righteous in Jesus Christ, to be as righteous as Jesus Christ, only 'in him'.

This is only part of the story; you cannot talk about that without going on to sanctification, of course; but we have to get this clear and accept it before we go on. If, on the other hand, someone preaches that but does not go on, that is wrong. But we must not reduce, minimise or weaken the force of justification in favour of sanctification—never.

Well then, this state that man is in through Adam and in Adam, means that we not only inherit the fruit and result of Adam's sin, but we share in Adam's one sin. Before we sin one sin of our own we are guilty with him of his one sin. This takes us back to Romans 5:14 which says, 'death reigned from Adam to Moses, even over those whose sins were not like the transgression of Adam, who was a type of the one who was to come.' Why did death reign over those between Adam and Moses? They did not sin after the likeness of Adam's sin in that theirs was not sin against a revealed command; they sinned in ignorance of the law. Why then did death reign between Adam and Moses? Because all men are guilty in and with Adam's guilt. All men without exception are guilty with him in his sin. Paul does not mean that all are sinners in the sense that all are born in sin, which is obvious. He says 'all *sinned*' (an active verb). The whole human race is guilty on account of that one transgression of Adam, as if there had never been another sin sinned by any man.

Now, I have no doubt that some will react critically and negatively to this. Others may be frankly puzzled by the whole thing. But this is what the Word states; it is the whole point of this passage, Romans 5:12–21. Look at verses 16, 17, 18 and 19. Paul is speaking about Adam's one trespass over against Christ's one act of righteousness. Coming to a climax he says 'by one man's disobedience many were made sinners' (v. 19). This is how guilty we are.

If you are willing to entertain what seems to me to be exceedingly plain in these passages, you will begin to understand why guilt is so deep in the human heart. This explains it as nothing else explains it. This is how guilty we are; not that we are enmeshed in the sin of another, but that we are caught in our own sin, in Adam. We were there and sinned that sin in Adam in a federal solidarity of rebellious action, and we are all condemned for that one sin even although we had never sinned another sin. This incidentally brings out the decisiveness, what I call the 'destinous' nature of these two beings: Adam and Christ.

Here, then, is the depth of our guilt: we are guilty of an almost almighty and categorical action by which we stand condemned, which nothing can atone for but the superior adversative, opposite action of Christ. Christ's action alone undoes its effects, and enables us to be translated from the solidarity of Adam's one sin to the solidarity of

Christ's one act of righteousness. Christ's righteousness, Christ's righteous act is imputed to us by faith. Here is what John Murray says, writing in the *New Bible Dictionary*, on 'Sin':

> Sin never consists merely in a voluntary act of transgression. Every volition proceeds from something that is more deep-seated than the volition itself, and so it is with sinful volition. A sinful act is the expression of a depraved heart. Sin must always include, therefore, the perversity of heart, mind, disposition, and will. This was true...in the case of the first sin, and it applies to all sin. The imputation to posterity of the sin of Adam must, therefore, carry with it involvement in the perversity apart from which Adam's sin would be meaningless, and its imputation an impossible abstraction. The depravity which sin entails and with which all men come into the world is for this reason a direct implicate of our solidarity with Adam in his sin.... 'Behold, I was shapen in iniquity and in sin did my mother conceive me' (Ps. 51:5) and our Lord 'That which is born of the flesh is flesh' (Jn. 3:6). The witness of Scripture to the pervasiveness and totality of this depravity is explicit. Genesis 6:5 and Genesis 8:21 provide a closed case. There is the *intensity*—'The wickedness of man was great in the earth'; there is the *inwardness*—'the imagination of the thoughts of his heart', an expression unsurpassed in the usage of Scripture to indicate that the most rudimentary movement of thought was evil; there is the *totality*—'every imagination'; there is the *constancy*—'continually'; there is the *exclusiveness*—'only evil'; there is the *early manifestation*—'from his youth'.
>
> That the indictment of Genesis 6:15 was not restricted to the period before the Flood is shown in Genesis 8:21. It is a permanent condition that no external catastrophe can remedy. There is no escape from the implications of this witness inscribed on the early pages of divine revelation. It leaves no loophole for any other verdict than that this depravity is total both intensively and extensively. It extends to the deepest movements of the human heart, and characterises all mankind.
>
> Later assessments of our human condition are to the same effect. 'The Lord searches the heart and tries the reins' (*cf.* Jer. 17:10), and his judgment is 'The heart is deceitful above all things, and desperately wicked: who can know it?' (*New Bible Dictionary*, IVP, pp. 1191, 1192).

Read again those verses from Romans 3:10–18. The quotations are taken from Psalm 14, Psalm 53, Psalm 5, Psalm 140, Psalm 10, Isaiah 59, Proverbs 1:16 and Psalm 136—all quotations from the Old Testament. Here Paul is dealing particularly with the Jews, professing, believing Jews in the Christian church in Rome. He is saying, 'Look, I'll deal with you and condemn you out of your own Scriptures, which you are supposed to know. This is what the Scriptures of the Old Testament say about man, any man, Jesus Christ apart.' Now, we all instinctively disagree with this. We say, 'I am not as bad as this.' But what I am trying to show is how bad we are. I am first trying to tell myself; I am far from excluding myself. I know myself better than that. That is not the end of the story and you must be patient, but we must learn how bad we are in God's sight.

'None is righteous, no, not one.' I always think when I read this verse of reading it about twenty-seven years ago in an evening service, when the words 'No – not – one' seemed to sound like nails being hammered into a coffin! 'No one is righteous; no, not one; no one understands, no one seeks for God. All have turned aside, together they have gone wrong; no one does good, not even one.'

Of course you could say that this is not true as far as your experience of men is concerned. But you are not the judge. It is God who is saying this, not man, not even a prophet or a psalmist. This is God's inspired Word. This is what God is saying about us. That must mean that in the ultimate analysis we must be very, very deceived about a great many so-called good deeds. 'No one does good, not even one. Their throat is an open grave, they use their tongues to deceive. The venom of asps is under their lips. Their mouth is full of curses and bitterness. Their feet are swift to shed blood, in their paths are ruin and misery, and the way of peace they do not know. There is no fear of God before their eyes.'

Now, just to answer someone who may be saying, 'No, no, no; you are giving a one-sided picture', let me give you the other side. Look at Romans 2:14, 'When Gentiles who have not the law do by nature what the law requires, they are a law to themselves, even though they do not have the law. They show that what the law requires is written on their hearts, while their conscience also bears witness and their conflicting thoughts accuse or perhaps excuse them on that day when, according to my gospel, God judges the secrets of men by Christ Jesus.' Of course there are good deeds done according to the law, but what does James say? 'You can do them all except that one and you are guilty of one?' Oh no, that is not what James says. 'Do them all except one,' he says, 'and you are guilty of all.' What a terrible book is the Bible!—devastating. So you see, that is the position according to Scriptures.

You may ask, 'Why rub all this in?' I have two answers to that: first, because according to the Holy Scriptures, it is a fact, and is God's truth about man. Secondly, to show what we can be saved from in Christ.

This is the 'bad news' which is the prerequisite of the gospel. Nobody could think that what I have been saying is good news, but it is in the Bible. It is the worst possible news you could hear. You will never read news like this in the papers. It is terrible. It is terrifying, but it is the prerequisite of the good news.

But this also shows what we are saved from in Jesus Christ; for you are not bad as you could be. You have never been as bad as you could be. You have seen other people who seem to have become—many of them friends of your youth—who seem to have become as bad as they could be. Brian Moore told me that he was involved in the funeral of a poor, helpless, inadequate, mentally defective boy in Belfast whose bedroom was invaded by a gunman who shot him down. That would seem to us to be almost as bad as could be. It seemed so deliberate, to seek out this helpless creature; but doubtless there is worse in the human heart, as indeed we know even from other contemporary history.

How can you know what you are saved from unless you know how bad you really were, and in a sense *are* in God's eyes? This is how bad you were, and in some ways still are in yourself. You were guilty of Adam's sin—*the* sin—in a sense the only sin, that one act. His sin is your sin; that is how God regards you. And it is from that point that God begins to deal with us, to redeem us. He says to us, Before I do anything for you, let me tell you what you are, and from what I am going to save you.

You will need to know this. For we cannot praise him properly unless we know what we are saved from. If our salvation is only a half salvation, if we are saved only from what we have become as sinners and not from what we have the potential to become in our heart, our praise to God is only, to put it in musical terms—*mezzo-piano*, there is no *fortissimo* about it. You won't shout and lift the roof in praise to God if you think he has only saved you somewhat. You need to know the depths from which he has saved you.

Satan doesn't want us to know this. That seems unbelievable, but it is true. We need to know it first of all to show us how bad *he* is. This is one of the things of which Christians tend to be ignorant. We do not hate evil enough. Sometimes we misguidedly hate men when we should hate the devil whence their sin flows. We need to know how bad the devil is, and therefore how bad he made us by our willing act. We have spoken of the heinousness of Adam and Eve's act against all the lavishness of God's grace which he gave them. We need to know that, but when the full force of God's holy law against our sin really hits us and God says to us, 'You are bad; bad; hellishly bad,' Satan begins to see how he can use God's holy law to keep us from coming to Christ. And even when we have come running to Christ, the devil still wants to use the guilt of what we were to keep us from the peace and liberty in Christ. He rakes up the past and implies of course that it is not forgiven and indeed cannot be forgiven. This comes from hell and it is from the devil. That is what he tries to do with us. He therefore seeks to induce in believers a false guilt.

Now, here is a word of comfort. The first word of comfort is that all our guilt can be expunged by Christ through his death and our repentance and faith in him. But you know that. You know the gospel. Maybe you know the gospel better than you know the bad news, the prerequisite of the gospel; but you need to know both. The second piece of good news to Christians—and, my word, we need this,—is that Satan induces a false guilt which is no real objective guilt at all, but is a fog which issues from his mouth. It envelops Christians even when they have been objectively, really, actually and finally delivered from condemnation in Jesus Christ. 'There is therefore now no condemnation to those who are Christ Jesus' (Rom. 8:1), but many Christians are belaboured by condemnation, simply because they allow Satan to brandish God's holy law at them to keep them in unwarrantable misery and in baseless, groundless, unjustifiable agony. This is from Satan. I therefore say; if, enlightened by Christ, we are angry at ourselves for our awful deed in Adam, along with that profound guilt which we need to get rid of, we must be ultimately far more angry at Satan for trying to perpetuate that guilt, after it has been completely expunged by Christ.

So, once we have come to Jesus Christ with all our burden of guilt, of Adam's one sin and all our other sins on top of it, and as Christians have found the burden roll away into Christ's grave—if Satan then comes and begins to accuse us to rake up the past, we learn to say to him, 'Get thee behind me, Satan.' My real objective guilt for Adam's sin and all subjective feelings in respect of it and all other sins, are all buried in the gracious salvation I have in Jesus Christ.

Remember Romans 8:31. If this teaching hurts you because you have taken it to heart, look at this. 'What shall we say to this? If God be for us'—how can he be for us, after all that we have said about our sin? He is for us in Jesus Christ, and in his one deed of righteousness, with complete exoneration and absolute freedom from guilt. Look, if you knew that in ten minutes—five minutes—one minute—you were going to die, could you from your biblical knowledge of what God thinks of sinful man, look up into the face of Jesus Christ and say, 'Come and take me. You are mine. I'm all right. I have no fear.' 'If God be for us, who is against us? He who did not spare his own Son but gave him up for us all, will he not also give us all things with him (and that includes peace, and heaven)? Who shall bring any charge against God's chosen ones? It is God who justifies; who is to condemn? (Will he let a poor, miserable little devil, a demon, or a fallen mortal condemn us, if he has justified us?) Is it Christ Jesus who will condemn us, who died, yes, who was raised from the dead, who is at the right hand of God, who indeed intercedes for us?'

Will he condemn us after all he has done for us? Who then can condemn?

'Who shall separate us from the love of Christ? Shall tribulation, or distress, or persecution, or famine, or nakedness, or peril, or sword? As it is written, "For Thy sake we are killed all the day long (this is the cost of being a Christian); we are regarded as sheep to be slaughtered" (does that mean we are to be destroyed because we suffer as Christians? Did Job go to hell? No!). No, in all these things (the worst that the devil can do and the worst that Adam did and we did with him) we are more than conquerors through him who loved us. For I am sure that neither death, nor life, nor angels, nor principalities, nor things present, nor things to come, nor powers, nor height, nor depth, nor anything else in all creation, will be able to separate us from the love of God in Christ Jesus our Lord.'

So, if you have looked into the depths of human sin—your sin and Adam's sin—as you have never done before, and have trembled at the thought and perhaps react with strong emotion, look at it again. Read some of the Scriptures. Face it even more bravely before you sleep tonight, and then when you have looked at the worst you are or could be, say—say this: 'BUT, Jesus died for me.' And go to sleep!

WHAT IT IS TO BE A CHRISTIAN

9. Made to Become Sin

In pursuing our theme 'What it is to be a Christian', we have discussed the question of justification by faith, that is, God declaring us to be righteous in his Son through faith. We have sought to go to the root of the biblical teaching to see something of the sin and guilt in man which necessitated the incarnation of God's Son to repair our ruin. We traced this back to Adam's guilt for his almighty sin, that one sin on which Paul keeps graciously harping in Romans 5:12–21. We have tried to uncover Paul's teaching that Adam's heinous guilt is also our guilt, we being identified with him in the solidarity of evil and sin. Our predicament is this as members of the human race: Adam's guilt is our guilt.

This is what the Scripture says, even if we cannot fully understand it. Indeed, the only way to understand it is first to accept that this is God's Holy Word and recognise the marks of divinity and divine authority upon it. We need to learn to say, humbly, 'Thus saith the Lord', and accept his Word whether we understand it or not. This is the best way to understand. It is 'by faith we understand' (Heb. 11:3a), not by understanding that we believe. So, we swallow first, or believe first; and then God by his grace is pleased to grant us understanding of these profound truths set before us in his Word.

We therefore speak about Adam's guilt as our guilt since we are bound in a solidarity of sin with him. If this were not so, then Romans 5:12–21 is nonsense. You can take other things out of it, but if you do not see Paul's identification of our sin with Adam's, you are being led astray, for that is what it says. This guilt is already brought out in Romans 3:10–19, which declares man's sin to be as great as it can be— he is totally a sinner, totally depraved. This is what this passage tells us

---

about man. It grants no concessions at all. The Old Testament, quoted in the New, says, 'As it is written, "None is righteous, no, not one; no one understands, no one seeks for God. All have turned aside, together they have gone wrong; no one does good, not even one."' Are both Testaments nonsense?

Paul goes on to elaborate that very statement. '"Their throat is an open grave, they use their tongue to deceive." "The venom of asps is under their lips." "Their mouth is full of curses and bitterness." "Their feet are swift to shed blood, in their paths are ruin and misery, and the way of peace they do not know." "There is no fear of God before their eyes."'

No doubt Paul is here saying how bad man is at his worst. But if it is true that we partake of the guilt of Adam's sin and Adam's sin is as heinous as it is, then it is also true that this is always the truth about man; whether or not he has had the opportunity to be as bad as he could be is not the point. This is what we are. You have only to see what happens in certain lands, or in other parts of the country—nominally Christian and Protestant lands—to see how bad man can be. This is the truth about man, which we see in the next verse, 'Now we know that whatever the law says it speaks to those who are under the law (the Jews) so that every mouth (Gentile and Jew, because of course he has been dealing with Gentiles in chapter 1, Jews under different categories in chapter 2, and at the beginning of chapter 3) may be stopped (every protester who says, 'It is not true about me. That is too bad. I am not as bad as that.' God says, 'Who knows? Do you know better than I, what I made you and what you have become by comparison?') and the whole world may be held accountable to God.' The whole world guilty—guilty of that, not guilty in general but guilty of that, summed up in the one sin of Adam in particular.

Well, there it is. So, you can see how totally depraved man is, as Adam must have been to have sinned against such grace and light as is described in the first two chapters of Genesis. These chapters are a record of the sheer, lavish goodness of God to man, to Adam and to Eve. It was in the face of all that, against all that light and grace, goodness and abundance—every conceivable provision for their health, their wealth, and their pleasure—that they turned against God and sinned the sin, the monstrous, heinous, unspeakable sin.

We must accept the fact, for what can you do but accept it? Then accepting, we begin to understand what Christ has saved us from, because we begin to know what we were in our sin. We begin to know how far Christ and his Father were prepared to go to save us. This is the subject of our present study. To understand this, we must first see who Christ is in relation to this work of redemption and justification. Who is this Christ who comes to us as the last Adam to undo the work of the first Adam, the sinner? He is not only God the Son, the second Person of the Trinity, but, being God the Son he also, I believe, became the pattern, the prototype of man (Gen. 1:26, 27). 'God made man in his own image' means that God made man in the image of his Son.

These two things are very important: he is God the Son, and he is God the pattern. As the Son, the second Person of the Trinity—not the first—he became the pattern, the prototype Son of man. Now, the results of that are:

Firstly, should God at any time want to come down to the earth he has made, to sojourn in his own world and survey his own estate, it would be natural to come down primarily to see and have fellowship with his prime creation which is not angels, nor beasts, nor rivers, nor trees, nor plants, but man. Should he want to come down to earth it would be natural for him to have fellowship with the creature nearest to himself, a creature made with understanding, reason, conscience and will.

Secondly, in coming down to earth and to man rather than to the beasts, or to the natural things, or even to angels, he would come as near to man as possible, because of course he wanted to have fellowship with him.

It seems natural to me that he would come in man's guise, as God did when he came to Abraham. He appeared before Abraham as a man, as men—a sensible thing to do! Man could not have fellowship with whirling, blazing worlds. Saul of Tarsus could not have fellowship with that flaming Being in heaven; he had to flatten his face on the ground. It was not possible to have fellowship with a flaming Fire. So God had to (the 'had' is his, not ours) accommodate himself to man (Phil. 2:5–11) and be made according to man's pattern. There is therefore a correspondence between the eternal Son, the prototype, and man the creature. Now, if in coming down to earth he sought to rescue man, all undeserving as he was, from enslavement to evil with all its consequences, it was open to God, incarnate in human flesh, to do so. Anything is open to God, but God being a perfectionist, as we have stressed, he obviously elected to do the thing totally. He was made of a woman and became a real, true man.

It was thus he came to deal with Adam's plight, by being, in his human generation, constituted not only a new man, as an individual, but by being constituted a new Adamic Head of a new race. As such he was and is our Representative, and it is as our representative man that he dies for us. Paul says so, quite plainly, 'One died for all' (2 Cor. 5:14). He represents man and dies for man. 'One died for all'—a few simple words, but how massive and far-reaching!

Now, go beyond his death to his high-priestly work in heaven. That is representative too. Jesus Christ now represents us at the throne and judgment bar of God, as John says, 'If anyone does sin, we have an Advocate with the Father, Jesus Christ the righteous (at the right hand of the Father); and he is the propitiation for our sins, and not for ours only but also for the sins of the whole world' (1 Jn. 2:1, 2). We have an Advocate, one representing us to God, speaking to God for us. That is what a high priest does: he speaks to God for man as a prophet speaks to man from God. And Christ is not only Prophet and Priest, but King as well. So, you see, he is our Representative also, and stands there at the bar of judgment at God's throne of grace (judgment and grace are both there) representing us and speaking for us as our Advocate.

But Christ is not only our Representative, he is our Substitute. He came and stood in for us. This is just expressing the one main idea in a different way, with different applications. He stood in for us as the 'Sinner', although he was personally sinless. 'In my place condemned he stood' as Philip Bliss puts it. That is the truth. He is our Substitute. 'The Son of Man came to give his life a ransom for many' (Mark 10:45). This is the wonderful message of Isaiah 53:4–6. It contains astonishing, tremendous truth, so great that many modern theologians won't stomach or swallow it at all. 'Surely he has borne *our* griefs and carried *our* sorrows; yet we esteemed him stricken, smitten by *God*! and afflicted. But he was wounded for *our* transgressions, he was bruised for *our* iniquities, upon him was the chastisement that made us whole, and with *his* stripes we are healed.'

This is taught throughout Scripture, as a variety of statements from different writers demonstrates. Consider Hebrews 9:27, 28: 'And just as it is appointed to men to die once, and after that comes judgment (no second chance), so Christ, having been offered once to bear the sins of many, will appear a second time, not to deal with sin (that has been dealt with finally) but to save those who are eagerly waiting for him.' Christ was offered to bear the sins of many on their behalf, in their place, in their stead. This is substitution.

An even clearer reference is 1 Peter 2:23. One would need to be ingenious to get round this. 'He himself bore *our* sins in his body (his own body) on the tree that we might die to sin and live to righteousness.'

Here, then, we have Christ not only as our Representative but as our Substitute, not only speaking for us, but standing in for us. But we need to go further. Even 'Representative' and 'Substitute' do not go as far, it seems to me, as the Scripture itself. Christ not only represents us, and stands in for us as our Substitute, but in doing so he identifies himself with us fully. This is clear, as we have seen from Isaiah 53:7: 'He was oppressed, and he was afflicted, yet he opened not his mouth; like a lamb that is led to the slaughter, and like a sheep that before its shearers is dumb, so he opened not his mouth.' He stood before them all, almost entirely silent, not only before Herod but also before Pilate. He did not need to say anything; that was in God's hands. 'He opened not his mouth' because he was standing in for us and we are guilty. It is a complete identification. When they were tempting him: 'Go on; speak. Justify yourself. Are you the King of the Jews?' without saying anything he was really saying (and this is implicit in his bearing): 'Go on; do it. I'm guilty.' Of course we cannot dare to say that without adding (as 2 Cor. 5:21 does) that he was personally sinless, stainless. But he identifies himself with us quite, quite fully.

In this context I find Romans 8:3 an exciting verse, if a frightening one. 'For God has done what the law, weakened by the flesh, could not do.' Let me paraphrase it: 'God sent his own Son in the likeness (similitude) of sinful flesh ('flesh of sin' says the original Greek) and for (for what?) sin.' That is *why* he sent him, and that is *how* he sent him. He came to be, not only our Representative and our Substitute, but to be absolutely and utterly identified with us, apart from sin. Of course you understand that the only one who could take the sin of others upon him was One who was himself sinless. It would be impossible for us. We could not take anybody else's sin upon us; we have plenty of our own. If you die for your own sin, you die for your own sin; you cannot die for anybody else's. You cannot simply say out of the goodness of your heart, 'I'll die for your sin, too.' But a sinless man can take upon his back the sins of others. And that is what he did. 'God sent his Son in the likeness of sinful flesh'. Miss this and you miss the point of his coming. He came to heal, he came to teach, he came to manifest the powers of the kingdom and all that—yes, yes, yes, but he came 'for sin', to identify himself with our sin.

These verses set the scene for the great verse! It is 2 Corinthians 5:21. I have been pondering this verse again. Years ago at Netherhall, Largs, with the students crowded one morning into the conference room, we looked into the depths of it and I sensed we all were afraid of what we saw. We had to ask God to give us grace to face the awe-fulness and yet the wonder and the glory of the truth. I remember I had on the rostrum a number of commentaries by various scholars, fairly conservative scholars, and ones whose works I use a great deal. I was quoting from these, but not one of these scholars would stomach what Paul is obviously saying, that Christ was made *sin* for us. They said, 'It cannot be true.' 'You cannot accept this as it is on the surface.' 'It is impossible, it is too contradictory.'

But God gave us grace then and God has given me grace until now, and please God, will give us all grace until the end to ponder this unsearchable, unfathomable mine of divine truth. Let me translate it in my own way: 'For God made Christ (the One not knowing sin) to become sin for us.' I do not read it as 'made sin' because that can sound like a verb; 'made to become' can not mean that he was made to become sinful. He was never that. It means he was made to become the *thing of sin* itself. Oh God! Can't you understand the scholars? They react against it. They say, 'Oh no, you cannot say that. You cannot say that, even if you immediately deny that it suggests he was a sinner.' But Paul said it. And he wrote it. It is there black upon white in the Greek. 'God made Christ, the One not knowing sin (either as a force or as an action) to become sin for us, that is, on our behalf.'

The other side is equally fantastic, in a sense more so. 'For our sake he made him to become sin, who knew no sin, so that in him *we might become the righteousness of God.*' If it seems absolutely unheard of that God should make Christ to 'become sin for us', how in the world could he have dared to make us to become 'the righteousness of God in him'? It does not merely say, 'to become righteous' or to be regarded as righteous. We sometimes say that justification by faith means that God has declared us perfectly righteous. That is one thing: but it is another to say that we might become 'the righteousness of God.' You can't say that! But God says, 'Yes you can. I do and I have made my apostle Paul write it. It is 'in Christ', not otherwise, of course. Do you see the solidarity of Christ with us in our sin and the solidarity of us with Christ in his righteousness? Do you see the exchange? He comes and takes our nature, 'Here; give me that.' He throws it away and says, 'Here, take mine. Take mine!'

This is complete identification. This is why I have called our Lord (and have even written it down although I still think it shocking when I look at it in cold print) 'God's Dustman.' When the dustman comes to your door he is heavily begrimed with *other* people's dirt, not his own. If you were to sit down on the bus beside him, you might want to edge away because he looks dirty and probably smells. God bless him for doing a good but nasty job! Christ is 'God's Dustman,' taking away our dirt also.

We may also dare to call Christ 'God's Criminal.' Because he came as representing, substituting for, and identifying himself with the first Adam in his sin. He was saying, 'I will bear the punishment for what he did, and I will bear the whole punishment, because I want this finished with, once and for all.' That is the expression in the Greek, *hapax* and *ephapax*, that you have over and over again in the Letter to the Hebrews: 'once and for all.' It occurs eleven times, nine of them referring to Christ's 'once and for all' work, his finished work on the cross (the other two references are to the finality of his second coming). He says, 'I want this matter finished. Let's finish with this transaction.' When we have a long drawn-out transaction with anyone, how wearying it is. We say, 'Let's get the matter finished.' So, Christ says, 'Let's get the matter finished. I'll bear all the punishment. I'll bear all the punishment for Adam's sin.' And he bore the undeserved punishment for it and all the sins that issued from it as if he were the only sinner who had ever sinned in the whole of history. Thus 'He opened not his mouth' in self-justification.

In my view there is nothing immoral in thinking of our Lord as our Substitute, our Representative, identifying himself completely and wholly with us. I see nothing immoral in our Prototype coming to represent us and stand in for us in our plight, however heinously we had sinned, thus identifying himself with his own elect. God the Father had chosen us 'in him' long before man sinned. It is therefore Christ as Adam, identifying himself absolutely and completely with us, who comes to us as the second and last Adam, bearing our punishment. It is no alien who comes to bear the punishment, no foreigner, no interloper pressed into this unwelcome service, but the One who loves us with an everlasting love and, God-like, the One who would do absolutely any-thing for us. This is what he has done for us. This is his love for us. He says, 'Yes, I'll be God's Dustman. Yes, I'll be God's Criminal. Yes, I'll shut my mouth and take it all as if I had done it all.' This he did.

Now, see what follows. I am going to express this rather startlingly and in an extreme fashion. In one sense there is nothing substitutionary or vicarious about Christ's bearing our sins. It is hardly right to say that he stood in for us, for it was simply our better Adam standing for our worse one. He identified himself, in a sense, with both. He identified himself with the first Adam absolutely, fully, yet sinlessly, and he was the second Adam. It is quite appropriate that if there is a solidarity of all mankind, that the second Adam should absolutely identify himself with the first Adam and bear that punishment as if he were that Adam. He became that Adam and therefore in that sense he was not punished for another but for himself as identifying himself with that Adam. So you have it in 2 Corinthians 5:21. He came and assumed our first Adam, not that he wanted to be associated with him, but the only way to get rid of him was to put him on. The only way to destroy him was to assume him and become one with him, sinlessly of course, and in death be destroyed with him, although the sinless part could not be destroyed—'death could not hold him.' He finished with our first Adam. No one else could do it. 'There was no other good enough to pay the price of sin.'

Christ finished our first Adam that he might begin our second. He identifies with both; the one to remove from him all the guilt, and penalty, and shame; the other to establish him. The one, to set him at naught, and the other to establish him that we might become, in that second Adam, the righteousness of God, and thus become acceptable to God, as Christ is acceptable to God. Notice that little word, 'as'. That we might become acceptable to God as Christ is acceptable. That is, as righteous in God's eyes as Christ is. Remember, we said that God was such a perfectionist he could not do with anything less than a perfect work, and we have to be absolutely perfect before he will accept us. So, he makes us as perfect as his Son.

Hence his indulgent kindness! This is the thing I find that Christians will not take in. A legal God, a grim God, a thrashing God, a stern God, a God that is waiting to strike, a policeman God, *that* is the God young Christians, trying to be good and trying to be holy, trying to follow the Master, *that* is the God they conjure and seek to follow. But a God who takes you and drenches you in his kindness, enfolds you in his arms and says, 'Don't let's talk about sin or anything nasty at all. Let me tell you how much I love you. It will take all of eternity as well as all of time, so let me begin now. Don't interrupt, don't interrupt, don't interrupt with all that long story about your sins. Listen to me telling you how much I love you.'

But Christians will not do that. We say, 'But this, that you know I

did!—and that! That which I am.' 'Oh,' he says, 'Hold your tongue.'
And it is because he has done such a perfect work that he has the right to
say, 'It is finished. That is an old story. Why rake that up? Do not be a
muck-raker!' It is the devil who is the muck-raker, 'the accuser of the
brethren' (Rev. 12:10). He is the muck-raker. 'I', says the Lord, 'am
not a muck-raker. Why rake up all that? Let's talk about something
good, about love, and loyalty, and devotion.' This is his indulgent
kindness.

On that ground the removal of all barriers to fellowship is assured.
'Come in,' he says, 'Come in to my royal apartments, my innermost
chamber. Sit by me, or kneel by me.'

Do you remember when Mary was with Jesus, and Satan said to dear,
hardworking Martha, 'Nag at them. The dinner will be five minutes late.
Nag at them.' And poor Martha, under the influence of Satan, nagged at
them. Jesus says, 'You, and your dinner! Leave her alone. She has
found what dinners were made for, and human bodies, and human
lives.' That is why you eat dinner, wear clothing, have a shelter over
your head, and have all the good gifts of God—so that he might bring
you to himself and take you in his arms and love you. They are means to
an end, and the end is that God might love, and love, and love, and
love.

I have brought the identification of Christ with man as sinner as close
as I can, in order that it may seem shocking and extravagant; but having
seen him as God's Dustman and God's Criminal, I remind you lastly
that it is God who does this. It is God, in human flesh, who becomes
this, and does this—no one else. That is what abases us to the ground. It
is *God* who became the Dustman. It is *God* who became the Criminal! It
is God who did the dirty work, and took man's filthy sin upon himself.
Only God in human flesh, absolutely morally and spiritually stainless,
could deal with all that filth, yet not soil himself. He does not go home
soiled like the dustman; it washes off him because he is God and he is
perfect man. That is the bit that makes us fall down and worship him.

Here, then, are two things we have been trying to consider: the excess
of vicarious merit that accrues to believing sinners because we become
the righteousness of God; that is the first thing. The second thing is this:
if there is an excess of merit there is an excess of debt on our part that
we will never be able to pay. Our gratitude must go on and increase,
forever and ever. There will never be a point in time or eternity when we
do not owe absolutely everything to this exclusive work that God did in

human flesh for us. So our lives have to be spent—even in mental energy as we think it all through again. I have done this many times from this passage in many years, and it is as fresh, and new, and wonderful as ever; indeed, ever more wonderful and deeper to me every time I do it. I need to do it periodically because I see depths, heights, wonders and glories in it each time that I never saw before. We are committed to that simply by the sheer intellectual (call it theological if you like) curiosity of our minds.

Here is an exercise for you: before you put your head on the pillow tonight, turn up your Bible to 2 Corinthians 5:21 and read it again. It would be a good thing to gather any translations you have and ponder them and do your own thinking. Do this sometimes, because you will never get to the end of it, or plumb the depths of it, because it is so great. It simply grows greater the more you think about it! You do not need to be an intellectual, or an academic to do this; you only need a little common sense to be able to read simple words, and as you do your gratitude to God will overflow.

Some people say, 'I can't pray. It is like speaking to a stone wall.' You'll pray after that! You'll say, 'Oh, God!' You won't ask for things. You'll say 'Oh, God, You're wonderful! You're wonderful!' And you will go scurrying to your work tomorrow saying, 'Oh God, You're wonderful! You're wonderful!'

WHAT IT IS TO BE A CHRISTIAN

10. Adoption

All that God decrees in heaven and then begins to work out in history on earth in regeneration and justification leads on to the idea of adoption. By creation we were made to be sons of God, but by the Fall we have become sons of the devil (1 Jn. 3:10) and are no longer sons of God. If God's mercy is to reach us in that awful state of rebellion against him, then he has got to do something wonderful before he takes us into his family, and calls us 'sons and daughters.' That 'rabble', sons and daughters? How in the world is he going to call 'good' all those horrid creatures who have rebelled against him in Adam, heinously turning against the God who gave him everything? How in the world is he going to call *them* sons and daughters? What can he do to justify such a thing? We have gone into that. We have seen what it cost him. So, having unfolded something of *our* justification in Jesus Christ, we go on to the point where he says, Now that I have justified them, I place them in my Son as 'derivative' sons and daughters in him. Thus Adoption is the bridge between Justification and Sanctification.

Justification has to do with what God does *for* us. Sanctification with what God does *in* us. He looks down and says, 'I'll have to get busy down there.' It is all very well to *say* this and that about so and so, but writing it down, even in heaven, will not make them become that. You can call anybody anything, but that does not make them what you call them! So the Lord has to do something about what he has written down. And the beginning of his doing is the placing of us as sons—adopting us.

Think about that word, 'adoption'. In Scripture 'adoption' is the act whereby God places as sons those who ceased to be sons by the Fall and have become by nature children of wrath (Eph. 2:3). All men descended from Adam and Eve, because of their sin and man's partaking in their sin, are children of wrath.

This is strong language, but it is used in Scripture. Jesus calls the Pharisees 'sons of the devil' (Jn. 8:44). He says, 'You are like your father the devil.' What a thing for him to say to those men! He stood and looked them in the eye and said, 'You belong to your father the devil.' Again, Paul calls Elymas, the magician (Acts 13:10), 'son of the devil', interfering with God's work. And he soon made short work of him, didn't he! Then John writes: 'He who commits sin is of the devil; for the devil has sinned from the beginning' (1 Jn. 3:8). Because he cannot do anything else.

What God does in adopting us in Jesus Christ is that by God's grace, sinners whom he has chosen to be his own are placed by him as sons, in the only begotten Son of God. This is an additional perspective to that of the indwelling of Christ. It is true that we know 'Christ in us, the hope of glory', and the hope of many other things, here and hereafter. But this is the other side. This is not Jesus Christ coming to dwell in my heart, but is God coming down and taking a whole flock of miserable sinners and saying, 'I'll take you.' He doesn't take them in the mass. He says, 'I'll take you John and you Mary—you Timothy—you Ethel'—singly like that. Then he 'dips' them in Christ. Call it 'baptism' if you like; this is what it means. You may represent it with water—that is what we do and continue to do—but the water represents the Holy Spirit. He dips them in Christ, places them in Christ, gives them a place as a son in the only begotten Son.

The important thing here about 'adoption' is that God has only one Son that he can own as a Son; every other man from Adam and Eve onwards has been a son of the devil. God could not own one of these sinners as his—never, never, never! 'I have,' he says, 'only one Son and that is he! Look at him, isn't he wonderful, my only begotten!' The description of Christ as 'only begotten' is used five times, as far as I can see, in the New Testament. God has only one divine, eternal Son whom he had in eternity before the world began; any other sons and daughters he is pleased to choose and call to be his sons and daughters can only be of a secondary or derivative order. And yet, what a privilege to be even that in him!

Here is an illustration: Prince Richard of Gloucester's right to the title of 'prince' lies exclusively in his relationship to the Queen. It is in her, the present monarch, that he has the right to be called 'prince.' So we are placed in Christ. This is a wonderful thing. We will never get to the bottom of this. You can read Ephesians 1 and 2 through and through, and never get to the back of this. You take Jesus Christ into your heart, but some people think he is so easily offended that when you grieve him he says, 'Good-bye, I'm away!' And out he goes through the door and that is that. 'No,' he says, 'I'll come in and *bide* with you.' That is what Revelation 3:20 means. 'I stand at the door and knock; if any one hears my voice and opens the door, I will come in and stay, and abide with him forever.' Those are the very words of Scripture. But in a sense, he can only say that because prior to his knocking at your door and your asking to come in is the fact that the Father had planned to place you in Christ. So, it does not merely depend on your opening the door when he knocks to let him in (although that is necessary and indeed is really his doing!). It is the fact that he has put his hand on you and said, 'Now, I am going to put him in Christ, and her in Christ.' And you are safe in him, for when he puts you in Christ he does it forever.

Of course, comes the time when he knocks at the door and says, 'Take me in.' He makes us want to take him in. If you want to take Jesus Christ into your heart and believe you have taken him in, and if you want to follow him, who made you want that? It was not you. You are not better than others, nor am I any better than any other man. Who, then, made you want to do it? Oh yes, other people have been an influence, and we could name some of those who have helped us towards Jesus. Oh yes, yes! I hope I have helped some people toward Jesus, but I have not actually united anyone to him. I have preached here for years (I hate to count!). And there may be some who have listened to me preaching during nearly all those years who still have not taken Jesus into their hearts, so I cannot do it. If I could make them, I would have had them all in Christ long ago. It is God alone who can make us willing.

Remember Ephesians 1:3: 'Blessed be the God and Father of our Lord Jesus Christ, who has blessed us in Christ with every spiritual blessing in the heavenly places, even as he chose us in him before the foundation of the world.' If you really are in Christ and he is in you (and these two 'ins' belong together), if it is really true of you, then God marked you down, chose you, elected you, selected you before he made the world, or angels, or anything. He knew you before you were born. He knew you before the world was made, and he put you in Christ. You see, 'even as he chose us in him before the foundation of the world, he destined us in love to be his sons in Jesus Christ according to the purpose of his will' (Eph. 1:4, 5).

Placed in Jesus Christ, we can never become exactly the same as Jesus Christ, because Jesus Christ was God. When we are placed in Jesus Christ we do not become part of God, but in him we are born of his Spirit and we become really his sons and daughters.

Turn to Romans 8:14–17 and follow closely what Paul says: 'For all who are led by the Spirit of God are sons of God. For you did not receive the spirit of slavery to fall back into fear (you aren't afraid of your father, are you? You shouldn't be) but you have received the spirit of adoption (sonship—you have received the Spirit that placed you in Jesus as a son; that is what the word in its original means), when we cry, "Abba! Father!" It is the Spirit himself bearing witness with our spirit that we are chosen children of God, and if children, then heirs (this is the bit I want: 'heirs'!), heirs of God and fellow heirs with Christ.' If your father had a great deal of money it would be a great wonder if you didn't share a lot of it, because you are his son or his daughter—and heir. As heirs of God we have a right in Christ to say, 'He is my Father; let me into heaven.' It is like the Prince of Wales saying to the guards outside Buckingham Palace, 'Excuse me sirs, I belong here.' Exactly— 'heirs of God and fellow heirs with Christ, provided we suffer with him (this is the test that we belong to him) in order that we may also be glorified with him.' Some people disown their parents; some parents disown their children when they disgrace them, but he will never disown us and we must never disown him and run away when things are hard.

Then consider these choice words in Galatians 4:4: 'But when the time had fully come, God sent forth his Son, born of a woman, born under the law (the Mosaic law) to redeem those who were under the law, so that we might receive adoption as sons. And because you are sons, God has sent the Spirit of his Son into your hearts, crying, "Abba! Father!" (recognising your Father because his Spirit is in your heart) so through God you are no longer a slave (or a servant, or even a nephew) but a son, and if a son, then an heir.' What does it say?—You are an heir!

There are different forms of adoption in different societies and ages, and also in different parts of the Scriptures. There is one idea of adoption in Genesis 15:2 where Abraham says, 'Look, if I die without a son, Eliezer my servant will inherit all I have got.' What he seems to be saying in a sense is, 'If I die without a son then Eliezer is my son by adoption and he will inherit all I have.' We find something of this kind of adoption in Semitic races. Here is another kind of adoption. When Jacob saw Joseph's sons, Ephraim and Manasseh, he adopted them to be his own. That is the strangest kind of adoption I ever heard of: the grandfather adopts his grandsons to be his own, so that there would be, in a way, thirteen tribes and not twelve, because Ephraim and Manasseh each became a half tribe. In fact Ephraim became the largest tribe of the lot (Num. 1:33; 26:37). Here is another unusual kind of adoption: Amram's son, Moses, became by adoption the son of Pharaoh's daughter. She adopted him as her son (Ex. 2:10). There is another lesser example of adoption in 1 Kings 1:20, but it is scarcely worth mentioning here, Egyptian adoption. Lastly, there is the adoption we have in Esther, when Mordecai, Esther's uncle, adopted her after her parents had died, to be his own daughter.

These are all examples in the Old Testament of different kinds of adoption. But as far as God's adoption of men is concerned, you could say that although it started in God's mind before the world began, we first read of it in his adopting a man, namely Abram, (although he does not use the word) down there beside the Persian Gulf. He was born and brought up there in Ur of the Chaldees and then God said: 'Here is another sinner, living in this city of Ur, but he is a special fellow to me. I will adopt him. I choose him to be a very special man. I will say to this man Abraham, "You are going right up the Valley of the Euphrates, and down into Canaan, and you are going to be special to me. You are going to be the beginning, not only of a new family of twelve tribes but the beginning of a new nation."' God had Seth before that, and Enoch, Noah and others, but he started this new kind of adoption with the man Abraham. God sovereignly gave him a command whereby he covenanted with Abraham in the symbolic rite of circumcision to make him the father of nations: 'Now you, my son Abraham, are to be the father of many nations.'

God told Abraham to circumcise himself and Ishmael, and Isaac when he was eight days old, but not only these: 'As for you, you shall keep my covenant, you and your descendants after you throughout their generations. This is my covenant, which you shall keep, between me and you and your descendants after you: every male among you shall be circumcised. You shall be circumcised in the flesh of your foreskins, and it shall be a sign of the covenant between me and you. He that is eight days old among you shall be circumcised; every male throughout your generations, whether born in your house, or bought with your money from any foreigner who is not of your offspring.' Every male on Abraham's estate was to be circumcised; not only his sons—Ishmael, maybe about fourteen years old, and Isaac, when he was eight days old, but all the sons of the servants and even of the strangers who were staying for a time with them, possibly on pilgrimage. They too were adopted into the family and made like Ishmael and Isaac, the sons. They were called, in that sense, 'sons of Abraham' and were in God's covenant with Abraham. God made a pact with Abraham that these would be blessed. If they remained within the covenant, even the servants would be blessed, too. In the fulness of time Abraham became a family and then became twelve tribes, and then there came a day when these twelve tribes of Israel were led out of Egypt and were born a nation. They were born a nation.

This is deeply embedded in the teaching of the Old Testament, as a few references will make clear: 'Who has heard such a thing? Who has seen such a thing?' says Isaiah in the very last chapter of his great prophecy (Is. 66:8). 'Shall a land be born in one day? Shall a nation be brought forth in one moment?' That refers to the day when Israel came out of Egypt and was baptised in the Red Sea (as Paul puts it) and became a nation. They were twelve tribes and a slave people in Egypt for hundreds of years, but then they became a nation so that God called them his son. If you turn back to the beginning of Isaiah 1:2 you will see a hint of it. 'Hear, O heavens, and give ear, O earth; for the Lord has spoken: "Sons have I reared and brought up, but they have rebelled against me."' Notice, they were 'sons'. Then look at Jeremiah 3:19: 'I thought I would set you (God is speaking of Judah and Israel) among my sons and give you a pleasant land, a heritage most beauteous of all nations.' But the loveliest bit of all is in Hosea 11:1. This is one of the most beautiful of all verses. Hosea says: 'When Israel was a child (that is when Israel was a newborn, baby nation) I loved him, and out of Egypt I called my son.' God adopted Abraham and all who were in Abraham's covenant, and then he adopted the whole nation as his son. This is what Paul calls the 'adoption' (Rom. 9:4). He is wringing his hands about his people, the Jews. He loves them and yet the Jews will not believe in his Jesus, and his heart is broken about it. 'I could wish that I myself were accursed and cut off from Christ for the sake of my brethren, my kinsmen by race' (Rom. 9:3). Like Moses he said, 'If I could give my life for them, as Jesus gave his life for us, I would do it.' Then he says, 'They are Israelites, and to them belongs the sonship...' They are God's sons. The people of the nation are God's sons. 'Sonship' here is 'adoption'. Paul uses the very word.

So here you have not only Abraham, Isaac and Jacob, but the nation, born in a day when they came out of Egypt, made God's son. Another interesting point is this: later on God takes the king and makes him his adopted son, in spite of the fact that he did not wish his people to have a king at all. They insisted on having a king to rule over them, when God wanted to be their king himself. He said, 'You don't need a human king; I'm your King.' 'Oh,' they said, 'we want to be like other nations. They have a king and we want a king.' God said, 'I don't want you to be like other nations.'

God does not want his people to be like other people. But they would have a king. So, God said, 'All right then; have a king.' And then God adopted their king to be his son. He says this especially of Solomon: 'He shall build a house for my name, and I will establish the throne of his kingdom for ever. I will be his father and he shall be my son. When he commits iniquity, I will chasten him with the rod of men (that is the Assyrians and the Babylonians), with the stripes of the sons of men; but I will not take my steadfast love from him, as I took it from Saul, whom I put away from before you' (2 Sam. 7:13, 14). What he is really saying is, 'Look, I am going to make him, this royal king of Israel, my son in a very special sense.' And when God makes someone his son, that cannot change.

Is there anything a boy could do to make himself not the son of his father? No, he could not. Even though his father threw him out or killed him, he would still die his son; he cannot change that. So, God does not change his sons. Here he is taking Solomon to be his royal son. In 1 Chronicles 28:6 he says to David, 'It is Solomon your son who shall build my house and my courts, for I have chosen him to be my son, and I will be his Father.'

In Psalm 2 God speaks through the psalmist about the royal son of Israel. He says, 'I have set my king on Zion, my holy hill.' Verse 7, 'You are my son, today I have begotten you.' When the writer to the Hebrews quotes this verse he says, 'That refers not only to Solomon, but to a greater than Solomon.' Solomon's name means 'peace' because he is a type of One greater than he, as David his father is also a type of a greater than David. It points to Christ of whom it is really said: He is the royal Son, and so that is why we are 'in him', the only begotten Son of God, the royal Son of heaven.

You see, then, the steps whereby God, through various kinds of adoption, particularly by adopting this family as his own, bringing them to the birth, taking them out of Egypt, points forward to the coming of his great Son, in whom we are adopted and placed as sons. Let me emphasise again: there is a vast distinction between him and us. He was eternally begotten. That is, he was from the beginning. There never was a time when God did not have a Son. The Son was with the Father from the beginning. He is eternal God, we are adopted sinners.

There was nothing specially good in Abraham but God said, 'I'll take you.' It is thus he chooses: God goes round the world, round the country, and lays his hand on this one, according to his books written up before the world began and says, 'You're in my books!' And in time he takes and places an individual in Jesus and makes him his own son. Suddenly someone says, 'I would like to go to Sunday School.' Sunday School? Or somebody says, 'I would like to go to church. We have a teacher at school and you know, she is a Christian and I like her.' Or, 'There is somebody at my work—rather a nice person—and it wasn't for quite a time that I found out that he is a Christian and that is what makes him so nice.' This is God's way of saying, 'I'll take him and I'll take her.' He sends somebody to them or sends them to somebody and something clicks and on they go; they are placed in Jesus before they know it! In a sense they were placed in Jesus before the world began.

Think of a boy who is the heir to a throne. When he is a little boy he is under a governess who no doubt punishes him when he is naughty (as all little boys are, sometimes!). This is how Paul puts it: 'The heir, as long as he is a child is no better than a slave (we would say, a servant), though he is the owner of all the estate; but he is under guardians and trustees until the date set by the father. So with us; when we were children, we were slaves to the elemental spirits of the universe (sons of the devil). But when the time had fully come, God sent forth his Son, born of woman, born under the law, to redeem those who were under the law, so that we might receive adoption as sons' (Gal. 4:1–6).

There is one other Scripture, in Romans 8: we looked at verses 15–17 of this chapter before. But later on in verse 23 the word 'adoption' appears again, 'and not only the creation, but we ourselves, who have the first fruits of the Spirit, groan inwardly as we wait for adoption as sons.' But, I thought as Christians we were already adopted? Paul, you are getting us all mixed up! 'No,' he says, 'I am not.' There are several stages in adoption. There was first, as far as mankind was concerned, the junior stage when we were junior heirs; that was until Christ came to the earth—junior heirs like the junior son of the sovereign who has to be treated pretty much as other little boys, until he comes of age. So when Jesus Christ comes, we become full heirs. That is what Paul is saying here: 'And we now, since Jesus Christ has come to the earth, have become full heirs.' We do not inherit as heirs until the senior dies. So, here, we do not inherit all that we inherit even as full heirs, until we die

and receive our resurrection bodies. Thus there is the prior adoption of
the Old Testament people until Christ comes. Then there is the full
adoption as heirs after Jesus Christ came, and that belongs to us. All his
wealth is ours because we are placed in Christ. Then when Christ goes
up to the Father at the consummation, at the end of the world he will say
to us, 'Come and sit on my seat with me, next to my Father.' That is
what we read in the Revelation, that we will be able to sit on Jesus
Christ's seat with him (Rev. 3:21). We are heirs of all that, but we will
not inherit it all, be fully adopted, until we get to heaven and are seated
with Jesus Christ on his throne. Then we will be able to look round and
say, 'In Jesus Christ all this is ours.'

So, there is a tremendous lot in this, a great deal to ponder, being
placed in Jesus Christ as sons and daughters. For although we will
never be God like Jesus Christ, we have his nature (2 Pet. 1:4). As
Christians we should grow up until people see the likeness of Jesus
Christ in us. Someone who knew your father and mother might meet
you and say to you, 'Oh, you're like your mother.' 'Oh, you're like
your father.' They see the family likeness. This is what is going to
happen to us, placed in Jesus Christ; if we allow him to grow up within
us, we will become like him. Somebody at work, somebody at school,
somebody at home will say, 'Oh, I know what it is that is special about
him (or her); it is Jesus I see in him (or in her).' So it will be until we are
fully like him. Then he will take us home and we will inherit all his
wealth and all his possessions. But my, how much of it we have down
here already—all his grace! So we live as sons and daughters of God.

Now, it is this that makes Christian friendships special. There is no
friendship in the whole wide world like Christian friendship, and this is
what makes it special: not that Christians are special of themselves, but
when Jesus Christ comes into their hearts and homes and fellowship, he
makes people see the best in one another and love one another, and care
for one another more and more and more so that people coming in say,
'Oh, we see where they belong. How these Christians love one another!
Where did they get that from?' They got it from their Father, and from
their Elder Brother, the one in whom they were placed by adoption, even
Jesus Christ.

That is what the Christian church and the whole Christian life are
about, letting Jesus Christ so work in our hearts by his Word and Spirit
that we learn more and more to love one another with Jesus' love which
is unique from heaven, so that people will sense a heavenly quality in
our friendship. That is the fruit of our adoption into the family of God.

WHAT IT IS TO BE A CHRISTIAN

11. Sanctification

Thus far we have discussed the objective justifying work of God in Jesus Christ to the point when we see that he takes his chosen ones (Eph. 1:4) and places them in Christ as adopted sons and daughters.

Having looked at all that side of it, we come now to think of the other side: God taking this very Jesus Christ by his Spirit, the seed of Christ ('the seed of God', *sperma*, 1 Jn. 3:8) and planting it in the heart of the believer. Thus we are not only placed in Christ, possessed by him and developed by him, but we are set in his kingdom. Christ is a whole kingdom, the only kingdom the world will know one day: the new heaven and the new earth, all will be Christ's and all in Christ. Christ is a whole kingdom, yet the essence of that kingdom, the personality of Jesus Christ, the eternal Son of God, who creates the kingdom and reigns over it all, is brought to bear upon our individual souls. That great Christ who fills all things and whose kingdom will fill all things is brought as it were to such a dimension that, losing nothing of that divine, infinite and eternal essence, God places him as a seed in our hearts.

Now, it is the linking of the two concepts that helps. It is this seed of Jesus Christ in the heart that transforms the personality. The aspects we have already considered are, in a sense, theoretical, although gloriously so, but we are coming now to practical things, what Jesus Christ does in a person's heart and life. This excites me more than the other, although the other is wonderful. This is what we are concerned with in the Christian church, making you better, a better man, a better woman— purer, cleaner, truer, humbler, more loving, more honest, more courageous in the world, wiser than the world, discerning, knowing when to speak and when not to speak, when to act and so on. This has

---

to do with the outside world and the witness of Jesus Christ, and can take us a long way.

I have been trying to think of figures, analogies, or pictures that would help us. You could think of saturating something in a fluid. The Bible uses the figure of baptising, dipping. You can dip something in water, steep it or stew it until the water saturates it. But that is not good enough for this; that represents only part of what we want to illustrate. First there is the act of placing the desired object in, and then leaving it in the liquid, until the work of saturating takes place. But that is not adequate to illustrate what God does, because the soul is not only placed in Christ, but Christ also comes to abide in the soul. There is a dual work here, his coming to envelop us but also at the same time entering into our hearts individually, secretly and privately to re-create us from within.

Think of planting plants in the soil. You plant a plant in the soil, and the moisture and the chemicals from the soil are drawn into the plant and absorbed into it. You have the stem rising, then the leaves appear and the plant, the flower, and the fruit. That gets a little nearer, but it is not near enough, because in a sense that is still only one idea, and there are at least two main ideas in what happens to us. The whole thing is complex, yet it can be stated simply in terms of simple propositions.

Justification is by God the Father, who writes us down as his in heaven; that is transcendent. That is the Godward side, what God does. Sanctification is really to do with the manward side, the immanent side, God in us—Immanuel, God among us. Some of the references to 'Christ in us' refer (perhaps there is a double reference here) to Christ in the fellowship. Christ is with us here in a double sense. Christ is in my heart. If he hadn't been I would have been a very, very different fellow. I may not be much yet, but my goodness if I had gone on without him all the years I have lived on the earth, that would have been a sight! But then he is also in the fellowship. He is among us. So, Christ within us can also be Christ among us. And Christ in the individual heart is the manward side.

The word 'sanctification' has to do with what is 'holy'. What is the basis or root meaning of the word 'to be holy'? There are two ideas involved. In the Old Testament it is to 'set apart'. And I would say that is pretty well equivalent to 'placing in'. It is to set apart something. I set apart *from*—negative; I set apart *for*—positive. I say, I don't want to set this there; I want to set it here. The other idea in holiness is that of brightness. The one is an action; the other a condition. The former underlying notion of sanctification is that of position (here, not there)—a relationship if you like—up there, not down here. The second notion of holiness as brightness is related to condition, to state, to the process of transformation.

Take the first idea: to sanctify is to set apart for a purpose. The Old Testament speaks about sanctifying the Sabbath. It is set apart for God. Similarly with the altar, the tabernacle, the garments of the priest and days of fasting. In fact the whole people were set apart for God himself, as a peculiar people (we know that is true in more senses than one, but we mean it in the better sense, now!).

Jesus set himself apart. We see this in the great prayer our Lord made not long before his passion. John 17:19, 'And for their sakes (his disciples) I consecrate myself, that they also may be consecrated in the truth.' That is to say, 'I set myself apart.' The notion here may seem more negative than positive, but it is not really. Jesus is a Man in the world, but he is not a Man of the world. He says at last, 'Excuse me, I have more important things to do than heal bodies; I have men to teach.' And as far as they were concerned, one day he said, 'I am going to the cross. You can come or not, but I am going to the cross.' Thus he set himself apart even from them so that he might do something for them. He is, by this action, setting himself apart from the world. 'I am not here to please the world and be their kind of king.' That is why they wanted to throw him over the cliff, wasn't it?

Having done that, he says, praying for his disciples, 'Sanctify them in the truth.' That is to say, 'Lord, sanctify them, set them apart by the truth' (Jn. 17:17). Or if you like to put it this way: 'Place them in the truth, dip them in the truth, baptise them in the truth.' And he is the truth. So, virtually it means, baptise them into Christ and into his inspired Word. Christ sets himself apart for the disciples and sets the disciples apart to be placed in the truth. He also sanctifies the church, the totality of believers (Eph. 5:26). 'Husbands, love your wives, as Christ loved the church and gave himself up for her.' He set himself apart for her that he might sanctify her. He did this, 'having cleansed her by the washing of water with the word.' The 'water' here is the Word. He has sanctified the church by placing it in the Word, the total Word of God.

One other concept here. We are placed *in Christ* and we are set apart *for Christ*, as Paul tells us in 1 Corinthians 1:30. 'He is the source of your life in Christ Jesus, whom God made our wisdom, our righteousness and sanctification and redemption.' We are placed in him and by virtue of this fact he is living in us.

Let us see the other side. Paul puts it as follows in Romans 5:6–9: 'While we were yet helpless, at the right time Christ died for the ungodly. Why, one will hardly die for a righteous man—though perhaps for a good man one will dare even to die. But God shows his love for us in that while we were yet sinners Christ died for us. Since, therefore, we are now justified by his blood (the first idea) much more shall we be saved by him from the wrath of God.' 'Saved *by his blood*', that is one thing; 'saved *by him*', that is another. This is made clearer in the next verse. 'For if while we were enemies we were reconciled to God by the death of his Son, much more, now that we are reconciled, shall we be saved by his life.' There you have the justificationary on the one hand and the sanctificationary on the other, which is what we are talking about. They come together in that wonderful way.

Many New Testament statements speak of 'Christ in us'—Christ placed in us. In 1 Colossians 1:27 the apostle speaks of 'Christ in you, the hope of glory.' Since the 'you' is plural some of the scholars say the reference is more to Christ in the church than in the individual believer. We do not really need to argue about that, for he is in both. But none the less many other texts suggest strongly Christ in the individual believer although the plural is used. Perhaps generally speaking both are implied, Christ in the individual and in the fellowship. Why should we set them over against one another?

I wonder how many times the phrase 'in Christ' or its equivalent appears in Ephesians 1 and 2? I think it may be sixteen. All the blessings of salvation are ours in Christ. But in the midst of that there is also reference to Christ in us. They interlace, you see, interweave, intermingle, these two ideas: we in Christ and Christ in us. Look at Ephesians 1:15. 'For this reason (that unfolded in the marvellous preceding passage), because I have heard of your faith in the Lord Jesus Christ and your love toward all the saints, I do not cease to give thanks for you, remembering you in my prayers, that the God of our Lord Jesus Christ, the Father of glory, may give you (that is, put into your heart) a spirit of wisdom and of revelation in the knowledge of him, having the eyes of your hearts enlightened (that is pretty inward isn't it?) that you may know what is the hope to which he has called you, what are the riches of his glorious inheritance in the saints, and what is the immeasurable greatness of his power in us who believe, according to the working of his great might which he accomplished in Christ when he raised him from the dead...'.

So, in the midst of all that is ours 'in Christ', we have got this 'Christ in us'; we in Christ and Christ in us. I am sure there are many Christians —and not only the younger ones—who have not yet taken these two ideas and held them together. If you take them together, with all you seek to study, understand, and follow through in the Word of God, that will of itself make you a balanced Christian, because you will balance what God has done *for* you with what God is seeking to do *in* you. If you forget what God has done for you, you will think that you are saving yourself; if you forget what God is doing in you or seeking to do in your heart by his Holy Spirit, you will take refuge, as do many old fashioned, archaic, legalistic, merely doctrinal Christians in worshipping the God of justification as a God afar off.

I recall being on a mission one week-end many years ago, and on the Sunday morning there was a gathering for prayer before the morning meeting. I was absolutely astonished at the prayers of the saints. They confined their prayers entirely to thanks to God for what he had done *for* them. There was no sense of enjoyment of God. It all seemed to have to do with tickets of justification. I found it a desolating experience. It was a great paean of praise for our justification, holding up the work of Christ on the cross and looking at it, as if to say, 'We are to spend the rest of our lives looking at what Christ has done *for* us and magnifying that'. Is there anything wrong in that? No, but that is only half. It is the first, most important half, but we must also come on to the second, and pray about what he wants to do in our hearts. I felt like crying out, 'Men, men, you have only half a gospel.'

This is why many evangelistic works are dying today; they have only half a gospel. If you went to some of these evangelistic missions of various groups and denominations and you took Romans 5–8 and taught that to them, do you know what they would say? They would say, 'That's not the gospel. Don't turn that on us. We want the gospel!' No; not that gospel, but this; which we turn on you to change you. The evangelical church today has largely forgotten the second half of the gospel—'Christ in you', changing you.

You have these two ideas side by side, or very nearly so, in 1 John 3:6, 9. Yet it overspills. I defy any scholar to be absolutely systematic about this because the Word of God overspills all our divisions. 'No one who abides in him sins.' That is one side: But 'abiding in him' is active, because it means choosing to rest in him. There is the fundamental idea of being placed in him and then there is the idea of abiding in him, keeping in with him, seeking him more, not less, as the days go on. But the fundamental idea is being placed in him.

John continues: 'No one born of God commits sin.' That is clearer, for 'God's seed abides in him and he cannot go on practising sin because he is born of God.' The two ideas you see: we in him and he in us. You get it again most beautifully in John's Gospel in chapters fourteen to seventeen. Wonderful! He in us and we in him. We in him and he in us.

Now, will you allow me to be even more difficult and complicate this further by introducing another idea found in Ephesians 4:20–22 and Colossians 3:10?

'You did not so learn Christ! (like those Gentiles)—assuming that you have heard about him and were taught in him, as the truth is in Jesus (I love these prepositions!). Put off your old nature which belongs to your former manner of life and is corrupt through deceitful lusts, and be renewed in the spirit of your minds, and put on the new nature, created after the likeness of God in true righteousness and holiness' (Gal. 4:20–22). 'Put off' and 'put on'—put off the old and put on the new. You could trace that back to the wedding garment. Remember the man in Jesus' parable who came into the wedding feast without the wedding garment (Matt. 22:11, 12). They said, 'How did you get in without a wedding garment? You can't get in here without a wedding garment.' The old garment must be exchanged for the new. To put off the old nature, cast it aside and not live that kind of life any more, is possible only when the Holy Spirit with Jesus' death to that nature is in your heart. You can put off the old nature only when Christ has come into your heart to give you the power to do so. Likewise, since the Holy Spirit of Jesus Christ includes the Holy Spirit of Jesus Christ crucified to your sin and raised for your righteousness, they are both in one. So it is by the Holy Spirit indwelling your heart that you are able to put off the old, day by day dispensing with more and more of this evil world and its practices. Is that the way you are going? Or, are you going the other way? Are you stripping off more and more of the old and putting on the new, putting on the Christian life?

Follow that idea into the Book of the Revelation where we find various references to 'white robes.' It seems to me that some of these refer to robes that are given us in justification, what God does for us that we cannot do for ourselves, but other references seem to apply to what we ourselves do by obedience to Christ in sanctification and devotion to him.

Take the 'justificationary' one first. In Revelation 3:18, Christ by the Spirit is speaking through John to the church at Laodicea. He says very hurtful things to them. Verse 15, 'I know your works: you are neither cold nor hot. Would that you were cold or hot!' I suppose that he means he would know where to put them, how to categorise them, but churches that are neither cold nor hot, that are absolutely indifferent, he does not know what in the world to do with them. 'Therefore, I counsel you to buy from me gold refined by fire, that you may be rich, and white garments to clothe you and to keep the shame of your nakedness from being seen...'. Don't be put off by the word 'buy'. What he is saying here is, 'You, church in Laodicea, it is Christ that you need. You have to put Christ on.' That is why we have the verse 3:20. 'Behold, I stand at the door (of the church in Laodicea)...'. He is really saying in effect, 'Let me come in and give you white robes, white garments to keep the shame of the nakedness, of your sin, like that of Adam and Eve in the Garden after they had sinned, from appearing.'

There is another important reference in Revelation 7. 'After this I looked, and behold, a great multitude which no man could number, from every nation, from all tribes and peoples and tongues, standing before the throne and before the Lamb, clothed in white and with palm branches in their hands...' (Rev. 7:9). These, I believe, are robes that God gave them in justification, that they could never, never work, achieve or produce themselves. 'Then one of the elders addressed me, saying, "Who are these, clothed in white robes and whence have they come?" I said to him, "Sir, you know." And he said to me, "These are they who have come out of the great tribulation; they have washed their robes and made them white in the blood of the Lamb"' (Rev. 7:13). I think here you have both ideas. You have the white robes given in justification but also sanctification. Surely even the dying thief was sanctified by his confession of Christ in his dying moments. Christ not only gave him the white robe of justification but he, by his act of confession of Christ, began his life of sanctification. Both are there. Now look back again to Revelation 3:4, 5, written to the church in Sardis. 'Yet you have still a few names in Sardis (Turkey), people who have not soiled their garments; and they shall walk with me in white, for they are worthy. He who conquers shall be clad thus in white garments...'.

Do you see what I am getting at? Later in Revelation 6:11, the martyred saints are portrayed. 'Then they were each given a white robe and told to rest a little longer, until the number of their fellow servants and their brethren should be complete, who were to be killed as they themselves had been.' They are given white garments, yet in another sense they also seem to be rewards. You could not say 'they earn them'; that would be Romish: yet it has something to do with achievement and holiness, with the works of faith which we discussed from James 2:14–26 in an earlier study.

Finally turn to Revelation 19:6: 'Then I heard what seemed to be the voice of a great multitude, like the sound of many waters and like the sound of mighty thunderpeals, crying, "Hallelujah! For the Lord our God the Almighty reigns. Let us rejoice and exult and give him the glory, for the marriage of the Lamb has come, and his Bride has made herself ready; it was granted her to be clothed with fine linen, bright and pure"—for the fine linen is the righteous deeds of the saints.' Here the very fabric of their robes is woven from what they did with Christ in their hearts: they were faithful, even unto death.

So, you have the two notions: you are in Christ and Christ is in you. You are in Christ because he has chosen you, placed you in himself, and says, 'You are mine.' Then, having gathered you into his kingdom and said, 'Now, you are mine. You are mine,' as if you were to take someone into your home—maybe someone who hadn't what you would call a home—and said to them, 'Now, this is your home forever, or as long as you live on the earth. This is your home. You are ours and we are going to call you by our name. We are adopting you into our family. We want you to be happy in our home and to fit in, but even if you are not and do not, we will never put you out because you are ours. We would, however, like you to be happy with the way we do things and fit in because we think that would be good for you as it has been good for us.' Then, having said all that, that this is their home, and we will never let them go, we nonetheless indicate that we are not pleased with them as they are and therefore with all the wisdom, prudence, patience, care and faithfulness God will give, we seek to change them.

The analogy stops short, of course, because we cannot put anything into others except, in one sense, by prayer and faith. But do you see the two sides? There is the security first: 'Come in. You are ours. We give you our name. We'll never let you go. Do what you like but we'll never let you go.' Then the other side: 'Oh, but we do want you to grow like us and fit in.' And it is thus the Lord, having given us his name, proceeds to change us. He plants himself in our hearts and says, 'Come on now, you are mine. You are mine; fit in.'

How are you getting on with your transformation? Are you becoming more like Christ? More like him in truth, faithfulness, loyalty, kindness, love, gentleness, thoughtfulness for others? Are you being delivered from pride, self-consciousness, backbiting, inferiority—all these horrid crippling things, these enslavements to evil? You are delivered by the power of Christ in your heart from the demonic forces working to destroy your life, aren't you? Jesus Christ is saying to a thousand demons, 'Out – out – out – out. Don't you know that my arms are around this person? You have no business here. Don't you know that my Spirit is in this life? You have no business here. Out!'

To be set apart for Christ, then, really means Christ is set in you to work out his will in your life. I wish, you know, that together in fellowship we would learn to grow up together into Christ, and let his gracious Spirit work his mellowing way in our lives. That means we have to change our attitude to some folk. We have to stop judging people. We are down in the midst of this world affected by the influences of evil, demonic forces, and Satan himself—the world, the flesh and the devil—and we are really very, very imperfect persons— and we need to know it. With people that we do not like—maybe it is because they make us feel small (which is a pity and it should not be)— but if they make us feel small, we may make them feel we are ten feet tall! We strut past them with our head in the air, we criticise them and dissociate ourselves from them. Is there someone you would never dream of going to speak to? He's so and so; she's so and so—and we judge. Sinners judging sinners! What an infernal cheek! Because that sinner does not partake of our particular brand of sinnerhood we don't like them and judge them, as if to say, 'Jesus doesn't like your kind of sinning; he likes mine!' Well! He hates ours too, as much as he hates theirs.

If Jesus gets half a chance, what he does in our hearts is that he mellows, sweetens, humbles, engraces, gracifies (if I don't know a word I'll make one up!); he dips us in pure, sweet grace and makes us loving and kind to all. He teaches us to turn even our enemies into our friends. Oh God, teach us this within the Christian church before we go out into the world, teach us to turn enemies into friends (Prov. 16:7).

We have been up on the mountain top in our earlier studies, looking at all that God has done for us. But now he is saying, 'Please come down to earth, and will you, Mr Minister, tell these people—and don't forget yourself—that Christ has done all that for you so that he might change you and make you better.' What we have said is part of this process.

May God help and prepare us for the next instalment by saying, 'I'm going to let his Holy Spirit have his way in my life in many, many things.' You'll see the difference. You'll soon know the difference.

A dear laddie was encouraged to tell me that he had received Jesus Christ into his heart. His daddy helped him. Do you know how the youngster put it? He looked up into my face and said, 'You see, I'm changed.' I hope so. I hope so. Daddy and mummy will know, won't they? And he'll know.

Are you changed?

WHAT IT IS TO BE A CHRISTIAN

12. The Indwelling Christ

To be a Christian is to become part of God's new creation because we have been placed 'in Christ'—in the kingdom of Christ, in Christ himself as the Person who fills all in all. To be in Christ is to belong to the total kingdom of Christ which kingdom will eventually fill all things. I do not know where hell can possibly be, although in *The Great Divorce* C. S. Lewis says that in heaven, hell will be seen to be a tiny crack in the pavement; it will be so small it will be quite, quite insignificant. We do not know. C. S. Lewis knew as well as anybody that there will be no cracks in the heavenly pavement. It is just a way of trying to describe how insignificant hell, the wicked and the devil will be in the kingdom of Christ that will fill the whole universe and the heaven of heavens.

We are placed in this total kingdom, this new world: translated from the kingdom of darkness, sin and evil, into the kingdom of light and glory, beauty and love, the kingdom that lasts forever. It was this invisible kingdom, which made the visible one. In the best sense it is just one of God's toys which he made for his pleasure, something given to his Son for him to enjoy. But then he wanted a help-meet for his Son, and so he planned that the church, Christ's church, should be his bride. I speak reverently.

We are placed then in Christ. But then you see there is another side to it, and they are very difficult to hold together. I think all these different 'ins' in Ephesians 1–2 attempt to bring the two together: we are 'in Christ', but we see that Christ is also in us. That is a different idea although it is to the same end. Justification and adoption have to do with our being placed in Christ. But sanctification has to do with Christ being placed in us, which is different. We dwell in Christ, the total eternal kingdom of God where evil shall be banished. Where in the world could it be banished to? It hurts my head to think about it, and yet it is marvellous! But then Christ dwells in me, this tiny unit of palpitating flesh! *That* Christ, who fills all things, the totality of the universe, in me? Here you see two things: first the greatness of the Godhead; and second the 'smallness' of Christ in his incarnation!

Let me put that in its proper context, so that we may clearly see the profundity and mystery of this. There are three Persons in the Godhead, the Father, the Son and the Holy Spirit. Yes, they were a family before the world was made. They are equal, these three, although in another sense they have their different roles. The Father and the Son are equal but the Son eternally honours the Father, although he is equal with him in power, glory, divinity and eternity. The same applies to the Holy Spirit. He is equal to both the Father and the Son in power, and glory, and eternity.

We need to see this particularly about the Son as the second Person of the Trinity; because, having spoken of the greatness of God, we are now going to think about (and this word is in quotation marks because we must say it very, very carefully) the 'smallness' of Christ. He became a baby you know.

One of the things one is inclined to ask on the birth of a child, after asking how the mother is and the little one, and the poor father(!), is its weight. Is it six, seven, or eight pounds? Now, think of the birth of Christ and of his tiny size. Here is how Edward Caswall put it:

> Lo! within a manger (the feeding trough of the beasts!) lies
> He who built the starry skies.

Christina Rossetti expresses the humility involved:

> A stable-place sufficed
> The Lord God Almighty,
> Jesus Christ.

Or think of Charles Wesley's words: 'Veiled in flesh the Godhead see.' That is God in the manger. The baby in the cradle is God Almighty! He made the stars, keeps them in their courses and he controls Herod, too. Yet, he is the Son of God that fills all in all.

Paul gives us the theology of all this in Philippians 2:5–11: 'Have this mind among yourselves, which you have in Christ Jesus, who, though he was in the form of God, did not count equality with God a thing to be grasped, but emptied himself, taking the form of a servant, being born in the likeness of men. And being found in human form he humbled himself and became obedient unto death, even death on a cross. Therefore God has highly exalted him and bestowed on him the name which is above every name, that at the name of Jesus every knee shall bow, in heaven and on earth and under the earth, and every tongue confess that Jesus Christ is Lord, to the glory of God the Father.' That does not mean that Christ is greater in power after his death and resurrection but that all the power of God is now in the hands of a man, as God gave it to Adam at the beginning,—although he sinned and forfeited all of his privileges. But Christ, by contrast, rises and is exalted to fill all things.

But turn now to Ephesians 1:15. 'For this reason, because I have heard of your faith in the Lord Jesus and your love towards all the saints, I do not cease to give thanks for you, remembering you in my prayers, that the God of our Lord Jesus Christ, the Father of glory, may give you a spirit of wisdom and of revelation in the knowledge of him, having the eyes of your hearts enlightened, that you may know what is the hope to which he has called you, what are the riches of his glorious inheritance in the saints, and what is the immeasurable greatness of his power in us who believe, according to the working of his great might which he accomplished in Christ when he raised him from the dead and made him sit at his right hand in the heavenly places, far above all rule and authority and power and dominion...'. Now, 'far above all dominion' refers undoubtedly to all the evil powers and authorities, the devil at the head of them, who are against God.

Christ is 'far above all power and authority' *as a man*; that is what staggers and obviously thrills Paul. God is always above all rule and authority, above the devil, and demons and wicked men and all that; but now it is the God-Man who is far above them. That is categorically, dimensionally different. Jesus Christ as the last Adam is still a Man and will be forever. Not only so, but God 'has put all things under his feet and has made him the head over all things for the church, which is his body, the fulness of him who fills all in all.' Christ is given to the church as its Head. Yet, one day, *every* created thing that is not banished to hell will be renewed, perfected and glorified in Jesus Christ and he will fill everything. He will fill the beasts, if there are any beasts, and they will not have any disease. He will fill the plants and they will not have any disease either. He will fill the oceans if there are any oceans (though according to Revelation perhaps there aren't. What do you think about that? It is a puzzle, isn't it?). But Christ fills everything. He saturates, Christises, Christianises everything. There will be nothing in the whole universe that is not purely and thoroughly of Christ. *And it is that One who became a baby.*

There are some things in Scripture so staggering that they nearly take my breath away. Look at John 1:16. 'And from his fulness have we all received.' Not merely 'from him', but 'from his fulness'. Now, that does not mean we each receive a little of his fulness. We could discuss that at length! But look now at Ephesians 3:19. What does Paul pray? 'That Christ may dwell in your hearts through faith; that you, being rooted and grounded in love, may have power to comprehend (that is embrace) with all the saints what is the breadth and length and height and depth, and to know the love of Christ which surpasses knowledge, that you may be filled with all the fullness of God.'

This is it! This is the church as the fulness of Christ. Ultimately, when every member of the church, every elect sinner is thoroughly saved and Christ comes and we all have resurrection bodies, then the whole church, holding hands and stretching arms together says, 'We have comprehended, we have embraced the fulness of Christ.' If it came to the glorification of the church and the Marriage Supper of the Lamb with the myriads of saints from all the ages to the end of time, and you were absent, there would be something lacking of the fulness of Christ in the church. He would say, 'We can't go on until we get him, or her. Where is he? Where is she? Bring her. The church is less than full.' The display of the virtues and qualities and graces of Jesus Christ would not be complete. It will be the exhibition, the demonstration of Christ's glory. When we say something is 'To the glory of God' we mean that everything that Christians do has in view the time when all the hidden glory of the eternal God, Father, Son and Holy Spirit will be, as it were, displayed by the church. The church, in a sense, is like a huge cinema screen on which all the inner virtues, and glories and wonders of God— the wisdom of Father, Son and Holy Spirit—are thrown, so that you see the whole thing. My great God, it is so big! What a kaleidoscope! We display in manifold, multi-colours the variegated glory of God.

Now, back to Ephesians. Paul is praying that you 'may have power to comprehend with all the saints what is the breadth and length and height and depth (of what, Paul? 'Ah', he says, 'half a minute'. Words can't get it all in) and to know the love of Christ which surpasses knowledge that you may be filled with all the fulness of God.' Oh, God, you are so great that I can scarcely contain the thoughts and feelings you inspire!

Here is another amazing statement, from Colossians 3:11. This is a different context but take the words at the end. In this kingdom of Jesus Christ 'there cannot be Greek and Jew, circumcised and uncircumcised, barbarian, Scythian, slave, free man, but Christ is all, and in all.' Are you a Christian? Then that is all that matters. Is Christ in you? 'Christ is all and in all.'

This is the perspective we need to have when we think of the greatness of God, and the smallness of the Christ, the Babe who was laid in a manger. But, go further: think of the invisibility of the now eternally human Jesus Christ planted as a seed of the Spirit in your heart. When I see a new Christian, one beginning to show the lineaments of the image, the likeness, the sweetness, the grace, the loyalty, the devotedness of Jesus Christ, I think to myself, 'I wonder how it happened?'

I do not mean the events, the decisions and all that. I wonder when the Spirit of Christ invisibly and silently stole into that heart. Talk about a baby of seven pounds in somebody's arms—precious bundle—oh, smaller than that, the eternally human Jesus by the Spirit stealing in invisibly and silently to take up room in my heart and yet to fill it. The ocean in a pint pot; qualitatively and quantitatively. All his Person, all his power bent to produce his image in my life, dwells in me! Is all the power of God, all his majesty and greatness, all the immensity of God directed to this end—to impress sinners?—to impress unbelievers?—to impress atheists with heavenly fireworks? No; that is a detail. Draw the curtains and hide it; that's nothing, but all the almighty power of God bent to this end that one day I should see Jesus Christ smiling out of the eye of someone who has been delivered from drink, drugs, prison, immoral sex—the whole lot. You see, God could do many things that he does not choose to do. What a book of science God could write! and doubtless is writing. When scientists go to the heavenly library, they will be able to spend the whole of eternity boring into how the world was made. What fun they will have! But the Bible is not a book of science, it is a book of salvation, directed towards making people Christians, true, kind, loyal, sweet, and self-sacrificing, to produce fully human characters—like Jesus Christ, being the only true and full man who ever lived.

This is expressed in a wonderful verse in John's Gospel, chapter 1:14. It says, 'the Word became flesh' (human flesh of course: there are different kinds of flesh as Paul tells us in the resurrection chapter, 1 Corinthians 15). God became a baby. Say it again! If this has not sunk into your minds, say it again: God became a baby in a cradle! 'The Word became flesh and dwelt among us, full of grace and truth; we have beheld his glory, glory as of the only Son from the Father.' The glory of God was seen in a shining human face, not a haloed human character; there was nothing outwardly supernatural or miraculous. He was not ten feet tall or twenty stones in weight. There was nothing odd about him. You could have lost him in the crowd. His gait, I think, would have been very poised. His eyes must have been marvellous. His voice—but if you saw him walking about the street you might miss him. They *did* miss him and even called him a sinner. 'Veiled in flesh, the Godhead see.'

The Son became a Man. He became the second and the last Adam, true man. And he has come by the Spirit, Christ in us, to work inwardly by sowing the seed (*sperma*) of the Spirit of God (1 Jn. 3:9) in our hearts that Jesus Christ might grow up in us. May I put it like this? Jesus Christ grows up spiritually in us as a baby naturally grows in the womb of its mother and at last demands to be seen and is evident.

I hear from various directions what it costs some ministers to teach this from God's Holy Word. Most evangelical Christians, even today, want a gospel that simply deals with coming to Jesus Christ and beginning. They will not go on. These people will not have Christian character and its fruits; they love to sit and hear a gospel that applies to others. Too many Christians will not have the gospel that applies to them, which says, 'This is the gospel to you: let Jesus Christ grow in your lives by his death and resurrection.'

When I say that Jesus Christ comes to dwell in our hearts to produce his image and to recreate his own human character within our lives, I mean that he comes to produce the fruit of his Spirit (Gal. 5:32)— always more important than the gifts of the Spirit. The gifts of the Spirit are for Christian service. But God did not save us for what we could do for him, he saved us because he wanted us. If you are married, or are just about to be married, you know you do not marry simply because it means someone else can serve you—make your breakfast, your dinner, and your bed! I hope not. I hope you married because you wanted your spouse, for his or her own sake—full stop; that's enough. Never mind the breakfast! In fact we know that the best gift is love; and love is not really, in that sense, a gift for service; it is fruit, it is character.

See then, sanctification has to do with the fact of Jesus Christ within us. It is *who* we have, not what we have. I must simply touch upon this, the fact of Christ within. In a moment we will think about faith. Have you heard the story of the three men called Fact, Faith, and Feeling? They were friends, but there has always to be a leader, even among friends. With these three the wrong chap was always getting in front. When Faith went in front, he went astray from Fact. When Feeling went in front, he went astray from both the others—even further astray. But when Fact went first, Faith followed safely, and Feeling came to heel. Feeling, the most difficult realm of all, is re-ordered. When faith follows fact our emotional life is ordered and its balance restored. The fact of Christ within includes the fact of faith. When Christ comes into your heart to dwell he comes with his own faith and enables us to believe. If you are supposed to be a Christian and you just cannot believe that Jesus Christ is in you, well, very likely he isn't. If he is, he is there to help you to believe that he is within (1 Jn. 5:10).

Who is this Christ who is within us? Think of him as a twofold Christ. He is Christ crucified and Christ risen. What is the necessity of this 'dual' Christ in our hearts? One aspect is to deal with the old, the other with the new. The one is to deal with the old Adam and the sinful nature, the other to give us the new; the one is to clear the old out, and the other to take its place. They belong together and are one seed. The death and resurrection of Jesus are not two events, spiritually speaking. Given the death of *this man*, the resurrection was certain and inevitable. He had to be raised on the third day because he died sinlessly with our sins, not his own. There was nothing in the world so sure as the resurrection. Christ's death and resurrection are two sides of a penny. Just as from the seed which rots comes, by germination, the fresh shoot that grows up to be the flower and the fruit, so the death and resurrection of Jesus Christ belong together.

When Christ comes to dwell in the Christian, by his Spirit, he is there to deal with all the past, all our sin, all our temptation, all our trials, all our preoccupations with evil things. He deals with that, radically, and says, 'Let's get rid of all that and let me come in and live my life in you.' We must believe that if we have invited him in, he is in. 'Behold, I stand at the door and knock; if anyone hears my voice and opens the door, I will come in to him and eat with him, and he with me.' If you have invited him in, he must be there. Surely you can believe that he is there, and know his presence and working by his death and resurrection? Passages like Romans 8:29; 1 Corinthians 11:7; 1 Corinthians 15:49; 2 Corinthians 3:18; Colossians 3:9, 10 are all about Christ producing his image in our lives. Wonderful! Marvellous!

But what about faith? Look at 2 Thessalonians 2:9–17, which has to do with believing and not believing. 'The coming of the lawless one by the activity of Satan will be with all power and with pretended signs and wonders, and with all wicked deception for those who are to perish, because they refused to love the truth and so be saved. Therefore God sends upon them a strong delusion, to make them believe what is false, so that all may be condemned who did not believe the truth but had pleasure in unrighteousness.' That is all about unbelief. By contrast, what follows is about believing. 'But we are bound to give thanks to God always for you, brethren beloved by the Lord, because God chose you from the beginning to be saved, through sanctification by the Spirit and belief in the truth. To this he called you through our gospel, so that you may obtain the glory of our Lord Jesus Christ. So then, brethren, stand firm and hold to the traditions which you were taught by us, either by word of mouth or by letter. Now may our Lord Jesus Christ himself, and God our Father, who loved us and gave us eternal comfort (the word often includes 'strengthen'—consolation—the old English is *confort*, to strengthen) and good hope through grace, comfort your hearts and establish them in every good work and word.'

It is all believing; believing the truth that Jesus Christ came, that he lived, died and was raised on the third day, and has sent his Spirit from heaven to indwell those who will believe. Then having received him by believing, you may believe that he is there. These are two kinds of believing. We receive him by believing. But this is not merely believing something in the head. I believe in New York although I have never been there! It is not that kind of faith. What use is that sort of belief to me? It is not of much personal importance to me whether New York is there or not. But if I had been to New York it would be different. Believing faith receives Christ—that is what makes the difference. Then, having received him, believes that he is there for a purpose, many purposes.

You say, 'Go on, Lord; do what you have come to do in my heart and don't let me stop you. Deal with that in me that would stop you. Deal with that in me that would say, "Don't do that kind deed you thought of yesterday, have a day off."'

Of all that, you see, we say, 'Lord, deal with that. You are there to do it. Stifle sin. Help me to put sin to death in my life. Enable me to clear out all the debris to make room for you. There's that hidden chamber, that attic up there with all that junk in it. That cellar down there, that musty, damp, dank cellar. Lord, help me to clear it out. Lord, let's have a removal. Let's have a displenishment. Then you come and decorate the rooms, tidy the place up, make it habitable, and then, you live in it. Every room in my house you may have.' That is what faith says. 'Lord, you are here to do it—then do it.'

To stress sanctification by faith, here are two words from the gospel. The first one is about two blind men who 'followed Jesus'(Matt. 9:27). I like that! I wonder how they were able to follow. Did they hear his footsteps? These two blind men followed Jesus, and cried aloud, 'Have mercy on us, Son of David.' When Jesus went into a house the blind men 'came to him' (I like that too). Jesus said to them, 'Do you believe that I am able to do this?' They said 'Yes, Lord.' Then he touched their eyes, saying, 'According to your faith be it done to you.'

Here is another passage: the father brought his son with the dumb spirit to Jesus, and the spirit in the presence of Jesus went mad within the boy and dashed him down foaming at the mouth. 'Jesus said to the father, "How long has he had this?" "From childhood.... But if *you* can do anything, have pity on us and help us." And Jesus said, "*If* you can!"' Was he quoting him? Was he repeating the man's words? I don't know. There is an exclamation mark in the RSV at that point. Or, was Jesus saying, throwing the ball into his court, 'If *you* can!' 'All things are possible to him who believes.' The father said, 'Oh, my son: I want him healed. I want him cured. Lord, I believe. I am trying desperately to believe. Help my unbelief.' Jesus said, 'That's the way. Stretch it, stretch it, stretch it. If you have got faith as a mustard seed in your heart, let it grow by exercise' (See Mk. 9:14–29).

That is not biology or botany, but it is truth.

All our problems must be related to the fact of Jesus in our life. It is he who fulfils all things in you and in me.

This is what has changed my life. It is not what it should be, but it is a lot better than it used to be, I can tell you. Christ lives in us, by his Spirit. 'Think what Spirit dwells within thee' says the hymn. Then let him work; that is what he is there to do. Let him work. 'But,' you say, 'there are hindrances.' Yes, but he is there to deal with them; that is what he is there for. He has already dealt with them by his death and resurrection and he has given that power to you to deal with them. He does this by saying, 'Here is my faith; use it. It is mine; I give it to you; use it.'

Your watch is broken and you need a new watch. I take mine off and put it in your hand. Use it! Tell the time! So, Christ says, 'My faith—here you are; use it.' So we grow and grow, and love one another more, and love God more, and go out into the world and love this needy, bedraggled, sin-sodden world more and more and more. That is sanctification by faith!

WHAT IT IS TO BE A CHRISTIAN

13. Into Christ's Likeness

Sanctification is dedication to God, being set apart for God for that kind of inner brightness shining out as in our Lord's experience of the Transfiguration. We are exploring how to give ourselves to God and live to his pleasure and to our beatification, so that ultimately the problems of our emotions or our feelings are dealt with. Get your facts right, get your faith right and the problem of emotions and passions will ultimately be solved. But in that order; not faith first, because you can have faith in anything. You can even have faith in something wrong and be led astray. It is fact first, the facts of the gospel truth in God's Holy Word, then faith upon these facts, and lastly our feelings. Sooner or later our emotions will come to heel and fall in line, even if imperfectly, until we are glorified.

If you want to see the first two of these in plain statements look at Revelation 12:10, 11, two of the most wonderful verses in the New Testament. Verse 10 speaks of Christ's once-for-all victory on the cross over the powers of evil. John says, 'I heard a loud voice in heaven saying, "Now the salvation and the power and the kingdom of our God and the authority of his Christ have come (by his death and resurrection), for the accuser of our brethren has been thrown down, who accuses them day and night (notice the present tense) before our God."' That is the fact: Christ has gained a final victory over all evil, over all that would hinder our sanctification and our beatification in glory in God's sight.

Where, then, does faith come into play? The next verse tells us: 'And they (that is believers, actually a company of martyrs) have conquered him (whom? the devil), conquered him (how?) by the blood of their Lamb (that is fact) and by the word of their testimony (*i.e.* to the fact;

that is their faith), for they loved not their lives even unto death (martyrdom).' They witnessed to the fact of Christ's victory even to death and would not let go. They held on to it even to death; that was their faith. So here you have an example of fact and faith working together, the one before the other.

Let me explain a little more what we mean by 'sanctification', because I really hate to use long words and I regret we have to use them. There are far more long words in Christian doctrine than there are in the Bible! I do not like long words. Sanctification is simply giving ourselves to God until we show the brightness of God. A little more explanation: in Jesus Christ through conversion, the new birth, becoming a Christian—any term you choose—we become new creatures. The newness begins with what we call a seed of God planted in the heart as a woman conceives a child, although this miracle is spiritual not physical. We are created in Christ Jesus for good works which God previously prepared that we should walk in them (Eph. 2:10).

John says that 'No one born of God commits sin (that is, practises sin); for God's seed abides in him, and he cannot sin because he is born of God' (1 Jn. 3:9). That does not mean that he never falls away or never makes a mistake. It means that he cannot go on living the old sinful life. He cannot sin as an expression of his true character. If he sins he is sinning against what he really is. He is sinning against himself when he sins. When you are sinning as a Christian, you are being untrue to yourself. You are not being your real self; you are going back to the old life. But if you are really a Christian you cannot go on living the old life because the new is there and it cannot be permanently ignored.

There is nothing in the world that makes a man or a woman so miserable as having Jesus Christ in their heart when they are sinning or want to sin against him. Think of that before you become a Christian. You will be far more unhappy as a sinning Christian, a disobedient Christian, a backsliding Christian than you ever were as a sinner in the world. Think about that. Count the cost! Make sure you are going to go the whole way, on and on with Jesus, here and hereafter; otherwise, if you turn back, there is nothing for you but hell, because you are sinning against great light (Heb. 6:4–6).

Let me take a crude illustration. It would be like a dog being changed into a man and wanting to go back to being a dog. It is incredible, and it cannot be done without hellish misery. Christians sometimes worry about this 'he cannot sin.' If you are worried about that, look at 1 John

2:1: 'My little children, I am writing this to you so that you may not sin. But if anyone does sin...' (I like the way that is put. It recognises that Christians do sin. Our Lord is very, very patient with backsliders. There is no licence to sin there. I like that. But sin is not the basic instinct of those who have been born again. But back to what we were saying.) 'Whosoever is born of God does not sin because the seed of God abides in him.' He can sin and fail but he cannot go on sinning.

The seed of God is in the Christian to grow, and it grows on one food only: the Bible. That is the food of the seed of God that dwells in your breast if you are a believer. But most of it has to be prepared. It is prepared by the Holy Spirit who brings it to you and you to it and also prepares the mind and heart of any intermediary who may be involved, so that the truth flows into you. God does not expect us to take great chunks of the Word and swallow great rocks of truth, but by the Spirit (especially the Spirit of prayer) he breaks the Word down, melts it down until it becomes a fluid that flows into your innermost soul and is absorbed into the very physiology of your spiritual life. That is why there needs to be prayer in the Holy Spirit. It is not merely learning a great lot of Scripture and being able to reel it off and talk about it. It has got to be broken down. It has to be melted and made soluble and absorbable, digestible.

What is the result of that? It produces the image of Christ. Other people, when they look into your face, should see something of Christ's grace and beauty. I could put it like this: one of the results of Jesus Christ being fed and growing up in new baby believers is that they are bonnier to look at. I can think of some whom I used to think (and I have no reason to speak, but never mind that!) were not very bonny, but, oh, when Jesus Christ comes into the heart and they learn how to smile (not to grin with hard, staring eyes, but smile), with their eyes smiling, dancing with fun and joy and peace, what a transformation! If you took photographs before and after you would see the difference. The food of the Word produces the image of Christ.

Here are some scriptural references concerning this.

1 Corinthians 11:7: 'For man...is the image and glory of God.' That is how God originally made him, but he lost the image; at least it was defaced through sin.

Romans 8:29: 'We know that in everything God works for good with those who love him, who are called according to his purpose, for those he foreknew he also predestinated (he predetermined, determined beforehand) to be conformed (to be formed) according to the image of his Son.' That is to become like Jesus Christ.

1 Corinthians 15:49: 'As we have borne the image of the man of dust we shall also bear the image of the man of heaven (the heavenly Man, Jesus Christ).'

2 Corinthians 3:18 is a wonderful verse: 'And we all, with unveiled face (the veiled face is the face that is veiled from the glory of the gospel. The veiled face is the face that sees nothing beyond the Ten Commandments and a system of legalism. It is a legalistic veil, trying to please God by our own efforts). But in Christ we have something better than the Ten Commandments. We have him of whom they speak (and the man is better than his description, surely!) beholding the glory of the Lord (looking at Jesus) are being changed (notice the continuous tense) into his likeness from one degree of glory (radiance, brightness) to another, for this comes,' says the apostle, 'from the Lord', the authoritative One, the Ruler of heaven and earth. We are being changed into his image. The way to get the marks of the sun upon you is to expose yourself to the sun; the same with the other Son. Look at him. Let the rays of his brightness shine until they change you; that is what it is saying.

Colossians 3:9, 10: 'You have put off the old nature with its practices and have put on the new nature which is being renewed in knowledge (spiritual knowledge, not merely head knowledge) according to the image of its creator.' This is Christ creating his own image within us.

The working of sanctification in our lives depends upon two things: one, knowing the potential negative and positive in Christ, and, two, drawing by faith upon it. We have said all this before. We have within us the potential of Christ's death and the potential of Christ's resurrection life. You have these two in one, and if the Spirit of Jesus Christ comes to you, or has come to you and brought you to the birth in him, you have the twofold Spirit of Jesus Christ in your heart. If you have Christ there you have all the potency of his death.

Let me put it like this: Jesus does not come to you direct from heaven. I believe that some of the epiphanies, manifestations of God, in the Old Testament were manifestations of the pre-existing Christ. But if Christ had come to you before he was born in Bethlehem that would have been a pre-incarnate epiphany. There is only one Christ, of course, you cannot have Christ in that way now. He is the same person, but he has been through earthly life. He was born of a woman. He lived a fully human life, then died a human death, and was raised in a supernatural resurrection. Then he ascended to heaven and sent his Spirit to his people. That Holy Spirit was not the Spirit of the Christ before he came to earth, but the Spirit of the Christ in all the virtue of his work.

If I meet someone that I knew twenty-five or thirty years ago he is a different person from the person I knew then because he has been through so much experience of life. We may very quickly get on to the same terms as before. He may not look much older and all that, but he is different. We have had experience in recent years of Christians we have not seen for twenty or twenty-five years and when we are together again, as, for example, one Saturday night when we had the Fiftieth Anniversary of the University Christian Union here, we had some fellows who hadn't been here for years and are now important men in Christian circles, but they were just like the lads they were at eighteen when they were converted here. Meeting them again was wonderful and glorious. But, you see, nonetheless they had gone through the experience of many years and when they got up to speak you could tell. You could tell that they had been through a lot.

The Jesus who comes to you has been through a lot too, and he comes with the ripe harvest of what he has been through. And this is the sum of his harvest: his death for your sin and his life for your new life in Christ. The two belong together in one seed of Christ. Are there not two parts to a seed? There is the bit that rots when you put it into the ground, but it does not all rot and die, or nothing would come up. Out of the midst of what rots germinates the new life. The one seed has two natures if you like. It is like that with the twofold Christ; the power of Christ crucified and risen—the one seed to grow up so that the death and resurrection of Christ both grow up in us. So that we are able to say, 'No', increasingly to sin, and, 'Yes', increasingly to the Spirit of Christ. Jesus died to the one and was raised to the other, but he brings both of them to our lives together. Yet the two, the death and the resurrection, are to work in orderly sequence. Sometimes it is the death and you say to the old within you, 'You're dead. Lie down.' Do you think that is a contradiction? Well, it seems to be, but there is something more here than logic. You say to the old life when Jesus Christ has planted his seed in your heart, 'You're dead, so you had better lie down.' We used to play as children at war games in what was waste ground at the foot of Albury Road where I lived as a boy. We played at wars and soldiers and fighting. And the blighters from Rosebank Place would not lie down when we had shot them! 'Lie down. You're dead.' Well, we must say to the old life, 'Lie down. You're dead.'

But then we turn away from that side to the other, and say, 'Ah, let's live to Christ.' But you see the integrity, the togetherness of the death and resurrection of Jesus Christ, as a seed in your breast.

Notice that Paul emphasises both of these aspects in Romans 6: 'We were buried therefore with him by baptism into death, so that as Christ was raised from the dead by the glory of the Father, we too might walk in newness of life. For if we have been united with him in a death like his, we shall certainly be united with him in a resurrection like his.... But if we have died with Christ, we believe that we shall also live with him.... The death he died he died to sin, once for all, but the life he lives he lives to God. So you also must consider yourselves dead to sin (that is, apply this to your own life) and alive to God in Christ Jesus' (Rom. 6:4, 5, 8, 10, 11).

Listen to what the *Westminster Confession* chapter XIII says about sanctification. This is a marvellous passage and is not too difficult. 'They who are effectually called (called by God's Spirit, not merely by hearing the gospel preached) and regenerated, having a new heart and a new spirit created in them, are farther sanctified really and personally, through the virtue of Christ's death and resurrection, by his Word and Spirit dwelling in them; the dominion of the whole body of sin is destroyed, and the several lusts (evil desires) thereby are more and more weakened and mortified (put to death), and they (who believe) more and more quickened and strengthened in all saving graces, to the practice of true holiness, without which no man shall see the Lord.'

'This sanctification is throughout (it is total) in the whole man, yet imperfect (incomplete; it is progressive: it goes on more and more) in this life; there abideth (notice) still (in the heart of the believer) some remnants of corruption in every part.' Strictly speaking we should not speak of Christians as having two natures, an old and a new, because we cannot have two natures in that sense at one and the same time any more than we can be an old Adam and a new Adam at the same time. But what we have is the remnants of the old nature (that is the better way to put it), the remnants of corruption in very part, 'whence ariseth (I love this) a continual and irreconcileable war (a war going on between the new man that you have become and the remnants of the old, with the devil holding on to the remnants of the old and saying, "Go on, make him sin. Go on, make him sin"); the flesh lusting against the Spirit, and the Spirit (lusting) against the flesh.'

'In which war (follow closely, and take this in) although the remaining corruption for a time may much prevail...'. Let me break off here. This is why we have got to be so patient with one another. I had an alcoholic at my door. He had been in a psychiatric hospital. I said to him, 'My dear man you know that alcoholism is one of the worst, if not the worst thing to deal with in the psychiatric realm.' 'Yes,' he said, 'I know that.' 'Well,' I said, 'if it is so hard, there is only one thing that will really transform your life and that is the grace of God.' 'Yes,' he said, 'I know that too.' 'Aye,' I said, 'but the point is whether you are willing to let the grace of God do it.'

This is why we have to be so patient with one another because someone with that particular trial and temptation may go back to it and back to it for years. We need to help some people for years maybe—especially in prayer—so that the remaining corruption, though it may prevail much for a time, 'yet, through the continual supply of strength from the sanctifying Spirit of Christ, the regenerate part doth overcome.' Is that a word of comfort? Are you being dragged down by your sinful evil nature? If Jesus Christ is in your heart he will get the better of the devil and his malicious influence in your heart. 'Jesus is stronger than Satan or sin.' Believe it, because it is true, and many have experienced it. 'And so the saints grow in grace (they do not jump into it either in one or two jumps, as some people think, but they *grow* in grace), perfecting holiness (completing holiness) in the fear of God.' What a chapter that is! It is absolutely wonderful and 'bang on' the Word of God.

Well then, talking about progress in this war against the remnants of corruption remaining in our lives, the way to it is to stand upon the Word of God, like those martyrs in Revelation 12:10. Christ had gained the victory over all the powers of evil and these saints said to the devil: 'Jesus has got the better of you. You can kill us if you like; but we will not yield to you.' That is what Jesus himself said on the cross. 'You can kill me if you like—and I'm sure you like. You can kill me, but you cannot shake me. I will not succumb to you any more than I did in my temptations. I would rather die than sin and give myself into your hands and be a slave to you.' So Jesus stood, and these saints similarly rested upon the verities of the truth and particularly upon the fact of the finality of the work of Christ. We have to stand upon the fact, not only that Christ did certain things, but that he did them once-for-all so that they do not need to be done again. The Letter to the Hebrews is full of that. What Christ has done he has done 'once-and-for-all'. It is never to be done again: it is final.

Look at three of these finalities. We have to stand upon the fact that Christ has finished his work. It is complete. It does not need to be done again. The first thing that is complete is his death to our sin. Look again at Romans 6:7: 'For he who has died has been justified from sin.' And verse 9, 'For we know that Christ being raised from the dead will never die again. Death no longer has dominion over him.' He will never die again. Lazarus died again after he was raised from the dead because Christ raised him a mortal body. But Christ himself was raised an immortal body that will never die again. His death to our sin is final. Romans 6:10: 'The death he died, he died to sin, once and for all.' That is the first thing; we have to stand upon the finality of Christ's death to our sin.

Secondly, stand upon the finality of his life with God; Christ is alive to God in a resurrection human body and will be forever. Romans 6:4b: 'As Christ was raised from the dead by the glory of the Father, we too might walk in newness of life.' Verse 8, 'We believe that we shall also live with him (because he is alive for ever more).' Verse 10b, 'But the life he lives he lives to God.' It does not need to say forever, because God is forever. Remember the words of Handel's Hallelujah Chorus, taken from Revelation 11:15, 'The kingdom of the world has become the kingdom of our Lord and of his Christ, and he shall reign for ever and ever.' Christ is alive as a man, possessing an immortal, indestructible human body in heaven for ever and ever. It is final. His death to our sin is final and his life is forever.

Thirdly, our death and life with him, these are final too. Read once more Romans 6:5–11 and see how it applies to us. 'If we have been united to Christ in a death like his, we shall certainly be united with him in a resurrection like his.... For he who has died has been justified from sin. But if we have died with Christ, we believe that we shall also live with him. For we know that Christ being raised from the dead will never die again; death no longer has dominion over him. The death he died he died to sin, once for all, but the life he lives he lives to God. So you also must consider yourselves dead to sin (because there is a new life in you, the seed of God. You are a new creature. Jesus Christ is in you and has given you a new nature. It is only the remnants of the former nature that remain) and alive to God in Jesus Christ.'

There is an interesting insight into this in Romans 7:17, 20. I was saying that we mustn't talk about two equal natures, the old and the new. You either belong to the first Adam who fell, or you belong to the last Adam, Christ who never fell and has given you his nature. If we belong to Christ all that remains is the remnants of the corruption of the old nature: that is made quite plain in Romans 7:17. So (says Paul) with regard to my temptations and with regard to my falling into sin (and even Paul fell into sin at certain points) it is no longer I that do it, but sin which dwells within me. I am a Christian. I side with Christ. I belong to him. I am a new creation. I cannot sin (*cf.* 1 Jn. 3:9), but sin within me drags me down and makes me untrue to my true nature. But the two things are not equal. Whatever you call the evil bit, the sinful bit in you, if you have Jesus Christ in your heart then that old part is not as strong as the new. The remnants of corruption, of sin in your life, cannot be as strong as Christ in your life. Now, you may often have thought it *was* stronger and have excused yourself and said, 'Lord, I can't be good. I can't do it; it is too much for me.' Well, it may be too much for you but it is not too much for Christ, and he is in your heart!

But what is he there to do? To watch you going down into corruption, yielding to temptation over and over again? Never! He is there to give you victory over sin. Look at what Paul says in Romans 7:20: 'Now, if I do what I do not want, it is no longer I that do it, but sin which dwells within me.' We must be careful here because some people when they have sinned say, 'I didn't do that, it was my sinful nature.' But, you cannot say that, because you are responsible for going on in sin. What the verse is saying is that you are being untrue to your own true nature.

Now gather that together in the two verses we mentioned before about putting off the old nature and putting on the new: Ephesians 4:22, 23 and Colossians 3:9, 10. The words in both places for putting off and putting on are in the aorist, that is the once-for-all tense. 'Put off' and 'put on'—once and for all. We belong to Jesus Christ and have put him on. But we have a polarity or tension between the fact that the act is done, once and for all, yet we have to keep reminding ourselves that it is done. If we are going to grow in grace as the *Confession* says, we have to live out the implications of our putting off and on.

What we are really doing here is acting on the finality of Christ's work on the cross and in ourselves. We are saying, 'I am a Christian. I do not belong to the old Adam. I do not belong to you. I will not live your life. I belong to this new life.' In Luke 6 Jesus describes two sorts of men in the world, under the illustration of good and bad trees. He goes on to speak about grapes and thorns. Notice, he does not begin to speak about good grapes and bad grapes. He speaks about good trees and bad trees; the good trees are vines and they produce fruit; thorns and thistles do not. So, he says, there are two kinds of men in the world, like the grapes and the thistles, the figs and the thorns, the olives and the weeds. Put it another way, as Paul says in 1 Corinthians 3. What is the product of your life going to be? If you are a Christian and you give yourself to Christ to live his life in you, it is a matter of producing for eternity, gold, silver, precious stones; the alternative is wood, hay, stubble. Gold, silver, and precious stones can stand the fire of God's love. Wood and hay and stubble burn up.

So sanctification leads to producing Christian character, the image of Christ, so that people, when they see you and meet you and get to know you, say, 'There's something special about that fellow. There's something special about that girl.'

We had a young man with us from abroad who later sent me a long letter. I was deeply impressed by him because of his insight into spiritual truth, and his wholesome, single-minded devotion to Jesus Christ. I saw Jesus Christ in him in a new way, and it was beautiful. It was manly. There was nothing soft, sentimental; nothing hard either! Very controlled, very dignified, very balanced, but suffused by the beauty of Christ. That is what it is all about. That is sanctification and it is beautiful. God makes us beautiful like that!

WHAT IT IS TO BE A CHRISTIAN

14. The Spirit Within

We have already begun to speak about the finality of the work of Christ for us. Let me explain what I mean by that: Christ's work on the cross was a final work; it does not need to be repeated. It is once-for-all (*hapax*). It is everlastingly, eternally efficacious, and is done forever. There is a sense in which it was done before the world began. John in the Book of the Revelation speaks about the 'Lamb slain from before the foundation of the world' (Rev. 13:8). It is true, because everything that happens in history has, in a sense, happened completely in God's mind and purpose. It was all complete.

How could that be? Simply because God was so sure that he could do it all. Anything that he thought, 'I will do,' he was sure would be done perfectly. He had everything in his hands because he made all things, and was in perfect control of everything, even evil. So what was determined in eternity in God's heart and mind in the fulness of time was done in a little middle-eastern country, Palestine, about the size of Wales, much smaller than Scotland. In time, in a certain year, in a certain place, Jesus was done to death, and had to be raised by the Father on the third day. Death and resurrection are a double event, the resurrection following inevitably from the death, as we have seen. No one could stop the Father from raising his Son on the third day, because Jesus had not sinned. He bore *our* sin, but he had no sin of his own and so death, Satan and evil could not keep him in the grave. Nothing in the world could have kept the sinless one in the grave! He died for the sins of others. So, 'Up from the grave he arose, with a mighty triumph o'er his foes'! What was done in the mind and heart of God in eternity was accomplished in history so that people saw it and testified that they had seen it, because he came and spoke to them and showed them the wounds in his hands, even although he had that new, immortal, indestructible body. So, what he has done is final.

That is what Paul was talking about in the sixth chapter of Romans, when he says that Jesus will never die again. 'Death has no longer dominion over him. The death he died, he died to sin once and for all'. Now he has an indestructible human body. We know it was *the same body* because he said to Thomas, 'Come and look at the wounds in my hands.' And we know it was a *human body* because he ate broiled fish; so Scripture says. It was a human body, but now indestructible. He has got it in heaven now, and will come back in it in glory one day! What he did was final.

Then, we have also emphasised that what he did he did for us. God did not need to send his Son to earth to have him hurt so. Why was it that he subjected his Son to such cruelty? It was for us. He did not even need to come to prove his loyalty or his obedience to the Father. The Father knew that his Son was perfectly submissive to him and loved him with utter obedience. The harmony in heaven was already perfect. All he did was for us, every bit of it. And if Jesus did anything on the cross it is all for you, in order to give you Christ's finality, as his eternal life in your soul. The whole of Christian faith begins, as far as we are concerned, with finality. It begins from completion, from what is finished. Christ gained the victory completely nearly two thousand years ago and comes and says, 'Here, have this that I have completed so long ago.' So he gives us the power, the effects, the harvest of his finished work.

I believe with all my heart that when God first comes to souls to make them his own by the Spirit of Jesus Christ, he gives them potentially all that he has. After all, the Holy Spirit is a person, and you cannot have him in portions any more than we can have you in portions! If you were taken to bits then you would no longer be a person. So you cannot receive the Holy Spirit in bits and pieces. You dare not think of him as quantitative, much or little. And this is important, because all the words that symbolise the Holy Spirit in the Scriptures, as far as I remember, are words that can be thought of quantitatively, such as breath, wind, oil, water, fire. These are inanimate things, and impersonal words. But the Holy Spirit is not an 'it'. He is not neuter. Even though the word 'breath' in Greek (*pneuma*) is neuter, the Holy Spirit himself is not neuter. He is a person. He is the third person of the Trinity, equal with God the Father and God the Son.

When God comes to a soul to quicken it into life, he gives his Holy

Spirit in the entirety of his person. I do not deny that he may add gifts of the Spirit. But then, where can the gifts of the Spirit come from but from the Spirit himself? In one sense even the gifts of the Spirit are present potentially when he first comes to us.

I have found over many years now that when people realise the Spirit is a person who cannot be divided into bits and pieces, it almost at once gives them a new stability as a Christian. They no longer claw, scrape, stretch or search for something more from outwith them. God has given us all he has in potential. It is ours to realise what we have; that is the important thing.

Once Christ has come to you the rest of your life is a matter of finding out from the Scriptures what you have. We have to know what we have, or better whom we have in all his potential power with all his gifts. He does not give them all to any individual. No one has a monopoly of them all, they are distributed among the saints. The only one who has a monopoly of the gifts of the Spirit for all kinds of service, is Jesus himself. He distributes the gifts but he does not distribute the Holy Spirit. He gives him as a person, in his entirety, to each one.

Now, it is the same Holy Spirit who is in every believer. How can the same person be in you and in me? Puzzle that out! What does that make us? It makes us one. This is so tremendous it takes my breath away. I cannot find words to express it. We speak of him as 'nearer than hands or feet,' and 'closer than breathing' and all that kind of thing, but even these are too weak and poor to express the truth that we are members of the same body. If I am the left hand, you are the right. Or if I am the left arm, you are the right—one body, in one organism; no mere organisation. Away with the church as a business; especially as a money-making business! God has plenty money and will give his people plenty without turning Christ's church into a business to make it. We have *him*. He is there. By the Spirit we have received the finality, the fulness, the completeness of Christ's work by his death and resurrection in our lives to work it out as a process. That is the great thing.

Paul gives us guidance for the practical application of this in Philippians 2:12, 13. 'Therefore, my beloved, as you have always obeyed (have they, Paul? They must have been wonderful Christians in Philippi. And of course they were!), so now, not only as in my presence but much more in my absence, work out your own salvation with fear and trembling; for God is at work in you, both to will and to work for his good pleasure.' Work out, for God has wrought in. Both these words, 'work out' and 'work in', are in the present tense. 'Work out' is a present imperative, a command: 'work out your own salvation with fear and trembling.' Go on working out your own salvation in fear and trembling, for God is at work in you (present participle). Work out, keep on working out your own salvation with fear and trembling for it is God who is continuously at work in you. That's it!

We have to work out in a process what God has given definitively and decisively and, by his active, living Spirit, is continuously working in us. It is a working 'engine', if I can reverently use a term that we understand. Scripture uses inanimate illustrations for the Spirit, so perhaps we may for once. You have the whole thing, every part. It is all there. So God says, 'Go on, you have a working engine.' Use it, work out what he has given and is working in.

Now we have to weigh two things here in the gift of God's grace: the once-for-allness of it and the continuousness of it. It is all given to us in conversion but we have to work it out as God is working it in. It may help clarify this if we go over some references and indicate the once-for-all and the continuous tenses in the Greek text.

Ephesians 4:22, 23: 'Put off (once-for-all) the old (because of course Christ did that. He slew the old Adam on the cross. He did not merely bind him or wound him and say, 'Now, you can't do any harm for a bit.' He said, 'You can't do any harm anymore because you are dead.' He slew him, and so if God has given us the gift of Christ's death to the sinful nature, then he says, 'Throw it away; it is dead. Put it off—the idea is that of taking off old clothes), and then put on the new.' Christ has given you that too; he has given you his life to God, resurrection life forever. So accept them both. 'Put off' and 'put on'.

Now you have the same thing in Colossians 3:9, 10. 'Put off' and 'put on'. Both again are in the once-for-all tense. 'Put off', once-for-all, and 'put on', once-for-all, because Christ has done it for you. It is complete. Back pedal for a moment here, because we have the same thing in Colossians 3:5: 'Put to death therefore what is earthly in you ('earthly' is a bad translation; it is nonsense, because if you put to death what is earthly in you, you would put to death your human nature, and that is not what it means). Put to death what is carnal in you (what belongs to the fallen nature): immorality, impurity, passion, evil desire, and covetousness which is idolatry.'

Let us stop here now and apply what this means. You have a desire to be impure in your actions, or you see a way of gaining an advantage over someone, or maybe gaining a bit of money by being dishonest, but Somebody knocks inside and says, 'Here, I'm here. You can't do that with me here.' And you say, 'Oh sorry, I forgot.' Yes we can forget! Christ could not do that. He did not do that when he was down here and he will not do it in me. God cannot do it either because he has joined himself with me. If I do it, it will be like making him do it too—and that is fearful. It is intolerable. Notice what I am saying; I am not saying, 'I must try harder not to sin, not to be so harsh with my tongue, not to be dishonest, to fly off the handle and do all sorts of things.' We are not saying, 'I must try harder.' We are saying, 'Remember who is inside you and who you are,' and say, 'Are you going to drag Christ into that? You cannot do it because you are not that kind of person. Christ does not do that!' Now, that is very different, surely? Do you realise how different it is? And it works. It is bound to work, not because I say so, but because it is God's truth.

How many times does Satan tempt you in a day?—a thousand? Or am I worse than you? That pestiferous creature keeps coming back and you have constantly to keep him from your door.

We have 'to put sin to death.' 'Put off' in Ephesians 4:22, Colossians 3:9 and Colossians 3:5 are in the 'once-for-all' tense, but the intriguing thing is that 'put to death the deeds of the body' in Romans 8:13 is in the present indicative. The idea is continuous: 'keep putting to death.' Christ has given the power of his death to your sin, but you have got to use it, and you have to remind yourself and particularly remind your tempter that you are dead to that. It is in this sense that Paul says 'Keep putting to death,' meaning, 'Keep telling yourself that that is dead, that Christ has brought you into death as far as that is concerned'. So, you say to the tempter who stirs up all your sinful and evil desires, 'That old horrid Adam that you led astray in the Garden is dead. Christ has given me his death. I have got his death certificate. He is a dead man; he must lie down. He is out of the battle.' That is what we have to do. But we have to keep on doing it because the old devil will not be vanquished in our lives by only one telling. He needs lots and lots of tellings. Up he comes again and we have to deal with him again and again.

That is the negative side of it, dealing with the sin. But we are not to live all the time thinking about sins. I have come to believe that if we are too preoccupied with sin, in a sense we are drawing the enemy. We must not become so obsessed with lamenting about our sins and how bad we are in God's sight that we never get round to anything positive.

That would be terrible. What hope is there looking at a sewer? No, we must go on to the positive. After all, the positive so often deals with the negative. Any mother with sense knows how to deal with the infant when it rummages in the coal scuttle (if there are coal scuttles nowadays!). 'Keep away from that dear; that's dangerous. You mustn't touch that.' Distract his attention, yes; but you must also give him something else to play with. There must be positive action. I know that in the home it does not always work, because children can be perverse little monkeys! But nonetheless the principle is fundamental, as Paul shows in Ephesians 4:23, 24, when he describes God's continuous work within us: 'and be renewed (present infinitive passive, God doing something in us) in the spirit of your minds, and put on the new nature, created (aorist passive participle; it is once-for-all) after the likeness of God in true righteousness and holiness.'

Paul makes the same point in Colossians 3:9, 10: 'Do not lie to one another, seeing that you have put off the old nature with its practices and have put on the new nature, which is being renewed (continuous tense) in knowledge (spiritual knowledge) after the image of its creator (who is God, and Christ).' So, there is the once-for-all gift of God in our hearts, and there is our continuous drawing upon its resources to put to death, to 'put off' and 'put on'. There must always be the *once-for-all* putting on the new nature, and the *continuous* being renewed in knowledge after the image of the creator. You have therefore both tenses in the tenth verse, the once-for-all and the continuous, the final and the ongoing.

But what is this that Christ has put in our hearts? Or how are we to think of the Holy Spirit of Jesus Christ in us? Remember 1 John 3:9! The seed (*sperma*) of God in Christ dwells in us, by the Spirit. Now, when a seed is planted and is nourished and the soil is not absolutely devoid of moisture, the seed grows. The moisture releases the chemical energies in the soil to nourish the seed; the outer part of the seed rots and releases the energy of the vital principle in the seed. Then, nourished by these chemical substances in the soil it grows. In the same way, the seed of God grows by feeding.

Here is an entirely different figure. Look once more at 2 Corinthians 3:18, and remember what I am saying, that the seed of God which is of Christ by his death and resurrection grows with feeding. But there is only one food for this seed. The only kind of nourishment that the life of God in your soul can stand is godly food, spiritual food, and that is to be found in only one place—the Bible.

Do you see how continuous and progressive the Christian life of sanctification, growing like Jesus, is? I have characterised it in terms of a seed growing within our life. Look at it another way. See the effect of the natural sun, when people expose themselves to it—they are changed by it. So it is when we are affected by the Sun of Righteousness! 'And we all with unveiled face (the veil is the Mosaic law which says, Look, the only way to get to God and to please God is by fulfilling these Ten Commandments. But we take the veil away when we see that is not the way to get to heaven. You will never get to God in heaven by trying to please him in your own strength. Take that veil away and look at Jesus! Expose yourself to Jesus by his Word), beholding the glory of the Lord, are being changed (continuous process—as long as you look, as long as you expose yourself to him) into his likeness from one degree of glory to another.' The sunburn analogy breaks down, of course; every analogy does. But never mind! 'We are being changed into his likeness from one degree of glory to another,' until we are perfectly like him and we become like miniature Christs, and he takes us to be with himself. 'For this comes from the Lord who is the Spirit,' working in our hearts.

Now think again about the seed of God in the soul of man. What is that seed? It is the Holy Spirit of Jesus Christ. But is there an abstract word that covers it? What word is there that covers, embraces, includes the Spirit of Jesus Christ dwelling in your heart? What is the word that fully sums up God's nature? What is God? God is love. LOVE. Now, there are many loves, but this is love of its own category and the Spirit of Jesus Christ in your heart is the God of love, and the seed that is in your heart is the seed of God's own love.

Paul connects all this together in Romans 5:5: 'God's love has been poured out (and I include the 'out' because it is in the original) from him into our hearts through the Holy Spirit who has been given to us.' Who is meant by 'us'? Believers, of course. Again writing to the Galatians, Paul says that the harvest of the Spirit, what the Spirit is in your heart to do, is to make you love God and Jesus, and your fellows, even.

I want to stress this. This is the test of the life of Christ growing in your soul and of the continuous work of the Spirit of God going on with your active co-operation. God who once-for-all sent his Son to die and be raised from the dead, and gave him to dwell in your heart in a process of life, is seeking to work love into you: love for God and his Son, love for fellow Christians who are bound together with you in the bundle of life, members of the same body of Christ, and love for this wicked world. But not love for the devil. Why not love for the devil? If God gives you love, he also gives you the opposite. You cannot have white without black. How in the world could you know what black was unless you knew white? The same is true here: you cannot love without hating the opposite of what you love. You learn to hate the devil. He cannot be saved; he has gone too far. You are to hate him, but you are not to hate men. We have to learn love in our hearts until we love our enemies. This is the way to change them, if they can and will be changed.

This is what Jesus did to Judas. Judas went to the chief priests and said, 'I'll get Jesus for you. Do you want to destroy this Jesus? I'm one of his followers you know (was he?); I'll get him for you if you give me thirty pieces of silver.' He got his thirty pieces of silver and he led them to Jesus and when he came, the wicked man kissed Jesus in the eastern manner and called him 'Master.' But Jesus, who knew what he was going to do, still called him, 'Friend.' He called him, 'Comrade,' 'Fellow'.

Was Jesus being a hypocrite in calling him a friend when he knew he was his foe? No, he was trying to win him. He was saying, 'Judas, I still want you to be my friend. I still want to be your friend. Oh, will you not change? You have brought these soldiers to arrest me and kill me, but will you not change? Will you not repent? We have been together for three years, and I have been trying to soften your heart. Change, Judas, this is your last chance! I gave you another chance in the upper room and you ran out on us because you were ashamed, for you had wicked work to do. In fact, I sent you out of the room and told you to do it because it had to be done. Yet, even though I sent you out of the room because it had to be done, even now Judas, I am appealing to you, will you not change?'

That is how *you* have to regard wicked men and women. It is not that you are not to be angry, incensed and shocked by what some people do. Oh yes, that's all right, but press it back to the devil. Hate him and say, 'You brute for doing that to men. You brute for enslaving men and making them do such wicked things.' And you pray, 'Lord, you could save these wicked people. You could send a Christian to witness to them; you could bring them to Jesus.'

Love your enemies! But, before you can do that, you have to feed this seed an awful lot with an awful lot of truth. It has to grow to a great big plant and flower and bear fruit before you will be able to love people who would seek to hurt you. I reckon that with most of us it will take time, so we had better begin by feeding our souls. We are to feed love with love, not love with prejudice to discolour, weaken and spoil it. Let us feed the life of God in our souls with the finest of the wheat!

We really need to look at 1 Corinthians 12–14 here, and at Romans 12 and Ephesians 4 which all deal with that, the gifts of the Spirit working for Christ. But these can be studied privately. But notice this: every list of the gifts of the Spirit given us to serve Christ ends in an ascending scale rising to love. At the end of 1 Corinthians 12 and the beginning of 13, Paul says, 'You must aim for higher gifts, but' he says, 'I'll tell you a better way, go higher still to love.' I believe there is a sense in which Paul is saying in the 'love chapter' that the way to serve Christ is not to think so much about what gifts of the Spirit have been distributed to you; the way to serve Christ is to learn to love more and more. Then you will serve without knowing it. You will not even know that you are *serving* him. And unconscious service like unconscious influence is best of all, for self-consciousness is bad here. You will be serving Christ, showing forth his fragrance, his winsomeness, his warmth, his grace, but you will not know it because you are just living Christ's life and his love is blossoming in your heart and glowing in your face. That is the way to serve him!

You say, 'How am I to serve the Lord? Am I going here? Am I going abroad as a missionary? Am I going to be a minister? Am I going to be a Christian doctor, lawyer, nurse, teacher, or whatever?' In one sense, it does not matter what sphere God has in mind for you. You could be a lawyer, doctor, teacher, or joiner, or whatever in the world you think you are fitted to be, a minister, or a missionary, but if you lack love, you had better stop because you are nothing. You are nothing without love. It is the only thing that counts, so let us get it. Let us get love—not soppy sentiment, mushy and sickly, but love that cares, that is strong, vital, manly and womanly. The love of Christ; that is what we need. That is the way, if you want to serve him.

This is it. Grow in grace means grow in love. Feed your soul with the truth, until you begin to love your enemies. And in the world outside people will soon know that there is a Christian, a Christ-one in their midst. It will tell, even when you do not know that it is telling. So, know the Spirit of Christ in you. And if you do not pull down the blinds and hide him from view, the Spirit of Christ will shine through your eyes and in the quality of your voice, in the way you walk, in the way you approach a person, the way you say, 'Good morning' tomorrow at work. That can minister Christ to somebody. They will see him. Believe it. I believe it.

Have you learned to live in this confidence? Are you able to say: 'Christ lives in me. What is he going to do today?' I do not *think* that, because *to think it* is self-conscious and would make me awkward and embarrassed and make me try to be pious. God save us from that! But I believe that Christ is seen and known in that way. It may be only in talking about the weather or in talking about their family, or maybe something very much more serious. Christ is a person. Christ is not sets of gospel words. He is in all that, of course, but he is a person and you can minister Christ to people by the way you say, 'Hello.' Did you know that? It is true. Of course it is true. It is also great fun! I for one am glad that we are not called forever to be going around merely intoning Scripture.

> O Jesus, King most wonderful,
> Thou Conqueror renowned,
> Thou Sweetness most ineffable,
> (O Bernard of Clairvaux, where did you get these words?)
> In whom all joys are found!

WHAT IT IS TO BE A CHRISTIAN

15. Recognising the Enemy

It would be very natural to think that, having studied the themes of justification and sanctification, we now need to think of glorification. But to do so at this juncture would be to leave out an absolutely critical area of what it means to be a Christian.

This is it: if Christ within us is greater than Adam who was within us, and if Christ is therefore much greater than the dregs of Adam remaining in us while we are in our mortal bodies, then why is it that these dregs of sin can be so powerful against Christ within us? A good question. If I can help to answer it I will have done you a signal service. I certainly mean to try.

This is an area of biblical teaching and pastoral need which even convention movements and literature about the deepening of spiritual life scarcely touch at all, even although more people are becoming aware that there is a devil and a kingdom of evil in the world that lies behind the wickedness of men. People today are so wicked you can scarcely credit it. It is almost beyond belief what happens today in so-called civilised lands that have had Christianity for hundreds of years. There is something—or rather someone—lying behind it, who is the author of sin himself.

Christians must speak about sin. But even sin must be set in its proper biblical context. For it is possible for even fine evangelical preachers to talk so exclusively about sin that all they accomplish in their hearers is a tremendous sense of guilt which weighs them down, depresses them, and tends to drive them further into the mire of sin. I do not like to talk too much about sin as such, except as a backcloth to Christ. It is Christ I want to talk about, for he is marvellous and the other fellow is horrid.

But we must not forget him; that is the point. And this is the next critical factor in the life of sanctification. In the life that pleases God you must reckon with the author of sin, as the Bible does from the beginning. Adam and Eve fell through the agency of the devil. The adversary who hates Christ is only trying to hurt man in order to hurt Christ. He does not care about man. There is only one thing the devil is caring about: that is to hurt Christ, indeed to destroy him if he could (*cf.* Gen. 3:15).

All through the Scriptures we are aware that beyond the wickedness of men lies a whole kingdom of evil. Christians, as individuals and as a church, local, national or international, forget it and him at their peril.

Sin in us is the mere remnants of the corruption of the old nature which is displaced by Christ. But (and this is one of the most important things I have to say. Miss this and you may get lost) these remnants of corruption within us, although they are far and away weaker than the power of the eternal Christ within us, yet they are open to the devil himself. He is able to stir up those remnants of sin, and so he sometimes makes us seem worse than we were before we were Christians. Do you sometimes think you are worse than you were before you were a Christian and find that temptations sometimes come that never came before you were a Christian? Are you led to conclude that they come from the depths of evil in your own heart? I tell you, the devil is a deceiver all right!

So we need to set forth this message of Christ's salvation as it applies to individuals and to the church in three dimensions since Christ came to deal with evil in three dimensions. He came to deal with the sins that we have committed. Then he came to slay the root principle in us of these evil deeds. First the deeds then the principle, the seed, the root of inbred sin which is the cause of them. Then, thirdly, he came to deal with him who sowed the evil seed in the heart of man, the devil.

We are therefore talking about: sins (deeds), sin (a fallen nature, a principle, a power), and Satan. You can put it like this: Fruit, Root and Brute. Many Christians know a lot about the first two. They know that Jesus died to take away the fruit of our sinful nature, all our deeds of sin; they also know that Jesus died to slay the old Adam. They know too, of course, that Christ died to gain final victory over Satan and snatch the whole universe out of his hands so that he, the God-Man, is now in control of the universe. But they do not apply the third of this trilogy to their own lives.

What is it that we need to know about Satan that will help us foil his attempts to spoil us as Christians? We need to know that although Christ has blotted out all our sins and has given us a new nature which is dead to sin and alive to God, Satan and the demonic powers still have access to the flesh, to the remnants of corruption within us. The devil loves to poke in these and stir them up and make us seem worse than we are and even than we were before, so that we see ourselves as a disappointment to Jesus. Satan laughs when he hears us say, 'Ugh, I've done it again. I'm hopeless. I'm a hopeless Christian.' He says, 'Hurrah, won't Jesus be mad!' That is exactly what he wants. Oh how he hates! If we only realised how much the devil hates Jesus Christ, that would solve all our problems. You would not need me to teach you all this! You would soon see it all, and apply it all, which is much more important.

Satan and the demonic powers have access to the remnants of corruption within us and he does three things. Note carefully what they are: he stirs up sin within us when we try to mortify it. We encourage ourselves by saying, 'Stop, stop, you can't do that, you're a Christian; that's against your nature. If you have Jesus Christ in your heart, you mustn't do that.' But you see, Satan stirs up the rebellion within us which says, 'Yes, I will. Yes I will.' And all the time we are saying to ourselves, 'I'm getting worse, I'm getting worse.' But that is not the truth. It is he who is getting hotter within us.

It is nothing less than tragic that Christians will not see this. I have given my strength throughout most of my ministry to help Christians to see this. Some will not see it; some who do see it, will not teach it, some who see it will not practise it. Do you know why? It is because Satan is a master deceiver and he encourages them to forget that this is the truth which liberates personality and makes people real Christians. He is behind the whole thing. He blinds us and refuses to let us see the light that would stream into our souls and give us health and peace, and would send us out to serve Christ. He pulls down the blinds. He says, 'Don't see that, don't practise that, don't preach that; it is embarrassing, all that spooky talk. Don't talk about devils, that is old fashioned.' It is not! It is the most modern thing of all. The British Isles are teeming with demons, absolutely! We are surrounded by false gods, demons, fallen angels, evil powers, 'nice' ones and 'nasty' ones. The 'nice' ones lead people away from Jesus Christ to what they call innocent pleasures. I was talking about sport. Have you ever noticed how incensed people become when you suggest that sport has become a god? Yet multitudes of people worship sports and sportsmen. I am not against sport, but watching sport is not sport! Play your football, play your games and

enjoy them to the full. But this is another thing. This is a religion. The
Olympics have become a substitute religion. Haven't you noticed the
sacred flame and the hymns and the marching? It is a religion and the
only reason people fail to see it as such is because they have been
glamourised and deceived. Footballers are gods to little boys—gods.
And if they saw one in the street—or if he came to their club! Even if
God came down from heaven it wouldn't be nearly so thrilling. I am no
spoil-sport. No one who knows me could think that, but I am deadly
serious about this.

By all means love your sport and be keen on it. But be keener on
Jesus Christ. That is the test. Everyone now knows the story about Eric
Liddell, the great runner. The final heat in the Olympics for the race they
said he would certainly win was to be held on a Sunday. Liddell was a
Christian and he said, 'No, no. Not on a Sunday to please all the
Olympics in the world.' And he refused. Then on a week day he ran in a
race in which they said he had far less chance of winning, and won it. I
have no doubt that God made that fellow win it to honour him! He later
became a missionary in the Far East and died in a Japanese prisoner-of-
war camp—guts, you see, stamina, proud of Jesus. 'No,' he said to the
Olympics, 'away with them. Jesus Christ is first to me.'

But, to return to our central theme: the first thing that Satan does is to
stir up sin within us, but then—this is the wicked thing—he turns and
accuses us of it. He stirs up the remnants of sin in us. Young Christians
frequently come and speak to me of a new force or power of temptation
in their lives: it gets harder to be good. Thus Satan tempts them to sin
and backslide. And as soon as they are down he whips round and says,
'Oh, look what you've done.' He becomes the preacher. The devil
becomes the holy one and stands over us dressed as it were in the high
priest's garment and looks down his nose and says, 'You horrid
creature; look what you've done,' when we should turn upon him and
say, 'Not what *I've* done; what *you've* done. That's what you started!'
He is the accuser of Christians. First he trips us up, then he says, 'Look
what you've done.'

Thirdly, he will even accuse us falsely where there has been no
conscious sin. He will go on to that. He will make us more and more
aware of sin. Some Christians lives are all taken up with sin. They can
scarcely draw a breath, but they are saying,—'I've sinned. I've sinned.
Have I sinned?' They do not know that Satan has got them on the run. I
have known people accused in this way get so depressed with
accusations that they are not able to come to church. They listen all the

time to Satan's accusations and say, 'It must be God who is telling me I am so bad.' But it is the devil. Of course we are bad, but Jesus is our Saviour, not our accuser (Rom. 8:33, 34). He says, 'Yes, you're bad, but come away into my arms and I'll sort that.'

Satan accuses of sins we have done that have been blotted out by the blood of Jesus, as well as accusing us of sins we have never done. Indeed he is so subtle that he can convince people they have sinned when they have not. Have you any idea of the deceptive power of Satan in the human mind? Or how he discolours and changes and works on our emotions? No? He is like a master actor. And all for ill, too.

The Christian life is, therefore, a tremendous battle, for we not only have to keep sin in check; we have to keep the rotten foe himself away from our sinful tendencies. We have to keep him out of the house because he loves to go down and stir up all the garbage and make a mess. He slips in, so easily, and hides himself, lurking in the corners and shadows of our life, hiding himself in the folds of our sinful selves.

Thus when we sin it becomes harder to be good. We are dragged down this way, and led away that way, and we say, 'I'm getting worse.' But what we need is a spiritual doctor to say, 'You are not getting worse, but there is someone under the garment of your flesh. Pull away the veil and see. You've got a bug. You've got a germ. There's someone working in your life.' But, instead, we blame ourselves and beat our breasts. This is what becomes of young Christians if they are not very, very careful to receive the full teaching of God's Word.

Sometimes, in wrongly responding to the discovery of this inner conflict, young Christians retreat into Pharisaism and become hopeless prigs. We heard of a church in a certain country which had become nominally Christian. As it became more nominal, people became more rigid in their traditions and their rules, about dress, about what Christians must wear and what they must do, all the rigid little rules, although many of them were not yet converted. This is a work of Satan to lead people into what is virtually a substitute for Christianity— legalism, whether it is Jewish or Gentile legalism. And people become so taken up with the rules, because they are afraid that they sin. But you see, when we walk happily down the road arm in arm with Jesus, we do not think about sin. Jesus is such a good companion and we are wholly taken up with him and with things that interest him—and there are so many! He tells us such interesting things in his Word and shows us such interesting things about nature. He is such marvellous company and such wonderful fun that he keeps us positively occupied and constructively active. He is the strongest medicine against the influences of Satan!

We need, then, to recognise that Satan is the greatest deceiver, the accuser of the brethren (Rev. 12:10). It is he who should be the prisoner in the dock, not the prosecutor, indeed the persecutor. He is the prisoner, he is the guilty one. Blame the devil. Who started it all, anyway? Was it poor Eve? Was it Adam who started it? Who started it? It is as simple as ABC, and yet Christians do not see it, or will not apply it, or teach it. Who started it?

Do you know the story about the spider? There was an old man who had become a backslider, but he still went to the prayer meeting in his little church. Because he had become a backslider he wasn't so interested in Jesus as he had been when he was younger, and his praying was in a rut and was always the same. He had nothing fresh to say to Jesus. One of the sentences in his prayer was, 'Oh Lord, sweep away the cobwebs from my heart.' Eventually the people used to say, 'Here it comes again,' and some of them used to mimic him saying, 'Oh Lord, sweep away the cobwebs from my heart.' But one day an evangelist came to that church and he not only preached the gospel, but he taught them God's Holy Word and everybody in that old church was stirred up. This old man became a new man just as if he had become a Christian for the first time. The first meeting after this mission his prayer was different from the beginning. He cried to God and was so happy and thrilled that he prayed a new prayer until out came the old sentence, 'Oh Lord, sweep away...'. But he stopped, and instead, opening his mouth wide, he shouted, 'Oh Lord, kill the spider, him who weaves the cobwebs in our hearts. Deal with him!' But before you can deal with him you have got to see that he is there.

We will blame ourselves, and we do not take the devil seriously. But sometimes we even blame God! We say, 'This Bible doesn't work. I've been reading Romans 6 about being holy and it doesn't work. I have tried to understand it. God, there is something wrong with your Bible; it doesn't work!' But all the time it is because there is a spider in your life that needs to be killed. But first you have to detect him. If there is a wasp or a bee buzzing around in your room, you have to find it before you can kill it. 'Where is he? Where is he? Where is he?' That is what we have got to say.

You cannot read very much about this in Christian literature, apart, perhaps, from Jessie Penn Lewis. I have had to go back through the centuries to the Puritans and to John Bunyan to read about it. John Bunyan certainly understood. Here is what he says in *Pilgrim's Progress* about how Satan comes to deceive and drag us down into sin.

> One thing I would not let slip, I took notice that now poor Christian was so confounded that he did not know his own voice, and thus I perceived it, just when he was come over against the mouth of the burning pit, one of the wicked ones got up behind Christian and stepped up softly to him and whisperingly suggested many grievous blasphemies (bad things about God) to him, which he verily thought had proceeded from his own mind.

He did not know the difference between his own mind and these wicked creatures.

> This put Christian more to it than anything he had met with before, even to think that he should blaspheme Him (*i.e.* Jesus) that he loved so much before, yet if he could have helped it he would not have done it, but he had not the discretion (the wisdom, the prudence, the judgment) either to stop his ears or to know from whence these blasphemies came.

That is fascinating. Listen to more from Bunyan: Christian is telling Hopeful, his friend, about Little Faith sleeping in Dead Man's Lane when three sturdy rogues, Faint Heart, Distrust and Guilt (these are thoughts and feelings and desires within us) came by and clung to him and stole his money. Christian then goes on to tell Hopeful that,

> although those three are very bad, they are but journeymen thieves; they serve under the king of the bottomless pit (you know who he is? the devil) who, if need be will come in to their aid himself; and his voice is as the roaring of the lion.

Christian adds,

> I myself have been engaged as this Little Faith was, and I found it a terrible thing. These three villains set upon me and I beginning like a Christian to resist, they gave but a call (you see; this is sin within us—Faint Heart, weak will, wobbly mistrustful of Jesus, full of guilt, all those feelings of being so bad) and in came their master. I would, as the saying is, have given my life for a penny,

but that, as God would have it, I was clothed with armour of proof, and yet though I was so harnessed, I found it hard work to quit myself like a man (against their master, Satan). No man can tell what in that combat attends us but he that hath been in the battle himself.

Christian goes on to speak of the three thieves and their king, Satan.

Besides, their king is at their whistle. He is never out of hearing, and if at any time they be put to the worst, he, if possible, comes in to help them, and of him it is said in Scripture, 'sword or spear, dagger or javelin, if they touch him, they have no effect. Iron he counts as straw and bronze as rotting wood. No arrow can pierce him and for him slingstones are turned into chaff. To him a club is a mere reed (a bulrush) and he laughs at the swish of a sabre, he is so strong (Job 41:26–29). What can a man do in this case? It is true if a man could at every turn have Job's horse and skill and courage to ride him he might do notable things, for his neck (the neck of the horse) is clothed with thunder. He will not be afraid of the locust. His shrill neighing strikes terror. He shows his mettle as he paws and prances. He charges the armour-line with all his might. He scorns alarms and knows no dismay. He does not flinch before the sword. The quiver rattles at his side. The spear and the sabre flash. Trembling with eagerness he devours the ground and cannot be held in when he hears the horn. At the blast of the horn he cries, "Aha," and from afar he scents the battle. But (says Christian) for such footmen as we are (soldiers on foot, not on horses, Christian and Hopeful) let us never desire to meet with an enemy nor vaunt ourselves as if we can do better, when we hear of others who have been foiled, nor let us be tickled at the thought of our own manhood, for such commonly come by the worst when tried; witness Peter of whom I made mention before. He would swagger: Aye, Peter would swagger as his vain mind prompted him to say, Do better and stand more for his Master than all the rest of the disciples, but who was so foiled and run down by these villains as Peter? When therefore we hear that such robberies are done on the King's highway, two things become us to do: one to go out harnessed and to be sure to take a shield with us (the shield of faith) for it was for want of that that although he laid lustily at Leviathan (the devil) he could not make him yield. For indeed if that shield be wanting the devil fears us not at all. Therefore, he that hath skill has said (that is, the apostle Paul), 'Above all, taking the shield of faith, wherewith he shall be able to quench all the fiery darts of the wicked' (Eph. 6:16). It is good also, says Christian, that we desire of the King a convoy, yes, that He will go with us Himself.

You see, if you cannot detect Satan rummaging in the remnants of your sinful nature, Jesus can. He will help you. He will say, 'Look, I say, somebody is approaching, somebody is climbing in at the window, somebody is creeping round that corner, watch him.'

So, he says,

It is this that made David rejoice in the valley of the shadow of death in the Shepherd Psalm, and Moses was rather for dying where he stood than to go one step without God. O my brother, if He will but go along with us, what need we be afraid of ten thousand that shall set themselves against us, but without Him the proud helpers fall under Him, slain.

Then he concludes,

I for my part have been in the fray before now, and though through the goodness of Him that is best I am as you see alive, yet I cannot boast of my manhood. Glad shall I be if I meet with no more such brunts, though I fear that we are not beyond all danger. However, since the lion and the bear have not as yet devoured me, I hope God will also deliver us from the next uncircumcised Philistine.

And John Bunyan makes Christian break into song:

Poor Little Faith, has been among thieves,
Wast robbed. Remember this, whoso believes,
And get more faith, shall then a victor be over ten thousand
Else scarce over three.

Come hither, you that walk along the way,
See how the pilgrims fare that go astray,
They are caught in an entangling net,
They are caught because they good counsel did forget,
'Tis true they rescued were, but yet you see,
They are scourged, whipped, lashed to boot,
Let this be your caution.

This is how Satan creeps into our lives and deceives us and leads us astray.

Now, what about Romans 7 where Paul apparently sees the conflict exclusively in terms of our sin? Here is something I wrote many, many years ago. 'If we read Romans 6:14 to 7:25 we will see Paul's continuing preoccupation with sin. Note that sin is characterised in increasingly personal terms. In 6:14 it is dominion; from 6:16 to 23 it is a tyrannical master, a slave driver; in 7:8, 11 it is an unscrupulous and wily opportunist, standing ready to use what is good, namely the law, for its own evil purposes. In 13, 17, 20, 23 it is a deadly enemy warring against the new Christ nature.' Although you do not find the devil's name in Romans until you come to Romans 16:20, you will find plenty about him in the rest of Paul's writings, as well as in James and in Peter, and in John. A careful reading of many biblical passages will show that we Christians are up against the devil himself, whom we have to detect as he pokes in our natures, trying to stir up the evil. If you fail to detect him, expose him, and chase him out, he will spoil your Christian life.

I have been teaching this many years, but time after time I meet Christians who after years of such teaching and practice sometimes forget and become mournful and depressed, full of guilt and condemnation as they look in and see how bad they are. Or, on the other hand, there are those led astray by other temptations who fail to see that a wily foe has slipped in to their lives. We must be on our guard (1 Pet. 5:8, 9).

I know some people who have grown cold towards Jesus Christ. These people used to love to share in the fellowship, prayer, and Bible Study, worship, and everything, because they loved Christ. Then they began to grow a little cooler, polite, still nice and friendly, but they can do with less and less, and there are more excuses. 'I must go here. I must do that.' All very well, doubtless; some at least are authentic and valid excuses. But somebody is at work in their lives, cooling them towards Christ, seducing them, leading them astray from Jesus Christ. If you were to speak about Jesus Christ and how marvellous he is, their eyes would go down and they would feel ashamed and embarrassed and would want to get out of your company. Perhaps they do not know that someone has done that to them. They have been enslaved, enmeshed in the cares of this world or something else, through Satan, and they have cooled towards Jesus. Someone who would perhaps be of great use to Christ and his church gets stuck, and it is Satan's doing. Oh, watch! He is subtle, he is cunning, he is silent, and he steals into our lives, colours our emotions, changes our minds and draws us away. Then we blame ourselves, we lose heart and give up. Oh, watch him!

You see the great thing is this: when you have someone to blame beyond yourself—it does not mean that you are not to blame, for often you are and you have to go and say, 'Lord, forgive me, I let Satan get a hold of me there. I'm sorry.' But when you have somebody else to blame it takes a great burden off you. There is someone to blame beyond yourself. Is that not a comforting word? I think it is absolutely tremendous. Never, never, never forget it; but time after time remind yourself of it.

But here is my final sentence. This is it! The closer you live to Jesus, the more you will be aware of the brute.

WHAT IT IS TO BE A CHRISTIAN

16. Resisting the Enemy

The unmasking of Satan and the detection of his wiles is a great burden on my heart, because I find that in personal and private pastoral work I am constantly having to speak about his vile influence on the lives of Christians. Those who are afflicted by these powers need to understand what is happening to them, for long after we think we understand what it is to be a Christian there rises a new wave and dimension of evil to hinder us. I can give instances of lives that are potentially spoiled because the enemy deceives them and leads them out of Christ's way. That is why I say this is a burden on my heart. I want all Christians and all prospective and potential Christians to try to grasp what follows. I would like to put it like this: I am going to say what, if these were my last words to you, I would want to say to Christians. It would be to tell them about the power of the evil one—not to concentrate upon him to the exclusion of our Lord; but we must never, never allow the evil one to get out of sight. We must constantly see him and watch him out of the corner of our eye. Jesus himself said, 'Watch and pray.' If we do we will discover that some of our struggles against what we believed was inbred sin, were not merely that, but were actually the cunning working of the evil one upon our lives to try to spoil them.

I think I can briefly summarise what I want to say. I am speaking of course to Christians. Once God is in our lives and we become new creatures in Christ, the struggle is not with ourselves but with the ultimate foe, the devil digging in and inflaming the dregs and remnants of our old fallen selves. If we are new creatures belonging to Jesus Christ, if Christ has come to dwell in our lives and unite our spirits with his and take the throne in our lives, then the struggle against evil is not with ourselves. We are new creatures; the fundamental struggle must be with something else—and something less; that is the important thing.

Paul makes a distinction between our new, Christ-born selves and sin, that still remains within us. But we will turn to that later in this study.

We are, therefore, concerned with the struggle between good and evil, the struggle that Christians have to be good and holy and serviceable to Jesus Christ. That is what we are concerned with. Who started it all? Who started the struggle in the first place?

What were the first creatures to be made? In Job 38 God addresses Job who had been presumptuous in speaking to God in his distress. God challenges him as to whether he was present when God created the universe. The Almighty almost taunts Job with this. 'Where were you when I laid the foundation of the earth? Tell me, if you have under-standing. Who determined its measurements—surely you know,' says God sarcastically. 'Or who stretched the line upon it (building the universe, you see, rank by rank of stones; that's the conception)? On what were its bases sunk, or who laid its cornerstone, when the morning stars sang together, and all the sons of God shouted for joy?' (Job 38:4–7).

What are 'the morning stars' here? Sometimes they are angels; they may not be here, but the sons of God certainly are angels. When we read that phrase in the Old Testament, 'sons of God' practically always refers to angels, not to men. It appears that before God created the heavens and the earth, he had already made the angels. They were the first-born in a sense.

One of these angelic beings, who may very well have been the brightest—I think he was the brightest of the lot—called Lucifer, in the Authorised Version, the light bearer—being taken up with his own beauty instead of ascribing his creaturely glory to the God who made him, said to himself, 'I think I'd look fine up there on that throne.' He aspired to God's throne and sought to usurp God's power and to be God. And so God cast him down for his pride and presumption: 'How you are fallen from heaven, O Day Star, Son of Dawn (that is Lucifer)! How you are cut down to the ground, you who laid the nations low! You said in your heart, "I will ascend to heaven; above the stars of God I will set my throne on high; (says the devil) I will sit on the mount of assembly in the far north; I will ascend above the heights of the clouds, I will make myself like the Most High." But you are brought down to Sheol' (Is. 14:12–15).

The pride that led him into this unhappy position seems to be described in Ezekiel 28:12–17: 'Son of man, raise a lamentation over the king of Tyre, and say to him, Thus says the Lord GOD (although this speaks of the king of Tyre it describes more than human sin, and looks beyond to the might and power of Satan): "You were the signet of perfection, full of wisdom and perfect in beauty. You were in Eden, the garden of God; every precious stone was your covering, carnelian, topaz, and jasper, chrysolite, beryl, and onyx, sapphire, carbuncle, and emerald; and wrought in gold were your settings and your engravings. On the day that you were created they were prepared. With an anointed guardian cherub I placed you; you were on the holy mountain of God; in the midst of the stones of fire you walked. You were blameless in your ways from the day you were created, till iniquity was found in you. In the abundance of your trade you were filled with violence, and you sinned; so I cast you as a profane thing from the mountain of God, and the guardian cherub drove you out from the midst of the stones of fire. Your heart was proud because of your beauty; you corrupted your wisdom for the sake of your splendour. I cast you to the ground; I exposed you before kings, to feast their eyes on you.'

So, the brightest of the angels in his pride and presumption is cast out. How in the world could a creature take the Creator's place? But he aspired to it. If he hated God because he aspired to his throne—and we usually hate those we want to pull down—how much more would he hate him when he was cast down? I stress this because the struggle between man and the devil has only one intent, though he uses many means. He wants to spite God and hurt him all he can. He does not care a fig for men. There is only one obsessive thought in his mind: *to hurt and spite God.*

How does he do it? Well, God has appointed Lucifer the governor of the universe. We have seen before that Jesus calls him the Prince of this world. He is no longer fit to be governor, but God does not take his position from him. He looks for another to take his place, and at the climax of creation he makes man and says, 'I'll give to man, Adam, dominion over all things created, and appoint *him* governor of the universe.' And Satan said, 'Ah, you will, will you? You will take my job from me? See if you will.' So he bent all his ingenuity, cunning, and skill to bring God's man down—and did, as Genesis 3 records. Out of pure spite against God he attacked man, enslaved him and brought him down. So if you can dare to think about it like this, God suffered two seemingly terrible defeats: one in that his first governor of the universe played false to him and became his implacable enemy, and a second in that Satan took God's second appointee as governor of the universe and brought him under his malevolent power.

So both God's creatures turned against him—far above the beasts and the natural, inanimate things, this angel with his tribe, the fallen angels and man. But God foresaw it all, and was not disturbed in his almighty power or in his inscrutable purposes. Indeed as soon as Adam and Eve had fallen, God promised a Saviour—not from sin, but from Satan: 'the seed of the woman (who is Christ to come) shall bruise the serpent's head.' God must intervene. God himself must intervene and must intervene as a man, to save man. There is no salvation for the devil and the demons, but man can be retrieved and can be redeemed, if God becomes a man to do it. Only a man can retrieve man's ruin, and only God can do it. There is no man fit: every man has fallen under the power of Satan. So God became man to seize the upper hand and defeat Satan. That is portrayed in Revelation 12:7 and 17 where we read of war in heaven, 'Then the dragon was angry with the woman and went off to make war on the rest of her offspring.'

This is what we are struggling against here and now. Paul sums it up when he says, 'For we wrestle not against flesh and blood.' Our struggles with evil are not against flesh and blood, evil men who have evil intent against us, nor do we wrestle against our own flesh and blood when we battle against sin, inbred sin, 'but against principalities and powers, against the world rulers of this darkness', this kingdom of evil that Satan has instituted.

The Christian life is warfare, as the chapter on Sanctification in the *Westminster Confession of Faith,* so clearly and simply says. There is, in the believer, an irreconcilable war that takes place. The *Confession* speaks of sanctification 'throughout in the whole man, yet imperfect in this life; there abides still in the Christian some remnants of corruption in every part (of his being) *whence arises a continual and irreconcilable war....*' This war is in your bodies, so do not become a Christian without thinking what you are doing, because you become a battlefield between God and the devil, in a way that you are not when not a Christian. When you become a Christian you become a battlefield between God and the devil; '...the flesh lusting against the Spirit and the Spirit against the flesh. In which war...'. Twice the *Confession* uses that word 'war', do you see that?

There are many references in Scripture to this conflict and war, all to do with the subject of sanctification, with giving ourselves to Christ to live the holy life. Peter speaks of it: 'Beloved, I beseech you as aliens and exiles, (not belonging to this world any more, although God has planted us in the midst of it to serve him. This world is going to pass away and we are going to pass away from it. We are going to another kingdom. We belong to the kingdom of God if we are Christians. So we are aliens and exiles, pilgrims and strangers here, here for a few years— seventy, eighty, ninety, maybe a hundred; but we don't belong here.) to abstain from the passions of the flesh that wage war against your soul.' That is the language used here, 'wage war'.

What is the nature of this war? I have hinted at it already. It is governed by the fact that we are new creatures in Christ Jesus. Jesus Christ has breathed his Spirit into us, so that we become partakers of the divine nature. We are new creatures in Christ Jesus. We are bound for heaven. The devil will hate us for siding with Christ. His spite and hatred of Christ are so great that anyone who turns to Jesus Christ is bound to face the full fury of the devil's hatred of Christ. Do not become a Christian until you have faced the fact that you have to face the devil!

Read Revelation chapters 2 and 3 about the seven churches in Asia Minor (Turkey, today). In every one of them you find words such as these: *Whoever conquers* shall attain to heaven and enjoy this honour and this blessing and this position. Seven times we have, 'Whoever conquers.' Now, what does it mean? Whoever conquers evil, whoever conquers sin, whoever conquers the devil. Every Christian must learn to do this. You cannot be a mature Christian until you have learned to face and wage war against the enemy, and win.

Since we are new men and women in Christ, there is a sense in which sin is the most unnatural thing in our lives. You can prove that, and doubtless you have proved it many times. I sometimes share in private the throes, struggles, and heartbreaks of some who have become Christians and have slipped. It has made them the most miserable creatures in the world, which is proof, you see, that Christ is there; that is why they become miserable, dissatisfied, ashamed and heartbroken because they have failed him. They could have said as others have said, 'Ugh, it doesn't work. It doesn't work. It is not worth it. Let me get back to my old life.' But that is not what they say; they are heartbroken. Have you seen young men and women, and some not so young sobbing their hearts out because they have disappointed Jesus Christ whom they have received, loved and want to serve? That, it seems to me, is proof that they have become new creatures.

Being new creatures in Christ Jesus, sin becomes unnatural and makes us miserable. That is why John's words are so important: 'My little children, I am writing this to you so that you may not sin; but if anyone does sin we have an advocate with the Father.' Some people come to Jesus Christ and they slip and fall. Satan, or some agent of Satan, trips them up and they say, 'Oh, it's hopeless, I can't do it. It doesn't work. I can't keep it up.' But, true Christians don't do that, however heartbroken they are at their failings and their stumblings, because they know that they can run back to Jesus Christ and be forgiven, cleansed and receive greater strength to face the enemy and temptation the next day. 'For we have an advocate with the Father, Jesus Christ the righteous, and he is the propitiation for our sins (he has borne the brunt of our sins upon the cross), and not for ours only but also for the sins of the whole world' (1 Jn. 2:1, 2).

John goes on to say: 'No one who abides in him sins.' That does not mean that we never sin again after we become Christians. We know that that is not true; we all sin every day, Christians though we be. None of us is perfect. But when he says, 'No one who abides in him sins,' he means, we do not go on practising sin, living the kind of life we were living before. We are living a different life although we may often be tripped up and have to run to the Lord for mercy and comfort. But we do not make a practice of sin. 'No one who abides in him sins. No one who sins has either seen him or known him.' This is the point: if you can go back to the old life and forget all about Christ and live the former life again without a thought, then nothing happened in your heart; you never were a Christian. You never were converted.

Sometimes people have to be allowed to turn back. Sometimes we may run after them and say, 'Stop, don't go.' Sometimes I have almost run out of church after people that way. At other times, no, no, no. One says it with sympathy, sorrow and sadness, but if they go, they have to learn the hard way. If Jesus Christ has been planted in their breast, they find that they cannot go back. 'Little children, let no one deceive you. He who does right is righteous, as he (Christ) is righteous. He who commits sin is of the devil; for the devil has been sinning from the beginning. (He does nothing else; and that is where all sin comes from. If you are sinning you are of the devil.) The reason the Son of God appeared was to destroy the works of the devil (in man's heart). No one born of God commits sin: for God's nature abides in him, and he cannot (go on practising) sin, because he is born of God. By this it may be seen who are the children of God and who are the children of the devil: whoever does not do right is not of God, nor he who does not love his brother.' Here are two things: you must do right, be honest, pure and true, and you must be loving as well. Two signs that you are a Christian—not merely that you believe the right things, but that you do the right things and care for people in the right way.

John continues this theme in chapter 5:4, 5: 'For whatever is born of God overcomes the world (and that means the fallen world, still in the clutches of the enemy); and this is the victory that overcomes the world, our faith. Who is it that overcomes the world but he who believes that Jesus is the Son of God?'

Now, what all this is saying is that, as new creatures, we become totally renewed by Jesus Christ, sons and daughters of God with new desires after Christ and holiness. We long to live the right life, associate with the right people, and then go out into the world to make known Christ's grace to those that so desperately need it outside in the world. But you say, 'Yes, but what about the struggles?' The whole of my life is involved with myself and other people struggling against evil. But we are new creatures in Christ Jesus if we have received him. We are not the old creatures; we are different, and it is only the remnants of sin and corruption that remain. This is the perspective we must have.

It is in this context that Paul's teaching in Romans 7:15ff is so vital: 'I don't understand my own actions.' How many people have said that? How many times have I said that to God myself? 'I do not understand my own actions.' Can you say that? Do you say that? 'For I do not do what I want, but I do the very thing I hate. Now if I do what I do not want I agree that the law is good. So then it is no longer I that do it, but sin which dwells within me' (Rom. 7:15–20).

Paul is not excusing himself here, but is speaking about his own struggles. He is not saying that he is not responsible, because sin has done something within him. If sin has done something within him it is with his consent it has been done. He was not anaesthetised or sedated. He was quite responsible. What he is saying is that it was not himself, that is, his true self, who did it. He had to become unnatural to his Christian self to do it. He had to go back to the old life to do it: 'Now, if I do what I do not want, it is no longer I that do it but sin that dwells in me' (v. 20).

We have to deal with the remnant of sin and corruption within us. But do you see that the violence and the virulence of sin within the saints arises from Satan's desperation to spite Christ and spoil Christians? So, what makes the struggle seem so unequal? What makes sin so attractive in the moment of temptation? You say, 'I am going to fight against it, I am going to resist', but then when you are actually faced with it, down you go. You seem to have no hope of resisting, and you just succumb. You may even say, 'I can't resist.' Answer me this question: How in the world can mere remnants of sin have such overwhelming power as that over Jesus Christ in your life? If it is only the remnants of corruption that remain in us after Christ has come to dwell in our lives, how can it be that this evil has so much power? The answer is clear: Satan's desperation to do despite to Christ, to spoil Christians and laugh at God. He does make messes of Christians—it may be that tonight there are more Christians in psychiatric hospitals than there are non-Christians. I would not wonder. I would not be surprised, and nor should you be, either. If there is one thing the devil loves to do above all it is to spoil Christians. What then, does Satan do? When we have been given over to Jesus Christ, and are determined to live his life, whatever comes, then Satan comes into play personally and stirs up the remnants and the dregs of our sin. Think of a pond. It is not a very clean pond but all the silt is at the bottom so it looks comparatively clear and bright. Then some naughty little boy comes with a stick and pokes it all, stirs up the silt and befouls the whole pond. That is what the devil is doing in your life, and that is why the struggle to live the Christian life is so fierce. That is why the remnants of sin and corruption can be terribly, overwhelmingly strong and overmastering. Do you understand?

Sadly, we are unlikely to learn this from modern books on the Christian life. That is why I have had to write about it, although I am not a writer. We have to go right back to John Bunyan to find it, as we saw in the previous study. Here is something else he says. Christian is telling Hopeful how Little Faith was sleeping in Dead Man's Lane. He was where a Christian should not have been, because he is not dead but living in Christ. Three sturdy rogues (here is the influence of inbred sin in our lives), Faint Heart, Mistrust (lack of faith) and Guilt come and club him and steal his money while he is asleep. Have you experienced this? You sin, and are covered in guilt. (I've done it again Lord. It is hopeless. I give up. You won't forgive me. You have forgiven me before but you can't forgive me again. Guilt will not let us believe that God forgives again and again. 'One slip and you are finished; give up', says the devil. 'Give up, it's hopeless.') Then Christian goes on to say that although these three rogues are very bad (they represent inbred sin, as I was saying, the dregs of our old nature) they are but journeymen thieves. There is not even a foreman amongst them. They are just ordinary thieves, these evil influences in our lives, and serve under the king of the bottomless pit (the devil himself).

The inbred sin, the remnants of corruption in your life are under the power of Satan. They belong to him, these dregs, and he has access to them. 'They serve under the king of the bottomless pit, who if need be will come to their aid himself, and his voice is as the roaring of the lion' says Bunyan. Inbred sin, when it is overmastered by the power of Christ, calls upon the devil himself. 'Come on Satan, we need your power to beat this man and do him down, and hinder him from being a real Christian. Come on.' And the devil comes with all his armoury. Christian goes on to say that he had experienced the same thing as Little Faith had suffered, and he says, 'I found it a terrible thing. These three villains set upon me and I, beginning like a Christian to resist (the sin), they gave but a call, and in came their master. He is at their whistle. He is never out of hearing and if at any time they be put to the worst, he comes in to help them.'

In my ancient copy of *Pilgrim's Progress,* Mason, its editor, has added this footnote: 'Who can stand in the evil day of temptation when beset with Faint Heart, Mistrust, and Guilt backed by the power of their master Satan?' That is the point. Learn it. We too often forget it. You have got to be constantly reminded that there is a Satan behind sin. 'But this is our glory,' says Mason, 'that the Lord shall fight for us and we shall hold our peace.' But we shall never fight successfully unless we recognise the malign power of Satan behind the downdrag of the dregs of our fallen nature. To fight him you need resources of power that belong to what I call the 'third dimension'. You need Christ's victory over the person of the devil himself.

John Bunyan here suggests that the powers of evil within us send for Satan to help them to get a good man down. But there is something even more subtle than that, as Bunyan points out elsewhere, Satan comes into play hiddenly. He hides himself within the debris of sin within us, so that we do not recognise his personal presence. He creeps into our lives, into the remnants of sin and hides himself among all that is capable of being drawn away from Christ. The result is that we fail to see that sin has been reinforced in our lives by the personal intrusion of the devil himself. So, watch the dregs of your fallen nature; watch them; do not be preoccupied with them so that you take your eyes off Christ, for he is the only help you have, but watch them, watch them, watch them every moment.

Think of it like this. Do you see that heap of filthy rags? Watch them; there is someone under them. I have a picture in my mind when I say that, of Hitler in the last days of his miserable life, hiding in his cellar.

He was nearly finished; not so Satan. You see, there is something alive there. There is a secret entrance, there is a hidden passage into your life. Satan has a way that he can walk in and you never know it. You begin to say, 'Dear me, that temptation is very strong. That temptation is stronger than before I was a Christian. Why do I feel so drawn to that? Why am I led so strongly away to this?' If you do not know the answer, you will never get the victory. You will, in Paul's language, never understand your own actions (Rom. 7:15), and you will not know why you go astray, because you are not facing the fact. The fact is that Satan is there and you must pull down the curtain and draw away the facade. Accept the fact that there is a devil who seeks to pollute your life as a Christian.

Sadly, this is the last thing we seem to be prepared to do. Do you know why we forget? He makes us forget. If the Holy Spirit is our remembrancer, bringing things to our memory, as Jesus says, then the Evil One is our forgetter. He makes us forget the things we need to know to save us from sin and from ruin and destruction. I say these things not only in view of biblical teaching, but from personal pastoral observation. We pastors are involved not only with people wrestling with ordinary temptations, but with extraordinary temptations of vice— not only sex and drink, but vice, drugs and demonic powers. These are certainly abroad today. The world is going mad. So-called worthy and honourable citizens, leaders of the nation, are blessing pornography; wicked creatures that they are. Do you know why it is this happens? Scripture explains: it is because the devil's time is short and he is mad (Rev. 12:12) and is doing the best he can to deceive the whole world. And we Christians are being deceived. We are not fighting. We have got to learn to see him, detect him, expose him, and drive him out!

A very important practical question arises here and we must deal with it briefly. How do I know that it is Satan working in my life? How am I to know that it is not merely the downdrag of my own fallen nature? Here is the answer. Once Jesus Christ is in your life it is only the remnants and dregs of sin that remain. But, you say, why are they so strong? Because Satan is there. But if you are still not convinced about this, how are you to know that the devil is dragging you down? When you are drawn to do what you do not really want to do, when you become other than yourself, and are deceived. Yes, you want to do it at the moment but your true Christian self does not and as soon as it is done you hate yourself. You say, Why did I do it? You do not succumb like others who say, 'It is all right. You will not worry about it so much after you have done it a few times, it becomes like taking a drink of water.' Well, no one with Christ in their heart could think or feel like that. Christians do worry because Christ has cast his anchor into their hearts and he will not let them go. But will we face the fact that we are waging war against Satan?

I remember a Roman Catholic man who came to the Bible Study one evening and afterwards asked if he could have an interview at the manse. He was a solicitor by profession, but had been dragged down to the depths of despair, and was thinking of taking his life. I do not know if it was the text on the board outside our church that made him think that perhaps a Protestant clergyman could help him; but he called. For about eighteen months we spent about an hour and a half together each week, and then because I was busy and he was much stronger spiritually we met less frequently. He soon went back to his own church. I thought that perhaps other things would happen, but he went back to his own church. However, as he grew stronger in the faith the thing that was absolutely new to him was the whole dimension of a kingdom of evil over against the kingdom of holiness and truth. He had been a devout Catholic in early days, a kind of humanist idealist who naturally wanted to make the world a better place. But now, he saw that there was a devil and it was this, particularly, that convinced me that he was seeking after and finding Christ. Our fellowship together grew. We became brothers in Christ. Of course there were lots of things we might not see eye to eye upon, but his hold on Christ's death for him, and his victory over all evil became vibrantly strong. Then he began to offer himself for service and became of greater and greater use, until one day he said, 'I believe God is calling me to the priesthood.' So he offered himself. There was no fund appropriate to his case, but he believed that God had called him and would provide. And he did. But then he arrived for our last interview before he went to college. I had someone with me and said, 'You must wait a little,' but I could see he was agitated. When he came into the room, before I could greet him he plunked himself down on the chair and said, 'It's all over. It's finished. I can't go on. It's hopeless. My sins have come up before me. I've even been to the authorities who say, "Just be patient for a day or two." But I can't go. I must cancel it.'

I said, 'My brother, what have I been teaching you for two years about the devil?' His face fell. He said, 'It couldn't be him could it?' I said, 'You naughty man.' He just collapsed in the chair. 'Oh,' he said, 'could I have been so deceived? I went to one of my friends in the church but before I got into the house my heart was broken and I put my head on the table and wept and said, "I can't go. It's hopeless."' So he left me a different man. I said, 'Ring tomorrow. I want assurance that this old devil will be kept from you.' 'Oh,' said he, 'It's all right. I've seen him now.' 'Well,' I said, 'I hope you have.' Next day there was a phone message—I knew by his voice—'It's all right. I'm off to train for Christ's service.' Do you see the point?

I could give hundreds of illustrations. Sometimes those who have been delivered wonderfully from Satan, quite suddenly are belaboured by him again through giving way to morbid thoughts. Others, in apparently 'chance' circumstances are ensnared by evil. It is happening all the time, alas. Do you wonder why I believe in the devil and his machinations in the lives of men and women? Unless we see it we are going to be deceived and defeated and Christ's cause will not prosper. Before there is a change in Christ's church in this land and a change in the land itself, we will all need to take a new dealing with the ultimate power of evil.

Look, it has taken God to deal with Satan. You cannot do it on your own. He is far too subtle and hidden, seductive and cunning, malign and clever. You need to run to Christ and let him deal with him. That is what the servant maid said, you know, giving her testimony one night to the power of Christ. 'Sometimes Satan comes to my door and knocks, but I begin to recognise his knock, so I don't go to the door. I send Jesus, and as soon as Satan sees Jesus, he says, "Sorry, wrong door!" and he runs.' You see? Keep him in view. Watch his approach from the distance. See him on the horizon. Admittedly there are dregs in us, but do not let him poke in them or our lives will be ruined and spoiled. God help us to learn this lesson!

WHAT IT IS TO BE A CHRISTIAN

17. On to Glory

Our final study in 'What it means to be a Christian' is on glorification. The Bible is able to speak of our glorification in the past tense (Rom. 8:30, 'glorified'), because God has declared it effectually before the world began, but of course it ordinarily views our glorification as the culmination of a process of sanctification in this life.

This is the perspective in 2 Corinthians 3:15–18. This passage is a long story about the 'veil' that has been taken from the eyes of the Jews who have seen Jesus Christ, such as the Apostle Paul and the disciples: 'to this day whenever Moses is read, a veil lies over their minds (the Jews); but when a man turns to the Lord (be he Jew or Gentile) the veil is removed'. He sees the Lord as the sum of the Ten Commandments and the answer to the Ten Commandments. He is the one who gives us the power to live according to the Ten Commandments, because he himself gave the Commandments and fulfilled them in his earthly life and then died to pay the penalty for our breaking them.

'Now the Lord is the Spirit (the Spirit of God within us, is the Spirit of Jesus the triumphant Lord who came to earth and lived his thirty-three years and died his death and was raised on the third day and ascended to the Father and is exalted and crowned) and where the Spirit of the Lord is, there is freedom (freedom to do what? Freedom to grow up in him. Freedom to store—notice this word—freedom to store glory). And we all, with unveiled face (the burden of the Ten Commandments being removed, not the commandments themselves being destroyed. It is Christ that saves us, not trying to fulfil the Ten Commandments) beholding (or reflecting) the glory of the Lord are being changed (it is a continuous tense in the original Greek) into his likeness (it is a process of sanctification) from one degree of glory to another; for this comes from the Lord who is the Spirit.'

There is no finer guide to the biblical teaching here than the chapter on sanctification from the *Westminster Confession of Faith*. It is not difficult to understand although written in the seventeenth century. 'They who are effectually called (that is the calling we have in Romans 8:30, which brooks no refusal. There is the outward call which everyone who hears gospel preaching can experience. But to be effectually called is when the Holy Spirit says, 'Here, this is for you; take it.' He makes you willing. You do not resist, because you no longer want to resist), they who are effectually called and regenerated (another word for 'born again') having a new heart and a new spirit created in them, are further sanctified by God's Word and Spirit dwelling in them' (*Confession of Faith*, XIII.i).

The compilers of the *Confession* say that when we are called and born again we have a new heart and a new spirit created in us. Further, we are sanctified by God's Word and Spirit dwelling in us. 'The dominion of the whole body of sin is destroyed'. (Our nature is changed. Christ has given us a new nature with new desires, and when he has done that, just try to go back to the old life! You may go on for a little time because you have been longing for some of the things you tasted before, and the old devil stirs them up and says, 'Go back. A little taste of this and a little taste of that wouldn't do you any harm. Away back and try to live the old life again.' But if God has done something in your heart, you cannot.)

Back to the *Confession*! 'The dominion of the whole body of sin is destroyed, and the several lusts thereof (we needn't necessarily take that in the ugliest sense. It means 'desires', but they are evil of course) are more and more weakened and mortified. (That is what the Spirit of God enables us to do when we come to him; we have the power to say, 'No, I will not do that again.') Satan may stir a desire in our hearts to want to do it again, when he catches us at our worst when we are tired, or forlorn or very vulnerable—the brute. But as far as our own heart is concerned, as Paul tells us in Romans 7, we do not want to do that again. So, 'the several lusts thereof are more and more weakened and mortified, and they (that is the new creatures) more and more quickened and strengthened in all saving graces (and that is a long story!) to the practice of true holiness (you could almost say, wholeness or health here; but that does not cover it completely, but it helps), without which no man shall see the Lord' (XIII.i).

'This sanctification is throughout in the whole man (it is total; we are totally new creatures. We may not always look like it. We may not always feel like it, but, you see, God has done a perfect work. That is to say, it is entire, see Philippians 1:6. It is as if God says, ' I have taken that man. He is mine. I have given him my nature. Oh, he'll have lots of struggles yet, and he may trip and fall many times, but he is mine, and I'll never let him go. You see, the work is potentially total), yet imperfect in this life (final and yet a process, a crisis and yet a process); there abideth still some remnants of corruption in every part (of his being): whence ariseth a continual and irreconcileable war; the flesh lusting against the Spirit, and the Spirit against the flesh' (XIII.ii).

Now, notice, the flesh lusting against the Spirit and the Spirit against the flesh, is not our mere human nature rebelling, because we have been taken over by Christ. No it is Satan poking and stirring up the remnants of sin within us. 'In which war (we are engaged in war against the devil and all his minions), although the remaining corruption for a time may much prevail, (and some sitting here tonight say, 'Yes, indeed, it may much prevail. What a struggle I've had. Would I have believed it when I became a Christian? Would I have believed I would still have had such moral and spiritual struggles?) yet, through the continual supply of strength (whence?) from the sanctifying Spirit of Christ (within), the regenerate part (really the new person we are in Christ) doth overcome; and so the saints grow in grace (not jump into it, but grow in grace), perfecting holiness in the fear of God' (XIII.iii).

Notice that our sanctification is 'imperfect in this life'. 2 Corinthians 3:18 speaks of a process. It is 'imperfect in this life' although you live to be a hundred and become the holiest soul on earth. Paul was still imperfect when he died. This process cannot be completed in this life, although much progress can be made.

The *Larger Catechism* and the *Shorter Catechism* which were also composed by the Westminster divines make it plain that the process of sanctification of the saints on earth is 'imperfect in this life,' and that this applies even to the holiest and longest-lived saints, whose sanctification is complete at the point of death. It is, of course, this completed work, spoken of as glorification, that Paul is dealing with in Romans 8:30.

The *Larger Catechism*, question 86, asks 'What is the communion in glory with Christ, which the members of the invisible church enjoy immediately after death?' The answer is: 'The communion in glory with Christ which the members of the invisible church enjoy immediately after death, is, that their souls are then made perfect in holiness.' But, you may ask, how can that completion be achieved so suddenly? Because Christ's perfections were always present by the indwelling Holy Spirit in the imperfect saint even although the potential of his resources were not drawn upon fully and perfectly. Not only so, but the mortal body while still living was open to Satan's attacks which hampered and hindered growth into. out-wrought perfection. But to continue the quotation: 'their souls are then made perfect in holiness, and received into the highest heavens, where they behold the face of God in light and glory, waiting for the full redemption of their bodies, which even in death continue united to Christ (that is really why we revere the remains of our loved ones), and rest in their graves as in their beds, till at the last day they be again united to their souls.'

Now, the *Shorter Catechism*, question 37, has it not only shorter, but better! I love this, and memorised it years ago. The question is, 'What benefits do believers receive from Christ at death?' The answer is, 'The souls of believers are at their death made perfect in holiness, and do immediately pass into glory; and their bodies, being still united to Christ, do rest in their graves, till the resurrection.' This is beautiful language, for one thing, but it is more than that: it is truth. The souls of believers are not asleep. Some people talk of departed souls remaining in a soul-sleep: not a bit of it! They are not yet complete, but when Christ comes at the end of the age, and we receive resurrection bodies like his, then will be consummated all that grace has done for us in his redeeming work. We shall then be fully human.

The believing departed do not yet have their bodies. Revelation 6:9 calls them 'souls'. But in heaven Christ has his resurrection body. He is the only one in heaven with a body. He is fully human. Christ will never again not be human. No one else in heaven, not even Moses or Elijah, have their new bodies yet. But at the general resurrection at the end of the age, the saints will receive their immortal bodies, indestructible and eternal, and will become fully human in heaven. They will be body and soul again. Heaven is a substantial place. It is no myth, no vapour. It is no mere figment of the imagination. Paul talks about a 'weight of glory'; and isn't it C. S. Lewis who says 'Spirit is heavier than matter.' I wonder what the physicists would say about that! I certainly do not understand it, but Scripture certainly gives us hints of it.

After all, what was it that made the visible, the tangible, the material what it is? The writer to the Hebrews says that the invisible made the visible (Heb. 11:3). To have made the visible so substantial, the invisible must be more substantial and durable and greater than the visible! Some people think that because they can't see God he doesn't exist. Yuri Gagarin, the first Russian in space, said he could not see God. Foolish fellow! Did he want God on an interstellar platter? God came in a human body and they would not believe it. No, Scripture teaches us that it is the invisible that made the visible.

Paul discusses this in 2 Corinthians 4:16: 'So we do not lose heart. Though our outward nature is wasting away, our inner nature is being renewed every day. For this slight momentary affliction is preparing for us an *eternal weight* of glory beyond all comparison, because we look not to the things that are seen but to the things that are unseen; for the things that are seen are transient (and pass away) but the things that are unseen are eternal.' Thus the *Larger* and *Shorter Catechisms* are one with Paul's statement in Romans 8:30 that declares that God views this work of glorification as he views the work of justification, as a sovereign work of his own, in an act which has an eternal dimension to it.

In this statement Paul is not thinking of our cooperation in sanctification at all. In one sense it cannot be excluded, but that is not what he is talking about here.

This eternal work of God applies to all who are effectually called, and who therefore persevere. The test that Christ has wrought a work in your heart is that you go on being a Christian, and make progress. When people fall away we could easily begin to wonder whether God has wrought a work in them. Some people talk after a mission about how many were converted; whereas they should say how many professed, and give them time to see if they go on.

Perseverance is the test as to whether a person is a Christian or not. We must not think that because someone has been to a meeting and has stood up or gone forward that they can therefore present themselves before God and say, 'Look, that is the day and date and place'. God looks on the heart, and when he does so he may say, 'I see no sign of anything having happened here. Your ticket is valueless.' No, this is the sign, that we persevere.

Here is what the *Confession* says about perseverance. 'They whom God hath accepted in his Beloved, effectually called and sanctified by his Spirit, can neither totally nor finally fall away from the state of grace; but shall certainly persevere therein to the end, and be eternally saved. This perseverance of the saints depends not upon their own free will, but upon the immutability of the decree of election (God choosing and calling them), flowing from the free and unchangeable love of God the Father (first of all); (secondly), upon the efficacy of the merit and the intercession of Jesus Christ.' (We have spoken about that already. This perseverance of the saints not only flows from the fact that God has laid his hand upon you and said, 'I'll have you,' but his Son in heaven has been praying to the Father for you constantly). Perseverance also comes from 'the abiding of the Spirit, and of the seed of God within them' (*Confession of Faith* XVII.ii). This is marvellous! The three Persons in the Trinity all work to ensure that what God has said about you will be true in eternity. God says, 'I have called him; he is mine.' Jesus is praying to the Father and saying, 'Bless him, and keep him, and preserve him, Father.' And the Holy Spirit is praying, too (Rom. 8:26, 27). The three of them are working night and day (although there is no night there!) to help us go on.

The *Confession* goes on to say that perseverance also flows from 'the nature of the covenant of grace. So, from all of these aspects of God's work in his people 'arise the certainty and infallibility' of their perseverance. It continues, 'Nevertheless they may, through the temptations of Satan and of the world, the prevalency of corruption remaining in them, and the neglect of the means of their preservation (prayer and Bible reading and worship) fall into grievous sins; and for a time continue therein: whereby they incur God's displeasure, and grieve his Holy Spirit; come to be deprived of some measure of their graces and comforts; have their hearts hardened, and their consciences wounded (and it appears to those looking on as if they were never converted at all); hurt and scandalize others, and bring temporal judgments upon themselves (like sickness and premature death, 1 Corinthians 11:30).' Nevertheless they go on because God has a hold of them, and will not let them go. Will not? *Cannot* let them go!

This applies to all who are effectually called and who therefore persevere. But we are concerned with the eternal stuff, the production of glory, and with what produces glory, the outshining of the character of God in men's lives.

When Christ went up the mountain (whether it was Mount Tabor or Mount Hermon does not matter at the moment), with Peter, James and John, he was transfigured before them. You know what happened? God switched him on, as it were—on went the glory! All the virtue of Christ shone out and was illuminated. The virtue of his perfect character shone out and made even his clothes to glisten; it seemed to shine through his flesh and through his robe. Now that is what is going to happen when we receive our resurrection bodies; all that Christ is within us and all that he has wrought within us, will suddenly shine out.

Let me stress this: glory has to do with glow. If we understand it rightly, everything involving the Christian church is to the glory of God; that is, to the ultimate outshining of God. In heaven every saint will shine with Christ's brightness. Yet we will all be different from each other. We will each have our own inviolable and unique personality. What a kaleidoscope! What glory! We will all be different because there are no two persons alike. There never have been two alike. In God's sight even identical twins are not alike. He knows the difference. In heaven there will be an innumerable company of reflections of Christ. This is what heaven is going to be: all the character of God, the grace, the love, the justice of the Father and in the Son, all that has been poured into us perfectly manifested—and every one illuminated with the virtue, the merits, the grace of Jesus Christ, and every one shining. That is what is called the fulness of Jesus Christ in his church (Eph. 1:23; Col. 2:9; Jn. 1:16).

Think of that in outward terms. The glory that came on Israel as they crossed the Red Sea, was the glory of God hovering in a cloud by day and a pillar of fire by night. Later on, when Solomon built the temple and had dedicated it, 'fire came down from heaven and consumed the burnt offerings and the sacrifices, and the glory of the Lord filled the temple' (2 Chron. 7:1). The place filled with smoke. The priests could not get in. What was the smoke? It was the smoke of the glory of God, the glory that had hovered over Israel in the wilderness and over the tent, the Shekinah glory filling the temple. That was visible to the Old Testament saints. But the glory now is in the face—not to say the heart—of a man. The former was outward; this is inward, the virtue and character wrought in men's hearts by Jesus Christ through his Holy Spirit.

Have you ever considered John 1:14? It says it all. 'The Word became flesh and dwelt among us, full of grace and truth; we have beheld his glory, glory as of the only Son from the Father.' Here is the fascinating thing: when the glory of God that could burn up the whole universe if he let it, came down to earth, it was contained and confined in a little babe—without a halo. From the moment of his birth to his death, he never had a halo. He did not need one. You do not need to decorate him because all the virtue and grace are inherent in his character and shine out of his eyes. If you had lived in Palestine in his day you might have passed him on the street, but I hardly think so if you looked into his eyes—pools of light, love, power, penetration, and kindness. 'His searching glance can scan the very wounds which shame would hide'. Here is glory! God took glory, his eternal glory with all its weight and power and confined it in a little baby thing. So he grew up and all the outward glory was unseen in this good boy and this good man, except in this one, unique instance when on the mountain God momentarily switched him on.

All that virtue was wrought in the growing infant, and as soon as he came to consciousness and to exercise reason, emotion and will, he had faith. His own development was a development of faith. Jesus, God's eternal Son, lived a life of faith on the earth. That is why there was no outward glory, no pomp. He came down to earth to show us how to store glory in hidden terms. He came down to earth to show us that faith in God is what living for him is all about. Those who receive the gift of God and live by faith—and to live by faith is to endure trials and temptations and to go bravely on, living for Christ though the devil goes mad and drives you almost to distraction with temptations, enticements and afflictions—go on and on. All the time they are storing glory in the present category of hidden faith. Yet it is not hidden, because you can see the results of it in people's faces and in their characters. It is this weight of glory that is being wrought in us by the Spirit. 'Christ in you, the hope of glory' as Paul describes him (Col. 1:27).

The manifold virtues of Christ are being poured by his Spirit into every believer, and so we are called upon to exercise faith, and as we exercise faith we are preparing for certain glory. For the deposit is already in us.

Ephesians 1:13–20 is a marvellous statement in this connection: 'In him (Christ) you (Gentiles) also, who have heard the word of truth, the gospel of your salvation, and have believed in him, were sealed with the promised Holy Spirit (as if he came to stand guard over you and said, 'Now, he's for God. God has chosen him.' The Holy Spirit therefore says to the devil, and the demons: 'Clear out; he belongs to God.') which is the guarantee of our inheritance (and what is our inheritance? our resurrection body. He stands over us and says, 'Now, he is for God, and he is to have a resurrection body, so devil; clear out!' That is what Paul is talking about there.) until we acquire possession of it, to the praise of his glory.'

Now, read on. 'For this reason, because I have heard of your faith in the Lord Jesus and your love toward all the saints, I do not cease to give thanks for you, remembering you in my prayers, that the God of our Lord Jesus Christ, the Father of glory, may give you a spirit of wisdom and of revelation in the knowledge of him, having the eyes of your hearts (it is inward you see) enlightened, that you may know what is the hope to which he has called you, what are the riches of his glorious inheritance in the saints (what he has deposited in us), and what is the immeasurable greatness of his power in us who believe, according to the working of his great might which he accomplished in Christ when he raised him from the dead and made him sit at his right hand in the heavenly places.'

Paul, then, wants us to know three things: first, the hope of our calling is that we are going to be glorified. The second is that, to that end, he wants us to know what Christ has deposited in us. Thirdly, he wants us to know how we may exercise that deposit, the gift of faith: 'what is the immeasurable greatness of his power in us who believe, according to the working of his great might.' Look, he is saying, the power of faith that God has planted in your heart is the power by which God raised Jesus Christ from the dead. And if God could raise Jesus Christ from the dead in an immortal, indestructible body, then he has given that very power into your heart. It is yours. You have it in your heart; nothing less—not a little of it, not a lot of it, but all of it. Now, go and live the Christian life; exercise faith, store glory and you will shine all the brighter. The process of sanctification will go on all the readier until he comes and, imperfect as we shall be at the end of our lives, we shall be perfect at the point of death when we immediately pass into glory.

No doubt some will say, 'I suppose I could be a backslider to the end of my days and still be perfected in holiness?' If you think that you are not likely to be a Christian at all. No Christian would ever think that. Sadly a lot of people do, because that is the way the gospel is sometimes preached. 'Come and be saved and go to heaven and be sure of your ticket, then go out into the world and make the best of this world and, you hope, of the next world, too.' But that is all wrong; it is a travesty of the gospel. God save us! The proof that you are a Christian is you have a new attitude to this world and a new attitude to the world to come. That is the real proof.

The deposit of faith is to be exercised until we are in glory. When Jesus' disciples came and said: 'Explain to us the parable of the weeds of the field;' he responded: 'He who sows the good seed of the kingdom is the Son of man; the field is the world, and the good seed means the sons of the kingdom; the weeds are the sons of the evil one, and the enemy who sowed them is the devil; the harvest is the close of the age, and the reapers are angels. Just as the weeds are gathered and burned with fire, so will it be at the close of the age. The Son of man will send his angels, and they will gather out of his kingdom all causes of sin and all evildoers, and throw them into the furnace of fire; there men will weep and gnash their teeth. Then the righteous will shine like the sun in the kingdom of their Father. He who has ears to hear, let him hear' (Matt. 13:36–43).

Do you know where these last words are taken from? Most of the things you find in the New Testament have come from the Old. Did you know that? They are from Daniel 12:2: 'And many of those who sleep in the dust of the earth shall awake, some to everlasting life and some to shame and everlasting contempt. And those that are wise shall shine like the brightness of the firmament. And those who turn many to righteousness (who do not waste their Christian lives by securing their ticket to heaven and then turning back to make the best of this world) shall shine like the stars for ever and ever.' There are two facts here: first basic brightness, the brightness of the glory of Christ in every believer's life; but then there is a second point (and this is dangerous truth, there are people who would not like this at all, but that does not matter!): all that we have suffered for Christ—truly suffered for him on earth, all resistance to temptation and trial, every moral and spiritual choice that has led us nearer to Christ, every death to self to win others for Christ, going out for them, caring for them, nursing them and showing them the love of Christ in every practical way, as well as telling them the gospel—every bit of that is faith stored up for the ultimate outshining. Scripture says that we shall be rewarded for every good deed in Christ.

So, I believe it is true that, in some sense, the better you live for Christ, the more use you make of the gift of faith down here (No, you don't do it for this reason: that would spoil the whole thing, but you do it for love of Christ), not seeking any reward but simply the reward of knowing you do his will, the greater will be your brightness up there. That does not mean that we devote ourselves to Christ in order to be very bright in the kingdom, but because he is so wonderful, and because he has given himself to us that he might conform us to his image, imperfectly as it must be, down here, but really so that other people see him in us. Then in heaven, the perfect image of Christ in his glory, his truth, his love and his brightness will be seen.

This is the Christian's life. And this is what it is to be a Christian in the end; it is to be illuminated with the inward grace of Christ through the exercise of faith. It is the will and the determination to keep going on and to be true to Christ in a world that hates him. That will be the test of whether what has been said from God's Holy Word has really stuck in your soul and found a permanent lodgement there. May it be so!

PRAYER

I was shocked to be reminded that in all the seventeen years we have met at Crieff, we have never discussed prayer as a formal topic.[1] Then I thought, in all my visits to the doctor throughout my entire life, I have never discussed the subject of breathing. I am not saying I might not have had to discuss it. Many have to, but I have never needed to. But I certainly think we need to discuss prayer now!

What do you think would be the best definition of 'spiritual'? A spiritual person? For my purpose now I think it would be one who really believes in prayer. By that I mean one who really believes that there is such a thing as substantial communication with the living God about things which concern us, and him. You might think there is no one here to whom that would not apply. That may be true as far as theory is concerned, but a theory which is not practised is only an inoperative notion, which may be of no practical value or importance at all.

I believe that inoperative notions are among the greatest temptations of our spiritual life. We need to *prove* the power and efficacy of prayer— not only in our personal lives but in our corporate life, particularly as companies of believers over whom we are generally set as leaders. You have got to believe that prayer, especially corporate prayer, makes a difference. I say, 'makes a difference', but someone may say, 'Are you crazy to think that we do not all regard corporate prayer as making a difference?' No; I am not crazy, I am absolutely realistic. I repeat that I think the thought that prayer might not make all that difference, is one of our greatest temptations. Satan sees to that!

This would not be a temptation, of course, or anything like it, to

---

[1] This address was given in October 1988 to 'The Crieff Brotherhood', an informal conference of colleagues and friends convened at Crieff since 1971.

nominal Christian ministers and elders who in church life would never dream of conceding importance, or even relevance, to corporate prayer. For they would regard prayer as a ritualistic exercise which happens to be part of conventional religion and worship.

But we are surely farther on than that. We have passed through the gate of the new birth, and believe in life after birth. We recognise that there necessarily must be communication between ourselves and God; just as there must be communication between each other as Christians for there to be fellowship and co-operation in God's work. But it is easy to believe in communication with our fellow-Christians when they are standing before us in flesh and blood; it is not so easy to believe that there is a world of unseen communication between us creatures of substantial flesh and blood and the unseen God—even if we are sure that he is there at all, or rather, is here!

For one thing, we have to believe that he cares; that he is sufficiently interested in us and in our lives to want us to communicate with him about them. There is such a great deal in the Bible that we take for granted, but do not really believe—I mean in the way we believe that the sun will rise tomorrow morning, or that if we put our hand in the fire it will be burned.

This all goes back to our personal relationship with God. How real is that? I could believe that even among the best of us it is often a rather uncertain, tenuous and somewhat random affair. Even if we fervently believe in a personal God who by the Spirit has taken up permanent residence in our lives, we may have notions about him which see him as someone of a rather unpredictable nature, who, like ourselves, may not always be in the mood to talk. Or he may be offended with us, or estranged from us, and refuse to talk. Fair enough, I could believe that that may be so; but there must be some rhyme or reason to him, if he is not as capricious as we his creatures often happen to be.

But we may be sufficiently uncertain of him, at times, to cause us to rush into prayer, almost panic-stricken, driving ourselves desperately to find a place of privacy. Perhaps we need adopt a particular posture, maybe with an open Bible before us, before we can believe that we have placated any offence or estrangement which may have arisen between us, for him to be ready to listen, even if not to talk. This frantic kind of prayer is perhaps too common in the private life of many devout Christians. I often feel that extempore resorts to prayer arise from sheer lack of confidence in our God (They can embarrass me!)—dropping on one's knees without a moment's notice. Yes, sky telegrams galore, of course, but inwardly, privately.

In that connection, I am reminded of the sermons published as 'The World of Grace'. These were preached in the sixties, because we had a race of student Christians in our congregation then who tended to grow weary of their faith. They therefore developed deep personal problems because they had tied themselves pietistically, and with not a little trepidation, to certain approved routines of personal devotion—like a certain currying of favour with the Lord, which eventually became a real bugbear and was boring them almost to death—the death of their Christian lives, that is. But they did not know how to deal with the problem, and some of them were consumed with guilt at becoming tired of what they regarded as life-saving exercises.

Their situation was this. They had been married, as they had assumed, to a legalistic God, and had consequently grown tired of him. They were ashamed and even frightened that if they failed to do this, that or the other concerning their devotional life, he would come down on them like a ton of bricks, or the sword of his wrath would fall upon them and slay them as Christians. They were fed-up with their tedious, pious routines, and would begin to accuse themselves of backsliding. While that may have been the case with some, and required investigation, the likelier cause with a sincere young person earnestly seeking help, was that he had become stuck with religious legalism of the sort about which Paul comments 'the letter kills'. This was bound to drive all the joy out of their walk with the Lord, whereas Nehemiah tells us that it is the joy of the Lord that is our strength (Neh. 8:10).

Now, my message to such is simply this: If you are truly born from above then Jesus Christ is for ever interlocked with your quickened and cleansed spirit ('one spirit' as Paul says in 1 Cor. 6:17). That is one of the most amazing things in the New Testament! That our poor human spirit being quickened and sanctified could possibly be joined with his Holy Spirit is so staggering that I can never get accustomed to the idea. Then the most natural thing in the world, if we realise that this is the case and see its potential for devotion to the Lord and for power for service, will be to live the whole of our lives together with him.

It is, I am sure, like marriage. Although I have no personal experience of that state, I know a good deal about it nonetheless from those who are married and from my own observations. One of the panics which does overtake some newly-married couples I know is the thought,

'Goodness, I am tied to him (or her) for the rest of my natural life, and I simply must begin to think in terms of the two of us and not of myself alone: I must consider him (or her) at practically every turn of my life henceforward as in double harness'. But the one spouse will soon put the other right on that!

Now, to say those things to those of you whose marriages are as near bliss as can be on earth, may sound the grossest misrepresentation of marriage as you know it. But it does happen, and before I say another word on the subject, let me make it clear that I have the profoundest belief in the institution of marriage, especially Christian marriage, and count the most of the three hundred marriages I have conducted in the course of my ministry as amongst the greatest joys of my life. But there are tensions even in the best marriages, so that it is necessary to become accustomed to the fact that you are now in permanent double harness till death do you part.

The parting, of course, if both are Christians, is only for a little; and I often wonder about those who have lived many years together in the love of the Lord and then are parted by death. Theirs surely has been an experience the richness of which will be gathered up in some way hereafter to find its heavenly counterpart too deep for now. Nevertheless it must be something very rare and beautiful to grow into one another until two hearts beat like one.

It is thus with our relationship with our Lord. We have got to get accustomed to the fact that we are married to him for ever, and we can not keep him out of anything, even if we wanted to. He is there! Maybe at times when he is somewhat estranged from us because he is grieved on account of our thought life, or our words, or our actions, he may withdraw from us the fulness of his blessing—alas! But he is still there, of course, for you cannot get away from him. You two have become one, and you have to live with him—for ever! And our life hereafter, as well as what we may call our prayer-life down here, is in fact the natural outcome of that union.

When Paul advised the Thessalonians to 'pray without ceasing', he is virtually saying, 'You two people, the Lord and you, now married and living together: do you speak with each other very much? not only with words, but with "looks", side glances, pats on the back, touches of the hand, or the equivalent of an endearing embrace? Do you walk out with your God? Do you go out with him? Do you take him on holiday with you?' Well, you have to, because you cannot leave him behind, even when you are intent on going somewhere he would not approve of. You can ignore him, of course, and he bears that sort of thing very patiently, although there is a price to be paid for it, for it does not make for a very happy marriage.

I have to confess that I regard my life with Jesus in exactly this way. For me it is largely a matter of keeping close to him. 'You're there, Lord?' I would say many times a day, as you would ask if your wife were in the next room. It is not so much a matter of keeping *in* with him; it is simply a matter of referring everything *to* him.

I have to, of course. I have no one else. But it is more than that. It is a matter, literally, of breathing the Lord Jesus, because I cannot live and breathe without him! How could I go on living if he were not there and were not the source and guide and guardian of my life! If he is the lover of my soul, then I want to be with him all the time, and never let him out of my thoughts. Then my whole life is bound to be a kind of prayer—or so it appears to me—an unending sense of the Lord's presence, like Brother Lawrence who practised the presence of God in his most menial duties.

There are two quotations from hymns which interest me here: one from John Ellerton on escaping from the ceaseless tide of business, toil and care. But 'the loom, the forge, the mart' are God's too, and he ends:

Work shall be prayer, if all be wrought
As thou wouldst have it done,
And prayer, by thee inspired and taught,
Itself with work be one.

Then William Piggott's wonderful hymn about the health and vigour of our life in heaven,

And praise, and work, and rest, are one,
With thee, O Christ.

Total integration!

But I must say (and I have a feeling that Brother Lawrence would agree with me concerning his menial service in the kitchen of the Carmelite Order in Paris) that that abiding sense of the presence of the Lord was tantamount to a kind of prayer. It would be unlikely for two people to be so much together as he with his Lord without some communication, even if it were just a sharing of thoughts and feelings, not only about themselves but about others.

This is the kind of communicating I have in mind, which seems to me practically to fulfil what Paul must mean by 'pray without ceasing'. As we travel into Christ, this sort of presence, sharing and communicating on an elemental level should form the character of our Christian lives. And the intriguing thing about it is, that then you are never alone—lonely, sometimes, but anyone can be that!—but practically always in heart communion, and indeed communication with each other, in two ways. I speak to him—often too little, seldom enough; and he speaks to me—when I am of a mind to listen, which I hope is most of the time. This must surely mean—not perfectly, but practically—that almost all my thought-life is tinctured with his presence. By that I mean not an idle, spectating presence—he could never be indolently present—but an active, creative, contributing presence, making every thought meaningful to him, and to me.

Say someone springs to my mind, one of you, and I think of that person before the Lord! If I am really in constant fellowship with the Lord—not always thinking of him consciously, but knowing he is there as he watches me, kindly and deeply interested in my thoughts—then we will therefore think our thoughts about that person, together, because I am living my life (and I have only one life, given over to him) before the Lord. If it should happen, alas, that my thoughts before the Lord are not such as please him, then that calls for instant confession (the sooner the better) and pardon, if the bond of blessed fellowship between us is not to be broken.

That is what John is speaking about at the beginning of his First Letter, when he says, 'If we walk in the light (and that should be the norm for children of the light), as he is in the light (There is no doubt about his being in the light, but there is doubt about my walking in the light.) then we have fellowship one with the other, and the blood of Jesus Christ his Son keeps on cleansing us from all sin' (1 Jn. 1:7).

I love this thought: this is not holy blood redeeming our souls, but washing them constantly clean so that it is possible for him to have fellowship with us. It is only by his blood redeeming us to the new birth and washing our regenerate souls clean, the Spirit answering to the blood, that we may have fellowship with the Lord at all. And he loves us to magnify the blood, both as to saving and as to sanctifying, for that endears us to him wonderfully—the two forgivenesses, the one enclosed in the other.

Now if we are living like that, not sanctimoniously, or with arch-spirituality, but simply and realistically in the light of the facts of our regenerate life with him, can there be any doubt that practically my every thought—about myself and about everyone else—should be shared with my ever-present Lord? That, to my mind, is the essence of prayer. Anyway, that is the bulk of my own prayer life, apart from corporate prayer which, of course, being mainly vocal, is likely to be more ordered, but not necessarily more effectual.

What you think of that? Of course I must admit that at times, especially when I try to explain and even expound this integrated rather than spasmodic life of prayer, I have horrible guilty feelings. These are mostly engineered, I must confess, by thoughts of what others may be thinking of me; and, as they may see it, my pathetically haphazard sort of prayer life—if they regard it as a life of prayer at all!

But how otherwise could I have continued in the Lord's service and been regarded as an ardent advocate and warrior for the necessity of corporate prayer? People come from the ends of the earth to be with us—not always for the preaching, but for the prayer meeting on Saturday evenings! Of course there are some preachers who seem to see no connection between the preaching, which they would hope and allege influences people, and the prayer without which it would seem to me the preaching becomes hollow and accomplishes little or nothing!

There are those who would not cross the street, let alone an ocean to come to a prayer meeting such as ours. And I must honestly say that I think a lot of folk, including ministers, are quite frankly apprehensive of such an arduous involvement, because of its cost. I can sympathise with that, for it is hard work for all involved. But is it not just here that we come to grips with the powers of evil at their most obdurate and threatening? But apprehension at the thought, or not, there is simply no other way to tackle the forces of evil; which forces, we are sure, would like us to think they have the upper hand, and that there is nothing we can do to hinder them, or frustrate their knavish tricks.

It is doubtless for this reason that some try to hope that they will get on with the work of the kingdom quite as well, without a burdensome involvement in a consistent regimen of corporate prayer. Indeed, to some it is a frightening thought, because they fear that it is going to exact a heavy toll on their lives. And it is; but it would be far harder if you were ministering in most places in America, if all I hear from American Christians is true. Christians in that vast country have become so activist that many fail completely to see what huddling together in an upper or nether room is going to do for a world in which the crying need seems to be—for action!

Many apparently do not believe in the realities of the spirit world, let alone the fearful conflicts that go on there. But for anyone anywhere sweetly to go on in the sanguine hope that there is an easier way to do the Lord's work fruitfully, and that the failure to engage in the battle of prayer in any serious way is not noticed must be one of the biggest fallacies and delusions ever to afflict misguided souls!

This is not to say that without such major emphasis on prayer a minister may not become what is called successful and run a very thriving socio-religious community and make a name for himself, even as a preacher. He may be exceedingly highly regarded, becoming quite illustrious as far as the general public, or even the Christian and evangelical worlds are concerned. And there may be converts, of a sort, and crowds of devotees; but as far as a seminal work is concerned, that produces seed-bearing fruit which abides and then itself dies to self and sin and Satan so as to produce fruit in the *next* generation—it will not be, and cannot be; because as our Lord says, 'except a corn of wheat falls into the ground and dies, it remains a single seed; whereas if it dies it produces many seeds' (Jn. 12:29).

Two elemental but opposite things are to be said about dying to sin, self and the enemy: the first is that it is always painful. It is much more painful to die a living death to these three bugbears, than to die a dying death. Dying is once-for-all whereas, as Paul tells the Romans, a 'living sacrifice' is in a sense a running sore (Rom. 12:1); for as he says elsewhere, he 'dies daily' (1 Cor. 15:31), and to the Romans again he says, 'For your sake we face death all day long; we are considered (by the enemy) as sheep to be slaughtered' (Rom. 8:36 from Ps. 44:22).

The second thing to be said about this 'living sacrifice' which is virtually 'living dying', follows on from that quotation from Romans 8. After Paul says that we 'face death all day long, and are as sheep for slaughter', he goes on in answer to the series of questions which begins: 'What shall we say to this about God foreknowing, our predestination; calling justification glorification?' And he continues, 'Who will bring any charge against God's elect' followed by, 'Who is he that condemns?' and by, 'Who shall separate us from the love of God?' In answer he replies: 'No, in all these things we are more than conquerors through him that loved us, for I am convinced that...(nothing) in all creation shall be able to separate us from the love of God which is in Christ Jesus our Lord'.

To put more plainly this point about 'living dying', we are more than conquerors because he has conquered before us, and we go on to conquer (in the matter of this daily and momentary dying), not only in his foregoing and prevenient strength, but in his foregoing and prevenient dying. We do it, we die—after him—and in his death. This means that we not only do it in his strength by the indwelling Holy Spirit, but as it were helplessly (this is dying) much more by drawing on his power than by driving ourselves to distraction by self-effort.

I am more and more convinced that what Christians need to know is the reality of God's sovereign Holy Spirit dwelling in their hearts with the gift of repentance and the yearning to draw upon the gift of faith. A great many Christians, even those of years of experience do not know this sufficiently, with sufficient conviction. It should be overpowering and overmastering; it should be the thought of all thoughts for Christians, that he is there, and is pleading with me to draw on the resources of his grace.

Do you see what I mean? When we do something after and in the Death and Resurrection of Jesus Christ, there is, paradoxically, an ease and sweetness of surrender which is quite extraordinary. Dying to sin, self and Satan in Christ is, when we come to terms with it, generally an exceedingly sweetening, albeit it may be a humbling experience. This stands to reason, for the one thing we are taught supremely in our evangelical and reformed faith is that it is a work of God and not of man. Have we learned that yet?

Man has to let God do it for him, and even his necessary co-operation has all to be like the action of any electrical appliance, an action consequent upon putting on a switch to receive power from beyond itself. Is your switch on? Or are you doing it all in your own strength? That is hopeless: you will never do it. The work of God has never been and never will be done but in his strength alone.

This calls for the armour of God. You remember how the Christian armour passage in Ephesians 6:10ff. ends. After standing in all the defensive armour of the belt, breastplate, shoes, shield, and helmet, Paul goes over to the offensive with 'the sword of the Spirit, which is the word of God', and continues, 'Praying in the Spirit on all occasions and with all kinds of prayer and requests. And with this in mind', he says, 'be alert, and always keep on praying for all the saints. And', he says, 'for me, that whenever I open my mouth, words, utterance may be given me, that I will fearlessly make known the mystery of the gospel. Pray', he says, 'that I may declare it fearlessly as I should' (Eph. 6:17–20). Fearlessly? That must mean that sometimes at least the great apostle was afraid. He tells us as much in another connection. And isn't that a comfort?

I have much less fear of man, and much greater fear of God today than ever I had before. Sometimes I am tempted to think it is a kind of nerves or nervousness, especially when I face a congregation to lead them in prayer or praise, or take a funeral, or a wedding service. I say to myself, What are you afraid of? For I could attribute those feelings nowadays to the increasing anxiety which comes upon older folk when they seek to do the simplest things they used to do without turning a hair; they now find them harder to do. But deep in my heart I know that this greater fear is of God, because the good Lord has brought me to live nearer—closer to him. Standing trembling at the door on Sunday morning before I leave the manse is a comparatively new thing to me, although I knew it in the earlier days. I say to myself, 'Why should that return?' But I do believe that it is fear of God because he has brought me nearer to him, and in more immediate awareness of his dear presence. That for me is the most exciting thing in the whole world. And—I call it —that life which I now live, with him—Prayer. What would you call it?

TWO SERMONS ON MORALS

'The body is not meant for immorality, but
for the Lord, and the Lord for the body.'
                                    1 Corinthians 6:13

1.   Ethical Questions

We are to consider some of the moral questions which exercise society these days. While I want to set forth the holy law of God in respect to them, I come to them with considerable delicacy of feeling. In consulting such subjects we always need to pray earnestly for chastity of mind, that nothing may cause any one the slightest sullying, but may rather sanctify our minds.

You may find that a good deal that follows seems to emphasise the legal rather than the gracious or dynamic side of Christianity. Let me explain why this is so. The laws that we are to set forth are the laws of God, not only for Christians, but for all men, who are the creatures of God and are subject to his laws. Some of these things apply particularly to those who are outside the Christian church and its standards of moral law and grace.

I begin with some basic statements from the Word of God, both from the Old and New Testaments, with regard to the question of sex. We are concerned now with what God says in his Word about it. It is perfectly clear here and throughout the Bible that this precious, necessary and holy gift of God is given for marriage only. Notice how early in the Bible this absolute statement comes (Gen. 2:24, 25): 'Therefore a man leaves his father and his mother and cleaves to his wife, and they become one flesh. And the man and his wife were both naked, and were not ashamed.' Thus 'They become one flesh.'

Jesus comments on this in Matthew 19, when the Pharisees came to him and said, 'Is it lawful to divorce one's wife for any cause?' Jesus' answer is one of the most important things on this whole question. When he was asked a question about divorce, and therefore about marriage, he drove the whole question back to the fundamental statement in the second chapter of the Bible. He stated it without qualification as being a sufficient and satisfying answer to his perfect heart and mind on the matter. He answered, 'Have you not read that he who made them from the beginning made them male and female, and said, "For this reason a man shall leave his father and mother and be joined to his wife, and the two shall become one"?' (vv. 4, 5). Then he emphasised and repeated this by saying, 'So they are no longer two but one.' There is no hint at all that he is speaking of union symbolically: 'What therefore God has joined together, let no man put asunder' (v. 6).

Notice these words, 'God has joined'. There is no question here of what you might call specifically Christian marriage. Jesus is implying that wherever two people come together in physical union, not only is that marriage in his sight, but the parties are joined together by God inasmuch as they act according to the nature he has given them. 'God has joined',—no explanations, no qualifications. 'God has joined', when a man leaves his father and cleaves to his wife. 'God has joined', and that covers every first union from the beginning. We might say, of course, still holding on to this passage, that this is in the Ten Commandments, negatively, in the seventh commandment. In Exodus 20:4 we are concerned with five words only: Thou shalt not commit adultery. Marriage is inviolable.

But the Pharisees cited Moses' concession in the matter of divorce, 'Why then did Moses command one to give a certificate of divorce and to put her away?' He (Jesus) said to them, 'for your hardness of heart Moses allowed you to divorce your wives, but from the beginning it was not so. And I say unto you: whoever divorces his wife, except for unchastity, and marries another, commits adultery' (Matt. 19:7–9; *cf*. Deut. 24:1–4). Nothing could be plainer. The whole thing is clear, without the slightest opportunity for compromise.

That leads on to the question of contraception, and all we need to say about that in relation to our Lord's words, is that all sexual relationships outwith marriage are absolutely out. Pleasure without lawful responsibility is absolutely out. God is against it all, in all circumstances. It is against God's holy law and the holy injunctions as we have read them. So that closes the matter! That doesn't make people conform? No: but God has a way of dealing with people who do not conform, because his holy laws take their toll, not necessarily, not often, at once, nor perhaps even soon; but ultimately. God is against it, and to be against God in anything is serious.

But even within marriage there is such a thing as self-control. Paul speaks of this in 1 Corinthians 7:1–7: 'Now concerning the matter about which you wrote. It is well for a man not to touch a woman. But because of the temptation to immorality...' He is not here discussing the whole question of marriage, because marriage can be set (and is normally set) in the Scriptures on a higher level than this. That is not the question. He is dealing with a specific question, in a sense a narrow question. 'But because of the temptation to immorality, each man should have his own wife...' That is to say, marriage, which has higher realms and reaches than this question of continence, is the solution to the problem of sexual continence, among others. 'Each man should have his own wife and each woman her own husband. The husband should give to his wife her conjugal rights, and likewise the wife to her husband. For the wife does not rule over her own body, but the husband does; likewise the husband does not rule over his own body, but the wife does.' This, in those days, was astonishing equality and mutuality. 'Do not refuse one another except perhaps by agreement (Paul is almost tentative here) for a season, that you may devote yourselves to prayer; but then come together again, lest Satan tempt you through lack of self-control.' There is no suggestion either here (or in any of the commentaries which I have) as to what the temptation is. Perhaps we do not need to be told very much more; we can use our imaginations. 'I say this by way of concession, not of command. I wish that all were as I myself am. But each has his own special gift from God, one of one kind and one of another.'

Here is what one commentator says about this passage: 'It is evident that refusal amounts to fraud. Three conditions are required for lawful abstention: 1. It must be by mutual consent. 2. For a good object. 3. Temporary. Even so, the advice is given very tentatively; but it is an exception for certain circumstances, not a rule for all circumstances.'[1]

Then he quotes Calvin, who uses this verse as an argument against monasticism:

[1] A. Robertson and A. Plummer, *A Critical and Exegetical Commentary on the First Epistle of St Paul to the Corinthians* (2nd edition, Edinburgh, 1914), p. 134

'To vow perpetual celibacy without having received the necessary charisma (gift of God) is to court disaster. (Celibacy without the aid of God is disaster! W.S.) Forcing it on the clergy prevents good men from taking Orders and causes weak men to break their vows.'

But suppose within this permission and the suggestion it gives of self-control, and especially within the interests of higher things, such as prayer and the pious life, there are reasons which make child-bearing dangerous? Is it not hard to expect husband and wife to live in the normal intimacy of married life continually without absolute continence? This is exactly what Paul is saying. If husband and wife abstain, it must be very temporarily, for we have to beware the tempter, by whom we may be sorely tried when we become unduly self-conscious about our abstention, and distracted by our unfulfilled desires. Does that suggest, and would Paul today suggest the possibility of some help, surgical, or whatever, in a case where there was real danger?

Many medics today, especially those not Christian, are easy on this. Even Christian medics or Christian ministers may want to suggest help, and may sanction this, that, and the other. But what is sanctioned must be sanctioned not only by those concerned, but by God in their consciences. This is a matter for God, in inward, intimate, personal guidance. It is surely in all relevant circumstances quite disastrous to exclude him and his guidance in such a matter—else how can the life continue to be blessed? If we do not consult him in what we do, and receive his counsel, guidance, and especially his assurance, then God will withdraw his blessing from our lives. Remember that the opposite of blessing is cursing; and those who are not being blessed are often nearer to cursing than we realise.

Now, on this matter, on which our words must be as few but as weighty as possible: it is not a question of who moralises. As Godber said to the Archbishop of Canterbury in a classic utterance, the only authority he had as a cleric was the authority of God's Word, and if he did not speak according to that authority, he had no other. So here. Our only authority is that of God's Word; and this is such a delicate, yet practical and burning question for so many, that it dare not be considered apart from the specific guidance of God the Holy Spirit. Let us be sure (for this is something that has often to be discussed, of course—usually in private) that none of us will find himself in the matter of sacred bonds of holy Christian matrimony, hard, harsh, or inhuman. But if God is grieved, all is wrong—and there is nothing worse in the whole wide world.

Another valid issue here is abortion. Here we are concerned with the value and status of an unborn child. As far as the Scriptures are concerned, we can set forth the most general principles in three scriptural references. The first one is from the words of the angel Gabriel to Mary when he announced the birth of the Son of God (Luke 1:35): 'The angel answered and said unto her, The Holy Ghost shall come upon thee, and the power of the Highest shall overshadow thee: therefore also that holy thing which shall be born of thee shall be called the Son of God.' In the RSV instead of using the word 'thing' the world 'child' is used, with a footnote; but it is of interest to note that the phrase in the Greek is in the neuter gender: 'Therefore also the holy thing being born (*to gennomenon*) will be called the Son of God.'

Now I do not want to overstress this. The name for the Holy Spirit, the word *pneuma* in the Greek, from which we have words like pneumatic, is in the neuter gender, and yet no sensible person would speak of the Holy Spirit as 'it', but 'he' and 'him'. Here the Greek is in the neuter gender, when the phrase might quite easily have been more specifically personal, as the RSV seeks in translation to make it.

The second Scripture is from Exodus 21:22–25—again a delicate passage. Moses says, 'When men strive together, and hurt a woman with child, so that there is a miscarriage, and yet no harm follows, the one who hurt her shall be fined, according as the woman's husband shall lay upon him; and he shall pay as the judges determine. If any harm follows (harm to whom? The mother) then you shall give life for life, eye for eye, tooth for tooth, hand for hand, foot for foot, burn for burn, wound for wound, stripe for stripe.' Note that the harm or hurt is to the mother, more than to the fruit of her womb, and the fine for loss of the unborn child is left to the husband's assessment. This also is interesting—and I think we may build upon that, because it seems wrong, therefore, to use the sixth commandment, 'You shall not kill' in connection with such a loss. This is not in any sense to condone sin, the sin of doing despite to such a precious burden; but surely it is going too far to use this commandment as such, in respect of an unborn child. Lest you think this is too concessive, and too negative and even harsh, let me also cite Isaiah 40:11 where the prophet, inspired of God, says these words: 'He will feed his flock like a shepherd, he will gather the lambs in his arms, he will carry them in his bosom and gently lead those that are with young.' The unborn child is a precious, precious burden surely.

What then of abortion? The Scriptures seem to make plain that the life of the mother is always more important than the life of the unborn child.

This gives no right to interfere with the fruit of the womb, and with the course of nature, unless, surely, the mother is in mortal danger, or unless her health is in danger of irreparable harm. These dangers will include imminence of death, or permanent injury to health, including, possibly, permanent mental derangement. The right to interfere will not include questions of personal inconvenience, or of mild, or even moderate upset: these are not grounds for interfering with the course of nature in the fruit of the womb. Would that this were believed in this country!

Nor is covering up, or getting rid of the results of sin any ground whatsoever for interfering. Look at it this way: the purpose of covering up the fruits of sin is to avoid painful consequences. But since no sin is hid from God, he is—this is what we as Christians must come to know more and more in our lives—far more to be feared than any other. Since sin cannot be hidden from him, what is the point of hiding anything that cannot be hidden from him? But you say, 'God is more merciful than men. Hide from men but not from God.' Yes, doubtless, but be careful. There is never any condoning of sin with God. You say, 'He forgives.' Forgiveness is a very costly thing, not only for God and his Son Jesus Christ, but for him who receives it. The hardest thing in the world, often, is to convince someone deeply convicted of sin by the Spirit, that God does forgive. But let me put it thus: if you were to receive a certificate from God to say that you were absolutely forgiven of all your sin through Jesus Christ, and perhaps especially of certain sins, and you then turned the certificate over on the other side, this is what it would say: 'Sin no more!' That is the obligation. There is not such a thing as an excuse. None!

To some an even more vexed question is that of homosexuality. This has been a vexed question in many civilisations. It is almost as common as normal behaviour in Mohammedan and Arab countries, as those who know these countries will tell. It has also been known throughout the centuries among peoples and nations that have been over-prosperous and therefore too idle. And the idle rich (and the idle rich are a different sort nowadays, like those pop star millionaires) are still so put to it, and so bored with life, that they have got to try everything, even the most ridiculous, obnoxious, horrid and unnatural things, for novelty.

I want to say a preparatory word here. It seems to me that the Bible thinks of this question as a matter of sin committed by comparatively normal people seeking sensual novelty. This, as far as I read the Bible, is what took place in Sodom and Gomorrah (Gen. 19) and in Judges chapters 19 and 20, in the horrid story of the Levite's concubine; and, remember, it was the sin of the tribe of Benjamin that caused that horrid story to be written.

In Leviticus 18:22 and 20:13 it is made clear that this sin is an abomination in the sight of God; that is, the sin of a man having sexual relations with another man. How abominable it is to God can be seen quite clearly (and this is one of the most terrible things) by geological facts by the change in the contours of that unique natural phenomenon, the Dead Sea depression. Here is what George Adam Smith says about the Dead Sea and Sodom and Gomorrah.

> In this awful hollow, this bit of the infernal regions come up to the surface, this hell with the sun shining into it, primitive man laid the scene of God's most terrible judgment on human sin. The glare of Sodom and Gomorrah is flung down the whole length of Scripture history. It is the popular and standard judgment of sin. The story is told in Genesis. It is applied in Deuteronomy, by Amos, by Isaiah, by Jeremiah, by Zephaniah, in Lamentations, and by Ezekiel. Our Lord Himself employed it more than once as a figure of the judgment He threatens upon cities where the Word is preached in vain, and there we feel the flames scorch our own cheeks. Paul, Peter, Jude, all make mention of it. In the Apocalypse the great 'city of sin' is spiritually called, Sodom.[2]

Now, after discussing various questions in the matter of the destruction of Sodom and Gomorrah, George Adam Smith goes on:

> The reality of the narrative however, has been questioned by many. They have argued that it is simply one of the many legends of overturned or buried cities, with the addition of the local phenomenon of the Dead Sea and with a very much grander moral than has ever been attached to any tale of this kind. But statements of this argument have hitherto been vitiated, destroyed, by three faults. They have been based upon facts that are irrelevant; they have omitted some that are relevant, and they have supposed that critics who maintain the historical truth of the narrative have some subjective or dogmatic reason for doing so. For instance, they appeal to the ease with which legends spring up everywhere of cities sunk in the depths of the ocean; but this is not relevant to our

[2] George Adam Smith, *The Historical Geography of the Holy Land* (14th edition, London, 1908), pp. 504–505

narrative, for the striking thing is that though the presence of the Dead Sea offers every temptation for the adoption of such a legend, it is nowhere in the Bible even suggested that the doomed cities are at the bottom of the sea, but we hear of this first from Josephus, the secular Jewish historian. This is surely a proof of the sobriety of the Biblical tradition.

Again, the argument against the Biblical tradition fails to deal with the fact that the phenomena it describes have all happened elsewhere in similar geological formations, and yet are so singular that it is not probable they can have been invented.

Thirdly, so far from being a dogmatic interest, which alone holds some to a belief in the narrative, the facts of the existence of the cities and of their overthrow in the manner described are accepted both by authorities in natural science and critics of Old Testament who have obviously no such interest to serve. The efforts to prove the story wholly legend may therefore be said to have failed.[3]

And that was the judgment of God—fire and brimstone for sin.

The New Testament takes up this theme in Romans 1:26, 27: 'For this reason God gave them up to dishonourable passions. Their women exchanged natural relations for unnatural, and the men likewise gave up natural relations with women and were consumed with passion for one another, men committing shameless acts with men and receiving in their own persons the due penalty for their error.' These verses show that this kind of conduct takes place (and notice that the New Testament is as concerned with this sin in women as in men) in situations so bad that God has abandoned men because of their depravity to sink into the depths of their soul-destroying ruin. It also shows that they receive in their own persons, in their own bodies, due penalty for their errors. Writing again in 1 Corinthians 6:10, Paul says, 'Do not be deceived; neither the immoral, nor idolaters, nor adulterers, nor homosexuals... will inherit the kingdom of God.'

In 1 Timothy 1:10, Paul warns young Timothy that the law of God is as much against this sin as against all other sin—as God is against all that is contrary to sound doctrine. That is to say, God is against it, absolutely, firmly and finally. Not much wonder, for it has sapped the

---

[3] *Ibid.*, pp. 509–510

vitality and ruined the manhood of more great empires than I care to mention, not least the Greek and Roman empires.

But let us distinguish, for a little, certain types of homosexual behaviour. The Bible is dealing most of all (and, doubtless, they are the most heinous sinners in this respect) with those who wickedly seek novel experiences; but there are those involved in this sin because they have been corrupted by others and are therefore not as guilty as those who have corrupted them. As Jesus says (if we can adapt this expression), 'Some have been made eunuchs by men' (Matt. 19:22).

It is against this danger in young people that part of the law of homosexuality stands. That part of it, we are all very glad of, to protect our young people from such a danger. But let it be observed that there are many more of the population prone to this temptation than is often realised or admitted; I suppose largely because of the dread of exposure. The question is covered by every degree of interest in either sex, and to those who are absolutely perverted and have a complete revulsion against the opposite sex and an innate attraction towards their own. There are far more people in the world who are almost equally, or quite equally bisexual, than most people know. This is a vexed question, and has to be dealt with often and carefully. Where an unnatural interest is almost equal with a natural interest, or where the unnatural is stronger than the natural, any marriage is in grave danger. A couple who find themselves in such a situation, if both know and understand, would be well advised to discuss the matter with some competent and worthy person who could at least afford them some understanding and, possibly, advice.

But there seems to be another category. Some appear either born that way (perhaps some psychiatrists would hardly allow the expression 'born that way', but would rather say they developed that way, without any outward corruption or interference whatsoever), or grow up with a complete revulsion against what is natural in the experience of the sexual emotions, and with a sense of complete natural inclination toward what is unnatural and which God has set his laws against. These, we may say, taking Jesus' further word in Matthew 19:12 are those who are born, not made by men, 'eunuchs'. It has to be said that there is a stage in nature, in the development of young people, as there is in the animals, when there is some such interest. But normally that passes and is not yielded to where there is strong moral influence and a keen, informed conscience. It is a passing—painful or pleasing, or just embarrassing— experience, to think such thoughts and feel such feelings, and it is normally comparatively easily dealt with.

Where it is innate and deeply bound up with the emotions, and indeed with the affections, this is, generally speaking (and has been stated more dogmatically in recent days) a twist that is often hard, if not seemingly impossible to untwist—although God can do anything. Indeed, it is often found to be far more intractable, far less willing to yield to any kind of treatment than corresponding physical kinks and malformations.

But however 'natural' such unnatural inclinations, tendencies and temptation may seem to be to one born a eunuch, this gives no licence whatsoever to sin. After all, if people who are natural in this regard must control their desires, in marriage and out of marriage, why shouldn't homosexuals? It may, of course, also be observed that such are often by nature highly neurotic, inhibited people, guilt-ridden because of the misunderstanding of their fellows and the dread of men knowing what they are and what they desire. Their desires on that account are often more intense, more clamant, and more demanding than other people's. But, here again, this gives no concession to sin.

Does this sound hard? Well, it would be but for the grace of God. What does the grace of God say? First, there is what the psychologists call sublimation, or redirection, by which a certain part of such emotional and physical energy is redirected, and often very usefully. This is never a full solution to the problem, but where it is a solution—and it can be considerable—it is a blessing. To the extent that it is not, these urges must be controlled. God gives no licence to sin.

Now, I have spoken of this partly to put the whole matter on a biblical, moral and gracious footing. I have also done so in the hope that what I say may help any such, or may help any who know such and desire to help them. There is help in the grace of God, and in the exquisite understanding and sympathy of Jesus. And, of course, such help ought always to be given in the strictest confidence. Surely no right-thinking person would want it to be known that they have such tendencies: it will only be in heaven that some of God's saints will be able to testify to the grace of God in this regard. God is able.

But to turn to another subject: Gambling. The gambling urge is, it seems to me, part of the spirit of adventure and daring, the desire in man to take risks, which is part of human life. There is that in many men, often the very best of men, which loves to live dangerously, and which finds great fun in so doing. Do you not think that Paul got great fun out of living as dangerously as he did? There are some who love rock-climbing and mountaineering. Others love exploring, as in the Antarctic. These urges are something so fundamental that they have to be fulfilled in some way. It is part of the sportsmanship which is a gift of God. Its highest satisfaction is for those who participate. This is too little understood.

But when the urge to gamble—using the word in its best sense, to risk, to venture—is handmaid with covetousness, then the gambling spirit is damnable. The principle of too easy gain destroys men's respect for honest labour, which was made an irksome necessity through the Fall (Gen. 3:17–19). God says we are to earn our living through the sweat of our brows. Covetousness destroys respect for labour, which is honourable, and destroys respect for labour as character-building. We all need to work. It is good for us to work—even if we do not need the money (see 2 Thess. 3:6–13)!

The principle of easy gain by chance also gives rein to a hell of evil practices, however high-sounding the names we give them. In modern days it was the Conservative Prime Minister, Harold Macmillan, with his Premium Bonds, who became the father of nameless subsequent political acts of degradation. I wonder if he ever regretted it. National lotteries? In other countries, but surely not here! 'Thou shalt not covet,' says God. To do so corrupts character and sows seeds of innumerable evils in the heart of man.

Whereas to gamble on Christ is not only safe, but blessed (although it involves many seeming hazards and much dangerous living), to gamble on any one or any thing else is to be a sure loser, first, in respect of our character, and second, as to what we hope eventually to win. If we lay up treasure in heaven, our treasure is sure. Jesus says that if we lay up treasure on earth and covet that which is upon the earth, moths, rust and thieves will do despite to it. If God had said to Jesus, 'I want you to go to the corner pinnacle of the precincts of the Temple and cast yourself down into the Kidron Valley as a display to man of my protecting power,' it would have been absolutely safe for Jesus to do so. That would have been a safe gamble or bet. When Satan asked him to do it, to comply would have involved absolute destruction. Do all your gambling in Christ according to his will. There is full scope for sport there, with no incentive to filthy lucre, greed or base gain. There we are sure winners.

I have one more subject: Drugs. This, of course, is another vexed question, especially since the distinction between hard and soft drugs has been blurred by the use of many so-called soft drugs which, it appears, increase the craving for those that are harder, more damaging, ruinous and disastrous to the personality. The aim of all drugs is to escape, either into oblivion (who does not thank James Simpson, who first used chloroform in surgical operations, for anaesthetics? What a blessed thing to go to sleep and wake up with the vile cause of disease and pain dealt with and removed!) or into what are called pleasurable hallucinations. But here is a question that concerns us: If you use the mildest sedative as a pain killer, or to induce sleep, you are seeking escape. How far is this legitimate? Would you say that the strain and pace of modern living, especially in cities, is so great, and the calls upon us as Christians to do our duty and faithfully serve our day and generation are so great that we sometimes need help?

The question arises: What is our duty? How much does God expect of us, and how much can our fellow men legitimately expect of us, considering the strain of modern life? I believe we must take very strict and disciplined steps to guard our health, and this includes guarding our rest and sleep in order that we may be able to continue to do our duty to God and man. Many men and women in the service of the Lord Jesus Christ end their usefulness, it seems to me, far too quickly because they have not had regard to their own health.

Take my own example—and you can apply this to yourself. How far is it my duty to try to attend to all the first priorities in my life, since I cannot possibly, without having a hundred hours in a day, attend to all the needs and demands made upon me? In the strain of such a life, am I justified in seeking escape from the pressures of life and the pressures of people? Is it legitimate to seek gentle help to induce sleep instead of tossing all night with the brain going hammer-and-tongs for hours? And how does this affect temptations? The likelihood is in such circumstances that the enemy will sweep in like a flood to bowl us over and knock us off our feet. Is a sleepless night now and then—even more often than that—always a bad thing? Some of the best thoughts that have come to man have come in the silent watches of the night. Some of the best thoughts that God has given me from his Word have been in the middle of the night. We know, of course, that this cannot go on night after night indefinitely, but it is not necessarily a bad thing to lie awake now and then, especially if one does not panic.

But if we are living in the Spirit and not on our nerves, we may say, 'Will not healthy exhaustion lead to healthy rest?' I suppose most of us would say that that is perhaps a counsel of perfection. Yet, as Christians who respect our bodies, and who have regard to our duty before God, we must aim at such an ideal more and more. Indeed, the whole life should be utterly under the governance of Christ. This is perhaps not what you expected would be discussed under the question of drugs; but this is what is most practical for us to look at, for we all need escape. Man needs escape. Man in the sinful motivity of his fallen humanity screams loudly for escape and for shelter. But escape from something is one thing, escape to another, is another. Men escape from the pains, the aches, the trials and the retributions of this life, to fall into worse—in hell.

What do they escape to? What have so many contemporary fugitives to India escaped in to? A nameless Nirvana, a world of complete illusion giving no real or lasting answer to their need? I do not think you are likely to find a healthy escape in India, except among the Christians. If this is mere escape from life and the responsibilities of life, and the pains and aches of life, then it is absolutely despicable and cowardly. But escape is necessary, and escape into Christ is utterly healthy. Why, this is the first part of our training as soldiers of Christ. We are called to shelter in Christ from the woes, ills and evils of this present world. But once we are sheltering in him, God is not only a refuge but also our strength. He strengthens us, then fortifies us and says to us, 'Now, I want you to go out into the world to stand and face the foe, and when he comes at you in the most fearful onslaughts, stand in my strength and face him, not moving an inch.' When you have learned to do that, he says, 'Now, I want you to take the sword of the Spirit, which is the Word of God, and all-prayer, and I want you to attack the evil in your own life, and as you find it in the lives of others, and be a router of Satan in other people's lives.' All this begins by seeking escape and shelter in Christ.

Do not misunderstand. This does not set us on a plane above infirmities. Jesus had infirmities. He suffered every infirmity known to men—sin apart (Heb. 4:15). He did not escape one of them. He knows all about human pain, more about it than we do. This does not set us above infirmities. We do not escape the ills of human life in this life.

I think of the late Isa Ross, who spent around thirty years in Morocco and won many women and girls for Jesus Christ in Southern Morocco. She came home a wreck at the end of thirty years of strain, living in that Islamic land. She was so distraught, disordered, weary and exhausted in her personality that some of her dearest friends could not understand her. I say this with the greatest tenderness, for we all loved her very much. She became, because of years of strain, such a changed person and so distraught, that it was difficult to know what to do to help her. Before she was taken to hospital, where she died, she moved from one furnished room to another until her state was pathetic and a great grief to her friends. What did God do for her? In the end he gave her blessed escape from the whole thing, but the last few years of that dear woman's life were agony and bewilderment because she had 'sold out', as they say, to Christ and exhausted herself for the souls of men and women in Morocco.

It is, first, escape into Christ for shelter; but it may ultimately involve us in being fitted for martyrdom—like Stephen, or Wishart, or Bonhoeffer. And let us remember that all Christians do not come through brainwashing successfully, as Geoffrey Bull did. Who knows what is happening to Watchman Nee and to the Peking Pastor at the moment? Some crack up and go under as far as this life is concerned, and many Christians end their days completely deranged, and mindless, in asylums and such places. We know that this is true, and in their confusion we may think that they have lost faith. Never! They are subject to the ills of life, and, perhaps, to the cost of living for Christ— sometimes, alas, the cost of not living for Christ, but that is another story. But at the last (and it is no royal way—although in another sense it is) theirs is the perfect escape from all the ills of mortal life, and from the cost of seeking to be faithful Christians (and, for some, the glory of a martyr's crown) and, beyond that, the glory of perfect health, in new bodies for old, by the resurrection of Jesus Christ. Hallelujah!

TWO SERMONS ON MORALS

**'The body is not meant for immorality, but
for the Lord, and the Lord for the body.'**
                              1 Corinthians 6:13

2. Overcoming the Flesh

We are now concerned with the workings of Satan on the desires of our
flesh. We are to look at what Christ comes to give us, and do for us,
which successfully combats the efforts of Satan to draw us downwards
to destruction away from Christ, by working upon the desires of our
flesh. What Christ does is simply to give himself to us, and take us,
who receive him, believing in him and repenting of our sins, to make us
his own. In fact, he marries us to himself. And while, of course, we
generally think of this marriage in relation to the whole Body or Bride of
Christ, the church, I want us now to think of our own personal union
with Christ.

Christ says, through the apostle Paul, 'The body is not meant for
immorality, but for the Lord, and the Lord for the body' (1 Cor. 6:13b).
We shall come back to that later. Again, 'Do you not know that your
bodies are members of Christ?... He who is united to the Lord becomes
one spirit with him.... Do you not know that your body is the temple of
the Holy Spirit within you, which you have from God? You are not your
own; you were bought with a price. So glorify God in your body' (1
Cor. 6:15, 17, 19, 20).

In Ephesians 5 Paul speaks of two things together, because they are
vitally related. He speaks of Christ's marriage to his church, and men's
marriage to their wives. In this passage it is sometimes a little difficult to
know which he is referring to, primarily, and in a sense it does not
matter, because the two are linked so closely. Listen to what he says:

> Be subject to one another out of reverence to Christ. Wives, be subject to your husbands, as to the Lord. For the husband is the head of the wife as Christ is the head of the church, his body, and is himself its Saviour. As the church is subject to Christ, so let wives also be subject in everything to their husbands (5:21–24).

On the other hand, he never deals with one side without dealing with the other: perfect balance.

> Husbands, love your wives, as Christ loved the church and gave himself up for her, that he might sanctify her, having cleansed her by the washing of water with the word, that he might present the church to himself in splendour, without spot or wrinkle or any such thing, that she might be holy and without blemish. Even so husbands should love their wives as their own bodies. He who loves his wife loves himself. For no man ever hates his own flesh, but nourishes and cherishes it, as Christ does the church, because we are members of his body. 'For this reason a man shall leave his father and mother (Gen. 2:24) and be joined to his wife, and the two shall become one' (5:25–31).

He then goes on to say:

> This is a great mystery, and I take it to mean Christ and the church (v. 32).

The two becoming one is a great mystery: first Christ and the church—Christ and sinners becoming one, and then a man and his wife becoming one, signifying a true union in marriage.

> However, let each one of you love his wife as himself, and let the wife see that she respects her husband (v. 33).

We are not concerned with marriage as such at the moment, except as it illustrates the marriage of Christ to his church and the marriage of Christ to the individual believer. Now, throughout the Scriptures, and in the Old Testament in particular, there are some beautiful descriptions of this. Here is one from the love song in Psalm 45:

> My heart overflows with a goodly theme; I address my verses to the king (the Bridegroom), my tongue is like the pen of a ready scribe.

The Psalmist proceeds to describe the heavenly Bridegroom, Christ:

> You are the fairest of the sons of men; grace is poured upon your lips; therefore God has blessed you for ever. Gird your sword upon your thigh, O mighty one, in your glory and majesty!

> In your majesty ride forth victoriously for the cause of truth and to defend the right; let your right hand teach you dread deeds! Your arrows are sharp in the heart of the king's enemies; the peoples fall under you.

> Your divine throne endures for ever and ever. Your royal sceptre is a sceptre of equity; you love righteousness and hate wickedness. Therefore God, your God, has anointed you with the oil of gladness (the Holy Spirit) above your fellows; your robes are all fragrant with myrrh and aloes and cassia.

Then the Psalmist speaks to the Bride, the church, or, if you like, the individual believer, for it is in the singular:

> Hear, O daughter, consider, and incline your ear; forget your people (your past life) and your father's house; and the king will desire your beauty. Since he is your lord, bow to him; the people of Tyre will sue your favour with gifts, the richest of the people with all kinds of wealth.

Then he describes her: this is what Christ thinks about you as a Christian, if you are a Christian. (Men must take this as well as women, although it is perhaps a little difficult, but Scripture says that as man is the head of woman, so Christ is the head of every man.)

> The princess is decked in her chamber with gold-woven robes; in many-coloured robes she is led to the king, with her virgin companions (bridesmaids, if you like), her escort, in her train. With joy and gladness they are led along as they enter the palace of the king.

There is something even more wonderful than that in the beautiful love poem of the Song of Solomon. The Bride, the church—in our context, the individual believer—speaking of herself against the glory of the Bridegroom, says:

> I am very dark (that is her sin), but comely (that is her new birth),

O daughters of Jerusalem, like the tents of Kedar (made from
black goats' hair), like the curtains of Solomon (glorious with
embroideries). Do not gaze at me because I am swarthy, because
the sun has scorched me. My mother's sons were angry with me,
they made me keeper of the vineyards; but, my own vineyard I
have not kept! Tell me, you whom my soul loves (and here she is
appealing to the Bridegroom), where you pasture your flock,
where you make it lie down at noon; for why should I be like one
who wanders beside the flocks of your companions? (1:5–7).

The Bridegroom replies:

If you do not know, O fairest among women, follow in the tracks
of the flock, and pasture your kids beside the shepherds' tents. I
compare you, my love, to a mare of Pharaoh's chariots. Your
cheeks are comely with ornaments, your neck with strings of
jewels. We will make you ornaments of gold, studded with silver
(1:8–11).

Keep in mind all the time that this is not a mere love poem. This is
God's revelation of his love to us in Jesus Christ. This is the one who is
going to make us pure because he loves us so much that he must have us
pure and will give us power to be pure.

Behold, you are beautiful, my love; behold, you are beautiful;
your eyes are doves. Behold, you are beautiful, my beloved, truly
lovely (1:15, 16).

Again, she says:

The voice of my beloved! Behold he comes, leaping upon the
mountains, bounding over the hills. My beloved is like a gazelle,
or a young stag. Behold, there he stands behind our wall, gazing
in at the windows, looking through the lattice. My beloved speaks
and says to me: 'Arise my love, my fair one, and come away; for
lo, the winter is past, the rain is over and gone. The flowers
appear on the earth, the time of singing has come, and the voice of
the turtledove is heard in our land. The fig tree puts forth its
figs, and the vines are in blossom; they give forth fragrance.
Arise, my love, my fair one, and come away. O my dove, in the
clefts of the rock, in the covert of the cliff, let me see your face, let
me hear your voice, for your voice is sweet and your face is
comely' (2:8–14).

Can you believe that Jesus is saying that about you? That is what he thinks of us. 'My beloved is mine and I am his' (2:16a). But something else. She is not perfect yet, and will not be. Thus, in the prophecy of Hosea, God has revealed to us the patience of his love for his unfaithful wife, Israel, under the figure of Hosea's unfaithful wife, Gomer. The Scripture is very blunt here. It even says that God said to Hosea to go and take a harlot for his wife. When the Lord first spoke to Hosea he said:

> Go, take to yourself a wife of harlotry and have children of harlotry, for the land commits great harlotry by forsaking the Lord. So he went and took Gomer the daughter of Diblaim, and she conceived and bore him a son.
>
> And the Lord said to him, 'Call his name, Jezreel; for yet a little while, and I will punish the house of Jehu for the blood of Jezreel, and I will put an end to the kingdom of the house of Israel. And on that day, I will break the bow of Israel in the valley of Jezreel.'
>
> She conceived again and bore a daughter. And the Lord said to him, 'Call her name Not pitied for I will no more have pity on the house of Israel, to forgive them at all. But I will have pity on the house of Judah, and I will deliver them by the Lord their God; I will not deliver them by bow, nor by war, nor by horses, nor by horsemen. When she had weaned Not pitied, she conceived and bore a son. And the Lord said, 'Call his name Not my people, for you are not my people (says God to Israel that he had betrothed to himself for ever) and I am not your God' (1:2–9).

And then the Lord speaks through the prophet to one of Hosea's and Gomer's children:

> Plead with your mother, plead—for she is not my wife, and I am not her husband—that she put away her harlotry from her face, and her adultery from between her breasts; lest I strip her naked and make her as in the day she was born, and make her like a wilderness, and set her like a parched land, and slay her with thirst (2:2, 3).

Right through this chapter the Lord makes plain what he is going to do to his unfaithful wife, Israel. But then, after all that, having thrashed her for her many sins, he says (for he would not let her go; God's marriages are for ever):

Behold I will allure her, and bring her into the wilderness, and speak tenderly to her. And there I will give her her vineyards, and make the Valley of Achor (*i.e.* The Valley of Trouble) a door of hope. And there she shall answer as in the days of her youth, as at the time when she came out of the land of Egypt.

'And in that day', says the Lord, 'you will call me, "My Husband", and no longer will you call me "My Baal". For I will remove the names of Baal from her mouth, and they shall be mentioned by name no more... And I will betroth you to me for ever; I will betroth you to me in righteousness and in justice, in steadfast love, and in mercy. I will betroth you to me in faithfulness; and you shall know the Lord' (2:14–17, 19, 20).

Apply all this to your own struggles with your passions. God deals faithfully with us in all of our sins because he loves us; but he will never let us go. When he has dealt faithfully with us he will take us back again—and again. He is determined to make us pure so that he might embrace us fully. His marriage with us is a transforming one, and in the fulness of time he will change us.

Now, we may ask, 'How is that related to questions that arise within marriage? Marriage to the Lord does not exclude marriage on earth.' (How could it?) Indeed not. But, in the first place, it should make it perfectly obvious that marriage on earth for a Christian must be to a fellow Christian, 'in the Lord' as Paul puts it (1 Cor. 7:39). This implies that one should not only marry only one who is a fellow-believer, but only that particular Christian whom God has made plain is to be our destined partner. I believe this with all my heart, and that conviction is simply confirmed by decades of observation and personal counselling of young people.

The trouble with many people is that they make the mistake of thinking that anyone they desire who is a Christian, or makes some Christian profession, may be right as their partner. But marriage needs nothing less than a clear commission from God, which he is surely prepared to give. This is of the utmost importance because marriage, that is the marriage of Christ and his church (and the individual believer in it) and the marriage of a man with a woman, is concerned with personalities—and the whole question of our passions is bound up with personalities.

It is precisely this that Satan would like us to forget. Our purity is not a passionless, statuesque frigidity, but a personal relationship to Jesus Christ and to our fellows on earth—whoever they may be. The Christian is married to the heavenly Bridegroom, and all questions about his or her relationships must be set in that fundamental context. That includes our passions, just as it includes the whole of our marriage. The marriage of two Christians is marriage in Christ. It involves relationships—each with Christ and then, in Christ, with each other.

I often say to young people when they are contemplating marriage (and afterwards!): 'See that Christ stands between the two of you. Do not stand so close to one another that he cannot stand between you, to bind you even closer together than you could bind yourselves.' He creates a true and full union. He alone, the Crucified One, can bind us together with the closeness he desires us to enjoy in this life.

The fact that all questions about our passions are related to personalities is important for this reason: we have a personal enemy, Satan. Sometimes a young man and woman purpose to marry and a third party comes between them as the enemy of their proposed union, hating it. So it is with the devil. How he hates our union to Christ, and all unions among those who are in Christ!

Peter's words are directly applicable to this: 'Beloved, I beseech you as aliens and exiles ('pilgrims and strangers' as the AV renders it) to abstain from the passions of the flesh, that wage war against your soul' (1 Pet. 2:11). 'Wage war' is literally, 'soldier'. James uses the same verb when he speaks about 'your passions that are *at war* in your members' as the cause of 'wars and fightings' among Christians:

> You desire and do not have; so you kill. And you covet and cannot obtain; so you fight and wage war. You do not have, because you do not ask. You ask and you do not receive, because you ask wrongly, to spend it on your passions. Unfaithful creatures! Do you not know that the friendship of the world is enmity with God?

The devil clearly hates our friendship with God!

> Therefore whoever wishes to be a friend of the world makes himself an enemy of God.

There cannot be three; this marriage is for two.

> Or do you suppose it is in vain that the Scripture says, 'He yearns

jealously over the spirit which he has made to dwell in us'? But he gives more grace; therefore it says, 'God opposes the proud, but gives grace to the humble'. Submit yourselves therefore to God. Resist the devil and he will flee from you. Draw near to God and he will draw near to you. Cleanse your hands, you sinners, and purify your hearts, you men of double minds.

This whole passage deals with Satan warring in our passions. What does he want? Not merely to defile us, but to destroy us. Doubtless he does not like the bad advertisements for himself that we see in the gutter; he is ashamed of the drug-addict who has become a shadow of a true human being, and of the drunkard and of the sad figure of the prostitute. His intent is to seduce us from Christ by more attractive, indeed by 'higher' means. For in the last analysis it is the marriage that he is against; the passions are the means he uses and on which he works, to separate us, or at least temporarily estrange us, from Christ.

Here then is something which is vital for all Christians to understand: Satan always seeks to depersonalise our problems. Take that in, and think about it. He wants us to see our struggles as problems of the passions, not as problems of relationships. Then, when he has interfered with, and even caused us to forget, the vital thing in our lives—being married to Jesus Christ—he can make a horrid mess of them. If we forget Christ himself and our relationship to him, the problems of our passions simply magnify. They always will.

Learn this lesson, therefore: Never allow Satan to depersonalise your problems and struggles. Remember, and remind yourself, that the Christ to whom you are married as a Christian is a person; he is a person to whom you can go; he is a person to whom you owe a duty of love because of all he has done for you in giving himself for you on the cross and to you by his Spirit.

The trouble with so many of us is that he is the last one we go to with our problems and troubles. *Christ is a person.* You in Christ are a person. He has constituted you a person, with a certain status, dignity and value. Do not see yourself merely as a moral animal, struggling with its passions. You are not merely an animal, although you may think you have animal passions. See Christ as a person, see yourself as a person dignified by Christ to be of his bride. See your rightful mate or spouse as a person in Christ's eyes; and see your fellow men, Christians and those not yet Christians, as persons of ultimate value to God. Never deal with a problem on the mere level of passion itself. Augustine was right when he said, 'Love God, and do as you like.' What he was really saying was that personal relationships are salvation, and when you are really saved into a close personal relationship with Jesus Christ, you can do what you like, and, in a sense, let your body do what it likes just because the governing principle in your life is 'What does God like? What has he revealed is pleasing to him?'

In 1 Corinthians 6 the apostle speaks about questions of the appetites. He speaks about hunger, how the body needs food. The body needs food. It would die without it, and it is our Christian duty to nourish it so that we may have health to serve God. But that does not mean that we are to live for food! The body will perish one day, as the apostle says. Here is a lesson: God has provided bodies which need food, and he has provided food for them, thank God (certainly, in the Western world: how grateful and generous we should be). But it is Satan who would incline us to live to satisfy our appetites for food and cause us to abuse what God has given.

So much for the appetite for food. What about the appetite for sex? C. S. Lewis compares the strength of the appetite for food with the clamant strength of the appetite for sexual enjoyment. 'The body is not for immorality', Paul says (1 Cor. 6:13). What are his next words? Let me change the Scripture a little, to point my lesson. You may think the next words ought to be, 'but for purity', but that is to de-personalise the matter. If 'the body is not for immorality', what is the body for? Purity? That is not good enough. The body is not merely for purity: this is where people go so far wrong. 'The body is for the Lord'! Purity will be taken care of in fellowship with the Lord. Does that mean there will be no struggles? Not in the least. Great struggles there may be, but the problem will only be solved in the Lord, through the Lord and in relationship with the Lord.

Some are appalled at the spontaneous and often involuntary spasms of their own passions, especially their sexual passions, as if mere animal bodies could sin of themselves. Because they hate what they call their vile passions, they seek to stifle their sexuality at its source, and stifle with it all the creative urge that God has given by these faculties and powers. They become eunuchs, in more senses than one. This is wrong. It is the mind that sins. The body of itself cannot sin; it is the mind, the will, with deliberate consent, that sins and seeks to abuse itself, its personality, and its body, and, alas, also seeks to abuse the personalities, bodies and lives of others.

Keep your personal relationships right, and you will exclude Satan, the mud-raker. If you keep close to Christ, Satan *cannot* get at you: it is a manifest impossibility, by the victory Christ has gained on the cross. Keep in constant communion with Christ.

What do I mean by that? Something very subjective, even sentimental? Not a bit. Your relationship with Jesus Christ might seem, if people knew your thoughts, very matter-of-fact, very prosaic, if you are that kind of person, and yet very real.

I sometimes fear to speak about what the love of Jesus means in my life, lest people misunderstand and think I am suggesting some sort of sentimental association. Not at all. It can be very business-like. What I mean is that he is the one I refer to, first. Not always, alas, but I am learning! He is my constant companion. I speak to him in a very objective, business-like manner, and matter of fact fashion, far more than I do to any one else.

This solves many problems, but in particular the one that I have in mind. All sexual offences stem from disrespect; for Christ, for ourselves, and for others, which causes us to misuse and abuse one personality or another. (There is much more that can be said about this in private, where I much prefer to deal with the subject. I do not want to make any one more self-conscious about these problems than they need to be, by talking of them publicly. God forbid!)

Whatever our problems or difficulties in this respect, let us learn to tell the Lord all about them; sexual problems, failures, the enormities of our thoughts and actions, the abnormalities, if there are such, the fatal biases. Do not get into the way of thinking that Christ is standing over you, frowning—although he is grieved and sorry when you sin, in thought, word and deed. If you see him like a great terrifying policeman standing over you saying, 'O, you wicked sinner!' you will never crawl to him and say 'Lord, help me.' Keep close to him and give him all your confidence. Tell him all about it. Tell him the worst. See him with the woman of Samaria. See him with the woman taken in adultery. See him even with wicked David, the adulterer. What patience! He understands!

Is this a word to you? You are married to the Lord. He is proud of you. He loves you. He wants to help you. Let him. We do not let Christ be our Saviour. How can he save us if we stand apart from him? I have said so often before, we get God and the devil mixed up. Christ is not standing frowning at us. Nobody was ever saved by frowns—ever. His sympathy with your struggles, his sympathy with your failures—grasp that! You do not know how much he cares and longs for you to come. 'Come on,' he says, 'tell me all. Tell me.'

Do that and keep doing it. God will save you wonderfully from ten thousand snares. That is my prayer.

THE CHRISTIAN IN THE HOME, CHURCH AND WORLD

1. Foundations

The over-all theme in what follows is the interrelation between the ideas of Christ in us and we in Christ as individuals and in the home, the church and the world.

We are believers incorporated into Christ's body, the church (Acts 2:47), chosen as an 'elect race' (1 Pet. 2:9; Is. 43:20), which began we may say with believing Abraham and his seed, who is the father of all who have faith (Rom. 4:16). But whereas in the Old Testament election begins in history, in the New it goes back to eternity before the foundation of the world (Eph. 1:4). This means that although we are instated fully as individual sons of God in Christ, each with his unique relationship to God ('the white stone' of Rev. 2:17), we are members of a Body, as integrated with it and integral to it as our limbs are to our human body.

This does not mean that (in Scots terms) we all 'muck in' indiscriminately and lose our unique identity in the fellowship, any more than we do, or ought to do, in the family. Even our personal relationship with Christ is a kind of marriage relationship (it is even closer than that!) in which there is inter-communication, in fellowship—although we may call it communion or private devotion. To combine each one's unique personal relationship with Christ with more complex relationships, with Christian marriage, in the home, in the church and in the world, would embrace worlds of knowledge and wisdom which, although they can be stated publicly in general principles, would need to be wrought out in more intimate discussion and even private conversation. Public exposition of Scripture should only be a beginning.

To be a Christian at all is to know the Lord personally. But from the beginning of the most intimate discussion of our personal relationship with the Lord we must never forget the other pole of truth about our relationship with him—not only is Christ in us, but we are in Christ. 'In Christ' is a far greater concept than 'Christ in us' as individuals. It is like the relation of the sea to the bucket plunged into it. The bucket contains sea water, but the sea contains the bucket. The bucket is full, but not apart from the sea. Our individual importance 'in Christ' is not only vital—God would not be happy without any one of his chosen—but is of eternal import. Moreover, we were chosen 'in Christ' before the foundations of the world!

So that it is in that mind-expanding context that we are to look first at the structure and functioning of the life of God in the soul of man. Here is my basic thesis:

Our life in God through Christ is fully human, not ethereal. Man is fallen and his image is defaced but not obliterated; we are still human. The life of Christ within the regenerate is his vital death and resurrection, as a dual or two-fold unity.

Now, follow as we unfold this in detail.

1. Man is God's highest creation (Gen. 1:26–28). We assume that the eternal Son was the prototype of man. Classical formulations of the incarnation seek therefore to guard Christ's humanity equally with his divinity. Here is a representative selection:

The Westminster Confession of Faith
After God made all other creatures, he created man, male and female, with reasonable and immortal souls, endued with knowledge, righteousness and true holiness, after his own image, having the law of God written in their hearts, and power to fulfil it, and yet, under a possibility of transgressing, being left to the liberty of their own will, which was subject unto change (IV.ii).

The Son of God, the second person in the Trinity, being very and eternal God, of one substance, and equal with the Father did, when the fulness of time was come, take upon him man's nature, with all the essential properties and common infirmities thereof, yet without sin, being conceived by the power of the Holy Ghost in the womb of the Virgin Mary, of her substance. So that two whole, perfect and distinct natures, the Godhead and the manhood, were inseparably joined together in one person, without conversion, composition or confusion. Which person is very God and very man, yet one Christ, the only Mediator between God and man (VIII.ii).

The Thirty-nine Articles of the Church of England
The Son, which is the Word of the Father, begotten from everlasting of the Father, the very eternal God, and of one substance with the Father, took man's nature in the womb of the blessed Virgin, of her substance, so that two whole and perfect natures, that is to say, the Godhead and manhead, were joined together in one Person, never to be divided, whereof is one Christ, very God, and very Man (Article II).

The Nicene Creed, 325 A.D.
We believe in one God the Father All-sovereign, maker of all things visible and invisible; and in one Lord Jesus Christ, the Son of God, begotten of the Father, only-begotten, that is of the substance of the Father, God of God, Light of Light, true God of true God, begotten not made, of one substance with the Father, through whom all things were made, things in heaven and things on earth, who for us men and for our salvation came down and was made flesh and became man, suffered, and rose on the third day, ascended into the heavens, is coming to judge the living and dead.

The Chalcedon Formulation, 451 A.D.
Therefore, following the holy Fathers, we all with one accord teach men to acknowledge one and the same Son, our Lord Jesus Christ, at once complete in Godhead and complete in manhood, truly God and truly man, consisting also of a reasonable soul and body; of one substance with the Father as regards his Godhead, and at the same time of one substance with us as regards his Godhead, begotten of the Father before the ages, but as regards his manhood begotten, for us men and for our salvation, of Mary the Virgin, one and the same Christ, Son, Lord, Only-begotten, recognised in two natures, without confusion, without change, without division, without separation; the distinction of natures being in no way annulled by the union, but rather the characteristics of each nature being preserved and coming together to form one person and substance, not as parted or separated into two persons, but one and the same Son and Only-begotten God the Word, Lord Jesus Christ; even as the prophets from earliest times spoke of him, and our Lord Jesus Christ himself taught us, and the creed of the Fathers has handed down to us.

2. Man is fallen and his image is defaced, but not destroyed. Otherwise Christ could hardly have come in the flesh, identified himself with us, taken our sin away, and established himself as the first everlasting Man of the heavenly order of eternal manhood. He came to take the fallen 'Adamness' out of man, and achieve God's purpose in the garden of making him partake of the tree of life, which is surely Christ! Thus the *Westminster Confession of Faith*, chapter VI, describes the state of fallen man:

Our first parents being seduced by the subtilty and temptation of Satan, sinned in eating the forbidden fruit. This their sin God was pleased, according to his wise and holy counsel, to permit, having purposed to order it to his own glory.

By this sin they fell from their original righteousness, and communion with God, and so became dead in sin, and wholly defiled in all the faculties and parts of soul and body. They being the root of all mankind, the guilt of this sin was imputed, and the same death in sin and corrupted nature conveyed to all their posterity, descending from them by ordinary generation.

From this original corruption, whereby we are utterly indisposed, disabled, and made opposite to all good, and wholly inclined to all evil, do proceed all actual transgressions.

This corruption of nature, during this life, doth remain in those that are regenerated: and although it be through Christ pardoned and mortified, yet both itself, and all the motions thereof, are truly and properly sin.

Every sin, both original and actual, being a transgression of the righteous law of God, and contrary thereunto, doth, in its own nature, bring guilt upon the sinner, whereby he is bound over to the wrath of God, and curse of the law, and so made subject to death, with all miseries spiritual, temporal, and eternal.

3. We are regenerated or born again of Christ. We speak a great deal about progressive sanctification or growing in holiness, but that can only be because our birth in Christ is one complete, definitive and final act—it is forever, it is eternal life we receive. We are new creatures, a new creation of God. You cannot exaggerate this. You could misuse it and distort its meaning, but you could never exaggerate it. It is almighty and eternal in its potential. We cannot begin to deal with all that accompanies it in forgiveness, justification and adoption. It would take too long and we would never get on. But if that has taken place in you, then it is forever. You can never be the same again, cannot go back and must go on to all eternity with Christ. He will at last make you willing, if you are not now, or are afraid. You are his, forever. Sit back and take it in.

4. The life of Christ within is that of both his (vital) death and resurrection. The Christ of who you are born forever is dual, that is to say, his effect on your life (which is now his life, as well as yours, you share the one life) is backward looking, and forward looking. Christ's eternal life, which he procured to be imparted to you by his death and resurrection contains the dual potency, the one potency (death) is as great as the other (life). It contains the potency of his death ('death works' 2 Cor. 4:12); it also contains the potency of his resurrection life. You are therefore by union with him (1 Cor. 6:17) dead to the old life of fallen Adam. There are dregs remaining, but not the old life itself; Christ has slain it, and that is surely final enough (see Romans 6:9–11). You are dead to the old life of Adam (his whole world and kingdom); and you are alive in God and to God, by the resurrection life of Christ within you, through the Holy Spirit. Therefore you have not two natures at once; you have two certificates, death, and birth, in that order (which is the opposite order from which the Registrar takes these two important documents!). Hallelujah! All this Paul expounds wonderfully in Romans 6:2–11; Galations 2:20 and Colossians 3:3.

We now go on to several following points in order to amplify the significance of this.

5. The New Birth, sanctification, although definitive, complete and final, is as a seed (*sperma*, Jn. 3:9). 'He who began a good work in you will bring it to completion at the day of Jesus Christ' (Phil. 1:6). Here is how the Puritan, John Owen, describes it:

> The work of holiness, in its beginning is but like seed cast into the earth—namely the seed of God, whereby we are born again. And it is known how seed that is cast into the earth doth grow and increase. Being variously cherished and nourished, it is in its nature to take root and to spring up, bringing forth fruit. So it is with the principle of grace and holiness. It is small at first, but being received in good and honest hearts, made so by the Spirit of God, and these nourished and cherished (by the Word, W. S.), it takes root and brings forth fruit. And both these, even the first planting and the increase of it, are equally from God by his Spirit

(but not automatically, *cf.* growth of a baby, by feeding).[1]

6. Over against the seed of God, the vital, eternal life of Christ, quickening and joining with, or uniting with our human spirit, you have the dregs, but only the dregs, remnants, residue, remains or remainder of the life of sin, which Jesus by the potency of his indwelling death has slain within you.

To call the power of indwelling sin within the believer mere remnants would enrage many a struggling and defeated Christian, and any intelligent Christian ought therefore to ask, Why, then, can mere dregs be so powerful? Well, although they lurk in the life of a born-again person, and that person is set in the midst of fallen world order, I do not believe that (of themselves) they are all-powerful, or can be. See how Paul contrasts our new nature with what remains in Romans 7:17, 20.

This idea is not easy. In Romans 6:18 and 22 Paul has just said that we are set free from sin, but in 7:17 and 20 he still calls the remnant 'sin which dwells in me', and in verses 18 and 25 he calls it his 'flesh', and in verse 23 'the law of sin'. But the power of sin in the life of a believer—am I minimising that? Never! Satan, the explanation of the baneful power lies beyond the believer, but yet has access to him, and to the remnants of sin within him. Satan's power has to be broken and defeated as well as the power of indwelling sin, and it can be; but only when the presence and malignancy of Satan is recognised, and Christ's supreme power over him by his victorious death and resurrection is involved.

The secret, therefore, of progress in sanctification lies in constantly reckoning with the tempter, and dealing with him, rather than with the mere dregs until they seem hellishly, mountainously high. And they will seem so high, as long as the devil is permitted to operate in your life, while at the same time he wickedly accuses you of what he himself is instigating in you and doing to you. When Jesus called Peter, 'Satan', he was recognising this. But it is hard for us to do that, because Satan slinks and sidles in, and lies so close to our humanity that he makes us sure that it is we ourselves who are doing the sinful things of which he accuses us, and not he.

7. Undue preoccupation with sin is a work of Satan that

---

[1] *The Works of John Owen*, ed. W. Goold, III, p. 388

takes our mind off Christ, and his threefold remedy for sin and Satan. Although we must know the depth of the depravity of sin in the fallen human heart, we must never forget that its pipe-line leads back to the bowels of hell, and that unless hell and its sordid master are dealt with, sin will never finally be overcome. Some of the greatest saints have unfortunately erred in a morbid and unhealthy preoccupation with sin, not placing sufficient emphasis upon its vile originator. I would dare, with great respect, to include Murray M'Cheyne and David Brainerd among these; and sometimes Puritans and Calvinists whom I revere so much have been deeply guilty of this. In this connection, however, John Owen speaks again with great insight:

> I confess sometimes it may come to this with a believer, that for a season he may be led captive by some particular sin; it may have so much prevalency in him as to have power over him. So it seems to have been with David, when he lay so long in his sin without repentance; and was plainly so with those in Isa. 57.17, 18, 'For the iniquity of his covetousness was I wroth, and smote him: I hid me, and was wroth, and he went on frowardly in the way of his heart. I have seen his ways, and will heal him.' They continued under the power of their covetousness, so that no dealings of God with them, for so long a time, could reclaim them. But, for the most part, when any lust or sin doth so prevail, it is from the advantage and furtherance that it hath poisoned it, inflamed it, and entangled the soul. So the apostle, speaking of such as through sin were fallen off from their holiness, says, 'They were in the snare of the devil, being taken captive by him at his will,' 2 Tim. 2.26. Though it were their own lusts that they served, yet they were brought into bondage thereunto by being entangled in some snare of Satan; and thence they are said to be 'taken alive,' as a poor beast in toil.

> And here, by the way, we may a little inquire, whether the prevailing power of a particular sin in any be from itself, or from the influence of temptation upon it; concerning which at present take only these two observations:

> (1.) Much of the prevalency of sin upon the soul is certainly from Satan, when the perplexing and captivating sin hath no peculiar footing nor advantage in the nature, constitution, or condition of the sinner. When any lust grows high and prevailing more than others, upon its own account, it is from the peculiar advantage that it hath in the natural constitution, or the station or condition of the

person in the world; for otherwise the law of sin gives an equal propensity into all evil, and equal vigour unto every lust. When, therefore, it cannot be discerned that the captivating sin is peculiarly fixed in the nature of the sinner, or is advantaged from his education or employment in the world, the prevalency of it is peculiarly from Satan. He hath got to the root of it, and hath given it poison and strength. Yea, perhaps, sometimes that which may seem to the soul to be the corrupt lusting of the heart, is nothing but Satan's imposing his suggestions on the imagination. If, then, a man find an importunate rage from any corruption that is not evidently seated in his nature, let him, as the Papists say, cross himself, or fly by faith to the cross of Christ, for the devil is nigh at hand.

(2.) When a lust is prevalent unto *captivity*, where it brings in no advantage to the flesh, it is from Satan. All that the law of sin doth, of itself, is to serve the providence of the flesh, Rom. 13.14; and it must bring in unto it, somewhat of the profits and pleasures that are its object. Now, if the prevailing sin do not so act in itself, if it be more spiritual and inward, it is much from Satan by the imagination, more than the corruption of the heart itself.[2]

8. One of the greatest dangers of undue preoccupation with inbred sin is that it may drive us to such distraction with ourselves that we want to jump out of our human nature, or at least deny it, in some of its essential elements.

Remember that Jesus is a man forever. Glorified man is the supreme fruit of creation and redemption. We must never denigrate our humanity or distend it or mutilate it, or try to dismember or fillet it into something ethereal (which will only turn out to be more ghastly) than human.

This can happen easily when we seriously hold what is called a tripartite view of man, rather than a bi-partite view of man's constitution. Man is essentially body and soul; the soul being that element in him which was formed when God breathed his life into the dust of the earth and thus made man. The danger is when some try to divide soul from spirit, and deny all that is called soul (*psyche*) as carnal and sinful, and therefore forbidden, and out for the Christian. Now someone might instantly throw back at me one of my own favourite quotations, Hebrews 4:11–13, where the inspired writer says the all-searching Word

---

[2]   *The Works of John Owen*, VI, pp. 203–204

of God penetrates, searches and sifts the essential elements of humanity. This is not done with a view to dissecting it (that will never be, unto all eternity, since Christ is a man forever; and also since our inheritance in Christ is not fully ours until our saved souls are united with our resurrection bodies at the coming of Christ), but to shaking out sin from it, exposing it and having it dealt with. That is very different from the subtle, albeit unconscious oriental, Buddhist element in Watchman Nee, for example, whose teaching on the nature of man leads to views of the world which verge on the gnostic. We must be careful here to observe a biblical balance.

9. In his work of restoration, God means to make us truly human—not less human. We could probably interpret Genesis 4 with its description of the rise of culture, crafts and music as the natural cause of and merely concerned with the emergence of polygamy and murder; but that would be such a gross, unsubtle analysis of the chapter, as to be no analysis at all. Indeed, we see worse than that in Genesis 6, when the demons invade human life, and monstrous creatures were born, and God was angry, and wanted to destroy them all, but saved eight persons by the deluge. You can see an even more flagrant and defiant culture in Genesis 11, where the tower of Babel is raised to heaven against God himself! God dealt with that too; but he did not extirpate the human race, nor deny its human constitution.

Indeed, after the Flood he said, 'I will never again curse the ground because of man, for the imagination of man's heart is evil from his youth' (Gen. 8:21). That was said, doubtless, on the basis of Noah's sacrifice (typifying and pointing forward to Christ's sacrifice). Therefore it is not merely a ghostly, spiritual element in man that is saved, but the whole man, body and soul, within its total cultural environment.

You see this in the prophecies of Isaiah: 'The wilderness and the solitary place shall be glad for them, and the desert will blossom as the rose' (Is. 35:1). You see God's care even for the beasts: 'The wolf shall dwell with the lamb, the calf and the lion and the fatling together, and a little child shall lead them (Is. 11:6). And in Amos: 'The plowman shall overtake the reaper, and the treader of grapes him who sows the seed; the mountains shall drip sweet wine, and all the hills shall flow with it. I will restore the fortunes of my people' (Amos 9:13, 14).

When Leslie Lyall, the missionary statesman, first returned, banished from his beloved China, he wrote, that among those missionaries who longest survived in China when the communists drove in, and on, and all were suffering from strain, those who cracked up first were those who had no cultural interest. Now, when Jesus floored me in my late teens and twenties, I had to give up practically all my music, like plucking out my right eye, because music was my god. But as soon as I put Christ in his rightful place, he gave it back to me, since it was, and is, part of my total life. It is not what God made that is evil, but what intervened. But all that—Sins, Sin, and Satan—Christ has dealt with, to make us not less but more human. Being fully human will never hinder us from being of service to him, as we shall see.

THE CHRISTIAN IN THE HOME, CHURCH AND WORLD

2. Primary Evangelism

Delivered from all three dimensions of evil, sins, sin and Satan, our poise and personality develops so that we are able to look out upon the world of others, in the home, church and world with Christ-like attitudes. All unhealthy preoccupation with self, crippling inferiority, twisted pride, touchiness and self-glory are dealt with at the roots. We now look out upon the world of others, with sincere interest, born of Christian knowledge and love, seeking to help them as we have been helped by Jesus and his servants ourselves.

To this end the Almighty God ordained human society to have a structure. As the body has a head, so the body domestic, politic, ecclesiastic or national needs a head. The head of Christ is God, the head of every man is Christ (who is also the head of the church) and the head of a woman is her husband (1 Cor. 11:3). Headship, then, runs through the whole of the higher creation, and this makes for unity in all its associations, from the most simple, domestically, to the most complex national and international alignments and alliances. (See the beautiful acknowledgement of divine headship in Genesis 24:26, 48, learned from Genesis 17:19, and its promise of preserving godly seed. See also Ephesians 1:22, 23; 4:15; 5:23; Colossians 1:18; 2:10.)

The headship immediately devolving on man comes from Christ's headship of the church (his body, bride) and applies to man's domestic marriage intriguingly with the heavenly marriage of Christ and his church, stressing both the headship and love. Peter likewise balances headship and love beautifully in his gracious phrase, 'heirs together of the grace of life' (1 Pet. 3:7). Many generations of happy Christian homes testify to the gracious workability and fruitfulness of this partnership, with the God-given authority in headship not at all abrogated or diminished.

Before we discuss further, living together in the home, we must go on to complete this subject of headship in respect of children. In Ephesians 6:1–4 Paul calls the fifth commandment (Exod. 20:12) 'the first commandment with promise', where 'honour' father and mother has wide application, embracing grown-up children as well as infants and youngsters. But Paul himself says, 'Children, obey your parents in the (Spirit of the) Lord, for this is right.' In that context, children are obviously juniors. Grown-up children, if converted, may well honour their parents by disagreeing on a matter of fact and disobeying them in a matter of conscience, although in a respectful, loving, and wooing way; whereas Jesus at the age of twelve submitted to Mary and Joseph and, presumably, for a long time thereafter.

Today many Christian parents have been conned by modern theories and practices (and by their offspring mouthing these theories) into fearing that even loving discipline will do their children harm. Never! Both parents and children know that they can get the better of each other if they undermine confidence in each other's dicta, rules or principles, which leads, not only to disorder, but disintegration of family unity.

Denial of covenant principles in bringing up children has undermined the authority of grace and faith in the Christian home. Faith, the gift of grace, claims the children of Christian marriage for Christ—even children of one Christian parent, according to Paul's dictum that such children are holy (not automatically saved, but holy, and to be believed for, and circumcised or baptised for a holy life).

Even Esau (non-elect and lost) was circumcised! But saving faith could not have operated in his case!—either in the case of his parents or himself. Theirs was a divided home, with Isaac and Rebekah each having favourites. But faith stands upon God's promises (going back to Abram the father of all who believe, but reiterated emphatically by Paul in that striking verse in 1 Corinthians 7:14 that the child of one believing parent is holy); it therefore brings them up with gracious authority as the Lord's children, and tells them so, and refuses to believe or let them believe anything else. Quietly, unfrantically faith holds to this even if they wriggle like mad as teenagers. Faith is prepared to hold on to them even throughout a wayward life until, on an aged deathbed, Christ overtakes them; faith dies believing for them. 'These all died in faith' (Heb. 11:13). Many are in the kingdom today because, known or unknown to them, parents or other loved ones, ministers or friends, would not let God go until he blessed them with salvation. This teaching works—as my years of experience proves—because God works according to his authoritative and gracious Word.

In this connection let me say in the context of headship that although the Christian family arises from conversion to Christ (and the life of the convert within the Christian church is centred in God's Word); yet the church in the home and household is more important for the Christian upbringing of children than the church. What should you do if you want them to grow up not merely as believers squeezed into the door of Christ's church but never coming right in, little more than lukewarm professors, living largely worldly lives with no burden of prayer or care for Christ's cause in the world, but rather as fighting soldiers of Christ? Family worship and the family altar daily, even twice daily is the way to enable your children to see that the life in Christ has something to do with daily living. The Christian life is to be wrought out in the context of life as it is lived every day and in every experience of life with bells ringing, babies crying, and people coming and going, and every sort of activity conceivable going on or being planned.

Some would say that an old bachelor is not the best person to discuss living the Christian life in the home! But I am not without some experience! I was brought up in the midst of a large family and have been able many times to apply that wealth of youthful experience to other situations. The principal thing to say here is that the regulating factor in the total home life is that the husband and father is head of the house under the headship of Christ, the real Head of the household. This governs all; and, as we see the beautiful balance of Peter's heirship in grace, and Paul's mutual obedience and love of husband and wife, so also with regard to the children, we are to see them obeying their parents in the (Spirit of the) Lord, and fathers not provoking their children to anger but bringing them up in the discipline and instruction of the Lord.

The New Testament's teaching can be summed up in the simple formula 'love rules all'. We do not mean that sentimentally, because such 'sickly drip' never copes with the realities of life, even in the best regulated household! So we need to work out our doctrine in terms of the difficulties in the Christian home.

Our guide here is, of course, the life and example of Jesus first, and then of his apostles. But that is external help. The Bible tells us fully how to be good, but what is the use of that if people do not have the will or the power to try to be good? But we, as Christians, have both the will and power by the presence of Jesus in our hearts by the Spirit. We must learn to draw not only upon our knowledge of him but on his power given to us. Nor must we regard living according to his standard of life as a mere responsibility, much less a burden or bore, but as a privilege even when it involves us (as it will and must) in the privilege of suffering for and with Jesus. We must be quite sure not only of the necessity of suffering with and for Christ if we are to reach glory (Rom. 8:17; 2 Tim. 2:12) but of the privilege of it. For we are called upon to share his death (2 Cor. 4:10–12; Col. 1:24; Jn. 12:24).

What may such an attitude to suffering within the Christian home entail? Well, what was the cause of so much of Christ's sufferings? It was that he put up with us. Look at the Lord's patience with wayward Israel for centuries before he really began to chastise them! Have you learned patience, forbearance, long-suffering and endurance in the home from Jesus? There is a limit, of course, and our limit is bound to be more limited than his! But he has promised never to allow us to be tried and tempted above what we are able to bear. There is a time when it is right to cry out. That is far better than bottling up resentment; otherwise it comes out in an uncontrolled and hurtful flood. Even the worm, the Christian worm, turns!—like Paul after they had beaten him and Silas (the charge against them remaining uninvestigated) when as full Roman citizens they ought to have been immune from such indignities. When the magistrates heard that they were Romans they wanted to shoo them out of Philippi quickly lest they get into trouble from higher authorities. But Paul said, 'Not likely, let the magistrates come in their Sunday best and their robes and regalia and conduct us out in a civic procession.' The door-mat, you see, which normally lies there and is trampled upon by all, occasionally stands on its end and says, 'And who do you think you're trampling on?' Normally, for Christ's sake, we take it all—but not to deify and pamper others in the home. If it is love all round it must be discipline all round, too. But to cherish and store up a resentful, censorious or judging spirit is bad for you and for others in the home. They will be dealt with sooner or later. God will see to that. 'Vengeance is mine', he says.

We can learn from the good psychiatrist here (Rom. 12:19). He suspends judgement until he has enquired as far as he may into why his patient behaves as he does. This is the way to understand. And this is where Jesus had the advantage over us: he knew all, even if you say it was by faith—his was perfect. But we too must try to find out as much as we can before adopting moralising attitudes. There may be sheer

badness which needs to be recognised, but we must also ask how far
human badness is reinforced by satanic or demonic intrusion, and how
far that intrusion has been sought or not. We must ask how far bad
behaviour is basically a cry for help—not excusing the wrong-doing, but
understanding its cause.

Take some examples: both Zaccheus and the Samaritan woman at the
well were lonely souls who had never really known love, as Jesus
loves. The woman, perhaps for all her husbands and men had never
been loved for herself, only for her body. And she had loved her own
body to the exclusion of any love for her soul and her higher dignity as a
woman in God's sight. Take Martha and Mary. If you have more
sympathy with Martha than with Mary you are at variance with Jesus!
Think about that! For Jesus would not be the last to appreciate a good
meal or a tidy house! Keep the searchlight on Jesus for a moment—he
can stand it. He was delivered from all self and had no problems of his
own, but discussed the 'problems' that he had concerning other people
every night and morning with his Father. He was therefore set free to
attend to the wants and needs of others, absolutely. Now, we are not
Jesus but we have his Spirit to draw upon, and he expects us to make
some progress in following not only his example but also in using his
power.

So often, just when we would take Christ's high road, because of a
bit of tiredness (sometimes false and satanic), our carnal mind takes over
and we see our situation with others as intolerable and are consumed
with self-pity. Then out comes the whine until it corrupts and poisons
the whole atmosphere of the home. Later, apologies are called for and if
there are no family prayers or worship to cleanse it all away, we may not
only let the sun go down on our wrath, but the blankets go over our
heads with a grudge and a hurt. Then we rise estranged from each other
in the morning. Silly, unloving, petty pride, pushing both Jesus and our
loved ones away from us!

We must learn the real secret of suffering the tantrums or moods of
others, not only patiently, but cheerfully. It is to remain detached from
all but Christ. Then, with no troubles of our own that are not constantly
laid at Jesus' feet and left there, we have time for others and *their* foibles
and quirks and queer bits.

Then you carry this attitude into the world of business or college or
factory. It will give people the shock of their lives because when, for
conscience's sake, you take exception to anything people say or do, you

do so plainly, but also cheerfully. You thus take the wind out of the sails of their upsurging anger and resentment. When all around are moaning about prices and restrictions and the failings of others, you are obstinately and consistently pleasant and cheerful. 'Has he no problems?' they ask. 'How does she spend so much time working for others with no time for pleasure, entertainment, indulgence?' (so they think who know not the pleasures of Christ!). Yet she is 'happier than we who plan for a whole week a weekend binge, or for a year a blow-out holiday abroad and try desperately to live it up and then return miserable because it's over for another year!' Then, 'He's so interested in us', and would be 'endlessly sympathetic however busy'. There is a 'quality about her', a kind of radiance or aura that seems to encircle her and make her so sunny that she seems holy. That is Jesus in her! Most people would not define it thus, but they see it and know that it is different (Matt. 5:16).

It is this indefinable but unmistakable aura which emanates from those who are letting the inner light of Jesus shine out of them, which not only sweetens home life but also—a very different thing—sweetens communal life because of its gentle, uncensorious acceptance of people very different from ourselves. When there are elements that are unpleasant, or unacceptable, or plain downright bad, we need to discover and understand the cause or causes (they are often complex). Then when we do find perhaps some horrid family background or some awful personal problem or tragedy in the life our sympathies arise. Jesus' sympathies rose too, when he was faced with great need like that of Zaccheus, or the woman at the well, or that of lepers, or the widow of Nain with her dead son, the breadwinner. Jesus' compassions simply flowed out. Then any objection to features in the other's life was swallowed up, not by being ignored but by being kindly aired, dealt with and got out of the way, so that loving friendship might be enjoyed to the full.

This self-same caring attitude must be carried out into the great big bad world. Not that we are to do so simply as we can in a Christian atmosphere! Just as we may share with Jesus, privately, what we would never share with the family, no more must we ever go out into the world and behave naïvely as if the world were the same as the Christian home. It is not—as we well know. Jesus was tough, very tough, in a bold, bad world—his world! and we must be tough, too; unhurtable, unshakeable and unshockable, with a hide as tough as Job's Behemoth (the hippo!) or Leviathan (the crocodile!). But this gentle, firm, gracious attitude which lets Jesus show himself shining through our lives (and it may take time, sometimes long time, even years of long-term witness to someone or to some group) may have to wait years for a crisis to galvanise others into decisive response. The trouble with the evangelical world is that it lacks patience. It does not believe in the efficacy of simply letting your light shine; consequently it does not reap its rewards. It does not wait to see the effect of a truly Christ-like life in the midst of an un-Christian community. Evangelicalism and evangelisticism has not been geared to that at all! I am not against meetings, campaigns, mission evangelism, but they may innocently enough obscure the value and use and superior quality of the other. It is in fact the easy way out. Where it is hard to live the Christ-life consistently and patiently, we say, 'Here is another way; raise a crowd, organise a mission, advertise like toothpaste or soap powder, plan a blitz, get up a stir, look how enjoyable it is and look at the fellowship you have, even if few or none are converted.'

God uses both quiet personal witness and large public meetings if they are in his holy hand, but converts from the one are generally far better than from the other. They have seen God in the flesh, they have seen Jesus in a human life (even if a far from perfect human life) but in one that unmistakably manifests his grace; and they want him just like that. Their eyes have been opened to see the beauty of Jesus (unlike Is. 53:2).

Even if you do not agree with this all, there is no doubt that this way of evangelising by living the life was God's first way of seeking to win the world. When Israel after her chequered career from Abraham to Samuel really began to shine in the land (in David and Solomon's day), the way they influenced other nations was not by going out (apart from David to subdue the ungodly nations that would have destroyed his), but by living the life so gloriously in Zion that people, like the Queen of Sheba and many others, came to see and said, 'the half had not been told' of Solomon's glory. The whole earth sought the presence of Solomon to hear the wisdom which God had put into his mind. Everyone brought his present of silver and gold, garments, myrrh, spices, horses, and mules.... Thus Israel (alas, for a very short time) fulfilled God's fundamental purpose of being God's evangelists to the Gentiles.

As early as Abram God had said that all the nations of the earth would be blessed through him and his seed, and this was God's first way of seeking to do that. They soon fell away, as you know, and became a public disgrace to God until in very shame he had to put them out of his land as a godly husband puts an unfaithful wife out of his house but never divorces her, that is not in the mind of God. He hates divorce (Mal. 2:16), but he puts her into a Babylonian wilderness (as Jacob's tribes earlier in an Egyptian wilderness) until she learns better. And it worked so far. Israel did not fully turn to God although Jeremiah, Ezekiel, Daniel, Ezra and Nehemiah helped a lot; but she was never again unfaithful to the husband of her youth, she was never idolatrous again. But she became guilty of a worse sin. Her God came in flesh, Jesus Christ, and even as a man was so unlike her that she did not recognise him and cruelly put him to death. So for that the people were sent out in 70 A.D. into, not one wilderness like earlier Israel went to Egypt, or later Israel went to Babylon, but into all the wild wildernesses of the world to be ill-treated in pogroms and persecutions throughout history until six million Jews were exterminated by Hitler.

But you cannot destroy what God has created and has called to be his own. Long before Christ came, indeed before the Jews had returned to their own land, Isaiah, by the Holy Spirit, foresaw a more glorious day for Israel. She would yet shine for her God in the world. She would be 'a light to the nations, to open the eyes that are blind, to bring out the prisoners from the dungeon, from the prison those who sit in darkness. I am the Lord, that is my name; my glory I give to no other, nor my praise to graven images. Behold, the former things have come to pass (Egypt's bondage and exodus), and new things I now declare (deliverance from Babylon); before they spring forth I tell you of them' (Is. 42:6–9). And from another of the Servant Songs: 'It is too light a thing that you should be my servant to raise up the tribes of Jacob and to restore the preserved of Israel; I will give you as a light to the nations, that my salvation may reach to the end of the earth' (Is. 49:6).

But that did not happen when Jesus came the first time because the Jews rejected him. Even those who formed the first Christian church as Jews were soon superseded by Gentiles, and so it has been almost ever since. But the Jews were not exterminated, even by the slaughter of six million of them. In fact, since from 1870 to 1880 Jews have been stirring in the ghettos of central Europe, longing for their own land (as they have not done for nineteen hundred years, nearly two millennia); but they are back in power there to the amazement and fury of Ishmael (and Marx, the renegade Jew). When we read Isaiah we see that what God promised (that Israel would yet be his evangelists to the Gentiles) must be fulfilled.

But when? Well, what would shake the world more than the conversion of that amazing people in one almighty, national movement?

Yet that is what is prophesied. A nation born (re-born, thinking of the Exodus)! But more of them later! Back to the local situation!

There is basic evangelism, 'living the life' according to God's primary way (*cf.* 1 Kgs. 10:24). Then there is preaching the gospel to every creature, God's secondary way (Matt. 28:18–20). That is our commission as preachers. This is primary or basic evangelism. But the one does not contradict the other. Everyone cannot go everywhere! But everyone can live the life where they are.

I believe this has something vital to say to those who belong to the Province of Ulster.[1] I am not being censorious. I am taking account of what Ulster men themselves have hinted to me over the years: trying to be realistic: somehow or other (by whoever or whatever influence) a superficial element entered into Ulster Christianity which has led to a superficial evangelicalism, a frothy evangelisticism which has done far too little for the character of Ulster. Now, do not in fury miss the point! The way to evangelise and build a nation is by Christian character, by the Word, Spirit, prayer, not evangelistic missions. The true witness is not primarily with banners in open-airs, and vast meetings in overcrowded halls but where you live and work and normally worship. Do you get the message? I hope so.

---

[1]   This material was delivered in Bangor, Northern Ireland in July 1977

THE CHRISTIAN IN THE HOME, CHURCH AND WORLD

3. Into the World, to the End of Age

Christ in us and we as individuals and together in Christ means that we begin to become fully human although fallen. We are regenerate in Christ (born again of him), with Christ within us to deal with all the negative needs of our lives (the destruction of evil on all levels), playing it down and playing up our new life in Christ by nourishing it and keeping the old devil away from the remaining dregs of sin. We thus healthily resist preoccupation with inbred sin, with all its de-humanising effects upon us, notably that of causing us to deny cultural elements of our humanity in a desperate attempt to deal with this huge bogus sin problem. The problem, as I said earlier (in one of the most illuminating simplifications which has ever occurred to me), is not temptation but the tempter!

Now, any personality governed by these elemental considerations is bound to look out on the world with healthy and happy eyes; and home, church and the world are going to be viewed with Christ-like attitudes thereafter.

The way this affects the home (as well as the church and the world) is that we see the whole of life as structured under forms of organisation which derive their character and constitution from what is called *headship*.

The headship which is universal (God having built the human race on this pattern of structure) works in the family through God's covenant of grace, which runs right through the Bible and history from the Fall. God conceives his chosen as organised in families under a headship that owes gracious authority to Christ and to God. By believing in the Lord Jesus at all we are committed to that structure and are blessed according to our submission to it, and our application of it to our human situation. The children of even one Christian parent are as a result, holy, which means that they are placed in a situation of advantage. They are brought up under Christian influence of course. The headship may devolve on a believing mother, as was my own experience. Not that she usurps the headship of the husband generally, but by putting herself under the headship of Christ she also assumes a certain believing headship for her children (and even in a sense for her husband; Paul's message in 1 Corinthians 7 covers that).

This is all a matter of faith of course, but if you mean by faith that it is done by man, not God, then that shows that you do not understand that Christian faith is not a human activity but is a gift of God's operation. It is as if he said to someone who had fallen into a pit, 'Here, stretch up your hand and I will pull you out'. There would be no point in a man stretching up his hand if there was no one there to haul him up!

A better illustration might be that of a Christian family in the Soviet Union where the children feared that they would be taken away from their Christian home and parents. But the father says one morning, 'God came to me in a vision last night and said "Do not fear that you will lose your children, I will see to it that they will never be taken away from you if you keep close to me, and keep doing as I say"'. The promise is God's but we have the covenant responsibility to keep in with him who makes the covenant. You do not make a covenant with God about your children, you merely keep the covenant he has made. You effectuate the covenant yourself by believing. You take God at his word and believe that as you exert Christian headship under Christ your children will grow up in the Lord. That is why paedo-baptists (those who believe in covenant infant baptism) are so sure and definite about baptising their infants. Their assurance is not the assurance of presumption if they are real, believing Christians, but the assurance of faith which is from God. They are simply taking God at his word and are acting upon it.

Although all this arises from the Bible, which is the charter of the Christian church so that this truth is said to be vested in the church, it is in the Christian home that it is seen most eloquently and practically as far as the children are concerned. The minister or under-shepherd along with the church family are seen to be standing between the head of the home and the head of the church (Christ) as communicators or teachers. The minister is never head of the church as the father (or a mother left alone with the responsibility) is head of the Christian home. So a tremendous onus rests upon the Christian father (along with mother) to take from Christ the true headship and work it out in the home not by turning the home into a little church, but by recognising that the Christian home *is* a Christian church and ought to be regarded as such and run accordingly. It is far easier to see how to run a Christian church in the rough and tumble of family life than before serried rows of well-dressed individuals on Sundays!

We have already discussed difficulties in the Christian home. Every solution must be sought in the knowledge and faith that Christ is there and his power can be drawn upon for every emergency, and for every chronic and protracted situation. Christ suffered for us that we, in him, might learn to suffer for others (Col. 1:24). There is a limit, of course, for just as Jesus occasionally asserted himself, as did Paul (Acts 16), so in Christ occasionally we need to assert ourselves in relation to others for their sakes as well as for ours and say, 'That's wrong, you can not do that. You must not do that'. But often, as between husband and wife, loving headship must involve bearing and forbearing with the other as a fellow-sinner needing to be understood and helped, and troubles and difficulties quietly prayed away.

What Peter says about the Christian wife and mother with an unbelieving husband is good. She does not preach to him but hopes to win him ('without the Word' if you please!) by living the Christian life as a woman (not a man!) in the home. The word is not in words and speeches and trying first to induce a sense of sin or need—Jesus scarcely ever did that. Rather we let the incarnate Word of a Christian life with its fragrance of Jesus do its own special evangelistic work.

This applies, by the way, to converted children in their teens and twenties, in a home with apparently unbelieving or nominally believing parents. The fifth commandment forbids a Christian son or daughter to 'preach' to their father and mother. Confession of Christ is in order and indeed required, but no more. Live the life, let them see that you are a new boy by helping in the house, and the same applies, even perhaps more so, to the girls. No brandishing of Bibles or tracts or leaving them with ostentatious carelessness by your bedside or elsewhere. There is nothing cunning about Jesus. He is as transparent as the day and trusts his Spirit to do his work without special pleading. Trust the Christ who dwells in you (if you are not hiding him deliberately under a covering) to do his work in your Dad and Mum.

More generally, in the home or anywhere, we must learn not to judge;

to discern is one thing, to pronounce judgement another. You never know the whole story about anyone else, as the Lord does. You must leave judgement to him as we leave vengeance to him; he will repay. We must love like Jesus did, to the end. We can never love as far as he does—and yet he is the Judge. Perhaps it is because he is the Judge that he suspends judgement for so long. We therefore in our inferior position to his must do so all the more. Only love wins, saves and builds up.

We must learn with Christ to be so detached from sin, self and Satan that we are increasingly set free to serve others. That is what life is about: not living for self and feathering our own nest, but for others within the home and outside it. The most of Christ's power, therefore, is to be geared and directed towards coping kindly, lovingly but firmly with all relationships. And it is this attitude that we are to carry with suitable realistic modifications and adaptations out into the world.

How are we to go out into the world? We may do so in a militant manner practically fighting with men for their salvation! But our wrestling is not with flesh and blood; that is why we prefer, and believe the Lord prefers, what we have called basic or primary evangelism to the more aggressive and confronting sort. But in view of the Great Commission (Matt. 28:18–20), we must state emphatically that they do not contradict but ought, in the total life of the church, to complement each other. But it stands to reason that God, drawing out evil to its destruction, is prepared to work hiddenly; then openly as he draws near to the final clash. Besides, character comes before service, qualifying it. Not, of course, character without prayer, which opens eyes (Is. 42:6, 7).

Now, having spoken of Christ within us and we in Christ, in the home, church and world, let us look at all this in the light of the total sweep of the Word of God, to see what God is doing, and will do in the world, and where, in Christ, we are going.

Taking a broad sweep of the Old and New Testaments and of subsequent history, some say converted Israel of old is lost in the church. Well, certainly believing Jews are incorporated into Christ, mourning their national disgraces (the captivities and the cross); but they still have their earthly task to perform as basic evangelists to the world. They have yet to shine (*cf.* Is. 60:1)!

Satan has sought to ruin man—trying to destroy Israel, and prevent Christ coming, destroying Christ on the cross (Jewish rejection), turning the church to heresies, swamping her with paganism and Islam in the 6th and 7th centuries, turning her into worldly Roman power, fragmenting her after Reformation, the Renaissance of arts putting man at the centre, trying to accommodate him to the surd in human nature—making the existential best of a bad situation with Hegel and then Marx building an earthly, temporal utopia practically denying individual human value, dignity and freedom. But Satan's greatest work (*cf.* Assyria and Babylon as rods of God to punish Israel but carrying their cruelties too far) has been to try to destroy God's chosen people (*e.g.* in Esther).

I do not know that any worthy history (Scripture apart) has been written of Israel's sufferings since she rejected Christ. Little did that comparative handful of Jews (who, when Pilate professed innocence of Christ's blood screamed 'His blood be on us and on our children') know what they were saying or doing. Yet it was Frederich the Great, sceptical of the existence of God, who asked his physician, Zimmerman, for proof of the Almighty's existence and was simply answered, 'The Jews, sire!'

We may take up the tale of the Jews about 1870–1880, partly with the help of such works as Leon Uris' (so called) novel *Exodus* (the fiction is only in the names of the characters), and Golda Meir's autobiography, *My Life*, to see that since the last third of the 19th century there has been an inexplicable, spontaneous stirring amongst Jews in the European land-mass (long before Hitler: was he not one of Satan's spiteful answers to it?) with a longing to return to their homeland. It was as if they felt there was no hope for them as a nation unless they did return and enjoy the security and dignity of a home of their own.

Wrote Golda Meir:

> A great deal has already been written—and much more will certainly be written in the future—about the Zionist movement, and most people by now have at least some notion of what the word Zionism means, and that it has to do with the return of the Jewish people to the land of their forefathers—the Land of Israel as it is called in Hebrew. But perhaps even today not everyone realises that this remarkable movement sprang up spontaneously in various parts of Europe.
>
> The first Jews who made the modern return to Zion came there as early as 1878 to found a pioneering village which they named Petach Tikvah (the Gate of Hope). By 1882 small groups of

Zionists from Russia who called themselves the Hovevet Zion (Lovers of Zion) had arrived in the country determined to reclaim the land, farm it and defend it. But in 1882 Theodor Herzl, who was to be the founder of the World Zionist Organisation and thus, essentially the father of the State of Israel, was still quite unaware of what was happening to the Jews in Eastern Europe...Herzl became interested in the fate of the Jews only in 1894, when he was assigned to cover the trial of Captain Dreyfus. Shocked by the injustice done to this Jewish officer—and by the open anti-semitism of the French army—Herzl, too, came to believe that there was only one possible permanent solution to the situation of the Jews. His subsequent achievements and failures—the whole amazing story of his attempt to create a Jewish state—are part of the history learned by all Israel school children and should be studied by anyone who wants to understand what Zionism is really all about.

Although the yearning of the Jews for their own land was not the direct result of pogroms (the idea of the Jewish resettlement of Palestine had been urged by Jews and even some non-Jews long before the word 'pogrom' became part of the vocabulary of European Jewry), the Russian pogroms of my childhood gave the idea immediacy, especially when it became clear to the Jews that the Russian government itself was using them as scapegoats in the struggle to put down the revolutionary movement.[1]

Not that there was anything godly in the minds of these Jews longing for a homeland and certainly not in Golda Meir's mind. They thought, and many still do, that they were absolutely on their own.

To the question, To be or not to be, each nation must make its own reply in its own way, and Jews neither can nor should ever depend on anyone else for permission to stay alive.[2]

I am grateful that I live in a country whose people have learned to go on living in a sea of hatred without hating those who want to destroy them and without abandoning their own vision of peace. To have learned this is a great art, the prescription for which is not written down anywhere. It is part of our way of life in Israel.[3]

---

[1] Golda Meir, *My Life* (Fortuna edition, London, 1976), pp. 10, 11
[2] *Ibid.*, p. 128
[3] *Ibid.*, p. 387

That is just Golda Meir's perhaps deliberate ignorance!

The fascinating story of the rise of Zionism, General Allenby's entry to Jerusalem in 1917 and the Balfour Declaration of that year and the British Mandate until 1948, the 1967 and the Six Days War, 1973 and the Yom Kippur War, is more than we can touch but in outline; but the epic of Israel's heroic survival and boldness to strike at her enemies (*e.g.* Uganda and Entebbe) as well as the fact of all the world's Jewish geniuses, from Paul to Einstein and Marx, is something that even the most bigoted and fanatical anti-semitic would have to admit. The mighty hatred and wealth of the Arab world, often desperately harnessing the organised odium and sinister 'know-how' of the Soviet (and maybe China) indicated the sheer giant quality of the Jews. And only the enormity of their rejection of their Messiah could explain how such gifted people could have suffered so much for nearly two thousand years!

But they are being thrashed by God under his specific orders for their ultimate good—not consigned to perdition and lasting destruction. Their affliction is temporal and temporary.

Meanwhile, it seems to me that the world hangs upon the significance of the Lord's imminent will for them—as if the poor Christian church, the *ecclesia* (like Jesus' gentle victory foreshadowed in Isaiah 42:1–4, *cf.* Matt. 12:15–21), weary with struggling against the highly organised and Satanic world of godless and cynical materialism, is desperately longing for a new fillip, a shot in the arm, an injection of new life from a hitherto startlingly unexpected quarter—Jewry. See her immemorial struggle with Ishmael, brought to a seeming head in our day; see the Arab's temporary ascendancy over the world through oil and Britain's shameful abdication of moral power and duty for filthy black oil; see the Soviet, planning world domination under the cloak of a working-class revolution—one of the biggest lies in history—see them using racial hatred and African and Asian under-privilege to foment discontent; poor/rich, brave, God-thrashed, yet God-protected Israel trembling with dread, and yet with supreme courage and set in the cockpit of history, waits, waits, waits...for what?

For something to happen that has not happened since Zerubbabel, Ezra and Nehemiah returned to devastated Jerusalem and was far less likely to happen after the Jews' rejection of Jesus and, practically, the extermination of those not already dispersed in A.D. 70 under the Roman Titus after the massacre at Masada in 94 A.D., or the horrid Bar

Chochba rising in 135—namely a mass return to Israel. For all the British cruelty to a people desperately swimming to the Mediterranean shores of the Holy Land and actually turning them back or arresting them and huddling them like cattle or West African slaves in the holds of inadequate shipping, Britain could not prevent them returning. Her pathetic Mandate was overwhelmed, and sheer native genius joined to the unknown and utterly unacknowledged power and will and prophesied Word of God established Israel in her own God-given land. And who is going to budge her? Only God; but will he? For her sin in rejecting Jesus she may yet have another terrible thousand or two thousand years' dispersion to undergo. Who knows how long Gentile ascendancy will last before Jewry converted rules the roost! But rule she will with her despised and rejected Jesus, when she mourns her colossal mistake and turns to him. She is only set aside. Read Romans 11:1–36, then Isaiah 60:1–5; 10–12; 21, 22; 66:10–14. Or hear Iain Murray as he concludes *The Puritan Hope*

> The glory of Christ has indeed been declared in the earth in past ages. In the apostolic age, 'His lightnings enlightened the world: the earth saw, and trembled' (Ps. 97:4). The Reformers and Puritans beheld him as the conquering King and it made them strong. The eighteenth-century Church knew his power and longed with Charles Wesley that
>
> > *he world might taste and see*
> > *The riches of His grace.*
>
> The same was true in revivals of the last century. 'It were worth living ten thousand ages in obscurity and reproach,' declared one minister in Ulster, 'to be permitted to creep forth at the expiration of that time, and engage in the glorious work of the last six months of 1859.' But this world, according to the word of prophecy, has not seen the last of such wonders of salvation; there are reserved for the future such evidences of the efficacy of the blood of Christ that the Apostle, as he anticipated them and contemplated the grandeur of the whole plan of God, exclaimed, 'O the depth of the riches both of the wisdom and knowledge of God!' There is no hope for the world apart from revivals, but it is not in revivals that the faith of the Church is to be rooted. Christ himself is the object of faith. The same faith which looks for his final appearing must also trust in his promised presence as the nations are evangelised. The Church, being united to him in whom the Spirit dwells without measure, will be built; she can no more be deprived of the

Spirit's aid than can the finished work of Christ—upon which the mission of the Spirit proceeds—be undone. When, therefore, the people of God find themselves with little evidence of spiritual prosperity, they are not to conclude that henceforth the Church can only be a dwindling minority in a pagan world, nor are they to suppose that they may suspend working until there be some new out-pouring of the Spirit: rather their present duty is to exercise a fuller confidence in the word and person of the Son of God. In doing so they will not find the Spirit who glorifies Christ to be absent. 'Christians', says Luther, 'must have the vision which enables them to disregard the terrible spectacle and outward appearance, the devil and the guns of the whole world, and to see Him who sits on high and says: "I am the One who spoke to you."'

When Christ is thus the object of faith, then will his promise always be fulfilled, 'Nothing shall be impossible unto you' (Matt. 17.20).

Murray then closes his book with the words of C. H. Spurgeon:

The fulness of Jesus is not changed, then why are our works so feebly done? Pentecost, is that to be a tradition? The reforming days, are these to be memories only? I see no reason why we should not have a greater Pentecost than Peter saw, and a Reformation deeper in its foundations, and truer in its upbuildings than all the reforms which Luther or Calvin achieved. We have the same Christ, remember that. The times are altered, but Jesus is the eternal, and time touches him not.... Our laziness puts off the work of conquest, our self-indulgence procrastinates, our cowardice and want of faith make us dote upon the millennium instead of hearing the Spirit's voice today. Happy days would begin from this hour if the Church would but awake and put on her strength, for in her Lord all fulness dwells.

Oh! Spirit of God, bring back thy church to a belief in the gospel! Bring back her ministers to preach it once again with the Holy Ghost, and not striving after wit and learning. Then shall we see thine arm made bare, O God, in the eyes of all the people, and the myriads shall be brought to rally round the throne of God and the Lamb. The Gospel must succeed, it shall succeed, it cannot be prevented from succeeding; a multitude that no man can number must be saved.[4]

Gathering all that together and summing it up—what does it say to us now?

First, we need nothing less than biblical world vision in time as well as in space. We need to know where we fit into the procession of history. We know what has gone before and from a study of that history, holy and secular, we should be able to see what must inevitably take place yet—although we do not know the gap, or the size or significance of the gap, between what has been and what must be. All we know is that we are sandwiched between these two, the future as predicted in clear but general outline in the Bible, just as sure as the past. Surely this knowledge should be sufficient to electrify us into the action likeliest to aid the ongoing process towards God's own consummation?

Vision, then, first; keeping within our knowledge and humbly seeking further light, as far as God may be pleased to give it to us. Then godly, sacrificial character to match the light we have. Godly character is always acceptable to God and hereafter, in and for itself. It is a total, inalienable everlasting gain. We must be, personally, bulwarks against the whole kingdom of evil—and that kingdom we must discern and delineate clearly from Scripture and from our knowledge of this present evil world. We must not remain ignorant of Satan's devices.

Next (and none of this is activist), we must intercede as we worship and praise and pray. Do not tell me that true praise does not lead to most specific and eloquent intercession. I do not believe it!

Then character and prayer go together. I will tell you why. It is possible for the very best life to be lived before men and for men to see it—and yet not see it because its divine proportions are hidden from their eyes: they are blind.

One question needs to be answered concerning the fact that so many Christians living in the midst of the community seem to bear little obvious fruit in their lives in the way of souls won. One would expect that if basic evangelism was God's prior way of influencing others towards Christ our churches would be full Sunday by Sunday with those who had seen Christ in their neighbours and friends and fellow-workers, and would crowd the gates of the Lord's house to hear what it

---

4   Iain Murray, *The Puritan Hope* (Banner of Truth, Edinburgh, 1971), pp. 237, 238

was that wrought such grace in them. But it is not so, is it? Because even a truly Christian life may not make evangelical impact upon the deeply-grained cynicism and unbelief of the present day.

It is one thing for Christ to shine out of the lives of others but another thing for men to see it. The people of Palestine during our Lord's three years of ministry (and surely in Nazareth before) saw the perfect life of our blessed Lord. But many did not believe, even within his own family. Were they jealous? Their eyes were not opened and their sin resisted what they did see, because it was directed like a sword at their corrupt hearts, calling for radical repentance and renewal of life. What is the use of light to blind eyes? Men's eyes have to be opened as well as the glorious truth of Christ exposed to them by life and lip. That is why another factor must be present along with the gracious, radiant life, and that factor is prayer that the truth of the Word of God in life and lip may be seen by the opening of blind eyes.

The prophet said, 'I have given you as a covenant to the people, a light to the nations, to open the eyes of the blind...' But, how can light open blind eyes? Only by the divine action of the Almighty can blind eyes be opened to see the lives of those who are shining for Jesus. Many worthy Christian lives, I believe, fail to tell for Jesus Christ just because although the life is lived all right before the Lord, yet the work of opening men's hearts to conviction of sin and need of Christ and thence to seeing his mercy, grace and beauty in other lives, has not been wrought by continuing fervent, believing prayer. It involves a real death. James says, 'The effectual, fervent prayer of a righteous man (righteous in and by Christ) avails much' (Jas. 5:16). But men's hearts have to be opened by prayer as well as the light made truly to shine before them. Travailing prayer, that is what we need.

Therefore, beyond the Christ-life received and truly lived, there is the responsibility to pray that our lives will tell and that men's eyes will be opened to the light even as we walk the streets, sit in buses and work in offices along with very needy people.

I would never walk into a hospital ward without becoming intensely aware that, poor though my light may be, and broken, alas, as it often is, Jesus in some sort or fashion is entering that ward with me. So one prays, Lord let my light shine and let these people see you in some real sense.

This kind goes not out but by prayer and fasting. Whatever you think about fasting (and some people think too much of it, and some too little) it suggests the cost of believing prayer. Read Daniel 10; Isaiah 53:10, 11; Colossians 1:24–29; 2:1–3. All these references are to travail. Without that there can be no births!

RHYTHMS OF REST AND WORK

'He saw that rest was good.'
(Genesis 49:15)

A consideration of rhythms of rest and work in alternate and simultaneous combinations, as applied to physical, psychological and spiritual health.

Nearly three decades ago the first sentence of *Towards Spiritual Maturity* declared: 'The fundamental blessing of salvation is peace. From it flow all God's richer blessings of love, joy, and glory.' Today this seems as true as ever. The more one shares with people the needs of their lives, the more one is convinced that the fundamental need of humanity is rest, in the sense that man needs to submit himself to God, in order that the divine life may be poured progressively into every part of his being. This is negative in as much as it requires man to cease from himself, that the Almighty may fill him with life-giving grace, but it is replete with the positive and vibrant blessings of God and will last to all eternity.

I pray that what I have written, and what is implied, lying comparatively hidden under the surface of holy Scripture, on this subject, may be heeded by those who read. For it must be realised that in our contemporary world, Satan, because he sees his time is short, becomes more urgent and insistent that we lose our heads, as well as our hearts, in fevered self-destructive activity.

The compelling reason for writing is simply this: much of my time in public and in private is spent expounding and applying the teaching of God's Word to those who greatly need the rest which God gives us in Christ. If some of that teaching is supplied in written form, it should save me and others much valuable time. I therefore appeal to those who have the Word of God as the source of their life, to take heed to this

---

teaching. I believe it will save their lives and make them happier, more efficient, and potentially more useful to God. This will be pleasing to God, than which nothing can be higher.

RHYTHMS OF REST AND WORK

1. Rhythms of Rest and Work

As in *Towards Spiritual Maturity*, before we consider the peace of God we must look at the God of peace; for if all God's blessings flow from peace, and peace flows from him, we must know him before we can know his peace.

Who is he, this God of peace? He is the Eternal, the Almighty, transcendent, self-existent, unchangeable, omniscient, 'immortal, invisible' (1 Tim. 1:17); the 'blessed and only Sovereign, the King of kings and Lord of lords, who alone has immortality and dwells in unapproachable light' (1 Tim. 6:15, 16); the altogether Other. 'I am the Lord, and there is no other' (Is. 45:5, 6, 14, 21).

The greatness of the almighty and eternal God is seen, amongst other things, in the complete satisfaction he derives from himself:

> When infinite intelligence finds infinite perfections in itself, infinite stability and integrity of character are assured. This integrity is simply another name for God's righteousness, or rightness.[1]

To see that this is true of God is instantly so commanding as to call forth all praise. It leads us to the contemplation of a God of such boldness and daring as to make us fear and wonder. Yet we also want to consider the unique phenomenon of a Being completely pleased with himself—and justifiably so. Indeed, he is looking to his creatures to recognise the fact, and charging them with sin, if they do not praise him with all their powers. This ought to be accepted by us human creatures as primarily proved by the sight of our eyes (Rom. 1:19, 20); and also

---

[1] Page 1 above

as regenerated sinners, we ought to see it, by reason of the gift of faith which God graciously gives to his own.

It is by revelation in his Holy Word that we see the greatness of God, and have confirmation of his complete satisfaction with his own perfections. The Son himself concurs and gladly worships the Father, 'I do always those things that please the Father' (Jn. 8:29); 'If it be possible...nevertheless, not my will, but thine be done' (Matt. 26:39); I and my Father are one' (Jn. 10:30). Likewise, we see this in the complete submission of the Holy Spirit to the will of both the Father and the Son.

There is therefore a 'family' agreement within the Trinity which forms an eternal consensus, and this is exceedingly satisfying for us to realise and contemplate. To be pointed away to the Father by the Son with perfect consistency throughout the revelation of the Gospel records, is one of the most stabilising influences afforded to man. And to have the Eternal Son descend from the infinite perfections of heaven, and dare to say in face of them, 'I am meek and lowly in heart,' (Matt. 11:29), as well as, 'There is none good but one, that is God,' (Luke 18:19), surely affords a wealth of confirmation of the transcendent nature of God, which even the sceptical mind of man can hardly gainsay.

Not only the greatness of God in his tri-unity and humility, but the love of the three divine persons for each other, is wonderful. David's expression of love to his deceased and lamented Jonathan, 'Your love to me was wonderful,' (2 Sam. 1:26), is but a pale reflection of the love that was between the Father, the Son and the Holy Spirit (see Jn. 17:22–26).

Now love, if it is true to itself and to its essential nature, loves to create. It seems inevitable, therefore, that such a wealth of divine love 'circulating' amongst the divine Three, should generate or reproduce that which is beyond itself—not out of outward necessity, but of inward desire. There was no other either to desire or bespeak, however deferentially; it seems to have been a necessity of the divine nature itself to create: it certainly proved to be so. And when God did create, we are, accordingly, not surprised at his own satisfaction with what he created (see Gen. 1:4, 10, 12, 18, 21, 25, 31): the inanimate and sub-human was 'good', and last of all, the crown of creation, man, was 'very good'.

Here we may comment on the order of creation. The chief hint as to the primacy of the angels seems to be taken from Job 38:7, as also in the form of words, 'heaven and earth', in many scriptural references: Genesis 1:1; Exodus 20:11; 2 Kings 19:15. Our friend William Mitchell, wrestling in Peru with the translation of the Old Testament into Quechua, raises the question of the meaning of the word 'host' in Genesis 2:1. There is no hint there as to any angelic priority in creation, but angels are surely included in that comprehensive statement.

The Almighty God's satisfaction, then, with himself in his triune Being and with his work of creation, may possibly provide a clue to the origin of the divine 'experience' of rest—not least since the Hebrew word for peace, *shalom*, has a rich, positive, creative content. There is nothing negative about the word. *Shalom* is no mere absence of trouble, strain, or stress: it is redolent of health, wealth and prosperity.

Interestingly enough, the usual New Testament word for 'rest', *anapausis*, as in, 'Come unto me, and I will give you rest,' (Matt. 11:28), is not as strongly positive as *shalom*, with the idea of cessation from labour and easement from strain. Indeed, modern men, possibly taking their cue from *shalom*, have tended to invest *anapausis* with the idea of positive satisfaction, and have been inclined to read 'refreshment' for 'rest', as in Matthew 11:28, 29—although the idea of relief is perhaps nearer the original meaning. Nevertheless, it is clear that the rest God enjoyed following creation cannot mean that the Almighty was tired, and needed respite! His rest was replete with satisfaction, in respect for his person and his work.

This contrasts with God's creatures, especially man, although we have no record of his experience between the creation and the Fall. Presumably, the ceaseless activity of the holy angels mentioned in Revelation 4:8 and the apparently constant movement of the living creatures in Ezekiel, chapter 1, is not the activity of unhappy restlessness, such as we see in Satan himself (*e.g.* in Job 1:7; 2:2) and in the wicked men spoken of in Isaiah 57:20, 21.

The other significant word for rest and peace is the Hebrew *Sabbath*, which we find first in Genesis 2:2, as the verb, 'to rest'; the whole idea of rest stemming from the fact that the Almighty God, infinite in power as in all other attributes, chose to rest after the work of creation. Of course, both 'rest' and 'work' apply differently to God from the way they do to us; but there must be some analogical relationship between them if Scripture is to have any meaning. The work which ceased was the work of creation, while the work of redemption went on. Even when that was completed, the task of working it all out in history still continued, and continues, with the Son now constantly active at the Father's side in heaven. Similarly with rest; the Father is not tired, but ceases from one form of work in order to engage in another. It is sometimes said that a change is as good as a rest! May this not suggest rhythm in the ongoing purpose of God, as in Genesis 2:1–3?

But when the concepts of work and rest are applied to man, because he is both finite and sinful, they take on added significance—and there can be no doubt that God intended the divine experience to be applied to man, as in Genesis 2:1–3, and Exodus 20:8–11. The Word states explicitly that God blessed the seventh day, the day of rest. That can hardly mean that he blessed it *in vacuo*. It was blessed for man as it had been blessed for God himself. How wonderful of the Almighty to order that his own 'experience' should apply to his frail and wayward creature, man! We should marvel at this and be the more inclined to submit to him, learn from it and follow on.

This is all of major importance since the Fall took place, because man, being not only finite but fallen, found that for him work became arduous and odious. After the Fall it consisted, not only of hard labour (Gen. 3:17–19), but of injurious restlessness, a work of undoing rather than of constructing and edifying. Thus the very idea of sabbath rest for man emerges as a clear and sweet parable of the gospel, in which restless sinners are able to rest from their own ineffectual labours in the effectual and fruitful redeeming work of God in Christ.

This idea of resting in God for salvation runs right through Scripture and when it becomes a commandment to man (Exod. 20:8–11) we begin to see its nature as a parable—in addition to the value of rhythms of rest in the world of say, agriculture, and the animal world (see Exod. 23:10–12). We may therefore deeply regret that in our land of Scotland sabbatarianism should so often be divorced from the glories of the gospel and become part of a legalistic religious system! The real message of sabbath rest is nothing less than that salvation is of the Lord (*cf.* Ps. 3:8; Jonah 2:9; Rev. 7:10).

This tremendous revelation, that salvation is of the Lord from beginning to end, and that man has no part in it but to receive it, and that even the strength and will to do so is from God, by the gift of faith, was what was lost so early in the history of the Christian church and had to be recovered—as it was, wonderfully, at the Reformation. This is what Luther saw and communicated powerfully to the other leaders of the

Reformation, that God was sovereign in his working and it was he who willed all the good done on the face of the earth; therefore, man's highest welfare was in seeking and resting in the God of his salvation.

The thesis of this study is, then, that on every level and in every department of life, the fundamental concept of resting in God and working only in co-operation with his sovereign, almighty, effectual will, is all. Every conflicting idea is vain, with the vanity of what the Scriptures call 'good works' done, or attempted, apart from the good will of God.

One can see, in a sense, how sinful it is to seek to do anything apart from God, for, in fact, it amounts to ignoring and refusing to believe that he is there to be consulted for guidance, direction, and the supply of strength to do his work in his way. We therefore see that the idea of resting in God is part of a total attitude, which includes the recognition that as finite creatures we are absolutely dependent upon him—as for our creation, so for our survival and well-being.

This would be all right if we were fit to receive and act upon that knowledge, and co-operate with the Almighty in all that pertains to his pleasure and our welfare, but the Fall has cut across all that. It has blinded us to our best and highest interests, so that under the influence of another god, Satan, we falter, flounder and make the wrong decisions. We become increasingly apprehensive, piling up strain upon strain, until we become enmeshed in ever greater complexities of life. In the end, we may almost welcome death as the only apparently decent solution to life's problems.

To such, the offer of the peace of God which passes all understanding affords a life-line and hope. It is far more than salvation; it is life itself, because peace with God is the road back to him, and to the heart of his love, and to real enjoyment in life.

Before we estimate the magnitude and depth of the peace God offers, with its unspeakable cost, we need to consider how man in the first place lost the peace and fellowship he had with God in the garden. The situation was this: Adam and Eve found themselves alive and well in the best possible world, with the eternal God in three persons to care for them. Of all creatures they were clearly God's favourite (see Gen. 1:26, 27). All that was expected of them in return was that they would go God's way, which was surely the most natural thing in the world to do to express gratitude to God for innumerable blessings. Indeed, so

generous was the Lord that he imposed upon them one prohibition only
as a sign of their creaturely finitude and subjection to their Maker: 'Don't
touch that tree!' It was under the influence of Satan, represented by the
serpent, that these two dared to touch the tree, against all that was God.
They then found that they plunged themselves into seas of trouble from
which none but the God they had despised and disobeyed could extricate
them.

The realism of God's challenge to the unhappy pair, not to say his
condemnation of Satan in the second half of Genesis 3, is beyond
compare. The repair of the damage to God's sovereign purpose would
take long, and cost much, but the great fiat promising a Redeemer, in
Genesis 3:15, was categorically stated in the first enunciation of God's
covenant of grace. Its promise thereafter ran through the Old Testament,
with increasingly specific references to God's grace in choosing men
like Noah (Gen. 6:8, 18; 9:9; 12:1–3), Abraham (Gen. 15, 17, 22),
Moses (Exod. 6:1–8); until, beyond the chequered rise and fall of the
chosen people, Israel, the promised Messiah himself came to fulfil the
gracious promises, and by the triune work of three specific deaths in
one, to deal with sins, sin, and Satan. All was to establish and secure
both negatively and positively, man's acceptable status with God, a
place in his heart, and, withal, fundamental peace in his own soul. This
is the peace we are to explore.

Nothing can exaggerate the heinousness of man's sin in rebelling
against God. It was in face of the sheerest kindness and lavish provision
of an altogether benevolent deity that the dastardly and disastrous
experiment was made. All the beguilement in the world of the subtle
serpent cannot mitigate its scandal, as far as man is concerned. It is in
the face of this that God instantly promised a Redeemer (Gen. 3:15).
Despite an appalling and mounting tale of perfidy, he persistently
pursued his declared saving purpose beyond the murder of Abel and the
sins of the Cainite stock, until, with a phenomenal upsurge of human
evil, joined by a demonic alliance of wickedness (Gen. 6), the Lord was
well-nigh at the end of his patience, and like to drown the whole
enterprise in a deluge.

His irresistible grace, however, lighted upon Noah, named in the
hope that he would bring relief from the wickedness of men after the
Flood (Gen. 5:29). God saved him and his family in an ark of salvation,
which, as Peter tells us (1 Pet. 3:20–22), is a type of our salvation in
Christ.

Then came the tower of Babel (Gen. 11) and what wicked men sought to do is to dispense with the God who had made them, so that after the manner of Satan's own attempt, they might impudently take his place.

But the greater the sinful attempt to foil the divine intention, the greater God's act of omnipotent saving grace. Take the choice of Abram from the Persian Gulf: God patiently led him into the promised land of Canaan when family loyalty would have held him back. Then he steadfastly brought him back to Canaan from Egypt when his wayward nature took him into that troubled realm, which is surely symbolic of the worldly world. But faith is rewarded despite Abraham's impatience for the birth of the promised son, resulting in Isaac's contention with Ishmael—a contention not yet over for their descendants! Abraham, nevertheless, by faith, laid his miracle son on the altar of sacrifice at Moriah, and thus another grim and hard-wrought parable of salvation in Christ was enacted before the eyes of men.

We could go on recounting the hellish acts of Satan working furiously overtime—his time is short (Rev. 12:12)—as well as the acts of his strategically placed human agents. But the sovereign Ruler of the universe more than matches these evils with acts both of grace and judgment. He preserves the Jews, yet punishes them at least as severely as other evil men, until, within a hairsbreath of survival, he affords them the deflated and demoted status of an oppressed people, back in their own land again, yet surviving. Although their royal house was now depressed until they were 'lost' in the hills, amidst the provincial paganism of Galilee, yet they were preserved: royal Joseph, descendant of David and Solomon, a Nazarine peasant, and his betrothed, Mary, related to Elizabeth of the house of Aaron (see Luke 1:5, 36), awaiting the birth of the second Adam.

Jesus, the second Adam, came to undo the evil wrought by the first Adam, to reinstate man as a fit companion for God. This he did by living a life of perfect obedience to the Father, and by taking upon himself the full tale of all elect man's disobedience and rebellion, and bearing punishment for the same, until nothing remained to obstruct the path that led from God to man and from man back to God.

Peace, fully and gladly acceptable to God through the action of his eternal, incarnate Son, was offered to man on absolutely free and unmerited terms. The repair of innumerable dastardly deeds of infidelity, rebellion and shame was perfectly completed. Thus man, still exceedingly imperfect and destined throughout history to grieve God and his fellows unspeakably, time after time, was nonetheless accepted by God upon terms of fully acknowledging Christ's work for him. He would thereby be absolved from all penalty, guilt and shame, being committed, of course, to the good life of holiness and obedience by the indwelling power of the Spirit of God. This was, not least, a sign of repentance, and of man's gratitude to God for the fundamental gift of peace with him. As such it must be understood as the mere commencement of all that was to follow God's lavish grace in time and in eternity.

The first great blessing of God, then, through justification, is that unspeakable peace which God establishes between himself and his rebel creature, man, on the ground of Christ's death, which by grace and the instrumentality of the gift of faith he gives to those chosen by him and destined for salvation. To know that a God who is implacably hostile to our sins, has reconciled himself to us by the death of his Son, and that all we need to do is accept this reconciliation as soon as we see that it is wrought for us—for me!—is so wonderful that we are not surprised Paul expressed the effect of it in terms of, 'peace which surpasses all understanding' (Phil. 4:7). Indeed, we are sure these words are so familiar to Christians and devout people that their astonishingly superlative character is far from realised. The apostle means that this peace between God and man is wrought finally and absolutely in Christ. It has the quality of the divine life of Jesus, and of his perfect, passive and active obedience, which made the offering of his blood so eternally valid and valuable. The peace is wrought so fully and finally that the security it offers sinner-man, when he is accepted as righteous, is beyond finite inspection, let alone understanding.

So much for the basic, objective fact of the peace established through righteousness on the Godward side. This is not to say how that fact may, or may not strike man: he may begin to see it, or he may scarcely see it at all, but if he has clinched the divine/human transaction by resting himself wholly upon the merits of Jesus' death, then this eternal fact of justification and peace with God is instantly open to him and is forever operative in respect of him.

Seeing it and understanding it, however, are two different things. Yet, when we do begin to understand it, we find that there is open to us a whole, subjective dimension of experience of the 'peace of God which surpasses all understanding.' It is this increasingly blissful experience which belongs to those whose pardon is sealed by his blood and by their faith upon that fact. There is an entire universe of possible experience for the believer to fathom and explore here, not for experience's sake only, but as the inevitable reward of discovering the wonder of Christ's death for us. Thus we enter into the enjoyment of its present fruits. It is then that earnest saints in all ages have come to know the joy of the Lord, until they have cried out to him in a pleasure amounting almost to pain, not to pour his peace into their hearts so lavishly, since mortal bodies are not able to contain such elation, and they are therefore tempted to an ecstasy (literally, standing out of themselves), in order to bear it.

There can, therefore, be hope of abiding welfare for creature-man only when he is in a state of enjoyment of the favour of God, because God in heaven is at peace with him in respect of sin, and because he accepts him as righteous in Christ. The multiple, healthful effects of God's peace are then known in his daily life only as the knowledge of God's deep transforming rest. This rest proves thereafter to be the basis of a far more reposeful and yet a more resourceful person. As death in one realm is the basis of life in another, so rest in one realm is the basis of energy in another. Do we not speak of 'giants refreshed'? How are they refreshed? Not by constant, unremitting activity, but by the recuperating effects of rest.

All that we subsequently have to say, therefore, applies in substantial measure to those only who base their search for personal peace upon the sure knowledge that they have peace with God (Rom. 5:1)—a word which means that God is at peace with them. The succeeding four verses of the chapter (2–5) go on to describe the fruits of the justification which procures peace with God. They include access into the grace of justification as a permanent standing with God, with the further joyful prospect of seeing and sharing the glory of God hereafter.

Nor is that all: so great and luxuriant are the fruits of the grace of justification flowing from God's peace with us, that entrance into them has the effect of transforming our character (see 2 Cor. 3:18), until we are able to contemplate and envisage experiences of affliction and trial which formerly we would have thought intolerable; experiences which are the antithesis of peace, and which would, therefore, have seemed impossible for us to bear because of the unhappiness and restlessness they would have caused.

Indeed, so deep is the peace founded upon God's saving act, that the first five verses of Romans 5 work from the fact of peace through justification into a standing in grace, and right on to the hope of glory. From that vantage point we view the sufferings consequent on attaining such a height. We are able to face them with equanimity, because the fruit in growth of character and spiritual stamina is now discerned. The hope of that end then brightens, being no mere future dream, because it includes the present reality of God's own love poured into the human heart by the Holy Spirit. The fact is, that when inward peace is established and ensured, outward dispeace and disturbance in the world may prevail and threaten heart and mind with all manner of fears and sinister forebodings, but made strong by God's own strength, and fortified by his grace, love and peace, the believer can face anything, because he faces it with him, and in him, who has already faced and finally defeated the worst possible in the whole universe. We shall never suffer as Jesus suffered.

> Thou, who once was thus bereft
> That Thine own might ne'er be left,
> Teach me by that bitter cry
> In the gloom to know Thee nigh.
>   (John Ellerton)

It is this category and dimension of peace which is the basis of what we are considering. It is well that we take stock of it although we may have occasion to draw attention to it a hundred times yet. That we will do, lest, under the influence of Satan (the arch-whittler of the truth), we see the peace of God as of diminishing importance and regard it more and more subjectively, until it becomes no more than a mood which sweeps over fortunate people, now and then, in felicitous circumstances.

RHYTHMS OF REST AND WORK

2. The Content and Substance of Our Peace

The peace Jesus Christ gained by his full and final work on the cross is immense. It contains three distinct elements or dimensions, without knowledge of which it is impossible to enter into the depth of enjoyment which is ours in Christ. There are, in fact, serious gaps in the knowledge of many Christians, because, almost as a matter of course, they become enamoured of particular aspects of the gospel. In their excitement they take the part for the whole, leaving out major elements of the truth, to their great detriment, thus paring it down far below what it is.

Christians who become obsessed with what I call 'evangelisticism' (the proclamation of the mere rudiments, or first principles of the gospel only), see Christ's death solely as a death for sins, and the blessing of the gospel simply as forgiveness. Of course, that is the fundamental blessing, but we must not stop there, as if we were to use only one storey of a three storey edifice of truth: what a waste! It was because so many Christians towards the end of the nineteenth century neglected the further dimensions of Christ's work, that the movement which provided conventions for the deepening of Christian life necessarily arose.

This movement, with its emphasis on sanctification, has done much to persuade Christians to consider the second dimension of Christ's death for sin. In such teaching sins and sin are set together in the relation of fruit to root. The great blessing of the truth of sanctification (as found in Romans 6) is that we learn that Christ died, not only to pay the penalty for our evil deeds, but to draw the sting of sin itself from our lives, and bring our fallen, perverse human nature to an end—not producing instant moral perfection (the erroneous expectation of some when faced with the finality of Christ's work in the second dimension), but the sure beginnings of progressive sanctification.

There is, however, another major dimension beyond these two, although most Christians think they have reached far enough when they have embraced (1) the blessing of sins forgiven (with its positive counterpart in the new birth) and (2) the belief and experimental acceptance of the fact of our death to sin in union with Christ; that is, the double truth, of putting to death the old nature, slain by Christ, and putting on the new nature, procured for us by Christ. This second involves the destruction of the old Adam by the last Adam, Christ, who presents himself to us in resurrection power, to dwell in our hearts and live out the Christ life within us (Col. 3).

It is one thing to deal with the fruit and root of sin, but quite another to challenge the originator, or instigator of sin, Satan himself, and tackle him! This also, and supremely, Christ has done (Gen. 3:15; Rev. 12:10, 11). We are convinced that the experimental peace of God in the believing heart is often sadly lacking. Christians may have been taught how to rest in God for forgiveness and peace through the blood of Jesus, and also for the victory of complete and final destruction of the sin nature—the 'flesh' remaining (Rom. 7:18, 25), as the *Westminster Confession of Faith* explains, being but 'remnants of corruption', the mere dregs or residue of the old nature, brought to an end when we received Christ. Yet many Christians are still completely nonplussed when temptations and accusations arise which throw the second dimension (death to sin), and even the first (sins forgiven), into serious question.

Not to know that rest in God as to the past, and victory over inbred sin in the present, can be insidiously questioned by subtle attacks of Satan the accuser simply means that Christ's work on the cross and our appropriation of its dimensions, are seen as, at least, inadequate. We fear we are not saved; our sins are not forgiven; we are still sinning as of yore; we are not 'dead to sin' (Rom. 6:11), for sin stalks ever more wildly through our lives. Satan is always ready with handy examples of our misdemeanours, and worse, stirs up the dregs of sin within us, and then, as soon as we succumb to his blandishments, he whips round and accuses us of what he made us do! There is vast ignorance of this technique, which is Satan's stock-in-trade; and often, alas, the ignorance is wilful. Consequently, many prefer the painful up-and-down experience of sinning and repenting, sinning and repenting, the sinister force within us taking over increasingly, because, obtusely and perversely, we refuse to believe the truth and take the wiles of the devil seriously. 'We wrestle not against flesh and blood, but against principalities, against powers...in heavenly places' (Eph. 6:12). We must never forget it.

Look at it this way: How can we possibly enjoy depth of peace with God, notwithstanding sins forgiven and our death to sin as long as the arch-enemy himself is loose and able to deceive us as to the efficacy, or even the reality of these two blessings? But you may say 'Satan is not loose; since Christ's victory he is bound and defeated.' Ah, but that is a half-truth, or a truth so complex that it ought not to be asserted so badly. He is bound, but by Christ's victory of faith, and we have no other means of controlling and vanquishing him! The Almighty's control of evil is now delegated to Christ, because he has won this power and honour. The new Man-for-men in heaven is reigning specifically for us. We enter his rule and reign only by the exercise of faith. We therefore need to know the facts, and apply them by faith to our lives, as well as to the lives of others. Since Satan and his agents are still free to work unsuspectingly in the lives of those ignorant of his devices, and since such agents certainly seek fleshly and sinful ground within us from which to stir up trouble to our dismay and undoing if possible, we need to be constantly on guard. We must not only cherish the former blessings of sins forgiven and the power of sin destroyed, but watch how the devil challenges them. He does this by casting doubt upon their reality and efficacy. In particular he stirs up the dregs of the old life, as perverse indications that we are deceiving ourselves, that our doctrine has not worked and cannot work.

It stands to reason that there can be no peace in the life of any one subject to such evil machinations. We cannot, therefore, know too much about the serpent's wiles and ways. It will help us to see the magnitude of the work of Christ's victory if we understand that, in fact, the rule and control of the universe is bound up with the redemption that is in Christ. A passage such as Romans 8:18–23, shows us this; all nature groans under the effects of the Fall, and waits the full redemption of the sons of God. But it is our experience of God's grace while waiting for full redemption that concerns us in this study. What healthful peace may we hope for? Since that is a matter of divine grace in a temporal situation, it must also be a matter of time, or, as we call it, rhythms. Indeed, we see that the universe itself continues by means of a system of revolutions, with, apparently, clock-work precision—we set our clocks by it, not the universe by our clocks. While this has its mechanical aspect, it also has its aesthetic and human aspects, as in musical rhythms; in the cycles of astral, solar, and terrestrial life; and in plant, animal, and human life. Deborah sang of 'the stars on their courses' (Judg. 5:20; Job 22:14) and the psalmist (19:6) tell of 'the circuit of the heavens'. We know that our years, months, and days are governed by the revolutions of the sun and earth, and even our weeks are related to the perfect number seven; which, we think, suggests motion towards perfection and completeness.

The importance of rhythm is also seen in God's commands to Israel concerning the need for different kinds of rest: the ground to lie fallow in husbandry, and the tilling of the soil (Exod. 23:10, 11; Lev. 26:34, 35); and rest for animals—even the dove sought rest (Gen. 8:9). There is rest for man (Exod. 20:8–11; 23:12); and even rest for God (Gen. 2:2, 3). As the revolving seasons and the sequence of day and night prescribe that man shall live rhythmically, so human nature, by its constitution, calls for rest and sleep as the restorer of its wearied frame and mind. Shakespeare in Macbeth speaks of,

> Sleep that knits up the ravell'd sleeve of care, the death of each day's life, sore labour's bath, balm of hurt minds, great nature's second course, chief nourisher in life's feast (II.ii).

It may be that our dis-health is often due in no small measure to the simple neglect of the basic and elementary rhythms of nature. Perhaps what we need, above all, is to return to nature by returning to the God of nature, who graciously reminds us in his Word that nature was made for man and God. We do well to study the God of creation, as well as of redemption, to see how these two fit together; for that is undoubtedly the great Designer's intention. Then we may make the most of life on earth in the interests of the heavenly life. Thus we may see how God, by his work of restoration, undoes, or minimises the quirks and snags of the Fall (see Gen. 3:14–21, and 1 Tim. 2:13–15). Indeed, a great deal of the teaching to be applied to the highest spiritual principles, begins most naturally in the realms of physical life, and leads on from the idea of rest and work as an alternating rhythm, to the idea of rest and work as simultaneous activity.

We will take the alternating rhythm first. I fear we may often expend and waste far more energy, physically, emotionally and mentally, than we need. The result is that we lack reserves of such energy for particular effort, and we, therefore, tire too easily. We must learn to know, from practice and experience, the length of periods of rest and work that are necessary and good for us as individuals. Ought it to be one long rest in sleep of six to eight hours per night, and then a long, continuous day of sixteen to eighteen hours? Or ought it possibly to be a shorter night's sleep, with rest and relaxation at a certain time, or times, during the day?

To expect the delicate and sensitive human frame and mechanism to maintain constant efficiency from early morning to late at night without any definite relaxation of tension during so many hours is, it seems to me, unreasonable, and explains why we often behave badly, and act inefficiently. I have noticed this, even in the most lively youngsters. Even in excellent health, I am sure they, no less than older people, need shorter rhythms of rest and work, if they are to maintain full efficiency in mental and physical effort and, what is at least of equal importance, to maintain an emotional equilibrium which keeps them, and those with whom they live and work, at ease and relatively happy. I am aware of how ridiculous this may seem to hearty young bloods who can easily lose a night's sleep, or several nights' sleep, without seeming to suffer unduly. Of course, the human frame can adjust wonderfully to strenuous and stressful conditions; but we are not discussing what the human constitution can do, by way of endurance in emergency situations, but what is best for it in order to preserve both health and length of life, and also to maintain efficiency of effort. In the case of Christians, this is surely vitally related to their participation in the Kingdom of God.

While the young may laugh at the thought of resting on the physical level during the long day, it should not be difficult for them to see how threadbare emotionally, or over-excited they may become by the end of the day. Those who are engaged in systematic intellectual activity, whether studious or not, should have even more of an inkling of how tired the mind can become, and how strained the emotions. Such may disdain any attempt to deal rhythmically with their life-style by periods of rest; the very fact of admitting to one kind of tiredness or another would appal them! Yet they should certainly come to see that some rhythm or cycle of rest and work is necessary for well-being and efficiency.

Lest any one should think we concentrate too much on the merely physical, and at an elementary level at that, let me quote from a volume of clinical theology which embraces the whole field of rest and work from the most physical to the most spiritual.

> For us, it is a fundamental fact of therapy that the fight against the phobias...should be given up in favour of the evangelical position of resting...in the finished work of a gracious God. The core of the Gospel is an invitation to step out of the arena of human

struggling to 'let go, and let God', as the old adage has it. Phobic (fearful) people cannot let go. The Gospel gives good ground for a change of mind in this respect.

It is impossible to discuss in detail the infinitely varied rhythms of rest and work that go to make up a harmonious way of life. The pattern, even for the same person, may be very different at different times: youth, middle age and old age; a young wife before and after the birth of her children; in health, or in invalidity; we might even say in the legalistic rigours of pre-Christian zeal and intensity as compared with both the rest and new incentives which Christ supplies.

The hardest battle is to convince zealous, industrious people of the necessity of rest in the midst of work, for both health and efficiency. It may take a thorough knowledge of the Bible, together with the conviction of the Holy Spirit concerning practical truths about resting in Christ, to constrain believers to put the Bible's many exhortations into practice. From long, practical experience of the rather dumb obtuseness of human nature in this respect, we stress the importance of becoming convinced that the example of the Almighty God himself in creation is the surest guide. As he rested after work, so he intends man to rest: he is to obey the fourth commandment (embedded in the ten). It is an important and mighty theme of Scripture.

We read of the Lord's passionate appeals to his people, at Kadesh-Barnea, to enter into the Canaan rest of the land—with Joshua's attempts to gain them rest from its vile inhabitants.

There is the major lesson of peace, provided by the history of militant David, followed by peaceful Solomon (see Ps. 95:11).

We have the Lord's earnest appeals to his people on the eve of, during, and in the throes of exile, to return to him, rest and be saved (Is. 30:15; 32:16–20). The prospect of that great peace to be brought by the Prince of Peace is prophesied (Is. 9:6, 7; 26:3).

There is our Lord's wonderful promise in Matthew 11:28–30. The climax, of course, is his procuring of this peace by his death and victory.

The mighty theme is continued and expounded in the writings of the holy apostles, the Epistles and the Revelation—not least in the great passage in Hebrews 3:7–4:13.

All this should convince an open-minded and teachable people that here indeed is a theme which requires instant and major attention. At least, there ought to be a beginning of a consideration of how the great theme of rest and peace is to be taken up in the practical details of life, to see how the foundations of a rhythmical life can be laid. For a start, there is the question of the lengths of these rhythms, or undulations, in each individual case, from the point of view of temperament and also the practical necessities and rigours of one's daily life-style of duty and responsibility.

I want to stress this to the point of belabouring the obvious, lest I seem to side-step the charge made by busy mothers with young families, that an old bachelor could not possibly understand the impossibilities of snatching rest periods in a household where young children are for ever around claiming full attention. What has surprised me in a number of cases is the indignant idea that a busy young mother should think of rest at all, whereas I know of no one who is in greater need of its regular rhythm! Of course, the practicalities are difficult, and one has often spent time with mothers and others (notably young doctors in their pre-registration year) who live lives of constant activity, working out with them ways and means of escaping from the grinding round to find even slight relief from perpetual strain. Ten minutes in a fully stretched out position may be made the greatest use of by those who have even begun to practise rest and relaxation. But, for some one, careering around at full speed, to think of such a thing may seem not only ridiculous, but also a too uselessly small amount of time in which to do any good. On the contrary, even the beginnings of a slumping into a restful frame, which one may learn in ten minutes, may have already done sufficient good to send one back to the hurried round with a real sense of relief.

The beginning of the secret of how to rest and relax is, of course, in one's attitude, and it may very well be that this is not only a psychological but a spiritual matter. Satan's work in the human heart is largely wrought by a kind of restlessness, and, therefore, the beginning of a real salvation here must embody a flat contradiction of the necessity of continual activity. The irrationality of being constantly on-the-go, without cogent reason, will soon appear; so that one may soon be able both to laugh and cry at one's former attempts to keep the pot boiling!

Once we see that, the battle is half won. It may be that to achieve so much involves admitting with tears of sorrow that we have been too proud to admit that we needed rest, and could not. Indeed, it may help us if we confess this to some understanding person. It may help them, too, to do the same more deeply.

After that beginning, the mind is then prepared to direct the body towards the desired end, which is that of healthful rest. The fact that God will look after the world while you take a little time off, should give a sense of real relief! 'Come ye apart, and rest awhile'; Jesus said it! For the time you have—it may be ten minutes only—give yourself to the serious business of rest. 'Strive to enter into rest,' says the writer of Hebrews.

First, whatever your physical situation, whether in a chair, couch, or, preferably, a bed (you really need your feet up and your head down; indeed, the floor, for all its hardness, may be better than trying to relax in an uncomfortable chair), begin to relax, from the head, right down to the feet, consciously trying to do it. You will be amazed how long it will take, because there are areas from the neck right down to the ankles and toes which tend to remain in a state of tension. Are you lying, dead weight on that bed, or are you gripping yourself as if you were holding up the bed, not it you? Are your shoulders slumped? Is your head relaxed? Is the pillow or cushion too high or too low for complete rest? Are you gripping your arms and clasping or clenching your hands? Are your ankles crossed and gripping each other like a vice, as if life depended on it?

Even when you have gone over the whole body and consciously sought to relax its various muscles and are in a state in which it is possible to rest, the sheer negativeness of it, or the impulse to be up and doing, or even involuntarily jerking yourself into some kind of action, may be more than you can resist. Before you know it, you have re-arranged yourself in your lying-down position, until all the tension is resumed and you are back at your favourite activity of gripping like mad! At this point you may want to give up trying and forget the whole thing, as more bother than it is worth! You may be surprised, when you consider it, how fiercely you seek to justify all this sheer waste of intense energy. You will then begin to realise that probably all your life you have been burning up various kinds of energy at a most extravagant rate, just wasting sheer effort on nothing but keeping yourself in this self-righteous state of tension. What for? For nothing, but Satan's satisfaction in seeing you wear yourself out uselessly.

Indeed, it may be that you are so full of tension that it is literally impossible to relax in the way described. This may have become a medical problem with you, and you may need to consult a doctor about your inability to relax and, therefore, to sleep refreshingly. There is around, a pious objection on the part of many good people to anything in the nature of sedation or aids to sleep, which, considering that we live by putting various kinds of chemical substances into our mouths every day, is rather puristic. Let me quote the recent experience of one under major satanic attack which was completely irrational, and who largely solved the problem of months of sleeplessness by being persuaded to take a normal dosage of a sleeping pill. After one really good night's sleep, he found the problem and its irrationality practically gone, so that he was able to cope. But it takes a good deal to convince some people of the necessity of relaxation and sleep for the continuance of healthy life and activity. It may be that a doctor ought to be consulted. Certainly, pills should only be taken under doctor's orders.

Perseverance is necessary to achieve real relaxation. It needs to be stressed again that the basis of such relaxation is a mind set at rest from all possible care by God through Christ: it is this that we are talking about. Nonetheless, the rigours of a duteous life may induce such a spirit of self-righteous legalism in the mind that it becomes hard to adopt an attitude which lets the whole world go by, for a while, until you are fitted again to take up your share, and only your share, of care and duty. We hope the point has been sufficiently stressed to be of help to those who want to benefit by it.

There is one thing more. From time to time we may be called upon to undergo a period of unusual strain of mind or body, and there is no possibility of relief until it is over. It is much easier to rest the over-tired body than the over-tired mind. The mind takes far longer to rest than the body. Normally, a tired body can be adequately rested by one good night's sleep, but if the mind has been strained through too much mental activity (students, in particular, know about this, but seldom understand it), it may take days, or weeks, or even months of nursing back to normal healthy mental activity, before it is delivered from the tendency to paralytic fixity or feverish racing. Some minds are so highly geared that they feed on intense, creative activity, and they may be totally unaware of the fact, or may even refuse to know that they are straining their mental equipment. The result can be infinitely pathetic; those engaged in highly intellectual activity need to watch themselves closely, albeit without distraction, to know when to stop and relax completely, or change to some physical activity which eases the strain, thus preventing the mind reaching the injurious stage of seizing up.

Intense, highly strung persons should be greatly encouraged by even the least progress in learning to relax as described. When, by persistence, a stage is reached where it is possible to achieve any real degree of restfulness for anything from ten minutes to half-an-hour— that is to say, until the exercise has become pleasing and one wants to linger over it—a great deal has been accomplished. Indeed, it is often at the point when a sultry, sleepy feeling actually overcomes one and one is slumping into a semi-coma that the healing and recovery has reached a beneficial stage. Even so, soon one may get up and continue the daily drag, feeling infinitely the better for the short rest. The fact is, a whole technique of resting and relaxing can be built upon even the slightest discovery of its benefit and pleasure.

There is a proviso to be entered here. I do not have the medical or psychological knowledge to know how to deal with it, but it can be stated. Such a period of rest as we are describing, is said to render some people incapable of resuming their work with any efficiency. They are rather like those so befugged by a good night's sleep that they need almost half the day to recover and wake up. This is a problem beyond me. Whether it is a fact that there are personalities so lethargic naturally that they tend to relax so deeply that that is their problem, I do not know. If so, they need to be exhorted to wake up, get going and not spend the most of their life in luxurious hibernation! It may be that such people live their lives at such a low level of tension that they do not expend as much nervous energy as the rest of us and, therefore, do not tire as easily or as deeply. If so, that is fine, and the rest may envy their equilibrium and ability to remain relaxed in what to others are strenuous and exhausting conditions. But it is unlikely that people who fear to rest, lest they incapacitate themselves for further work, then go on to work themselves to a standstill. There may be those who tire themselves so deeply that, when they get the chance, they slump into the deepest sleep, from which it is hard to rouse them, because they are in need of it! Each person with such a problem must work it out in his or her own way. Indeed, this is what this is all about—that, under God and the governance of his over-all care for us, we learn to know ourselves, how we tick, or not, when and where.

To return for the preparation for rest: the practice of relaxing the mind is said to be much better accomplished psychologically by drawing in stray thoughts than by excluding them, as is also often advised for straying thought during prayer and meditation. Once that has been learned a little, and also the accompanying practice of relaxing the muscles of the whole body from head to foot until one is lying dead weight upon couch or bed, attention ought to be given to breathing. It is sometimes said that singers are far more healthy folk than others because they have learned to breathe properly. There is much in this. One of the beneficial results of a hearty sing in church on Sunday is the fruit of the sheer physical effort of exercising one's lungs, not to speak of the emotional release and religious exaltation of praising God, looking away beyond one's puny self to Another, greater and better. The fact of doing this in a group has also a beneficial effect, for we are social, gregarious creatures.

There is a great deal to be learned about health through breathing and, indeed, concentration on breathing as the only conscious physical activity continuing when lying down and otherwise motionless, is an excellent way of distracting and disentangling the mind from the preoccupations and worries of day-to-day life. Try it. Try to prolong the time you can hold your breath and then practise letting it out slowly. Evenness of tone in singing has to do with the even outflow of breath. In fact, unpractised singers use far too much breath, and waste it, having to breathe far too frequently and shallowly, because they let it out in gusts, not controlling its outflow from the diaphragm (waist). The practice of relaxing from a position of complete rest, along with concentration on the physical mechanics of breathing, will do a great deal to ease tension. It is at such a time that the sheer luxury of resting in the Lord for salvation, in all its aspects and dimensions, becomes the most precious experience of life.

We have spoken of salvation in three dimensions, but we need also to distinguish more clearly its two areas of justification and sanctification. The former involves utter acceptance of all that Christ has wrought for us. The latter, sanctification, involves our appropriation of all that he gives us in the three positive dimensions of a new world, a new nature, and a new Master. These three correspond to the three expansions of peace, love and joy (Jn. 15:11). Think what this does to worries, or, rather, attitudes towards real worries. One returns to them, if necessary, with an entirely different attitude of mind, having sweetly consulted the Source of all wisdom concerning them.

All of this is good when we have begun to see the necessity and, even a little, the practical benefits of rest; but until we do, it is clear that the whole exercise is a burden we do anything to avoid. The thought of suspending normal routines and work is regarded as a 'perfect nuisance'. This is the device the enemy of God and man uses to deceive us (deceit is his name, nature and constant activity) into missing the best in life because we are ignorantly 'on the run' from the restless one himself, Satan.

Obviously, we could multiply words on this theme and add many practical hints; but perhaps enough has been said to help any who really want to learn how to rest in the Lord, and make the most of their rest periods, in the interest of efficiency which this rest affords in every conceivable sort of activity.

Perhaps a personal testimony may help here. If I have been busy with calls and have not had sufficient time to study, say, for an address, or Bible exposition, and I have half-an-hour before I must go out, which is the better course of action? Spend the time in rather feverish study, trying to make sure I have all my facts right, and, in the process, almost exclude the blessed aid of the Holy Spirit when I come to minister? Or, rather, sit, or lie down, relax and prepare myself physically, mentally, emotionally, spiritually for the inflow of the Spirit's grace and power, so that I may be a communicator of his truth and blessing to others? Normally, I would not have the slightest hesitation. I would plump for rest every time. For, while I might be ill-prepared for ministry, the Lord who, in his grace and mercy, knows how necessarily busy I have been seeking to care for others and their needs, will look after what I have not been able to do. With real rest I can come to the occasion—including the fact of inadequate preparation—with a fresh, relaxed, rested mind.

In fact, rest is the first priority, because it concerns fundamental health, and here is the analogy of our salvation: that all depends upon him, not upon us, and, therefore, nothing can be as important as resting in him, since all fruitful work issues from him and from our rest in him. It is the pre-condition for anything worthwhile.

May God help us to see it, and do it!

RHYTHMS OF REST AND WORK

3. Simultaneous Rest and Work

We now consider the more complex exercise of learning to combine the greatest degree of restfulness and relaxation with the activities of daily life, so as to understand and know how to adopt them, to enable us to do our work with the maximum of efficiency and the minimum of injurious, wasted effort.

The relation between sequences of rest and work and the simultaneous action of controlled relaxation is exceedingly interesting. Undoubtedly the depth of repose and relaxation we seek to enjoy when resting should help us to find the proper degree of controlled relaxation in our active service.

How does one rest and work at the same time? It is a fascinatingly complex idea, enshrining the dual principle which governs all human skill, from the most physical to the most intellectual. See what it means from a simple illustration of the working of the mind. Try in vain to remember some fact, or piece of practical data, and someone says, 'Forget it, and you'll soon remember.' And you do, because, whereas a tense mind tends to paralyse, a relaxed mind is soon able to recall. There is, in fact, a correlation between relaxation and efficient action, with emphasis on 'controlled', not sloppy, mindless relaxation. It is practised, directed ease of action which makes for efficiency.

In the fundamental biblical sense in which the writer to the Hebrews means it, striving to enter into rest (Heb. 4:11) is that simple, yet difficult activity of ceasing from clumsy, injurious, even sinful effort, and learning to relax completely on the Lord and on his finished work of salvation. This is the fundamental idea we have stressed from the beginning.

There is, nonetheless, the Lord's call to action. On the one hand he says, 'Rest in the Lord' but within that absolute and complete command there are equally the commands to 'Make your calling and election sure' (2 Pet. 1:10); 'Put on the whole armour of God' (Eph. 6:11); 'Love one another' (Jn. 15:12). Therefore, we must learn to act properly, with a due balance of rest and attitude of rest. It is this spiritual secret of working from rest (a secret paradoxically open for all to observe in innumerable physical illustrations) that we are seeking to learn.

In physical actions, which would you practise first, the skill, or the controlled relaxation by which the skill becomes easy and efficient? Spiritually speaking, we may say rest comes first, because we rest in God, who made us and redeemed us; we can do nothing but accept. Yet, as fallen creatures, we have learned too well from our false father Satan, the injurious practice of trying to work for our own salvation, and thus we have disdained the help of God. So we need to begin by seeking to rest and relax, as God did, after the activity of creation and before that of redemption. Sooner or later, we tell ourselves that the whole purpose of such profound resting in Another is that we may be possessed by his powerful and purposive activity, and begin to act co-operatively with him in his strength.

This is where the analogy may seem to break down, because there is no physical counterpart to our drawing upon another, spiritually, for life and strength. Yet, we need these physical illustrations, since the combination of rest and work in physical activities (which require controlled relaxation) affords excellent examples of how we ought to behave, emotionally, mentally, spiritually, as well as physically. It is in learning physical skills—an infant learning to walk, a child to ride a bicycle, or an adult to play the piano, drive a car, use a hammer, or wield a paint-brush—that we understand the necessary tension which exists between relaxing with a view to freedom of movement, and taking a grip or hold of a tool, in order to gain firmness of movement. So we adjust the relaxation and control as economically and finely as possible.

I learned from James Ching, a pupil of Tobias Matthay (himself the music teacher of Myra Hess and Irene Scharrer), that when the pianist lowers his finger to perform the simple action of depressing the piano key (however unconsciously), he must neutralise the potential action of the opposite set of muscles by which he raises his finger. That is to say (almost in terms of the positive and negative in alternating electric current) the 'up' muscles remain inactive to let the 'down' muscles act freely. If the two sets of opposing muscles act together, due to tension in the mind and will of the performer, there is virtual muscular paralysis, since nothing happens for much expenditure of energy. It is rather like the action (or lack of it) in a tug-of-war, when two sides pull with equal strength. Think how wasteful of energy it is for two rows of sturdy men to pull with all their might and yet achieve nothing, because the strenuous efforts of one side are being neutralised by those of the other. There is a complete 'waste' of effort, with, ultimately, exhaustion, all to no end!

The lesson is clear, and its application to the emotional, mental and spiritual levels of life, obvious. Of two sets of conflicting muscles, the one must rest to allow the other to act properly. The rapid movement of a finger, wrist, or forearm in the skilled activity of playing the piano, clearly involves the rapid alternation of action and inaction, of relaxation and activity in the interaction of two opposite sets of muscles. Only so could any rapid repeated action be performed. What this involves in, say, the high skills of triple tonguing in trumpet playing, or in the fantastically rapid alternations of a pianist's or drummer's wrists, is hard to imagine. Perhaps few skilled performers know more about controlled relaxation than these. Nor is it unimportant to stress the personal satisfaction which such a skilled performer derives from the practice of his art, when he sees the extent to which controlled relaxation is contributing to the efficiency of his performance.

These actions, nonetheless, are not simultaneous, but their rapidity points to the simultaneity of rest and work in controlled relaxation. In this, it is the degree of relaxation which contributes to the skill of the action and this is a matter of learning the skills of: (a) proper relaxation and, (b) properly directed activity, so as to combine or co-ordinate these in techniques which (since such skills are generally harnessed to the higher aims of art or craft) must eventually become unconscious and practically automatic.

For example, no one but the youngest child needs to think about the physical action of walking, since it soon becomes a virtually unconscious action employed in the interests of another activity than that of mere walking. Simple activities are learned in infancy and early childhood, and we need only look at an infant learning to walk, or a child learning to ride a bicycle, to see how laborious it is at first. Indeed, see the look of intense concentration and anxiety on the face of a learner-driver, to be reminded how difficult the simple(!) activity of driving a car once was. We learn by practice, both the skill and the ease with which the skill can ultimately be performed. Do any of us, I wonder, ever learn to relax sufficiently to reduce the strain of our activity to the minimum, while at the same time paying attention to the efficiency of what we are doing, in order to bring it as near as possible to a state of perfection, or, at least, efficiency? That is the question.

One point needs to be stressed. It stands to reason that to attain efficiency in a particular skill calling for full concentration, the mind requires to be released from competing cares and anxieties. This is the cost of attaining simplicity in such activities, and of disentangling the mind and body from competing activity. This thought must have caused the writer of Hebrews to pen the highly suggestive words, 'Strive to enter into rest.'

Take an example of grace and ease, if not skill, in activity, which may have something to say about the combination of rest and work in the complex exercise of controlled relaxation: it is from the animal world— the litheness of movement of the feline species. We may marvel at the grace of the larger wild cats, when we see them in their natural habitat, or in zoological gardens, but we can see something of the same grace in the domestic cat in the back garden. The beauty and seemingly effortless grace of movement which the feline species display when they leap walls, show a perfectly natural and unconscious combination of ease and skill within their powers. But, let a bird, or another cat, or a dog appear on the scene, and we instantly see the difference; the cat suddenly becomes tense and rigid with excitement at the possibility of adventure, or danger, and becomes virtually a different animal.

Transfer these tensions to the experience of human beings, who, because more rational than animals, have, therefore, a correspondingly greater potential and complexity of tension. We then see the difference between how we too often live (our whole beings tensed up over various matters which we allow to worry us unduly), and the way, as Christians, we ought to live. Our life should be one of restful ease, even in busy-ness and energetic activity, which ought to enable us not only to get through our work but to do so more efficiently, and therefore, more satisfyingly.

You see how complex even the simplest action must be, which calls for any degree of ability or skill and yet must be performed, not only with the minimum of necessary effort, but with that effort directed towards its end, and unimpeded by contrary, or conflicting action. It may help us to see how important this is if we consider some of the skilled activities in which the technique of controlled relaxation is essential for efficiency. Musical skills naturally occur to me, such as piano-playing or violin-playing. See the practised skill of the expert violinist as he poises his bow upon the strings and makes it seem to bounce with seemingly phenomenal freedom; yet the cascading notes are true and articulate. The beauty of movement of the bowing hand is fantastic. No rigidity there, but perfect muscular ease and control.

The same with singing: the human voice is the most perfect musical instrument in the world. Even in speech, an understanding of the use of the vocal mechanism is helpful, especially for public speakers. One principal reason why ministers and school-teachers lose their voices is that they have not learned to produce the voice with the minimum of strain. The firm diaphragm, for good breathing, and the relaxed throat (larynx), for ease, are absolutely essential for proper voice-production.

The voice is really a stringed instrument, working by means of a column of air passing through the vocal chords, vibrating them. This causes a tiny volume of sound to be amplified, as it reaches the cavity of the mouth and resounds in the caverns of the head, before being emitted through the mouth. On the way, that sound, if deep enough, may receive considerable resonance from the sounding board of the chest walls.

This is how basses and contraltos produce their lower notes; whereas higher notes find their resonance in the vault of the head—sopranos' notes from the second G above middle C, on the piano, are for that reason, called 'head notes'. The singer may direct the column of sounding air against any part of the head, such as the teeth, for sharpness of tone, or the nose for nasal tone. The point is, that a column of air passing through the body and the head should be unimpeded in its course, since a tight throat will affect the quality of the tone and strain the apparatus, as over-tense breathing muscles hinder the free, controlled action of the air supply. The relaxed throat may not be easy to achieve, since the skilled action of singing requires much mental and emotional activity, for example, in understanding the music, not to speak of the mood of the song and the true interpretation of its message.

Someone has suggested that the right sensation for speaking and singing alike is that of a 'yawning' feeling, and I have known nothing in singing teaching which has been as effective for controlled relaxation as this. In the days of my musical training, I used to go to the fields and walk beyond the hearing of any but birds and beasts, and there practise both the relaxation that makes for ease and richness of singing tone, and, also the skills (a whole world in themselves) of articulation and diction.

The whole aim is to combine skill of action with the appropriate relaxation, let it be emphasised again, not only for ease, but for efficiency.

Another realm of such skilled action is that of the surgeon, perhaps especially the eye surgeon. I remember when Eric Sinton (an eye surgeon in Red Deer, Alberta) was a boy, he used to love to make and work with miniatures. I have marvelled at the fineness of his muscular control as he performed fine actions upon tiny objects.

The balance of tension and relaxed control in athletes and sportsmen and sportswomen is an entirely different area. Whereas power of movement is often very important, the sheer weight of the body, or the members of the body, must be a powerful factor in the success of some athletic activities. It would be interesting to know how much weight and how much force is used in the shot putt!

To return to piano-playing, there is an unbelievable difference in the quality of tone emanating from piano strings when struck by fingers and hands using sheer weight, and alternatively, using force. Perhaps a guitarist would appreciate this. It may be possible to strike the strings of that kind of musical instrument with the hand and fingers in such a way as to break the strings; yet in loud playing tremendous power is called for: weight rather than force is surely the answer, and the difference between the two is a matter of the degree of relaxation. Perhaps this is also relevant to boxers and all-in wrestlers(!) and, certainly, ballet dancers, who must know a great deal about it.

Could it be that much that pertains to ease of living in a hard-driving, tense age (though true in any age), can be learned from these two extremes—religion, and physical activities? Geoffrey Lester, of Bath Abbey, quotes Charles Morgan speaking of,

> the stilling of the soul within the activities of the mind and body, so that it might be still, as the axis of a revolving wheel is still.

And he goes on,

> It is something we need to discover. How to be still. How to acquire peace within the sanctuary of our souls, and within the revolving wheel of our many activities and relationships and obligations.

'Rest in the Lord' from a whole world of strain, and acquire the greatest degree of skill in performing useful and fruitful actions in a consciousness that one is not on one's own, but is divinely aided to do one's best with the greatest economy of means.

Of course, the mind must take hold of these truths, and we must learn to adopt that good-humoured, cheerful attitude to life which comes from having a Father in heaven and being indulged in the lap of luxury by a Saviour who has done everything that he could do for us. That is the secret of secrets, since all shallower attempts at mental relaxation may founder on the results of not having found ultimate peace and confidence. That is why we go to the two extremes of the spiritual and the physical, and learning from these, apply all we learn to that area of tension which can and does do so much harm to the human personality, namely, the mind. With a heart at rest ('Let not your heart be troubled', Jn. 14:1) and learning practical lessons from the muscular and physical, we can apply the whole gamut of truth to the mind, so that it begins to relax and progressively reduce tension, until we hardly know ourselves. Others, too, may not recognise us—we are so peaceful, so cheerful and easy to get on with.

Let us state this again briefly. With fundamental rest in the Lord, and some basic knowledge of how to relax physically, we can then go to work on the mind, since the body influences the mind, as any kind of pain easily proves. Although it may take a long time for the mind to adopt a more relaxed attitude to life and see its fears, doubts and dreads in a more detached, trustful and philosophical frame, it will come, with quiet and calm determination. 'Strive to enter into rest.' May God help us to do so, and prove its benefits and blessings in our own experience!

My plan was to end there although there are worlds of application of the principles of rest and work and controlled relaxation not yet touched on. These include social worlds, which seemed too great a subject to tackle here. Certain things, however, can, and ought to be said.

Underlying the complications of applying principles from the individual to his social relationships in the home, at work, in the community and in the church, certain basic realities must be considered. The first of which is that, before there can be any social relationships at all, there must be basic acceptance of others as personalities other than, and different from our own, even if that acceptance may seem initially to be grudging and interim. After all, at best, we are raw material in the divine manufactory of soul-making, and need to learn at least as much patience with others as with ourselves! Even if our hopes of changing people are high, we must begin where they are.

It will, therefore, be well to begin the consideration of rules of rest and relaxation as applied to social relationships, by suggesting what must be the hardest thing for sinful human nature to contemplate, namely, the application of the same rules to others as we apply to ourselves. The famous biblical rule which sums up the prophets—'Do as you would be done by' (Matt. 7:12)—covers it. Since we are all good at allowing ourselves every possible consideration in order to appear in our best light and make the best of ourselves, we must get it fixed in our minds, too, that others with whom we live and work, deserve like consideration. It is, therefore, ours to combine the highest degree of rest and relaxation with the same desire for others. As we would claim to be, and doubtless are, fully realistic about the peculiar needs of our own unique personalities, and are ignorant of the needs of others, we must allow them a large degree of tolerance. The more we know of others, the better equipped we ought to be to understand them, for to know is often to understand, at least where there is Christian goodwill, which is what we are talking about. To the basic truth of Romans 13:8: 'Owe no one anything, except to love one another,' we add that more explicitly evangelical truth of Romans 13:14, 'But put on the Lord Jesus Christ, and make no provision for the flesh, to gratify its desires.'

The Christian requirement in ourselves (as well as in others) takes into consideration not only that we are new creatures in Christ Jesus (2 Cor. 5:17), but also that Christian character is by growth; God has ordained it that way, however suddenly and dramatically he can work otherwise. God in nature can, in an instant, produce earthquakes, tidal waves and tornadoes, but our food is produced by processes of growth, whether we are vegetarians or not.

Part of the rest and relaxation we have learned, or begun to learn, we want to share with others and recommend by example, or exhortation, is good-natured tolerance, which, nonetheless, has a high degree of expectancy of higher things, from others as well as from ourselves. It is a positive attitude, but it is patiently so. It rests on the basic facts of our unity as humans and on our much richer unity in Christ (Eph. 2:19–22; 4:1–6), as, also, on our diversity (Eph. 4:7). It goes on to rejoice in the richness of life within the body of Christ (Eph. 4:11–16; 1 Cor. 12:12–26), waiting with buoyant good humour and expectancy to see babes grow up into God's salvation (1 Pet. 2:2) and as living stones into Christ's church (1 Pet. 2:5) as a spiritual house.

Not only so, but the man or woman who can go out into the world in which we live and view it with charity because he or she emerges from a happy home where life is satisfying, and from a church which is enriching, will make impacts by sheer cheerfulness and stability.

Not that to go into the world with that cheerful attitude will always receive a like response. Jesus did not and we will not. We may react in several ways. We can say, 'Here am I, seeking to be as open and transparent as the air: I now know no other way to live; ought I not to expect others to lift their blinds also, and be as open with me as I with them?' We may not expect that. How do we know how far those we encounter dare lift their blinds, even a little? That which a man at peace with God and enjoying frequent pardon may not be afraid to admit may bring terror and complete demoralisation to others. Jesus never forced people. He was gentle and profoundly respectful, even to those considered by others to be very bad, like the woman of Samaria, Zacchaeus and the woman taken in adultery. We are always in such a hurry to get 'the work done', especially in other people's souls, that we are prepared to use a little, if not always a lot of force, to accomplish it. But what does hurry speak of? Certainly not rest. What we call 'the work', the running of groups, or organising people in series of meetings, is not really the work; the work is learning to work together. That learning takes time.

Don't rip up other people's blinds! Count it time well spent to learn, however slowly, painstakingly and discouragingly, to work with others whom you may find difficult. Ultimately, you will learn to love them dearly, and they will love you. And that is what life is about—love. Contrast the clarion call to love in Romans 13:8–10 with the sensitivity of Romans chapters 14 and 15:1–16; and read also 1 Corinthians 8:1–10; 9:1–24; 10:31–11:1, to see what tremendous work God is prepared to do for us and through us, if we learn to work with him and follow him from a position of fundamental rest and relaxation.

See a captain standing on the bridge of his ship, the whole vessel gently vibrating and pounding as the propellers drive the great craft forward through the waters, and there you have a man at rest, because everything is working according to plan. He has the right idea; a sequence of rest and work before departure leads to a combination of relaxed control and activity which synchronise rest and work—not to speak of co-operation from the crew in the common endeavour of reaching the desired haven. But, paradoxically, we need the peace of the haven in our hearts before we arrive. That is what life is about.